CATHERINE
de' MEDICI

ALSO BY MARY HOLLINGSWORTH

The Medici
Princes of the Renaissance
Conclave 1559

CATHERINE
de 'MEDICI

THE LIFE AND TIMES OF
THE SERPENT QUEEN

MARY
HOLLINGSWORTH

PEGASUS BOOKS
NEW YORK LONDON

CATHERINE DE' MEDICI

Pegasus Books, Ltd.
148 West 37th Street, 13th Floor
New York, NY 10018

Copyright © 2024 by Mary Hollingsworth

First Pegasus Books cloth edition July 2024

ISBN: 978-1-63936-701-6

10 9 8 7 6 5 4 3 2 1

Printed in the United States of America
Distributed by Simon & Schuster
www.pegasusbooks.com

For Nel and Bonnie

Contents

Dramatis Personae

Alava, Francisco de (*c.* 1519–86), Spanish ambassador to France 1564–70.

Alba, Fernando Alvarez de Toledo, duke of (1507–82), soldier, diplomat and trusted adviser to Charles V and Philip II; governor of Milan 1555; viceroy in Naples 1556; Philip's representative at Treaty of Cateau-Cambrésis 1559; the king's proxy at his m. to Elisabeth of France 1559; his emissary to conference with Catherine de' Medici at Bayonne 1565; Spanish governor in the Netherlands 1567, with task of quelling Protestant rebellion.

Albany, duke of, *see* Stuart, John.

Albret, Henry d' (1502–55) King of Navarre.

Albret, Jeanne d', *see* Navarre, Jeanne of.

Alençon, *see* François, duke of Alençon and Anjou.

Andelot, *see* Coligny, François de.

Anjou, duke of, *see* François, duke of Alençon and Anjou; Henry III.

Aumale, *see* Guise, Claude of Lorraine, duke of Aumale.

Beaujoyeux, Balthasar de (*c.* 1535–87), Italian (born Baldassare di Belgioioso), violinist, composer and choreographer for Catherine's masques and entertainments; one of her *valets de chambre*.

Bellièvre, Pomponne de (1529–1607), diplomat, French ambassador to the Swiss cantons, *surintendant des finances* for Henry III 1575; loyal ally of Catherine.

Birague, René de (*c.* 1509–83), Milanese lawyer who took French citizenship; diplomatic appointments for France, lieutenant-general in Piedmont; Keeper of the Seals 1570; chancellor of France 1573; one of Catherine's protégés.

Biron, Armand de Gontaut, baron of (*c.* 1524–92), lieutenant-general in Guyenne; marshal of France 1577.

Bochetel, Bernardin de (d. 1570), bishop of Rennes and French ambassador in Vienna.

Bourbon, Antoine de, duke of Bourbon-Vendôme (1518–62), first prince of the blood; elder brother of Louis of Condé and cardinal Charles; m. Jeanne d'Albret, heiress to Navarre 1548; king of Navarre 1555; lieutenant-general of France 1560; father of Henry IV (qv).

Bourbon, Charles de, cardinal (1523–90), brother of Antoine and Louis of Condé' (qqv); acquired red hat 1548; archbishop of Rouen 1550; Catholic League declared him the rightful heir to the French throne after Henry III made the Protestant Henri of Navarre his heir.

Bourbon, Charles de, prince of La Roche-sur-Yon (1515–65), younger brother of Louis de Bourbon, duke of Montpensier (qv); governor of Paris 1561; governor of Dauphiné 1563; m. Philippa de Montespedon (qv), Catherine's *dame d'honneur*.

Bourbon, Henri de, prince of Condé (1552–88), son of Louis, prince of Condé; leader of the Protestants with Henri of Navarre.

Bourbon, Louis de, prince of Condé (1530–69), younger brother of Antoine and cardinal Charles (qqv); governor of Picardy; leader of Protestants with Gaspard de Coligny.

Bourbon, Louis de, duke of Montpensier (1513–82), m. (1) Jacqueline de Longwy (qv); m. (2) Catherine of Lorraine, sister of Henri, duke of Guise (qv); governor of Dauphiné 1565; initially a moderate in religious matters, like his first wife, he changed sides to become a militant supporter of the Catholic cause.

Brantôme, Pierre de Bourdeille, abbé of (*c.* 1540–1614), aristocrat who abandoned church career for the military and, after a fall from his horse, retired from the army to write his *Memoirs*, an account of the illustrious men and women of his acquaintance; a strong supporter of Catherine.

Brulart, Pierre (*c.* 1535–1608), seigneur de Crosnes, secretary of state.

Chantonnay, Thomas Perrenot de, *see* Granvelle.

Charles V (1500–58), king of Spain and Naples 1516; Holy Roman Emperor 1519; abdicated 1556/7.

Charles IX (1550–74), king of France; Catherine's second son.

Charles, duke of Orléans (1522–45), third son of Francis I.

Châtillon, *see* Coligny, Odet de.

Cheverny, Philippe Hurault, comte de (1528–99), chancellor of the Order of Saint-Esprit; Keeper of the Seals 1578; chancellor of France 1581.

Claude of France (1499–1524), daughter of Louis XII, first wife of Francis I; mother of Henry II of France.

Claude of France (1547–75), duchess of Lorraine 1559; Catherine's second daughter.

Clement VII (Giulio de' Medici), pope 1523–34; b. Florence 1478, illegitimate son of Giuliano de' Medici, brother of Lorenzo *il Magnifico*; cardinal 1513; governor of Florence 1519, Catherine's guardian; elected pope 19 November 1523; cousin of Catherine.

Clermont, Louise de (*c.* 1505–96), duchess of Uzès, one of Catherine's *dames d'honneur* and a close confidante.

Coligny, François de, seigneur d'Andelot (1521–69), brother of Gaspard and Odet; converted to Protestantism *c.* 1556 and became one of the movement's leaders.

Coligny, Gaspard de, seigneur de Châtillon-sur-Loing (1519–72), brother of François d'Andelot and cardinal Odet, and nephew of Anne de Montmorency (qqv); admiral of France 1552; converted to Protestantism *c.* 1560; lieutenant to Louis of Condé in early civil wars and took over as leader of the Protestants after Condé's death in 1569.

Coligny, Odet de, cardinal (1517–71), brother of Gaspard and Odet; archbishop of Beauvais; created cardinal in 1533 by Clement VII, who was in France for Catherine's wedding; participated in the Council of Trent; converted to Protestantism 1561; deprived of his offices by Pius IV 1563; married his mistress in December 1564; sought asylum in England 1568, where he died.

Condé, Louis de, *see* Bourbon, Louis de, prince of Condé.

Constable, *see* Montmorency, Anne de.

Cossé, Artus de (*c.* 1512–82), seigneur of Gonnor; royal treasurer (*surintendant des finances*) 1563; marshal of France 1567; governor of Anjou, Touraine and Orléans 1570.

Crussol, Antoine de (1528–73), duke of Uzès, m. Louise de Clermont; Catherine's *chevalier d'honneur* 1559; commanded Protestant troops during the civil wars.

Damville, *see* Montmorency, Henri de.

Elbeuf, *see* Guise, René of, marquis of Elbeuf.

Eleanor of France (1498–1558), queen of France, second wife of Francis I; sister of emperor Charles V and Mary of Hungary.

Elisabeth of Austria (1554–92), daughter of emperor Maximilian II; queen of France 1570.

Elisabeth of France (1545–68), queen of Spain, Catherine's eldest daughter.

Elizabeth I (1533–1603), queen of England.

Épernon, Jean-Louis de Nogaret de La Valette, duke of (1554–1642); admiral of France; governor of Metz, Toul and Verdun, Touraine, Anjou and Normandy; disgraced 1588.

Este, Anna d' (1531–1607), daughter of duke Ercole II of Ferrara and Renée of France (qv); duchess of Guise 1550; duchess of Nemours 1566 after marriage to a Guise ally, Jacques of Savoy, duke of Nemours; friend of Catherine.

Este, Ippolito d' (1509–72), brother of duke Ercole II of Ferrara; archbishop of Milan 1519; cardinal 1538; cardinal-protector of France 1549; Henry II's governor of Siena 1552; legate to France 1561; uncle of Anna d'Este (qv); close friend of Catherine.

Étampes, madame de, *see* Pisseleu, Anne de.

Farnese, Alessandro (1545–92), duke of Parma and Piacenza; governor-general of the Netherlands for Philip II, his half-brother 1578; son of Ottavio Farnese and Margaret of Austria (qqv).

Farnese, Ottavio (1524–86), duke of Parma and Piacenza 1547; m. Margaret of Austria (qv), illegitimate daughter of Charles V.

Ferdinand I (1503–64), Holy Roman Emperor 1588 on abdication of his brother, Charles V.

Ferrara, cardinal of, *see* Este, Ippolito d'.

Fourquevaux, Raymond de Beccarie, seigneur of (1508–74), French ambassador to Spain.

Francis I (1494–1547), king of France; Catherine's father-in-law.

Francis II (1544–60), king of France; Catherine's eldest son.

François, dauphin (1518–36), eldest son of Francis I.

François, dauphin, *see* Francis II.

François, duke of Alençon and Anjou (1555–84), duke of Alençon 1566; duke of Anjou 1576; Prince of the Dutch Provinces and duke of Brabant 1582; Catherine's youngest son.

Gonzaga, Ludovico (Gonzague, Louis de), *see* Nevers.

Granvelle, Antoine Perrenot de (1517–86), brother of Chantonnay; cardinal, participated in Council of Trent; diplomatic career in service of Charles V and Philip II; Philip II's representative at negotiations for Treaty of Cateau-Cambrésis 1559; principal adviser to Margaret of Parma, governor of the Netherlands; created cardinal 1561; Spanish ambassador in Rome 1571.

Granvelle, Thomas Perrenot de, sieur of Chantonnay (1521–71), brother of cardinal Granvelle (qv); diplomatic career in service of Charles V and Philip II; ambassador in France 1560 and Vienna 1565.

Guise, *see also* Lorraine.

Guise, Charles of Lorraine, cardinal (1524–74), second son of Claude, first duke of Guise; younger brother of François, duke of Guise; archbishop of Rheims 1538; cardinal of Guise 1547; inherited title of cardinal of Lorraine after the death of his uncle Jean (qv) 1550; chief minister to Henry II and Francis II.

Guise, Charles of Lorraine, marquis of Elbeuf (1556–1605), son of René, marquis of Elbeuf, youngest son of Claude, first duke of Guise.

Guise, Charles of Lorraine, duke of Mayenne (1554–1611), second son of duke François of Guise and Anna d'Este; leader of the Catholic League after the death of his brother Henri 1588.

Guise, Claude of Lorraine, duke of Guise (1496–1550), created first duke of Guise by Francis I as reward for military service; his wife, Antoinette de Bourbon, gave birth to twelve children.

Guise, Claude of Lorraine, duke of Aumale (1526–73), fifth son of Claude, first duke of Guise; governor of Burgundy 1550; m. Louise de Brézé, daughter of Diane de Poitiers.

Guise, François of Lorraine, duke of Guise (1519–63), eldest son of Claude, first duke of Guise; m. Anna d'Este 1548, daughter of Renée of France; *grand chambellan de France* 1551; governor of Dauphiné and Savoy; lieutenant-general of France 1557; leader of Catholic faction; with his brother Cardinal Charles, the power behind Francis II's reign.

Guise, Henri of Lorraine, duke of Guise (1550–88), eldest son of duke François of Guise and Anna d'Este; governor of Champagne and Brie 1563; *grand maître de France* 1563; leader of Catholic League 1581–88; reputedly had affair with Catherine's daughter Marguerite.

Guise, Louis of Lorraine, cardinal (1527–78), third son of Claude, first duke of Guise; cardinal of Guise 1553 and inherited title cardinal of Lorraine after the death of his brother Charles (qv) 1574.

Guise, Louis of Lorraine, cardinal (1555–88), third son of duke François of Guise and Anna d'Este; cardinal of Guise (1498–1550), archbishop of Rheims 1574; crowned Henry III 1575; actively involved with Catholic League.

Guise, René of Lorraine, marquis of Elbeuf (1536–66), youngest son of Claude, first duke of Guise.

Henri of Anjou, *see* Henry III.

Henri of Orléans, *see* Henry II; Henry III.

Henry II (1519–59), duke of Orléans, dauphin 1536; king of France 1547.

Henry III (1551–89), duke of Orléans 1560; duke of Anjou 1566; king of Poland 1573; king of France 1574; Catherine's third son.

Henry IV (1553–1610), son of Antoine de Bourbon and Jeanne d'Albret; king of Navarre 1572; king of France 1589.

Henry VIII (1491–1547), king of England.

Johann Casimir von Pfalz-Simmern (1543–92), son of Friedrich III, elector-palatine; leader of mercenary troops fighting for the Protestant cause in France and the Netherlands.

Joyeuse d'Arques, Anne de (1561–87), duke of Joyeuse; m. Marguerite of Lorraine, sister of queen Louise; *premier gentilhomme de chambre* 1581; admiral of France 1582; governor of Normandy 1583; one of Henry III's favourites.

La Mothe-Fénelon, Bertrand de Salignac, marquis of (d. 1589), marquis of La Mothe-Fénelon; diplomat; French ambassador in London 1572–74.

La Noue, François de (1531–91), Protestant army commander and senior figure in the movement after the St Bartholomew's Day massacre; also fought for the Protestant cause in the Netherlands.

Lansac, Louis de Saint-Gelais de (1513–89), illegitimate son of Francis I; served in Henry II's household before diplomat career that included post of ambassador to Council of Trent 1554 and to Spain 1564; Catherine's *chevalier d'honneur* 1573 and one of her close allies.

La Rochefoucauld, François III, comte de (1521–72), brother-in-law of Coligny; successful military career for Henry II; a committed Protestant, he was one of its leaders to be killed on St Bartholomew's Day.

La Tour d'Auvergne, Henri de (1555–1623), viscount Turenne, ally of Henri of Navarre and lieutenant-general in Languedoc; a distant relation of Catherine and reputed lover of her daughter Marguerite (qv).

La Tour d'Auvergne, Madeleine de (1498–1519), daughter of Jean III de La Tour d'Auvergne and Jeanne de Bourbon; duchess of Urbino 1518; Catherine's mother.

L'Aubespine, Claude de (1544–70), secretary of state under Henry II, Francis II and Charles IX; close confidant of Catherine.

L'Aubespine, Sébastien de (1518–82), bishop of Limoges and diplomat; French ambassador in Spain; uncle of Claude de L'Aubespine (qv); close confidant of Catherine.

Leo X (Giovanni de' Medici), pope 1513–21; b. Florence, 1475; created cardinal 1489; elected pope 11 March 1513; Catherine's cousin.

L'Hospital, Michel de (*c.* 1507–73), councillor of the Paris *parlement* 1537; chancellor to Marguerite, duchess of Savoy; chancellor of France 1560.

Limoges, *see* L'Aubespine, Sébastien de.

Longwy, Jacqueline de (*c.* 1520–61), duchess of Montpensier; Catherine's senior *dame d'honneur* and close friend.

Lorenzo *il Magnifico*, *see* Medici, Lorenzo de'.

Lorraine, *see also* Guise.

Lorraine, cardinal of, *see* Lorraine, Jean of; Guise, Charles of Lorraine; Guise, Louis of Lorraine.

Lorraine, Charles III (1543–1608), duke of Lorraine; m. Claude of France; Catherine's son-in-law.

Lorraine, Christine of (1565–1637), daughter of Charles III of Lorraine; duchess of Florence 1589; Catherine's granddaughter.

Lorraine, Jean of (1498–1550), brother of Claude of Lorraine, first duke of Guise; cardinal of Lorraine 1518; archbishop of Rheims 1532; diplomatic missions for Francis I.

Lorraine-Vaudémont, Charles of, cardinal (1561–87), brother of Queen Louise; created cardinal 1578.

Lorraine-Vaudémont, Louise of (1553–1601), daughter of Duke Nicolas of Lorraine-Vaudémont; queen of France 1575.

Lorraine-Vaudémont, Philippe-Emmanuel of, duke of Mercoeur

(1558–1602), brother of Queen Louise; governor of Brittany 1582; prominent member of the Catholic League.

Louise, queen of France, *see* Lorraine-Vaudémont, Louise of.

Magnifico, Lorenzo il, *see* Medici, Lorenzo de'.

Margaret of Austria (1522–86), illegitimate daughter of Charles V; duchess of Florence 1536; after assassination of Duke Alessandro in 1537, married Ottavio Farnese to become duchess of Parma and Piacenza 1538; governor in the Netherlands for her half-brother Philip II 1559–67; Catherine's cousin by marriage.

Margaret of Parma, *see* Margaret of Austria.

Marguerite of Angoulême (1492–1549), sister of Francis I; m. Henri d'Albret, king of Navarre; mother of Jeanne d'Albret; grandmother of Henry IV; author of *Heptameron*, a collection of short stories inspired by Boccaccio's *Decameron*, and of *Miroir de l'âme pécheresse* (Mirror of the Sinful Soul), which was condemned by the monks of the Sorbonne as heresy.

Marguerite of France (1523–74), duchess of Savoy 1559, Catherine's sister-in-law and close friend.

Marguerite of France (1553–1615), daughter of Henry II; m. Henri of Navarre 1572; Catherine's youngest daughter.

Marguerite of Navarre, *see* Marguerite of Angoulême.

Mary of Hungary (1505–58), regent in the Netherlands for her brother Charles V.

Mary, queen of Scots (1542–87), daughter of James V of Scotland and Mary of Guise, eldest daughter of Claude, first duke of Guise; inherited Scottish throne when only six days old; dauphine of France 1548; queen of France (1559–60); Catherine's daughter-in-law.

Matignon, Jacques de Goyon, comte de (1525–97), marshal of France 1579; lieutenant-general in Guyenne 1580.

Mauvissière, Michel de Castelnau, seigneur de (*c.* 1520–92), French ambassador in London.

Maximilian II (1527–76), Holy Roman Emperor 1564.

Mayenne, *see* Guise, Charles de Lorraine, duke of Mayenne.

Medici, Alessandro de' (*c.* 1511–37), illegitimate son of Clement VII; first duke of Florence 1532; m. Margaret of Austria 1536; Catherine's cousin.

Medici, Catherine de' (1519–89), b. Florence; m. Henri of Orléans 1532; dauphine 1536; queen of France 1547–59; regent for Charles IX 1560; queen mother.

Medici, Clarice de' (1491–1528), m. Filippo Strozzi, papal banker 1509; Catherine's aunt.

Medici, Cosimo de' (1519–74), duke of Florence 1537; Catherine's cousin.

Medici, Giovanni de', *see* Leo X.

Medici, Giulio de', *see* Clement VII.

Medici, Ippolito de' (1535), illegitimate son of Giuliano de' Medici, younger brother of Leo X; Catherine's cousin.

Medici, Lorenzo (*il Magnifico*) de' (1449–92), banker; Catherine's great-grandfather.

Medici, Lorenzo de' (1492–1519), duke of Urbino, Catherine's father.

Mercoeur, duke of, *see* Lorraine-Vaudémont, Philippe-Emmanuele de.

Mondoucet, Claude de, French ambassador in Brussels 1573–4.

Monluc, Blaise de (*c.* 1502–77), marshal of France 1574; during civil wars acquired reputation for brutal treatment of Protestants.

Monluc, Jean de (*c.* 1503–79), bishop of Valence; brother of Blaise de Monluc; ambassador to Poland 1572; a close ally of Catherine.

Montespedon, Philippa de (*c.* 1510–78), princess of La Roche-sur-Yon; Catherine's senior *dame d'honneur* 1561.

Montmorency, Anne de (1493–1567), marshal of France 1522; *grand maître de France* 1526; governor of Languedoc 1526; constable of France 1538; duke of Montmorency 1551.

Montmorency, François de (1530–79), eldest son of Anne (qv); governor of Paris and Île-de-France 1556; marshal of France 1559; duke of Montmorency 1567.

Montmorency, Henri de (1534–1613), second son of Anne (qv); count of Damville, governor of Languedoc 1563; marshal of France 1567; duke of Montmorency 1579.

Montmorency, marshal, *see* Montmorency, François de.

Montpensier, duchess of, *see* Longwy, Jacqueline de.

Montpensier, duke of, *see* Bourbon, Louis de, duke of Montpensier.

Morvillier, Jean de (1506–77), bishop of Orléans 1552; Keeper of the Seals 1568–70; close ally of Catherine.

Nassau, Louis of (1538–74) count of; leader of the Dutch Protestants with his brother William of Orange (qv).

Navarre, Henri of, *see* Henry IV.

Navarre, Jeanne of (1528–72), queen of Navarre, daughter of

Henry II d'Albret and Marguerite of Navarre; m. Antoine de Bourbon (qv).

Navarre, king of, *see* Albret, Henri d'; Bourbon, Antoine de; Henry IV.

Navarre, Marguerite of, *see* Marguerite of Angoulême.

Nemours, Jacques de Savoy, duke of (1531–85), m. Anna d'Este, widow of Francois, duke of Guise; ally of the Guise faction.

Neufville, Nicolas de, seigneur of Villeroy (1543–1617), secretary of state under Charles IX and Henry III; son-in-law of Claude de L'Aubespine (qv); close ally of Catherine.

Nevers, Ludovico Gonzaga, duke of (1549–95), third son of Federigo, duke of Mantua; m. heiress of duchy of Nevers; one of Catherine's Italian protégés.

Orange, William of Nassau, prince of (1533–84), brother of Louis of Nassau; leader of Protestant rebels in the Netherlands.

Orléans, duke of, *see* Charles, duke of Orléans; Henry II.

Paul III (Alessandro Farnese), pope 1534–49; b. 1468; created cardinal 1493; elected pope 13 October 1534; as pope began process of reforming abuses in the Catholic Church with the opening of the Council of Trent; a famous nepotist, he exploited his position to establish his family in the European aristocratic elite.

Perron, Catherine de Pierrevive du (*c.* 1500–70), m. Antonio Gondi, Florentine banker and seigneur of Perron 1516; *dame d'honneur* to dauphine Mary Stuart; one of Catherine's closest confidantes.

Philip II (1527–98), duke of Milan (1540), king of Spain (1558), Catherine's son-in-law.

Pinart, Claude (d. 1605), seigneur de Cramailles, secretary of state under Henry III.

Pisseleu, Anne de (1508–*c.* 1576), duchess of Étampes; mistress of Francis I.

Poitiers, Diane de (1499–1566), m. Louis de Brézé, *grand seneschal* of Normandy; duchess of Valentinois 1548; Henry II's mistress.

Renée of France (1510–75), daughter of Louis XII of France, sister of Francis I's first wife Claude; duchess of Ferrara 1528; returned to France after the death of her husband in 1559 and settled at her castle of Montargis.

Retz, Alberto Gondi, comte de (1522–1602), son of Catherine's close friend Catherine du Perron (qv); marshal of France 1573; governor of Provence 1573; one of Catherine's Italian protégés.

Saint-André, Jacques d'Albon, seigneur de (*c.* 1505–62); son of Jean d'Albon, Catherine's *chevalier d'honneur*, member of Henry II's household as dauphin and as king; lieutenant-general of the Lyonnais; marshal of France 1547.

Saint-Sulpice, Jean Ebrard, seigneur de (1519–81), French ambassador in Spain 1562.

Savoy, duchess of, *see* Marguerite of France.

Savoy, Emanuele Filiberto, duke of (1528–80), son of Charles III of Savoy and Beatrice of Portugal, sister-in-law of Charles V; m. Marguerite of France, sister of Henry II; fought for the Habsburgs in the Habsburg–Valois wars.

Strozzi, Filippo (1489–1538), Catherine's uncle, papal banker.

Stuart, John (*c.* 1481–1536), duke of Albany; grandson of James II of Scotland and regent for James V of Scotland; Catherine's uncle by marriage.

Stuart, Mary, *see* Mary, queen of Scots.

Tavannes, Gaspard de Saulx, seigneur de (1509–73), lieutenant-general of Burgundy, Dauphiné and Lyonnais; marshal of France 1569; governor of Provence 1572.

Tournon, cardinal François de (1489–1562), archbishop of Bourges 1526; cardinal 1547.

Turenne, *see* La Tour d'Auvergne, Henri de.

Uzès, duchess of, *see* Clermont, Louise de.

Uzès, duke of, *see* Crussol, Antoine de.

Valentinois, duchess of, *see* Poitiers, Diane de.

Villequier, René de, baron of Clairvaux (*c.* 1530–86), first gentleman of the chamber 1574; governor of Paris and the Île-de-France 1580.

Villeroy, *see* Neufville, Nicolas de.

Vivonne, Jean de, seigneur of Saint-Goard (*c.* 1530–99), French ambassador in Spain.

FAMILY TREES

Note: these family trees are not complete, but relate to the people in the text.

* indicates illegitimate birth

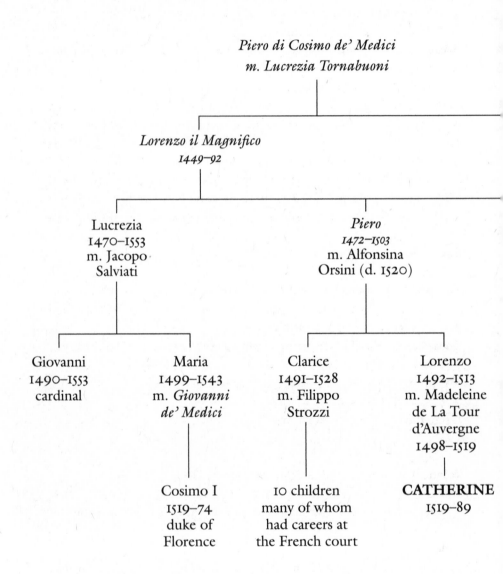

Piero di Cosimo de' Medici
m. Lucrezia Tornabuoni

Lorenzo il Magnifico
1449–92

Lucrezia
1470–1553
m. Jacopo
Salviati

Piero
1472–1503
m. Alfonsina
Orsini (d. 1520)

Giovanni
1490–1553
cardinal

Maria
1499–1543
m. *Giovanni
de' Medici*

Clarice
1491–1528
m. Filippo
Strozzi

Lorenzo
1492–1513
m. Madeleine
de La Tour
d'Auvergne
1498–1519

Cosimo I
1519–74
duke of
Florence

10 children
many of whom
had careers at
the French court

CATHERINE
1519–89

*Names in italic indicate individuals who were no longer alive at
Catherine's birth on 13 April 1519.*

Catherine's Medici Ancestry and Her Relations in 1519

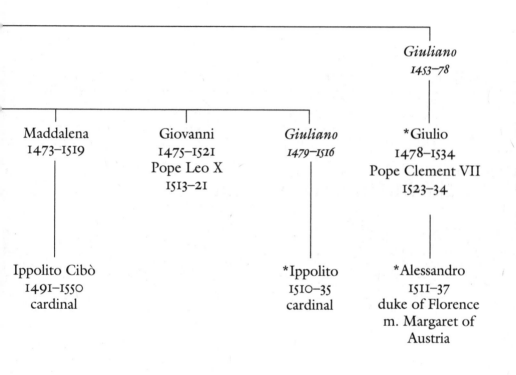

Giuliano
1453–78

Maddalena
1473–1519

Giovanni
1475–1521
Pope Leo X
1513–21

Giuliano
1479–1516

*Giulio
1478–1534
Pope Clement VII
1523–34

Ippolito Cibò
1491–1550
cardinal

*Ippolito
1510–35
cardinal

*Alessandro
1511–37
duke of Florence
m. Margaret of
Austria

The Valois

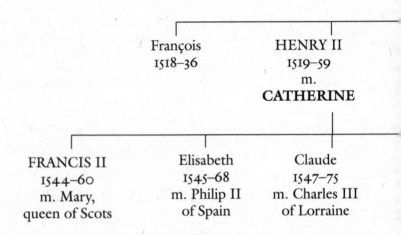

François
1518–36

HENRY II
1519–59
m.
CATHERINE

FRANCIS II
1544–60
m. Mary,
queen of Scots

Elisabeth
1545–68
m. Philip II
of Spain

Claude
1547–75
m. Charles III
of Lorraine

The Montmorency Family

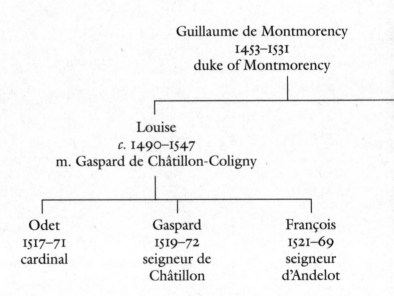

Guillaume de Montmorency
1453–1531
duke of Montmorency

Louise
c. 1490–1547
m. Gaspard de Châtillon-Coligny

Odet
1517–71
cardinal

Gaspard
1519–72
seigneur de
Châtillon

François
1521–69
seigneur
d'Andelot

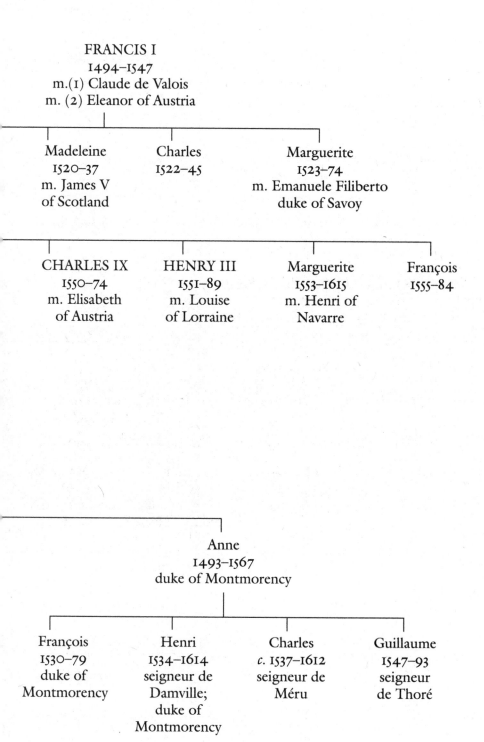

FRANCIS I
1494–1547
m.(1) Claude de Valois
m. (2) Eleanor of Austria

Madeleine
1520–37
m. James V
of Scotland

Charles
1522–45

Marguerite
1523–74
m. Emanuele Filiberto
duke of Savoy

CHARLES IX
1550–74
m. Elisabeth
of Austria

HENRY III
1551–89
m. Louise
of Lorraine

Marguerite
1553–1615
m. Henri of
Navarre

François
1555–84

Anne
1493–1567
duke of Montmorency

François
1530–79
duke of
Montmorency

Henri
1534–1614
seigneur de
Damville;
duke of
Montmorency

Charles
c. 1537–1612
seigneur de
Méru

Guillaume
1547–93
seigneur
de Thoré

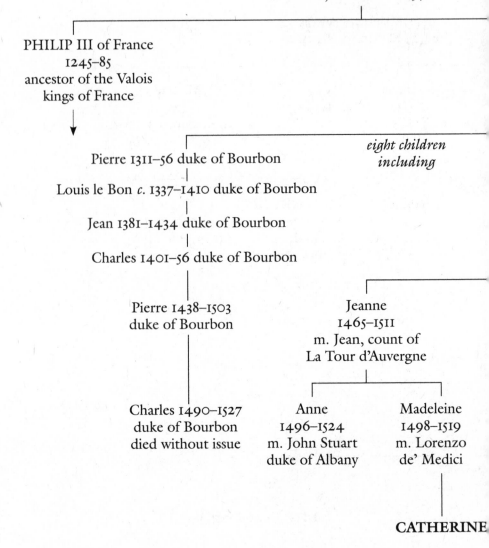

LOUIS IX of France 1214–70
St Louis, canonized 1297

PHILIP III of France
1245–85
ancestor of the Valois
kings of France

*eight children
including*

Pierre 1311–56 duke of Bourbon

Louis le Bon *c.* 1337–1410 duke of Bourbon

Jean 1381–1434 duke of Bourbon

Charles 1401–56 duke of Bourbon

Pierre 1438–1503
duke of Bourbon

Jeanne
1465–1511
m. Jean, count of
La Tour d'Auvergne

Charles 1490–1527
duke of Bourbon
died without issue

Anne
1496–1524
m. John Stuart
duke of Albany

Madeleine
1498–1519
m. Lorenzo
de' Medici

CATHERINE

The Bourbon Family

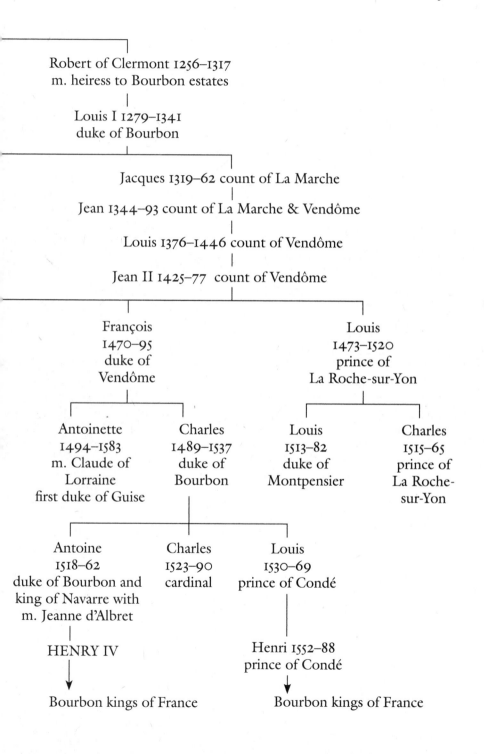

Robert of Clermont 1256–1317
m. heiress to Bourbon estates

Louis I 1279–1341
duke of Bourbon

Jacques 1319–62 count of La Marche

Jean 1344–93 count of La Marche & Vendôme

Louis 1376–1446 count of Vendôme

Jean II 1425–77 count of Vendôme

François
1470–95
duke of
Vendôme

Louis
1473–1520
prince of
La Roche-sur-Yon

Antoinette
1494–1583
m. Claude of
Lorraine
first duke of Guise

Charles
1489–1537
duke of
Bourbon

Louis
1513–82
duke of
Montpensier

Charles
1515–65
prince of
La Roche-
sur-Yon

Antoine
1518–62
duke of Bourbon and
king of Navarre with
m. Jeanne d'Albret

Charles
1523–90
cardinal

Louis
1530–69
prince of Condé

HENRY IV

Henri 1552–88
prince of Condé

Bourbon kings of France

Bourbon kings of France

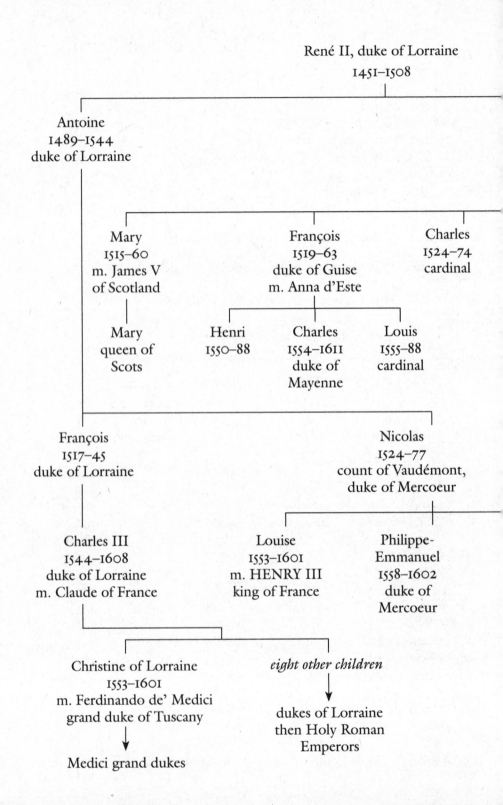

René II, duke of Lorraine
1451–1508

Antoine
1489–1544
duke of Lorraine

Mary
1515–60
m. James V
of Scotland

François
1519–63
duke of Guise
m. Anna d'Este

Charles
1524–74
cardinal

Mary
queen of
Scots

Henri
1550–88

Charles
1554–1611
duke of
Mayenne

Louis
1555–88
cardinal

François
1517–45
duke of Lorraine

Nicolas
1524–77
count of Vaudémont,
duke of Mercoeur

Charles III
1544–1608
duke of Lorraine
m. Claude of France

Louise
1553–1601
m. HENRY III
king of France

Philippe-
Emmanuel
1558–1602
duke of
Mercoeur

Christine of Lorraine
1553–1601
m. Ferdinando de' Medici
grand duke of Tuscany

eight other children

dukes of Lorraine
then Holy Roman
Emperors

Medici grand dukes

The House of Lorraine-Guise

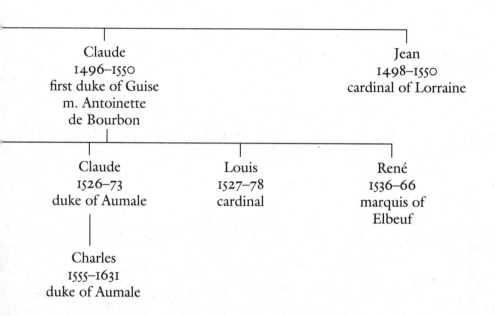

Claude
1496–1550
first duke of Guise
m. Antoinette
de Bourbon

Jean
1498–1550
cardinal of Lorraine

Claude
1526–73
duke of Aumale

Louis
1527–78
cardinal

René
1536–66
marquis of
Elbeuf

Charles
1555–1631
duke of Aumale

Charles
1561–87
cardinal of
Lorraine-Vaudémont

Marguerite
1564–1601
m. Anne, duke of
Joyeuse

France in the Sixteenth Century

Calais
Boulogne
ARTOIS
Thérouanne
Arras
Cambrai
Abbeville
St Quentin 1557
Dieppe
Somme
Amiens
St Quentin

English Channel

Le Havre
Rouen
Seine
Compiègne
Villers-Cotterêts
Charleval
ILE-DE-FRANCE
Rheims
Caen
DREUX 1562
ST DENIS 1567
DORMANS 1575
Meaux
NORMANDY
St Germain-en-Laye
Paris
Montceaux
CHAM PAC
Ollainville
St.-Maur
Alençon
Fontainebleau
Seine

BRITTANY
Rennes
MAYENNE
ORLÉANAIS
Montargis
BURGUNDY
Orléans
Yonne
ANJOU
Blois Chambord
Loire
Angers
Amboise
NIVERNAIS
Nantes
Saumur
Tours
TOURAINE
Romorantin
Chinon
Chenonceau
Bourges
Nevers
Loches
BERRY
MONCONTOUR 1569
POITOU
Poitiers
F R A N C E
Moulins
BOURBONNAIS
La Rochelle
MARCH
Loire
SAINTONGE
ANGOUMOIS
Charente
LIMOUSIN
AUVERGNE
LYON NA
Cognac
JARNAC 1569
Angoulême
Issoire
Allier

ATLANTIC
OCEAN
COUTRAS 1587

Bordeaux
Dordogne
GUYENNE
Garonne
K I N G D O M   O F   N A V A R R E
Nérac
Montauban
Av
LANGUEDOC
Bayonne
Toulouse
Montpellier
Pau
Pamplona
ROUSSILLON
Perpignan

0   100   200 km
0   50   100 miles

S P A I N

Br
A

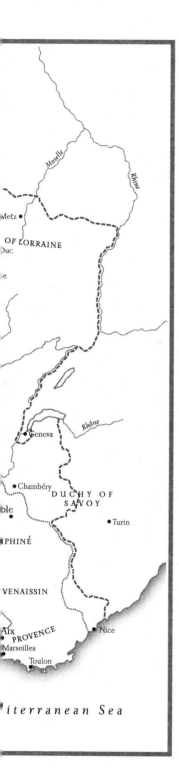

Moselle

Rhine

Metz

OF LORRAINE

Duc

le

Rhône

Geneva

Chambéry

DUCHY OF
SAVOY

ble

Turin

PHINÉ

VENAISSIN

Aix
PROVENCE
Marseilles
Toulon

Nice

iterranean Sea

.... frontier of Kingdom in 1515
------ present frontier
♜ royal châteaux
✕ battles

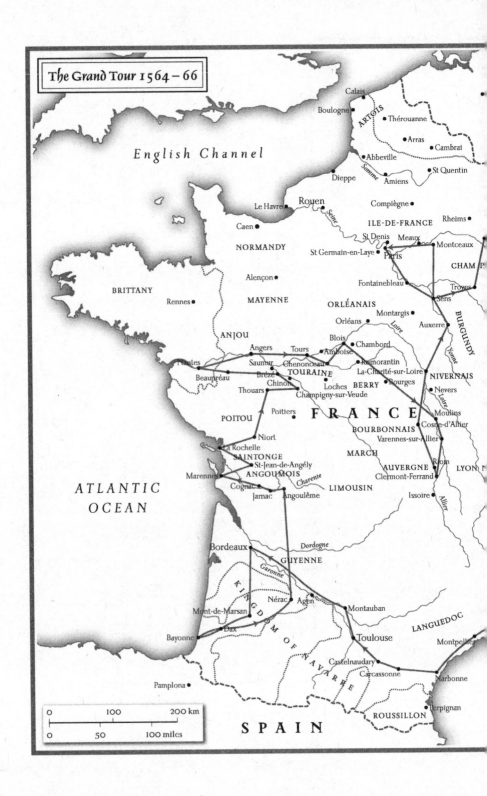

The Grand Tour 1564–66

English Channel

Calais
Boulogne
ARTOIS
Thérouanne
Arras
Cambrai
Abbeville
St Quentin
Somme
Dieppe
Amiens

Le Havre
Rouen
Compiègne
Rheims
Caen
ILE-DE-FRANCE
St Denis
Meaux
Montceaux
NORMANDY
St Germain-en-Laye
Paris
CHAMP
Alençon
Fontainebleau
Troyes
BRITTANY
MAYENNE
Sens
Rennes
ORLÉANAIS
Montargis
Auxerre
BURGUNDY
Orléans
Loire
Yonne
Blois
Chambord
Angers
Tours
Amboise
NIVERNAIS
Nantes
Saumur
Chenonceau
Romorantin
La-Charité-sur-Loire
Beaupréau
Brézé
TOURAINE
Nevers
Chinon
Loches
BERRY
Bourges
Loire
Thouars
Champigny-sur-Veude
Moulins
POITOU
Poitiers
FRANCE
Cosne-d'Allier
BOURBONNAIS
Niort
Varennes-sur-Allier
La Rochelle
SAINTONGE
MARCH
St-Jean-d'Angély
AUVERGNE
Riom
Marennes
ANGOUMOIS
Clermont-Ferrand
LYON
Cognac
Charente
LIMOUSIN
Jarnac
Angoulême
Issoire
Allier

ATLANTIC
OCEAN

Bordeaux
Dordogne
GUYENNE
Garonne
Nérac
Agen
Montauban
Mont-de-Marsan
LANGUEDOC
Dax
Toulouse
Montpellier
Bayonne
Castelnaudary
Carcassonne
Narbonne
Pamplona
Perpignan
ROUSSILLON

SPAIN

0   100   200 km
0   50   100 miles

Metz •

CHY OF LORRAINE
pagne
e-Duc

ngres

sur-Saône

Geneva

Rhône

• Chambéry
DUCHY OF
SAVOY

Grenoble •
• Turin

AUPHINÉ

T-VENAISSIN

Aix PROVENCE
• Nice

Brignoles
les
Toulon • Hyères

diterranean Sea

Moselle

Rhine

.... frontier of Kingdom in 1515
------ present frontier
⟶ the grand tour route

Note on Money

Renaissance France had several different currencies. The coinage that was used in accounts – known as money of account – was the *livre tournois*, which was worth 20 *sous*, or 240 *deniers*. There was also the gold écu (the *écu au soleil*) that weighed 3.357 grammes, broadly similar to the Italian gold currencies: the Venetian ducat, the Florentine florin and the Roman *scudo*. The value of the two currencies fluctuated against each other in response to market forces. In 1533, the year Catherine arrived in France, the *écu* was worth 45 *sous*; by 1563 this had risen to 49 *sous*; and in 1575 its value was fixed at 60 *sous*. To simplify this I have converted all sums into the equivalent gold currency, giving the original amount in brackets where relevant.

PROLOGUE

The Serpent Queen

The legend of Catherine de' Medici (1519–1589) as an evil, vicious and corrupt queen has proved one of the most durable myths in history. It has its roots in one of the bloodiest events of the sixteenth century: the brutal massacre of thousands of Protestants in Paris on St Bartholomew's Day, 24 August 1572. For Protestants it was her hands that were red with the blood of these innocent men, women and children, an accusation all the more compelling after Pope Gregory XIII warmly congratulated her on what he saw as a stupendous Catholic victory; so stupendous, in fact, that he had scenes of the triumph painted on the walls of the reception hall in the Vatican. But his enthusiasm was short-lived: she was soon a figure of hate for him and for most Catholics after it became clear that she had no intention of embarking on a campaign to eliminate the rest of the kingdom's Protestant heretics.

Her reputation for evil mushroomed among Catholics and Protestants alike far beyond the issue of the massacre. For many at the time she was a witch, steeped in the arts of poison, sorcery and other malicious practices she had brought to France from her Florentine homeland. Others accused her of using the duplicity and deviousness applauded by her compatriot Niccolò Machiavelli to foment the civil wars that ravaged France during the second half of the sixteenth century and threatened the kingdom's survival. She was despised for her ignoble ancestry; she was blamed for debasing the French language with her Italianisms. And the legend of this 'maggot from the tomb of Italy' was taken up with gusto by writers from Alexandre Dumas, whose *La Reine Margot* (1845) painted a lurid picture of Catherine as a greedy, power-crazed mother surrounded by her debauched court, to Jean Plaidy and her 1960s trilogy *Madame Serpente, The Italian Woman* and *Queen Jezebel.*

The power of this myth has made Catherine's own achievements all but invisible. Her story may be less colourful but it is fascinating nonetheless. The daughter of Lorenzo de' Medici, parvenu duke of Florence, and Madeleine de La Tour d'Auvergne, a French royal princess, she was orphaned within a month of her birth when her mother died of puerperal fever and her father of syphilis. Her unfortunate start, combined with the storms and uncertainties of sixteenth-century European politics, guided her trajectory from orphan to queen; and then to widow when her husband, Henry II, was killed in 1559 in a jousting accident. Thrust suddenly into the limelight, she sat at the heart of power for the next thirty years, a central figure in the regimes of three sons who succeeded their father to the throne.

Catherine's greatest handicap was her sex. Women rulers of the period were routinely despised: a threat to established (male) social norms, they were invariably dubbed domineering, devilish or just plain stupid – and even more opprobrium was heaped on those who were powers behind the throne, particularly in France where women were barred from wearing the crown itself. Fashioning herself first as loving, dutiful wife to a husband who flaunted his mistress in public and then, after his death, as devoted widow and mother to their children, she created an image for herself that enabled her to rule in a country where females were not welcome in the structures of power. It also provided appropriate themes and subjects for both state occasion and private ornament. She had an instinctive understanding of the propaganda value of the arts and staged magnificent festivities that exploited theatre, music and ballet for marriages, visits and other court celebrations.

Above all she promoted herself as generous patron of the arts, a subject to which few of her biographers – past or present – have paid much attention. A builder of superb palaces and châteaux, which she lovingly embellished with beautiful gardens, she surrounded herself with luxury, amassing huge collections of artworks and valuables: her inventory listed quantities of paintings and sculpture, tapestries, books and manuscripts, maps and curios and, one of her most famous possessions, a large collection of chalk portraits depicting her children and the men and women of the French court. Her importance as one of the leading female patrons of the arts of her time is rarely aired outside academic circles: but, in the words of one leading art historian, 'no woman of the Renaissance left a greater mark on the history of architecture than Catherine de' Medici'.[1] Nor is it generally known that she took an unusually close personal interest in all her projects to the extent of being involved in the process of design itself and, as such, must be considered partly responsible for the emergence of the distinctively French style of the late Renaissance.

Catherine's havens of luxury and beauty were a stark contrast to the world outside, where she faced formidable problems, not least the frailties, physical and mental, of her sons, none of whom conformed to the Renaissance ideal of a king, a painful contrast to the strong, athletic and undeniably regal figures of their father and grandfather, Henry II and Francis I. Four of her five sons died of tuberculosis and other diseases before the age of thirty; the fifth was assassinated soon after she died; her daughters too caused her considerable distress. As one historian recently noted, 'whatever we may think of Catherine herself, there is no denying that her children were all dreadful'.[2] Her greatest challenge was to ensure the survival of the crown through the seismic upheavals born of the Reformation: it was her task to navigate not only the wars between Catholics and Protestants that devastated France and came very close to destroying the kingdom, but also the peace that was so often sabotaged by the total absence of trust between the two sides.

Too many of her biographers have become immersed in her role in the civil wars that engulfed France for much of her life, preoccupied with evaluating the extent to which she was responsible for the bloodshed through the prism of religious bigotry. There was so much more to this redoubtable woman: she was intelligent and played an excellent game of chess; she was unusually well informed on subjects as diverse as geography, physics and poetry; but she also laughed a lot, enjoyed good food and chose to wear beautiful clothes. She was no whiner but put duty first, even when this was difficult: she maintained her dignity in spite of the opprobrium heaped upon her by her enemies and in the face of her husband's very public adultery. Most impressively, she learned to survive at the French court, no easy task. It may have been the most magnificent in Europe, but it was also the most treacherous, a venomous hive of gossip and intrigue; and its courtiers were a truly villainous cast of arrogant, ruthless, devious and self-serving characters, who plotted and murdered to attain their own ends, placing their own ambitions before loyalty to the crown.

Catherine, who was always loyal to the crown, became one of the most influential figures of her time, playing a pivotal role in the political, religious and social changes that transformed Christian Europe during the sixteenth century. In this male-dominated world she was one of the few women to write their own page of history – and this is her story.

1

The Little Duchess
1519–1531

atherine's story begins, very appropriately, in France in April 1518 at the royal château of Amboise, where Francis I hosted the wedding of her parents as part of the splendid festivities he staged to celebrate the birth of his son, François. After four years of marriage and the birth of two daughters, both barred from inheriting the throne by the Salic law, Queen Claude had finally produced an heir to the Valois dynasty. It was an occasion for much rejoicing. It is difficult to overstate the importance of festivities as part of the rituals of court life across Europe – and Catherine herself would play a significant role in their development. While the passing of the Christian year was marked with a regular cycle of processions, feasts and rites, for the court there were other more unexpected occasions for celebration. The spectacular entries that welcomed the king into the cities of his realm, for example, the solemn pomp of coronations and funerals or the noisy fireworks and parties that acclaimed victory on the battlefield and the signing of political treaties. Above all, the ruling dynasties of Renaissance Europe celebrated the marriages that were designed deliberately to forge political alliances in Renaissance Europe, and the birth of heirs to guarantee their futures.

The christening of the dauphin provided Francis I with the occasion not only to celebrate a dynastic milestone but also to promote his political agenda. Since his accession to the throne on 1 January 1515 his priority had been the restoration of the honour and prestige of the French crown which had been damaged by the ignominious failure of the Italian campaigns conducted by his two predecessors, Charles VIII (1483–98) and Louis XII (1498–1515), to assert their rights to Naples and Milan. Francis had inherited legitimate claims to both states, though these were hotly contested by the emperor, the king of Spain and the papacy. As the legitimate great-grandson of Giangaleazzo Visconti, the first duke of Milan, he had a better claim to the title than the Sforza family, an illegitimate branch of the Visconti who had usurped the title in 1450; the situation was complicated by the fact that Milan was an imperial fief and Emperor Maximilian I refused to recognize Francis's claim. In Naples, which he claimed as heir to the medieval Angevin kings, Francis faced opposition from Spain, who had forced Louis XII's armies to retreat from the kingdom in 1503. Moreover, both Charles VIII and Louis XII had also earned the enmity of the pope in Rome, a mistake Francis I himself was determined to avoid.

Within months of his accession Francis I began assembling an army to invade Italy. Having surprised his enemies by avoiding the customary passes over the Alps, he won a resounding victory at Marignano on 13 September 1515 and entered Milan in triumph a month later. Winning the battle for Milan, however, was only the first step: maintaining his authority in the duchy, and pursuing his campaign for Naples, could only be achieved with the support of at least some of the Italian powers. Having placated Milan's neighbour Venice, the other major state in northern Italy, Francis held a summit meeting with Leo X in Bologna that December and signed an alliance with the pope. The terms were very favourable: in return for Francis promising to support papal policy, Leo X agreed to back the king's plans for the invasion of Milan and Naples. As a bonus Francis also negotiated a vast increase of his powers over the Church in France, including the rights to tax the clergy and to appoint his own bishops and abbots. Both his new Italian allies sent appropriate gifts to commemorate the birth of the dauphin. The Venetians sent Queen Claude an altarpiece of the *Visitation* by one of their leading painters, Sebastiano del Piombo, while Leo X sent two works by Raphael: a *Holy Family* for the queen and a *St Michael*, the patron saint of the French royal chivalric order, for the king.[1]

It was with the intention of increasing Italian support for his campaign in the peninsula that he invited several Italian aristocrats to join his own courtiers for the two weeks of jousting, balls, banquets and parties that followed the dauphin's christening on 26 April. For all those taking part it was an opportunity to show off their wealth and status in lavishly expensive outfits. Display mattered. The marquis of Mantua, who was too ill with syphilis to attend in person, sent his son Federigo Gonzaga in his place and made sure that the youth would be suitably dressed. He ordered lengths of cloth of gold from Florence, at great expense, advising Federigo to get the outfits made up by the royal tailor once he arrived in France.[2] It was also important to show skill in the jousting lists and he warned his son to take extreme care as the heavy lances in use in France could cause serious injury; 'we think they are very dangerous'.[3] Indeed, the jousts, sword fights, mock battles and other games played by these knights were designed to showcase military prowess and were not for the faint-hearted. A 'battle' in which the king himself led a team of 600 men proved so realistic that several of the competitors were killed; 'it was the finest battle ever seen,' enthused one member of the audience 'and the nearest to real warfare'.[4]

Of the Italians present at Amboise, one was conspicuously favoured above the others: Lorenzo de' Medici, duke of Urbino and Leo X's nephew. Francis I heaped honours on him, including the French title of duke of Lavaur.[5] It was Lorenzo who held the infant dauphin at the baptismal font (acting as proxy for his uncle, the pope) and he was admitted into the royal chivalric order of St Michael. As one of the knights of this order, which was largely reserved for the upper echelons of the French nobility, he could boast his membership with the coveted gold badge embossed with an image of the archangel suspended from an elaborate gold collar. And, importantly for this story, the king agreed to Lorenzo's marriage to one of his own cousins, the twenty-year-old Madeleine de La Tour d'Auvergne.

Royal approval of the match was evident for all to see. Francis I gave the bride a pension of 10,000 écus; his gift to the groom of the duchy of Lavaur brought an annual income of 4,500 écus (10,000 livres) and the king also signed a guarantee that this French title would pass to any children the couple might have, male and female.[6] The wedding itself, financed by the king, was certainly grand enough to befit a royal princess and it was one of the highlights of the festivities at Amboise. It was celebrated with a grand banquet, followed by a ball that went on into the early hours of the morning. With no room large enough to host the party, the courtyard of the château was specially decorated for the occasion with a parquet floor for dancing, tapestries hung over the walls and an awning of 'blue cloth decorated with lilies' to protect the guests from the elements.[7]

Bride and groom were not socially well-matched. Madeleine de La Tour d'Auvergne belonged to the Bourbon family, the premier dynasty of the French nobility which claimed descent directly from Louis IX (1214–70), as did the Valois themselves. They were styled princes and princesses 'of the blood' and, significantly, the princes held the distinction of being next in line to the throne after the royal family. Her sister, Anne, had made a far grander match: her husband was John Stuart, duke of Albany, grandson of James II of Scotland (1437–60), regent for the infant James V and, until the boy had children of his own, next in line to the Scottish throne. He was also Madeleine's legal guardian following the death of her father in 1501. Lorenzo, by contrast, could claim no royal connections and very little noble blood. His mother, Alfonsina Orsini, was the daughter of the Neapolitan branch of a Roman baronial family but his father, Piero, came from a family of bankers – Piero and his father were addressed as *Magnifico*, an honorific reserved for wealthy men who were unable to claim an aristocratic title of their own. Moreover, as we shall see, his Italian title, duke of Urbino, had been obtained illegally.

It was not just Francis I who had compelling reasons for arranging the marriage; for Leo X the priority was safeguarding the future of his family. The Medici family had made a spectacular fortune as bankers during the fifteenth century and had used their profits to buy their way into power at the head of Florence's republican government.[8] For much of the century the family had been careful to hide their princely pretensions behind a show of loyalty to the republic but they were far from popular. Eventually the Florentines, outraged by the arrogance and sense of entitlement shown by Lorenzo's father, Piero, sent the entire family into exile in 1494. It was eighteen long years before they were able to return, and then only because of the political acumen shown by Piero's brother, Cardinal Giovanni, who had negotiated this favour from Julius II in 1512. When Giovanni was elected as Leo X the following year, he put his determination to protect and magnify his own family before the governance of the Church in order to avoid a repeat of the disastrous exile – one of the clauses of the alliance between Francis I and Leo X required the king to provide military support if the authority of the Medici in Florence came under threat.

In 1513 Leo X installed Lorenzo, his twenty-one-year-old nephew, as ruler of Florence – under the guise of 'leader' of the republic – and sent the papal banker Filippo Strozzi to act as his adviser. Filippo, who was three years older than Lorenzo, was married to his sister Clarice and the brothers-in-law were close friends. They shared a reputation for loose living; apparently Strozzi regularly climbed into convents at night and had a house outside the walls for other assignations.[9] The banker, who was in charge of both the papal and Florentine treasuries, was also a financial wizard, adept at diverting Florentine public funds to finance Medici ambitions: a little judicious bribery, for example, persuaded the republic to appoint Lorenzo as captain-general of the Florentine army with a salary of 35,000 florins a year.[10] With this appointment Lorenzo was effectively lord of Florence in all but name; but what he really wanted was a proper title and his uncle duly obliged. Exploiting his power as pope for his own in the interests of his family, Leo excommunicated Francesco Maria I della Rovere, the rightful duke of Urbino, and made Lorenzo duke instead. Within months the new duke, at the head of a papal army funded by the Florentine public purse, forced Francesco Maria I into exile.[11] It is no coincidence that Niccolò Machiavelli dedicated his book *The Prince* to Lorenzo: it is a work that has much to say about rulers who secured their states by luck and by the assistance of foreign troops, rather than those who acquired them through the more conventional route of inheritance. It was certainly Lorenzo's good luck to have a pope for an uncle and a king in need of an alliance. In early 1518 he left Florence in the company of his brother-in-law for France, to obtain more money, more titles and a royal bride.

Lorenzo and his new duchess remained in France for several months after their wedding in April 1518. That summer he accompanied Francis I on a hunting expedition to Brittany, leaving Madeleine behind at Amboise in the company of Filippo Strozzi, who, to his disgust, was charged with teaching her Italian.[12] By the time the couple left for Florence in late July, Madeleine was already pregnant. She made her formal entry into the city on 7 September 1518, an event recorded by coppersmith Bartolomeo Masi in his diary, who judged it to have been done 'with the greatest honour and magnificence'.[13]

One wonders what Madeleine, accustomed to the grandeur and etiquette of the most illustrious court in Europe, made of Florence and the Florentines. The city was prosperous, certainly: with a population of around 70,000, it was one of the largest in Europe, in fourth place after Paris, Milan and Venice, all of which could boast over 100,000 inhabitants. The city was filled with grand palaces and splendid churches ornamented with expensive marble façades. The enormous cathedral with its inlaid marble cladding and elegant bell tower was one of the largest churches in Christendom. However, although Leo X had made her husband effectively titular head of Florence, he did not have the absolute power of a king. Authority in Florence was vested in the *Signoria,* a committee of nine men elected to serve three-month terms of office in charge of government affairs.

Lorenzo's power was circumscribed by the need to pay lip service to the republican constitution. Leo X had felt it necessary to advise his arrogant young nephew to mix a little more with the citizens: Cardinal Giulio de' Medici, the pope's cousin and right-hand man, suggested that Lorenzo should 'make a show of affability and kindness ... and invite [Florentines] to dine with you not just in the city but also at the villa, because these are two ways in which you can show favour and this will surely increase their good opinion of you'.[14] The Medici were not popular and many resented the hold Lorenzo exercised over the city. Staunch republicans measured their success in their ledgers not their ancestry; and they proudly traced the origins of the *Signoria* to 1293 when the city's merchants and shopkeepers had written their own unique constitution banning the aristocratic elite from power.

It was Lorenzo's mother, Alfonsina Orsini, who organized the celebrations that were staged for Madeleine's official entry into Florence. The daughter of a Neapolitan baron and no fan of the republic, Alfonsina was determined to showcase Medici wealth and prestige in order to welcome the royal bride in an appropriately grand manner. The festivities were staged at the Palazzo Medici, the family palace on the Via Larga, which must have seemed rather modest by the standards of the royal châteaux in France. However, as at Amboise, the palace lacked a suitably large indoor space for gatherings of this size so Alfonsina ordered the garden at the rear to be paved with flagstones to enable it to be used for the nuptial banquet, while the theatrical entertainments and dancing took place on an enormous raised wooden platform in front of the palace, which extended across the entire width of the Via Larga and was hung with tapestries.[15]

Among the guests were cardinals, churchmen, local aristocrats and merchants but Leo X, the architect of the event, was unable to attend. He was present, symbolically, in his portrait by Raphael that was rushed to Florence so that it could hang above the diners for the nuptial banquet, 'and it really brightened everything up', Alfonsina reported that evening to one of Lorenzo's household.[16] Madeleine herself was seated between the two guests of honour, who, in the absence of the pope, were cardinals: Luigi de' Rossi and Innocenzo Cibò, both of whom were Medici relatives and had been given their red hats by Leo X. Alfonsina was evidently relieved that all had gone well; 'indeed, today passed very agreeably, and God gave us lovely weather … and there were lots of people at their windows, on the rooftops, on the streets and on the platforms that had been set up everywhere'.

The lunch parties, evening banquets, dances continued for five days. The quality of the musical performances and plays were much enhanced by actors and musicians sent up from the papal court in Rome.[17] Florentine painters, carpenters and sculptors had been busy for weeks assembling and painting stage sets as well as the decorations on the carts representing the triumphs of Venus, Mars and Minerva that formed the procession on the final day, concluding with the arrival of Hymen, the god of marriage.[18]

The following months passed quietly enough. Later in September Lorenzo hosted a tournament in the piazza at

Santa Maria Novella with two teams of eight knights mounted on horses 'that even the greatest men in the world could not rival for beauty and quality', reported the coppersmith.[19] During the autumn Lorenzo and his brother-in-law Filippo were in Rome hoping to persuade Leo X to use his power to terminate the Florentine republican constitution and allow him to become duke of Florence but the pope refused, fearful that this would provoke a revolt against the Medici in the city.[20] Then in November Lorenzo fell ill and soon developed a fever, joint pain and loss of appetite, symptoms which lasted into the winter.[21] He was still far from well on 13 April 1519 when Madeleine gave birth to a daughter in the Palazzo Medici.

There must have been some disappointment that the child was female – a son would have given Lorenzo an heir who might have done much to safeguard the Medici position, but women were excluded, by law, from political life in Florence. Three days later 'the baby girl was christened at the Baptistery and the customary font', reported coppersmith Masi, and named 'Caterina, Maria and Romola'.[22] The name Caterina might well have been the choice of Alfonsina as it had belonged to her own mother. Masi also named her six godparents, most of whom held religious positions, including the prior of San Lorenzo, the Medici family's local parish church, and the abbesses of two Florentine convents, the Benedictine nunnery of the Murate and the Dominican nunnery of the Annalena, both of whom were represented by proxies. The coppersmith added ominously, 'Duke Lorenzo her father was not at the baptism because he was ill'. As the duke's secretary explained, 'every hour he gets worse and it is more dangerous'.[23]

Tragically, within a month baby Caterina was an orphan, left in the care of her grandmother Alfonsina. Madeleine died from puerperal fever on 28 April, a fortnight after giving birth, and the next day she was 'buried at dawn in San Lorenzo without celebration and this was because Duke Lorenzo her husband was also gravely ill and had not been told of the death of his wife in case it precipitated his death'.[24] Less than a week later, on 4 May, Lorenzo died, probably of tuberculosis: Masi judged he had been poisoned; others thought syphilis the most likely cause. The coppersmith recorded that he was not much mourned by the Florentines 'and the cause I think is that it was believed that the said Duke Lorenzo had the desire to make himself lord of Florence'.[25] Nevertheless, Masi continued, three days later 'he was buried with great magnificence in San Lorenzo' after a funeral service that lasted four hours.

Lorenzo's death was a disaster for Leo X, who had optimistically assigned him the task of siring a male heir to secure the future of the dynasty. Apart from the pope himself and his cousin Cardinal Giulio – himself a bastard, but legitimized in 1513 to receive his red hat – Caterina was the sole legitimate descendant of the branch of Medici family that had been exiled in 1494. The only males left were illegitimate boys: Ippolito, aged eight, who was the acknowledged son of Leo's younger brother, Giuliano; and Alessandro, a year younger, whose origins are shrouded in mystery. There is no record of this boy before 1519 when he was presented as the son of Lorenzo and an African slave; however, there is good evidence, as we shall see, that it was Cardinal Giulio who was the father of this boy.[26]

By contrast to her cousin and 'half-brother', little Caterina was not only legitimate but also a wealthy heiress in her own right. She was given the title of duchess as her father's only child – and she was known more affectionately as 'the little duchess' (*La Duchessina*). In May 1519 Francis I issued an order confirming her right to inherit her mother's possessions in France.[27] These were quite extensive: Madeleine and her sister, Anne, had inherited the family patrimony in the Auvergne on the death of their father in 1501. Moreover, the king confirmed

Caterina's rights to Lavaur in south-west France, which had been a gift to Lorenzo as part of Madeleine's dowry. In February 1520 Caterina's grandmother Alfonsina Orsini died and, though she left the bulk of her fortune to her brother-in-law Leo X, her will charged the pope with providing for Caterina.[28] The girl's fortune increased substantially in 1524 when her aunt Anne died, leaving her as heiress to the other half of her French patrimony. Such wealth and connections made her a valuable asset to both the Medici and Francis I and each took steps to claim her as their own. Unfortunately for the king, the Medici held all the cards and Leo X firmly refused the king's formal request to be appointed guardian to the baby girl.

In order to maintain the Medici presence in Florence after Lorenzo's death, Leo X had sent Cardinal Giulio to take the reins of government and in March 1520, following the death of Alfonsina, the cardinal took steps to ensure that Caterina remained legally in the charge of the pope. According to Florentine law, as Caterina was without parents or grandparents, she was the responsibility of the *Ufficiali de' Pupilli* (the officials in charge of orphans); however, Giulio announced, given the unusual circumstances, that her legal guardian was to be her great-uncle Leo X.[29] Unfortunately in December 1521 Leo died and responsibility for the orphan again reverted to the *Ufficiali de' Pupilli*.[30] This time Cardinal Giulio was named as her new guardian: one of his first tasks was to appoint an agent to recoup all the monies and goods that had been confiscated in 1494; and he later sent agents to France to get hold of the arrears of income owed to Caterina.[31]

The death of Leo X was a blow for the entire Medici clan. He had been only thirty-seven years old when elected and the family had expected to enjoy several decades of power, but he died after less than nine years in office. So it was an amazing stroke of good fortune when Giulio was elected as Clement VII just two years later. For Caterina, it brought some stability, as he would continue in his role as her guardian until she married. She was now four years old, probably too young to remember the excitement of his splendid coronation procession making its noisy way through the streets of Rome in November 1523 or the celebrations for Carnival two months later when she went out to see the horses racing down the Corso in the city centre together with her two cousins, Ippolito and Alessandro, all three dressed in specially made velvet and gold outfits.[32]

We know little about Caterina's life at this point, although it is safe to assume that she had an upbringing typical of girls of her background, who were kept in the seclusion of the nursery and surrounded by women, playing and learning her letters until her formal education started, at around the age of seven. We cannot even be sure exactly where she was living. She was in Rome, where she had been taken after the death of her parents in the care of her grandmother Alfonsina, who remembered Caterina's nurse in her will and bequeathed her the substantial sum of 150 ducats – skilled workmen on Florentine building sites only earned 34 florins a year.[33] There is some evidence that after Alfonsina's death she was brought up by her aunt and uncle, Clarice de' Medici and Filippo Strozzi, who acted as banker for Clement VII as he had for Leo X. Soon after Clement's election Strozzi moved into the Palazzo dell'Aquila,* a jewel of a Renaissance palace with an elegant stuccoed *all'antica* façade designed by Raphael, which was close to the Vatican and gave him easy access to the pope's private apartments. A population census taken in 1526 recorded Strozzi living in the palace with his wife and children (they had ten) and a modest number of servants, a total of twenty-five people in all.[34] There is also some evidence that Caterina's Medici cousins, Ippolito and Alessandro, were part

---

* The Palazzo dell'Aquila, built for Giovanbattista Branconio dell'Aquila, an official in the Curia, was demolished in the seventeenth century to make way for Bernini's colonnades that enclose the piazza in front of St Peter's.

of the household at the Palazzo dell'Aquila; or at least that she was living with them somewhere in Rome in early 1524 when she received a visit from her uncle, the duke of Albany.[35]

Meanwhile the world outside Caterina's nursery was growing increasingly insecure. Clement VII faced an alarming state of affairs on the international front. When Martin Luther nailed a list of complaints about indulgences on the door of the castle church at Wittenberg in October 1517, he had hoped to precipitate much-needed reform of the Church but the situation quickly spiralled out of control. Although Luther had been declared a heretic and his writings banned, Catholics in northern Europe were converting to Protestantism in vast numbers, severely depleting the papal coffers in Rome. The Turks, under the leadership of Sultan Suleiman, were expanding their authority to threaten Christian Europe. In the Mediterranean, despite the heroic efforts of the Knights of Rhodes, that island was captured in December 1522; and, with Suleiman's armies advancing through the Balkans to the borders of the empire, there was panic in Rome the following spring when several Turkish spies were arrested.[36]

Moreover, a new superpower had begun to flex its muscles on the European political stage. The Holy Roman Emperor Maximilian I had died in 1519 and his successor was his grandson Charles V, who was already duke of Burgundy and king of Spain. The authority of the new emperor, who was only nineteen years old at his accession, now extended over the Low Countries, the German states, Naples and Spain, even across the Atlantic to the New World. Like Francis I, he had ambitions to extend his authority in Italy and the two rivals were soon locked in a bitter enmity that would transform the political map of Europe. Clement VII urged the two men to settle their differences and present a united front that would challenge the threats posed by the Protestants and the Turks, but his insistence on a policy of neutrality infuriated both sides. 'The poor pope is buffeted on all sides like a ship battling through a storm at sea,' reported one ambassador.[37] Clement proved incapable of preventing the violence from spreading across northern Italy. In February 1525 the French were heavily defeated at the Battle of Pavia; Francis I was taken prisoner and sent to Madrid, from where he was released a year later after signing a peace treaty with Charles V, promising to relinquish his claims to Milan and Naples and leaving his two sons, François and Henri, behind as hostages for his good behaviour. Within two months Francis had broken his word and signed an alliance with Clement VII against the emperor.

Many, including Filippo Strozzi, warned Clement VII of the dangers posed by this new alliance which was in direct contravention of the treaty Francis I and Charles V had signed at Madrid. Strozzi also had his own worries: his financial assets were increasingly tied up in loans to the pope which were secured on papal revenues and taxes, and would be worthless in the event of Clement's death. Both the pope and his banker had a vested interest in taking steps to safeguard all potential Medici assets. It was about this time that rumours began to circulate suggesting that Clement intended to secure Caterina's substantial fortune for his own family by marrying her to Ippolito, who, in May 1524, had been installed in the family palace on the Via Larga as the figurehead of the Medici regime – the pope also sent a close ally, Cardinal Silvio Passerini, to Florence to keep a watchful eye over the thirteen-year-old. By 1526 Caterina and Alessandro had also been sent back to Florence and were living in the family villa at Poggio a Caiano, some 10 miles west of the city, when disturbing news arrived from Rome in early May the following year.

It was fortunate that they left when they did: on 6 May 1527 Rome was brutally sacked by a mutinous imperial army who, lured by tales of the fabulous wealth of the Church, had ravaged the city, butchered and raped the inhabitants and plundered their palaces. The bodies of thousands of men, women and children, monks and nuns were left dead or dying on the streets. When the dramatic news that Clement VII was a prisoner in Castel Sant'Angelo reached Florence on 11 May, an angry mob took to the streets to challenge the Medici regime. With the threat of violence very real, the eight-year-old Caterina was fetched from Poggio a Caiano and placed in the Dominican convent of Santa Lucia for her safety.[38] On 14 May Clarice arrived in Florence, having escaped from Rome with her husband just before the sack, and two days later she collected Caterina from Santa Lucia and moved her into the Palazzo Medici.

Support for the revolt against the Medici was gathering force. On 17 May Cardinal Passerini was forced to leave the city with Ippolito and Alessandro; the following day the *Signoria* ordered Clarice and Caterina to leave the palace, which was sacked by rioters determined to destroy all traces of the hated family. There is some confusion about what happened to Caterina but at some point she was moved to another Dominican nunnery, that of Santa Caterina di Siena, where she spent the next six months or so being 'raised there under the instruction and care of these holy and religious mothers', as one nun recorded in her chronicle.[39]

It was soon apparent that it was not just Clement VII and Francis I who were keen to exploit Caterina's value as a political pawn. There was now a third party involved: the new republican regime in Florence, installed after the exile of Ippolito and Alessandro. Amid the euphoria of victory had come the brutal shock that the city's coffers were empty: between 1512 and 1527 more than four million ducats had been taken out of the Florentine treasury to finance various projects of the Medici popes, not least the war to conquer Urbino for Caterina's father.[40] Even the wealthy had been so heavily taxed that they were unable to pay any more in forced loans. In an attempt to raise necessary funds the government set up a commission on 4 June 1527 to investigate charges of fraud against the Medici and their supporters.

One of the first targets of the investigators was Alfonsina Orsini, who had been in charge of Florence during her son's frequent absences and was particularly reviled for her lack of regard for the city's republican institutions. She was widely condemned for her avarice, not least for the way she had acquired properties in and around Florence which included shops and farms, as well as a property near Fucecchio, west of the city.[41] They accused her of not paying anything for this estate and then of stripping it of its assets by cutting down the woods and draining the lake, thus depriving local fishermen of their income.[42] As Alfonsina was dead, it was Caterina who was ordered to answer the charges in court in person.[43] The court announced its verdict on 7 September: the eight-year-old was required to pay 2,400 florins, a sum increased a fortnight later by 2,000 florins to repay a debt her father owed the city, and another 6,749 florins to cover taxes and other charges due on Alfonsina's land, a total of 11,149 florins – though it should be said that this looks fairly modest in contrast to the sum of 212,000 florins which Clement VII was deemed to owe.[44] That same September, orders were issued from the Palazzo della Signoria to the nuns at Santa Caterina 'in future not to allow the duchess, daughter of Duke Lorenzo de' Medici, to leave the nunnery'.[45]

In its search for allies, the *Signoria* had re-established Florence's traditional alliance with France and one of the tasks of Francis I's ambassador was to keep the king informed about Caterina's wellbeing. It must have been some comfort to her to know that the king's interest would mitigate to some degree the republic's anti-Medici stance, though when Francis's ambassador requested the government to send Caterina to France, he was met with blank refusals. The republic certainly knew the value of its little prisoner, whom they had placed in 'the care and custody' of the city's police force (the *Otto di*

Guardia).[46] By the autumn of 1527 reports reached France that she was not being particularly well treated in Santa Caterina di Siena though the reasons for this are not clear. Possibly her family name made her unpopular at the convent, which had been founded in 1500 by a follower of the Dominican friar Girolamo Savonarola whose sermons attacking the pomp and sleaze of the Medici had substantially contributed to the exile of the family in 1494. The convent, which was under the authority of Savonarola's own friary of San Marco, attracted many of his supporters and had grown rapidly, reaching eighty nuns by 1515.[47] Or perhaps it was the wrong sort of place: the convent was unusual in that it had been established to cater for the daughters of shopkeepers and artisans rather than those of wealthy merchants, who would have been more in keeping with Caterina's background.[48]

Although the *Signoria* refused to release Caterina to Francis I's guardianship, it did bow to pressure from the French ambassador to move her to a different nunnery and to improve her living conditions. On 7 December 1527, after six months at Santa Caterina di Siena, she arrived at Santa Maria Annunziata delle Murate, on the Via Ghibellina, apparently escorted there by the French ambassador himself. By the end of the month the *Signoria* had issued an order to pay 20 florins a month for the eight-year-old's living expenses, monies that were to be deducted from confiscated Medici funds.[49] She would remain at this convent until she was eleven, formative years in the life of a young woman. Although technically a prisoner of the republic, in reality she was now a paying guest living in the safety of a community of women who made their own decisions and followed their own rules, largely independent of the masculine world outside. It was an experience that would have a lasting impact on the little girl.

The option of convent life had become popular among women from the mercantile elite during the late fifteenth century. By 1515 there were over 2,500 nuns in Florence and the number was rising rapidly, especially for daughters of families unable to afford the increasingly expensive dowries demanded for a good match: the average dowry for a husband was around 2,000 florins; that for a bride of Christ could be as little as 50 florins.[50] However, few of these institutions were able to survive on dowry income alone. They supplemented their meagre resources with bequests and ran small business ventures – some convents sold second-hand goods, for example, others specialized in making scented waters or medicines; and there was good money to be made in producing silk thread, ribbons and luxury textiles for trousseaux, or plaster figurines of saints and angels. Another source of funds was the fees they charged for board and lodging: a small nunnery could double its income by taking in boarders.[51] They offered places of safety, albeit in rather austere surroundings, for girls temporarily without protection of a father or brothers while these men were away from home on business; they also functioned as retirement homes for wealthy widows with no family of their own; in particular, they were the solution of choice for the wards in the care of the *Ufficiali de' Pupilli*. For girls like Caterina life in a convent was not unlike a modern boarding school: they were taught to read and write, while some were even given Latin lessons; the nuns also instructed them in the Catholic faith and they could practise their needlework skills.

The Murate,* as the nunnery was popularly known, was an enclosed convent, named for the walls (It: *mura*) that surrounded it. Access was restricted: female visitors were permitted but men were forbidden except for close relatives; letters and presents could be delivered by means of a revolving shelf inserted into the stonework. The convent was founded in 1390 by a woman determined to lead a pious but

---

*   After the suppression of the convents in the nineteenth century, the Murate was used as the city's male prison, which closed in 1985; the building has recently been converted into an upmarket leisure centre with bars, restaurants, shops and an area for exhibitions.

independent life who walled herself up in a house on what is now the Ponte alle Grazie, where she was joined by several more like-minded women. In 1424 they moved to the house in the Via Ghibellina, where they established their closed community. Although the nuns joined the Benedictine order in the early fifteenth century, over the intervening years they acquired an unusual degree of independence from local Church authorities.[52]

By the time Caterina arrived, the Murate was one of the grander religious foundations in Florence and its fame had spread through Italy and beyond: by 1515 it was home to 200 nuns, making it one of the largest convents in the city and one of the richest. When Caterina's uncle, the duke of Albany, asked the Florentine ambassador in France about her new accommodation, the diplomat replied that it could not be more honourable as the convent was one of the most venerated in Florence.[53] The Murate was richer than most Florentine nunneries. Patronized by the city's elite families, it was the beneficiary of many wills, through which it acquired money and property: the nuns owned a pork butcher's shop on the Ponte Vecchio and one of the convent's grandest patrons, Queen Eleonora of Portugal, sent regular supplies of Madeira sugar to the nuns.[54] Inside its forbidding walls were comfortable dormitories, private rooms, a scriptorium, a garden and an orchard, where the nuns grew fruit, herbs and flowers, which they used to make syrups, potions, lozenges, soaps and distilled waters to augment their income.

During the late fifteenth century the Murate had attracted the opprobrium of Savonarola, who ordered the nuns to reform their 'sinful' activities: they were famous for their expensively embroidered goods, for their illuminated manuscripts and for their musical skills that included organ playing and the singing of polyphonic music, a practice that Savonarola castigated in his fiery sermons as 'satanic'.[55] Nevertheless, by the time Leo X visited the convent in 1515 – on his way to Bologna to draw up his alliance with Francis I – the nuns were

again plying their needles with gold and silver thread and
singing their intricate harmonies. It was a convent with close
ties to the Medici family. Caterina's own godmother had been
abbess of the Murate and many of the nuns came from families related to the Medici by marriage. Her great-grandfather
Lorenzo *il Magnifico* – father of Leo X – had been generous in
his support, giving regular gifts of grain, wine and oil as well
as occasional parcels of marzipan and other treats.[56] There
may have been some hyperbole in the charming account of
Caterina as recorded by sister Giustina Niccolini in her chronicle of the Murate, who described the eight-year-old as 'small,
graceful in style who, by her own behaviour, made herself
beloved by everyone'.[57] But it is likely that little Caterina
felt more at home in this socially prestigious community of
unmarried women.

In Rome events had taken a turn for the better. On 6
December – the day before Caterina arrived at the Murate –
Clement VII finally completed the tediously long negotiations
with Ugo de Moncada, Charles V's viceroy in Naples. In
exchange for his freedom the pope had promised to take a
neutral stance towards the Habsburg–Valois struggle and to
assemble a general council for the reform of the Church. As
guarantee of his good behaviour, he had handed over seven
wealthy hostages to his captors and surrendered various papal
fortresses to the imperial army. He had also paid an indemnity
to the emperor of some 400,000 ducats, raised by melting
down all his valuable jewels and selling a quantity of red hats.[58]
In a sign of how little he trusted Moncada, Clement escaped
from Castel Sant'Angelo that night disguised in the clothes of
his major-domo and rode north to the papal city of Orvieto.[59]
Despite being humiliated and beggared, and unable to wear
those costly vestments and valuable mitres that had been the
visible signs of his authority in the past, he was pope again.

Orvieto was soon inundated with diplomats from courts across Europe with conflicting requests for the pope: from Francis I urging him to drop his alliance with Charles V; from Henry VIII demanding a divorce from Catherine of Aragon, the emperor's aunt; and from Charles himself, urging him to refuse Henry's request, and proposing a more formal alliance with the pope.

Also part of Clement VII's political agenda was the three-sided tug-of-war over Caterina's future, in particular how to solve the problem posed by the refusal of both Francis I and the Florentine republic to countenance any solution that involved this valuable asset returning to his protection. Francis I for his part feared that the pope would be forced to bow to pressure from Charles V and agree to Caterina's betrothal to a Habsburg prince, thus giving the emperor a very unwelcome interest in French affairs. For the *Signoria* it was the pope's own designs on Florence that caused the greatest concern. There was little doubt that Clement would use all means in his power to enable his family to return; what worried the republic was that the pope would force a Medici government on the city or, worse, dissolve the republic completely and install a hereditary Medici dynasty – headed, perhaps, by the cousins Ippolito and little Caterina.

The volatile political situation was complicating the tug-of-war over Caterina's future. In April 1528 Francis I launched an attack on Naples and destroyed the imperial fleet, but it ended in failure that summer after a catastrophic outbreak of the plague decimated his army. However, he had been more successful at finding support in northern Italy. In May he cemented an alliance with Alfonso d'Este, duke of Ferrara, with the marriage of Renée of France, younger sister of Queen Claude, to the duke's heir, Ercole. He could now count on Ferrara as well as the Florentine republic. Clement VII, in an attempt to re-establish his alliance with Francis I, confided to the commander of the French army that Caterina was being ill-treated in the Murate and his pleasure at hearing that the

French ambassador in Florence had asked the *Signoria* to allow Caterina to leave the city.[60]

The response of the republic to these manoeuvres was quick. In May the *Otto di Guardia* issued the first of a series of injunctions ordering the abbess and nuns of the Murate to keep a watchful eye on their young ward.[61] The *Signoria* certainly believed that it would be better to send Caterina to France than allow her to join Clement VII but, as they informed their ambassador in France that July, 'we judge that it is no bad thing to keep the little duchess in our territory'.[62] As a favour to Francis I, however, they gave permission for the king's envoy to Rome to visit Caterina. This envoy was a distant kinsman of the orphan: François II de La Tour d'Auvergne, viscount of Turenne and a member of the cadet branch of Caterina's maternal family. Turenne informed the duke of Albany that Caterina 'is still in the convent keeping her spirits up with few visits but little esteem from these Florentine lords who wish with all their heart that she was in paradise'.[63] He added that she would very much like a present from France and, in a very remarkable comment on the composure of Albany's nine-year-old niece, judged that 'by my faith I promise you that I have never met any person of her age who has a better understanding of the good and the bad that is done to her'.

It is at this point that we have our first real glimpse of Caterina herself. In a letter to Turenne, written in Italian and dated 16 March 1529, she thanked him for the 'kind demonstrations and offers that your lordship has done for me on many occasions' and asked him for a favour for a certain Rosso Ridolfi, 'a Florentine gentleman who has been the head of my household for six years and has looked after me excellently'.[64] As she explained:

> Loving him like my own father, I want to do something for
> him in his old age and, having no other way of doing this,
> I thought that with the help of your excellency that his

Most Christian Majesty [Francis I] would do me the favour of helping me to pay this debt. The way of doing this is through his son Vincenzo Ridolfi who is a priest and his majesty might give him an abbey or another benefice in his realm worth 500 or 600 scudi, and permission to hold it despite not having been born in France. Asking you with great affection to intercede with the aforementioned Most Christian Majesty, for this is the first favour I have asked of him for one of my good servants.

Caterina's gesture suggests that she was a kind, thoughtful child, imbued with a strong sense of duty. Still a month away from her tenth birthday, she comes across as unusually self-assured and well versed in the language of patronage, though one suspects that she may have had help in composing the letter. What is really striking, however, was her decision to appeal to Francis I for this benefice for her governor's son, a favour that surely could have been granted more easily by her cousin the pope. It seems that already at this young age Caterina was aware that her dynastic identity was more French and royal than Medicean and Florentine.

Outside the protective walls of the Murate Catherine's world was becoming increasingly turbulent. In early January 1529 there was a moment which threatened disaster for her future when Clement VII fell seriously ill after celebrating mass for the Feast of Epiphany in a chilly Sistine Chapel. On 10 January, worried that he might die before having the opportunity to restore the fortunes of his family, he summoned the cardinals to his bedside and asked them to agree to give a red hat to the eighteen-year-old Ippolito de' Medici. As a boy Ippolito had briefly been destined for a career in the Church to complement his uncle Lorenzo's secular role as head of the family in Florence but the situation had changed radically with Lorenzo's untimely death. Leo X had chosen Ippolito to take on the role of secular head of the family and ordered him to move into the Palazzo Medici in Florence. It was certainly Ippolito's expectation that he would take the senior role, and that his younger cousin Alessandro would have the Church career. Clement VII's decision to reverse this is one of the compelling reasons to identify Alessandro as the pope's own illegitimate son. The result caused Ippolito much anguish – and the two cousins were henceforth estranged.

In Florence anger against the Medici family was growing in intensity. Medici supporters, real or suspected, were spat at on the streets and a priest was denounced for not removing a Medici coat-of-arms from his church.[65] Although the elected leader of the regime Niccolò Capponi was a moderate, his opponents were beginning to play a more strident role in political debate. In an early sign of what was to come, in January the *Otto di Guardia* had issued an order to the abbess and nuns of the Murate to prevent Caterina from speaking to any foreigner.[66] Clement VII had returned to Rome back in October and had begun to reassert his influence on the international political stage. Capponi knew that it was only a matter of time before the pope turned his attention to the restoration of the Medici and in November he sent envoys to Rome in the hope of negotiating a compromise. Intransigent as ever on this issue, the pope demanded not only the restoration of all Medici property but also Caterina's release as the price of peace.[67] That spring there was panic on the streets of Florence when it was rumoured that Clement was about to reach an agreement with Charles V, and in April the hard-line anti-Mediceans forced Capponi out of office and replaced him with Francesco Carducci, one of their own.

The rumours turned out to be true. In June 1529 came the shattering news that Clement VII had signed the Treaty of Barcelona with Charles V and that the emperor had promised the loan of his own army – the wages of the men to be paid by the pope – to force the capitulation of the republic and the restoration of the Medici. The alliance was, as usual, to be guaranteed by a betrothal between the two sides, and here came another surprise, as well as proof of Clement VII's ambitions for his son. Alessandro's bride was to be Charles's illegitimate daughter Margaret of Austria; and the groom was to be installed as head of the Florentine state with imperial approval. A month later came even worse news. In August Charles V and Francis I signed the Treaty of Cambrai, guaranteed by the betrothal of the dauphin and the one-year-old Maria, Charles V's eldest legitimate daughter. Francis had renounced all his claims to Italy, agreed to withdraw his troops back across the Alps and promised not to interfere in Italian affairs.

It was two massive blows for the republic though, outwardly at least, the *Signoria* maintained a positive attitude, determined at all costs to resist this double assault on the city's independence. They could still count on the friendship of Ferrara, and hoped for the tacit favour of France. Above all, they were optimistic that Charles V, who was about to sail across the Mediterranean on his first visit to Italy, would be open to negotiation in order to avoid conflict. They also had possession of Caterina and continued, politely but firmly, to refuse requests from Francis I's envoys to have her sent to France.

That August, Charles V sailed into Genoa at the head of a large fleet carrying a majestic entourage of courtiers, secretaries, servants and troops. The emperor had extracted a promise from Clement VII, as part of the negotiations for the Treaty of Barcelona, that the pope would crown him Holy Roman Emperor* though for logistic reasons it had been agreed that the ceremony would take place in Bologna rather than Rome. The wider significance of this summit between pope and emperor is beyond the scope of this book but two

---

* The first emperor to receive this honour was Charlemagne, who was crowned in St Peter's in Rome in AD 800; Charles V would be the last to receive a papal coronation.

issues under discussion at Bologna touched Caterina directly.
The first was that Charles V confirmed, with Clement's reluctant agreement, that the duchy of Urbino should revert to
Francesco Maria I della Rovere, depriving the girl of any claim
to this title. The other issue was of far greater significance for
her future: the conquest of Florence.

Within days of Charles V's arrival at Genoa, some 7,000
imperial troops, the remnant of the army which had sacked
Rome so savagely two years earlier, finally left the city under
the command of Philibert of Orange to march northwards
towards Florence. Determined to avoid war, the republic sent
several diplomatic missions to see Charles V. In Genoa their
attempts to negotiate met a with blunt refusal: the emperor
would not even see the envoys though he evidently did see
diplomats from other states and the Venetian ambassador
reported hearing imperial courtiers boasting that Florence
was to be sacked.[68] In early September the Florentines offered
Charles V the huge sum of 400,000 ducats if he let the city
retain its liberty.[69] It was a tempting amount of money for a
penurious ruler but Charles refused to negotiate a separate
deal, insisting that the republic must first reach an agreement
with Clement VII. However, he did order Orange to slow his
advance to allow more time for negotiations and, in the hope
of avoiding the violence of a siege, suggested a compromise by
offering the pope a fief for the Medici in the duchy of Milan.

Unfortunately both sides were adamant in their views:
Clement refused to budge from his initial demands for the
restoration of the Medici to Florence, rejecting the emperor's
offer of another duchy out of hand. He also insisted on the
return of all the family's property and the release of Caterina.
The republic was equally adamant: 'Florence in ashes rather
than under the Medici'.[70] When the pope added the outra-
geous demand that the Medici family should be declared
exempt from all taxation, negotiations broke down completely.[71] Caterina must have known something of the progress of
the talks and she would certainly have known of their failure.

By September, Florence was preparing for war. That month the government ordered the complete destruction of all buildings within a mile of the city walls: villas, orchards, vineyards, monasteries, all burned to the ground and crops destroyed. Fortunately it had been an excellent harvest and the city's granaries and larders were filled with supplies but all building trades were ordered to close their businesses and work on the fortifications. As the imperial army approached, wealthy Florentines fled in droves, as many as 500 a day, all declared outlaws by the republic, their property confiscated to fund the war effort.[72]

Orange and his troops finally arrived in late October to set up camp along the southern perimeter of the walls. The Murate was on the opposite side of the River Arno but Caterina would have been able to hear the barrages of artillery fired into the city. The two sides skirmished and attacked each other's convoys bringing food, saltpetre and other supplies. It was not until late December, when troops arrived from Bologna to reinforce the imperial army and set up camp along the northern perimeter of the walls, that the blockade around the city was complete. The enemy was now very close to the Murate, which was situated just inside the eastern gate, and the noise of battle must have penetrated its walls. Inside Florence the siege had begun to bite – food stocks were low; it was too dangerous to gather firewood outside the walls. The *Signoria* ordered a series of religious processions to appease God's wrath, the penitential guilt on the streets providing a telling contrast to the glamorous celebrations taking place in Bologna.

The Murate was inundated with refugees: a chronicler recorded that 'a great number of women of all ages and backgrounds, gentlewomen, widows, wives and girls' flooded into the convent.[73] By the beginning of 1530 there were as many as 1,000 women taking refuge in the Murate, sleeping on floors and in the scriptorium.[74] Stores of meat were running low, though bread and wine were still available as well as what sustenance people could grow in their gardens. Both Clement VII and Francis I were worried about Caterina's safety. In January the king sent an envoy to Florence to request that Caterina be sent immediately to the French court, but yet again the request was refused. As Clement's secretary informed the duke of Albany, 'it is certain that the pope has asked many times for his niece and has always been refused, so the French ambassador's request for her restitution is also fruitless'.[75]

In February the *Signoria* issued orders that when the great bell tolled on the Palazzo della Signoria to announce that the soldiers were going out to fight, 'all persons not adapted and fitted for arms, such as priests, friars, monks, nuns, children and women of all ages ... shall be obliged to kneel and pray continually to Almighty God' to will the soldiers to victory.[76] By Easter the siege was causing serious hardship. As many as 200 people were dying each day of their wounds, of hunger, of typhus and of other diseases; and, terrifyingly, there were rumours of cases of the plague. Caterina was safer behind the walls of the Murate, where the nuns took the precaution of disinfecting any coins left as alms on the revolving shelf in a vat of vinegar.[77] Anti-Medici fervour gripped the city: on 16 May a solemn religious procession took place to celebrate the overthrow of the hated family three years earlier. At the end of the month the town of Empoli surrendered to the imperial army, closing off the sole remaining source of supplies. In June, with the city's inhabitants surviving on water and bread made from bran, the government appointed a committee to search houses to requisition all hidden supplies.

Hunger, fear and the relentless roar of the guns were fuelling a rising tide of suspicion and hundreds were denounced as Medici sympathizers. Even the inmates of the Murate were divided between supporters of the family and its enemies. With the regime's anti-Medicean rhetoric reaching a crescendo in an effort to rouse the starving Florentines to further sacrifices in defence of their city, there was much discussion in the Palazzo della Signoria about what to do with Caterina. One hardliner suggested putting her into a brothel in order to ruin her chances of a prestigious marriage, indeed of any marriage at all.[78] In the end, fortunately, it was decided not to punish the eleven-year-old but to move her to a safer environment. On 19 July four officials arrived at the Murate to take Caterina to a different convent. The eleven-year-old burst into tears, assuming she was to be killed, and the nuns persuaded the men to grant her twenty-four hours' respite.[79] The next day, when chancellor Silvestro Aldobrandini came to collect her, 'she replied in a calm and respectful voice', asking him to tell the *Signoria* 'that I have decided to become a nun and I will not be separated from my reverend mothers'.[80] So Aldobrandini got another order and this time she dutifully mounted a mule and was taken to Santa Lucia.

Less than a month later, on 12 August, Florence surrendered and Caterina returned to the Murate. The Medici were restored as rulers of the city and Charles V added yet another client state to his Italian empire. An edict of 28 October appointed Alessandro as head of the government, though it took another two years before he officially acquired the title of duke. Clement VII was ruthless in punishing those connected with the republican regime. In the aftermath of the siege they were all arrested and imprisoned; many were tortured and the leaders were condemned to death and beheaded. Caterina herself intervened on behalf of Silvestro Aldobrandini, who had treated her with kindness and respect when he took her out of the Murate, and he escaped serious punishment. It was an act that would have surprising ramifications after her death. And Caterina never forgot her years in the Murate, corresponding with the abbess and her successors for the rest of her life.[81]

2

Bride
1530–1533

Caterina returned to Rome in the autumn of 1530; 'the duchess arrived here last week,' the French ambassador's secretary reported, 'and his holiness gave her an affectionate and paternal welcome, receiving her with open arms and tears in his eyes'.[1] Clement VII's obvious relief that she was now back at the papal court was not solely personal concern for her welfare; it also had a political edge to it. He had emerged the victor in the three-way struggle with Francis I and the Florentine republic for control of his little cousin, now eleven years old, who, at the time, was usually described as his *nipote** or 'niece'. With the Medici future in Florence all but settled, the pope now turned his attention to realizing the value of his prize. Like so many girls of aristocratic lineage, not least her own mother, Caterina's marriage would be arranged according to the wishes of her (male) elders and their choice would reflect their political priorities. In Caterina's case, the negotiations would involve many of the crowned heads of Europe, not least those bitter rivals Charles V and Francis I.

---

* The Italian 'nipote' was an ambiguous term which could be used to signify not only nephew or niece but also grandson or granddaughter.

❧

As the pope's niece, Caterina was a valuable commodity on the marriage market. Names which had been under consideration in those far-off days before the catastrophic Sack of Rome in 1527 included James V of Scotland, who was the preferred choice of her uncle the duke of Albany; Henry Fitzroy, duke of Richmond and illegitimate son of Henry VIII; Ercole d'Este, heir to the duchy of Ferrara, but he was no longer in the running since his marriage to Renée of France in 1528; Caterina's cousin Ippolito de' Medici, also no longer available after becoming a cardinal; Federigo Gonzaga, marquis of Mantua, and Guidobaldo della Rovere, heir to the duchy of Urbino, had both been suggested as possibilities, as had the younger brother of the duke of Lorraine. It was even rumoured that Philibert of Orange, who had commanded the imperial army during the siege of Florence, had demanded Caterina as his price but that Clement VII had firmly rejected this offer.

Inevitably, given the size of Caterina's estates in France and her status as a granddaughter of a princess of the blood, it was Francis I who would take the greatest interest in her future. As early as 1524, when Caterina was just five years old, rumours had begun to circulate that the king was seeking to betroth her to his second son, Henri, duke of Orléans, but given the political turmoil in Italy at the time, Clement VII had been reluctant to conclude such an overt alliance with France for fear of angering Charles V.[2] Now that the siege of Florence had ended in such a satisfactory manner for both the emperor and the Medici, Francis decided to reopen negotiations and this time Clement VII was prepared to listen. Ironically, Henri, who was just two weeks older than Caterina, had also endured several years of captivity – as a hostage in Madrid for his father's good behaviour – and he too had only just been released, leaving Spain in July 1530, a few weeks before Caterina herself left the Murate.

After initial discussions Francis I drew up a draft contract
that was taken to Rome by Cardinal Gabriel de Gramont in
April 1531. In it the king offered to settle an annual income
of 13,000 écus (30,000 livres) on his son and give Caterina a
present of 4,500 écus (10,000 livres) as well as a château for
her own personal use.[3] In a secret codicil to the contract the
pope agreed to settle several papal fiefs on the couple and, significantly, to provide political backing for Francis I's plans to
launch yet another campaign to assert his rights to Milan and
Naples. It is worth underlining that this clause was in direct
contravention of the treaty Francis had signed with Charles V
at Cambrai less than two years before, in which the king had
renounced all his claims in Italy. When the rumours reached
the emperor in July that Clement was negotiating with Francis
he warned the pope against any alliance with the king. His
ambassador in Rome, Cardinal Garcia de Loaysa, was quick
to reassure him that nothing had been fixed but the cardinal
was evidently ill informed.[4] By the end of the month Gramont
was on his way back to France carrying the pope's response to
Francis's offer.

Clement VII now outlined which papal fiefs he intended to
settle on the couple: Parma, Piacenza, Modena, Reggio, Pisa
and Livorno.[5] It was an impressive list, but Francis would have
been aware that the offer was not at all what it seemed. Parma
and Piacenza were papal city-states which would almost certainly be withdrawn by the next pope; Modena and Reggio
were imperial fiefs and it was unlikely that Charles V would
agree to them becoming French territories; the Tuscan ports
of Pisa and Livorno, however, were in Clement's gift. In addition, he offered to pay a dowry of 100,000 scudi, though he
required Caterina to renounce any claims to Medici property
in Florence. He also refused Francis I's request that she was to
move to France immediately to live at court until old enough
to be married; he insisted that the move could not take place
until after the marriage had been consummated. On this last
point Gramont persuaded the pope to accept a compromise

by allowing the marriage to take place on the French borders. All seemed settled in September 1531 when the duke of Albany completed a visit to Rome having given Clement VII an engagement ring for Caterina.

However, it was soon evident that Clement VII was having second thoughts, under pressure from several directions to change his mind about this match. Some members of his own family, particularly those who remained sympathetic to the republican cause, such as Jacopo Salviati and his wife, Lucrezia de' Medici, Caterina's great-aunt, considered it inappropriate for her to marry the son of a king.[6] More worryingly there was serious political pressure from Charles V, who wanted Caterina as a bride for one of his own client-princes, Francesco II Sforza, recently installed by the emperor as duke of Milan. In an audience with Clement VII in late August, the English ambassador to Rome had been informed that the pope would never consent to Caterina's betrothal to Henri if Francis I insisted on conditions that would cause trouble with Charles V.[7] Clement's advisers were divided: the hawks who thought the emperor's power in Italy needed curbing and the doves who were unwilling to upset this powerful ruler. The French themselves were bullish; 'the pope has more need of my king than my king has of him,' boasted Gramont.[8] But Charles V warned Clement 'to concentrate on the preservation of peace in Italy' and urgently requested a meeting with the pope.[9]

By the beginning of 1532 the arguments about whether or not the betrothal between Caterina and Henri of Orléans could go ahead had become important enough to fill the diplomatic bags with rumours and counter-rumours. In January it was reported in Rome that Clement VII intended to wait for the emperor's approval before agreeing to the match.[10] A week later there was disconcerting news from London where, according to the Venetian ambassador, negotiations were now underway for an entirely different bride for Henri: Mary Tudor, Henry VIII's daughter by Catherine of Aragon.[11] Though, as the envoy warned, this scheme would be hampered by Charles

V's stubborn opposition to allow the pope to grant Henry's petition to divorce Catherine, now under review in Rome.[12]

On 29 April Clement VII sent Caterina back to Florence and inevitably the gossipmongers at the papal court assumed that this move was of some significance. While the pope insisted it was for her health, the Venetian ambassador in London claimed that Francis I had 'urged the pope to send the young duchess to some Italian city whither his majesty would despatch his son, the duke of Orléans, to consummate the marriage but his holiness denied this saying that he was sending the young duchess to Florence to avoid the summer heat of Rome'.[13] Evidently she was safer in Florence with her family but, more significantly, she could be protected from the gossips and their rumours in Rome. Hopefully nobody mentioned the rumours of negotiations between Francis I and Henry VIII for a marriage between Henri and Mary Tudor; or passed on the unwelcome news that she had been abandoned by her erstwhile royal champion.

The meeting that Charles V had requested with Clement VII took place at Bologna in December 1532. In an undisguised show of force, the emperor arrived in this small city (population: 50,000) with his entire court accompanied by 10,000 armed soldiers, 700 of whom were on duty every night to guard the town hall where Charles V was lodged.[14] Moreover, he was confident enough to boast his hegemony over Italy with the presence of his client-princes, the dukes of Milan, Mantua and Florence, evidence of his very real political influence in the Italian peninsula. As in 1530, Bologna was again the political and social hub of Europe as its illustrious visitors celebrated Carnival. In public Charles V and Clement VII maintained a show of unity and friendship but the negotiations that went on behind the scenes were far from amicable.

When the results of the talks were made known on 24 February 1533, it was clear that Charles V had bullied the pope into submitting to most of his demands. Clement VII promised to hold a general council on Church reform, one of the emperor's priorities, and he agreed to refuse Henry VIII's petition for a divorce from Catherine of Aragon – indeed, he went so far as to order the English king to drop his mistress Anne Boleyn within thirty days or face excommunication. More significantly, Clement had also been forced to join the emperor's league for the defence of Italy, a powerful coalition which included the rulers of Milan, Mantua, Ferrara, Genoa, Siena and Lucca, with Venice giving its tacit agreement, while the commitment of Duke Alessandro of Florence, Charles's future son-in-law, was taken for granted. It was an alliance aimed exclusively against Francis I: all its members, including the pope, had been obliged to promise not to sign a treaty with any foreign power (for which read France) without the consent of Charles V, nor to assist any foreign power to interfere in Italian affairs. Clement VII had been naive to hope that the enmity between Charles V and Francis I had begun to abate; on the contrary, it was as bitter as ever.

The one point on which Clement VII had remained adamant throughout the two months of negotiations at Bologna was his refusal to agree to Charles V's proposal to marry Caterina to Francesco II Sforza. At this point it was Charles V who was guilty of naivety. The emperor was well aware, from personal experience, of Francis I's capacity for mendacity and double-dealing and decided that the king's offer to betroth Caterina to Henri of Orléans was merely a ruse. So he urged Clement VII to call Francis's bluff and demand that the marriage must take place immediately. However, the king's response was not what the emperor had expected. Francis I promptly instructed his envoys in Bologna to fix a date for the wedding, suggesting Nice as the location, and invited Clement VII to join him there for a joint summit meeting. Charles V was incandescent with rage, but the pope was triumphant at his modest victory.

In France the Venetian ambassador was informed by Francis I that the pope 'has renounced plans to marry Caterina to the duke of Milan' and in April confirmed not only that the negotiations for the betrothal had been concluded but that both the marriage and the summit between king and pope would take place at Nice that summer.[15] In May the same ambassador reported that all the arrangements were in place for the duke of Albany, Caterina's uncle, to command the French fleet that was to escort Clement VII to Nice.[16] He also confirmed that the pope had promised to include the papal cities of Parma and Piacenza as part of the dowry, though there was no mention of the other, more contentious, fiefs. The ambassador also confirmed that Caterina's marriage would take place on 24 June, a nice touch as this was the feast of the patron saint of Florence, St John the Baptist.

Over the past two years Alessandro had established his authority in Florence. His position had been confirmed in July 1531 in a speech in the Palazzo della Signoria given by Charles V's representative, who intoned the imperial decree appointing the emperor's future son-in-law as 'governor of the republic', and declared that the position would be hereditary.[17] However, it took several more months of argument to persuade Clement VII to grant him a more convincingly noble tag. In April 1532 the pope made his son 'duke of the republic', a clumsy title by any standards, but even now Alessandro's authority needed to remain circumscribed in order to avoid angering those who were proud of Florence's traditions. Nevertheless, it was a victory and the new duke celebrated in lavish style. Caterina was expected to attend the festivities on 1 May but her arrival in Florence was delayed until the following week – perhaps a sign that in future her loyalties would lie with Francis I rather than his enemy Charles V – when she was given a warm welcome by her cousin.[18] Alessandro may have been 'duke of the republic' in name but he entirely ignored the subtleties of his official position and behaved like any other Italian prince. He minted his own coinage, with the image of the Medici patron saints Cosmas and Damian in place of Florence's patron saint,

St John the Baptist. He also destroyed the great bell of the Palazzo della Signoria, using the metal for coins and cannon, and symbolically silencing this seat of the old republic.[19]

There were many in Florence who objected to Alessandro's new position, but his most powerful enemy was Cardinal Ippolito, whose anger at being sidelined by Clement VII to pursue a career in the Church in order that his younger cousin could take the secular honours had developed into a bitter enmity between the two childhood playmates. Ippolito set up a rival court in Rome and, as opposition to Alessandro's rule grew, so did the number of exiles who gathered at the cardinal's palace, where they plotted and schemed against the new duke. Among the high-profile names were many with close Medici connections: Jacopo Salviati, for example, the brother-in-law of Leo X and another of Caterina's uncles, and he was joined by his son Giovanni and his nephew Niccolò Ridolfi, both of whom had been given red hats by Leo X. Another important figure to gravitate to Ippolito's side was Caterina's uncle Filippo Strozzi, who had been hounded out of Florence with his family because Duke Alessandro distrusted him, and the power of his enormous wealth. The duke's standing among the Florentines in general was also on the wane. Particularly unpopular was the massive pentagonal fortress under construction on the northern flank of the city walls that would soon house a garrison of imperial troops. In fact, Alessandro, like his father, was little more than an imperial poodle and the real power in Florence, as in Rome, was Charles V.

Visible proof of the city's alliance with Charles V came in April 1533 with the state visit to Florence of Margaret of Austria, the emperor's illegitimate daughter and Alessandro's bride-to-be. Margaret was just ten years old, far too young to be married, and she was on her way from the Netherlands, where she had spent her childhood, to her father's court, which was then at Naples. The celebrations staged by the new duke for the occasion had more than a whiff of bread and circuses. It was reported that, in a gesture worthy of a powerful prince,

Alessandro ordered the release of all the prisoners from the city's gaol, 'whatever crime they had committed except, for those few citizens who were there for their debts'.[20] Caterina, whose fourteenth birthday had taken place just days before Margaret's arrival, played a prominent role in entertaining the little princess.

The festivities, which lasted for ten days, were exceptionally grand: there were banquets, tournaments, horse races and bullfighting as well as spectacular fireworks displays and much music and dancing. One banquet consisted of forty-six courses 'of every sort of food it was possible to have' including live birds in a pie.[21] Another entertainment that both girls would have enjoyed was the staging of a mystery play recounting the story of the Annunciation to the Virgin in the church of San Felice.[22] It must have been a thrill to watch the Archangel Gabriel swoop down from heaven, which was located on a platform above the main door to the church, where a bearded God sat enthroned, surrounded by dancers and a choir of angels. Gabriel 'flew like a bird' up the nave, thanks to an ingenious contraption of ropes, pulleys and winches, to land on the top of the rood screen, where the Virgin sat in her bedroom beside a sumptuous bed, awaiting the Incarnation, after which Gabriel flew back down the nave to Heaven to the roar and flash of fireworks exploding from candelabra.

On her return to Florence in May 1532 Caterina had been placed in the care of Maria Salviati, the daughter of her great-uncle and aunt, Jacopo Salviati and Lucrezia de' Medici. Maria had been married to the famous war hero Giovanni de' Medici – known as Giovanni delle Bande Nere – who came from the cadet branch of the Medici family. She had been widowed in 1526 when he died after an operation to amputate a leg. Wearing widow's weeds for the rest of her life, she honoured her husband's memory and devoted her energies to promoting the interests of their son, Cosimo, who was just three months younger than Caterina. We know very little about Caterina's relationship with Maria but the widow's piety and stoicism in the face of grief were lessons that the bride-to-be did not forget; and Cosimo would play an important role in Caterina's future life.

Maria was in charge of preparing Caterina for her move to France. We know that she was learning French, and was able to speak and write the language by the time she left. Rumours of her 'dreadful Italian accent' are not borne out by contemporary sources and presumably belong to the development of the myth; in fact she spoke good French 'despite being Italian', as one Frenchman remarked.[23] It is likely that she continued her lessons in Latin and Greek, reading the works of the historians and philosophers of the ancient world, and the other subjects that were part of the humanist education typical of aristocratic girls and boys of the period. She also learned more courtly skills such as dancing, singing and playing musical instruments. It is evident that she much enjoyed riding: in October 1532 after Clement VII sent Duke Alessandro a horse as a present, she wrote to the pope to remind him, 'I think your holiness might send me the one you promised'.[24]

Clement VII's secretary informed Alessandro that Caterina had 'a wisdom and prudence beyond her years', while the Venetian ambassador thought her 'alert by nature and a gentle spirit'.[25] Many commented on her natural grace and lively character. The young painter Giorgio Vasari, aged twenty-two in 1533, was evidently charmed by her: 'I am fond of her for her own particular character traits and for the affection she has not only for me but for all my compatriots who adore her,' he wrote to a friend; 'it is impossible to depict her charm so I will have to make a memory of her with my paintbrushes.'[26] He had started on Caterina's portrait and told his friend an amusing anecdote 'which made me laugh this week': returning to his easel after lunch he found that the mischievous

fourteen-year-old had used his brushes to make some colourful additions to the work.

For much of the summer of 1533 Maria Salviati was busy
supervising the making of Caterina's trousseau. She was joined
by her cousin Caterina Cibò, duchess of Camerino, another
niece of Leo X, who had arranged her marriage to Giovanni
Maria Varano and given him the title of duke. In July 1533
Alessandro instructed his government to raise 35,000 florins
ostensibly to pay for supplies of grain and repairs to the city's
dilapidated fortifications, but the word on the street was that
this enormous sum was destined to pay for Caterina's finery.[27]
The formal betrothal contract specified a long list of items:
fine lace, linens, precious textiles, clothes and bed hangings
made from cloth of gold as well as a large quantity of gems
and other valuables.[28] The jewels Caterina took to France were
valued at 27,900 scudi and included a gold belt studded with
rubies and diamonds worth 9,000 scudi as well as a diamond
ring worth 6,500 scudi. It was not just the tailors of Florence
who were busy stitching outfits for Caterina: the duchess of
Camerino asked Isabella d'Este, marchioness of Mantua, to
have two bodices and two skirts made in Mantua for the bride,
and sent a large quantity of gold and silver thread with which
to embroider them. The marchioness was a fashion icon in
Renaissance Europe and even Francis I had sought her advice
over the style of dresses and headgear for his court ladies.[29]

The plans for the wedding itself, however, were not going
so smoothly. In May, just a few weeks after the Venetian ambassador had reported the agreement that the wedding was to
take place on 24 June after the conclusion of the summit
between Francis I and Clement VII, he informed his masters
that the French king had had twenty-four galleys prepared for
the fleet that would take the pope and his court to Nice 'and
he has taken all the malefactors and felons out of prison to
man them'.[30] Two days later, however, came the news that the
king had delayed their departure because some of the galleys
needed repairs and would not be ready until July.[31] Later that

month it was rumoured in Venice that the conference might not take place at all.[32] There were also rumours of problems in Rome, where it was being said that Clement VII was 'irresolute and in great suspense about this voyage for the meeting and is awaiting letters from Spain'.[33] Fortunately this ominous warning came to little: when the letter did arrive from Charles V, it instructed his ambassador just to inform the pope that the emperor disapproved of the whole plan.[34]

Francis I himself was worried enough to ask his diplomats in Rome to make a formal request to the pope that the marriage between Caterina and his son should take place as soon as possible, whether the summit went ahead or not, but Clement VII refused to comply.[35] In London it was reported that the meeting had been postponed 'and that many suspect it will not take place', though in France the word was that it would be held 'as soon as the weather cools down'.[36] Poor Caterina: it is to be hoped that she was ignorant of all the diplomatic machinations going on between the various European courts but she certainly would have known that her wedding had been delayed and must have worried that this delay might be the prelude to its cancellation.

However, by early July, Clement VII was beginning to put a more positive spin on his plans for both the marriage and the summit, though it was evident that he was fearful of the dangers inherent in provoking Charles V. It was also evident that he did not entirely trust Francis I. On 5 July it was reported in France that the pope had insisted that Caterina's dowry was not to include any Italian properties: that meant no Medici properties nor the imperial fiefs of Modena and Reggio which Charles V had recently awarded to Alfonso d'Este, duke of Ferrara. Moreover, the pope intended 'to witness the consummation of the marriage with his own eyes'.[37] It was not until 13 July that Clement VII held a consistory at which he made the formal announcement that he did intend to travel to Nice for the meeting with Francis I, 'though it was observed that he made no mention of his niece's wedding'.[38] Then at the

end of the month there was yet another delay after Francis
I fell seriously ill and, though the king recovered, one more
hiccup remained. It was fitting that it was the emperor who
was behind the final difficulties. In the middle of August,
Carlo III, the duke of Savoy, bowed to pressure from Charles
V, who was his brother-in-law, and announced that he was no
longer prepared to make his castle at Nice available to the
king and the pope for their conference. The result was a significant coup for Francis I, who was now able to host the visit
of Clement VII in his own realm.

On 1 September, after bidding farewell to family and friends at
a splendid banquet in Florence, Caterina left on the first leg of
her journey to Marseilles. She would never return to the place
of her birth, nor indeed to Italy. She was escorted by her uncle
Filippo Strozzi, recently appointed papal nuncio to France by
Clement VII for the occasion, and a large entourage of ladies
including Maria Salviati and the duchess of Camerino. Several
of these ladies had been reluctant to attend the wedding
because of the costs involved, so Strozzi agreed to pay their
expenses and loaned the duchess an extra 600 ducats for her
own use.[39] It was an expensive business for the banker. Having
made loans to the pope to cover Caterina's dowry, he was now
obliged to spend another 30,000 scudi bankrolling the cost
of the journey.[40] The party travelled north to La Spezia and
on 6 September arrived at the harbour at Portovenere, where
Albany was waiting with the royal galleys for the two-day voyage
to Villefranche. Caterina and her ladies were to stay at this
small port near Nice while Albany returned to Italy to collect
Clement VII. The pope had left Rome on 9 September and
travelled overland to Pisa, where he arrived on 24 September.
Unfortunately, the weather was bad and they were delayed for
ten days before finally sailing from Livorno to Villefranche,
which they reached on 7 October.

The papal party was huge, deliberately so in order to impress the French. Travelling with Clement VII were the staff of the Curia to attend to the business of governing the Church as well as his own personal household, his secretaries, his master of ceremonies, his valets, his chefs and servants as well as an armed escort of twenty-four lancers and two companies of infantry.[41] Also on board were his physician Paolo Giovio and his legal adviser Francesco Guicciardini, who were both historians and wrote accounts of the event. Thirteen cardinals made the journey to Marseilles, each with their own courtiers and servants. Caterina's cousins, Cardinal Ippolito and Duke Alessandro, displayed their rivalry in their choice of expensive clothes and liveries. Sadly, her great-uncle Jacopo Salviati, who had had the onerous task of overseeing the preparations for the voyage, died just three days before the party left Rome. And it was not only men that embarked on the galleys: there must have been at least as many horses and mules as all but the most menial servants were mounted, and many travelled with a spare or two.

The importance of display was evident in the vast amount of baggage that had to be carried on board: jewels, clothes, silverware, bedding, tapestries, table linen, kitchen pots and pans. Clement travelled with his official robes and ornaments; he also took the Eucharist in its tabernacle and his throne, the *seda gestatoria*. Travel by sea had many advantages. The veritable mountain of crates, chests and other bulky items could be stored in the holds of the galleys and did not have to be roped each morning onto the back of a reluctant pack mule. Nor was there the often tricky task of finding accommodation for the travellers; dinner and beds for the men, fodder and stabling for the animals horses had to be found each night on the road. The greatest advantage, however, was that it was significantly faster than travelling overland. It took the papal cavalcade fifteen days to cover the 200 miles or so from Rome to Livorno: at that rate it would have meant another three weeks on the road to reach Nice, probably longer; in Albany's galleys the journey took only three days.

However, travel by sea was fraught with danger. Guicciardini had tried several ruses to avoid the voyage: 'I fear the sea excessively,' he wrote to a friend.[42] It was a fear shared by many. Although ships of the period did have compasses, sailors relied heavily on the portolan charts that mapped the features of the coastline in great detail and avoided straying out of sight of land whenever possible. The Mediterranean was notorious for sudden storms. On the journey back from France one of the galleys carrying the papal court was driven off course in heavy seas and it was several days before it became clear that all on board were safe. There was also the danger posed by pirates, who seized ships and charged huge ransoms for the release of wealthy passengers and valuable cargo. There was also the very real threat from Turkish corsairs, and their famous leader Barbarossa (Khair ad-Din) – the following year, 1534, Barbarossa attempted to kidnap Cardinal Ippolito's mistress, a noted beauty, for the sultan's harem.

Caterina, too, had her own brush with Barbarossa. After she had arrived safely at Villefranche she informed Albany of rumours she had heard 'that the ships which were left behind at La Spezia were unlucky enough to fall into the hands of Barbarossa's *fuste** which, if true would distress me greatly and so I beg your excellency to let me know when you have reliable news'.[43] The second half of the letter shows that the ladies of the party were entertaining themselves with dancing. Caterina herself was keen to learn French dances and asked Albany for a favour: 'I understand that captain Gianazo has a tambourine that plays these French dances and I would very much like to have it; it would give me great pleasure if you could get it for me.' She passed on to her uncle the best wishes of the duchess of Camerino and Maria Salviati, who particularly wanted to

* *Fuste* were light Turkish biremes, which were fast and very manoeuvrable.

thank Albany 'for the great kindness you showed her during the voyage'.

Other important figures seem to have interested themselves in Caterina's welfare and comfort at Villefranche, not least the duchess of Savoy and Francis I himself. The duchess – this was Beatrice of Portugal, the sister-in-law of Charles V – was evidently looking after the party. On 14 September Caterina wrote to thank her for her letter and for a message delivered to her in person by one of the duchess's senior courtiers 'for which I send you infinite thanks for your affection and great kindness; I will forever be in your debt, and thanks to you we are well accommodated here and lack nothing'.[44] Ten days later she wrote to Francis I, in Italian, to express her gratitude to her future father-in-law for his kindness towards her, 'praying that God will grant me the grace to be humbly obedient to your majesty for all the days of my life'.[45]

Caterina spent a month at Villefranche before Albany arrived with the sixty galleys that had brought Clement VII and the papal court, who were now joined by Caterina and her ladies for the last leg of the voyage. On 11 October the fleet anchored off Marseilles and the following day the pope made his formal entry into the port to a noisy welcome of ear-splitting artillery salvoes fired from the castles guarding the harbour entrance and the pealing of bells in all the city's churches. After his formal welcome by Anne de Montmorency, Francis I's senior courtier, the pope was carried on his gilded *seda gestatoria* through the streets, accompanied by the Eucharist, mounted on a white mare, and a cavalcade of courtiers, prelates and cardinals.

The procession made its way to a temporary palace built specifically to accommodate Clement VII and his entourage across the street from the medieval castle of the counts of Provence where Francis I would be lodged. The two residences were linked by a bridge over which carpenters had constructed a great hall to be used for the festivities staged for the entertainment of the two courts. Francis I's own entry into Marseilles took place on 13 October, the day after that of the pope. Reversing the usual protocol whereby the host welcomed his guests, Francis made an ostentatious show of his obedience to papal authority, and thus avoided boasting his diplomatic coup by which he had been permitted to host the head of the Church in his own realm, an honour that the pope had not granted to Charles V.

Francis I had spent extravagantly on the decoration and embellishment of the two palaces. Montmorency had been in Marseilles since August supervising the building works on the temporary palace, arranging accommodation for the huge numbers expected in the city for the summit and preparing for the formal entries of pope, king and bride. Back in April the master of the royal tapestries had been ordered by Francis I to collect 'many pieces of furniture, gold and silver vessels, tapestries and other items from our châteaux of the Louvre, Blois and Amboise'.[46] These were then carefully packed and taken to Orléans, where they were loaded onto two large barges to be shipped up the Loire to Roanne and then trans-ferred to ox carts to be carried overland to Lyons, where they arrived on 24 June; it was not until 12 August that orders came to transport the goods down the Rhône to Marseilles, where they were displayed in the apartments for king and pope.

For the next ten days Francis I and Clement VII spent long hours in secret discussions, even eating their meals together in private on occasion. Paolo Giovio recorded that 'not even a servant with a candle was permitted to interrupt their evening conversations'.[47] The agenda for their talks covered the three most pressing issues of the day. The spread of Protestantism posed a threat across Europe and, although there was wide-spread support for the need for Church reform, there was no agreement as to how this should be done. The issue of Henry VIII's divorce from Catherine of Aragon was equally divisive. The most important task facing the two men, however, was to negotiate a highly secret agreement that would enable the king to reconquer Milan and install his son Henri as duke.

Despite all the treaties he had signed with Charles V, Francis I still refused to accept defeat regarding his rights to the duchy. Here the details of Caterina's dowry were central. A draft agreement in Francis I's hand suggests that Clement VII agreed to support the French campaign for Milan and would make a gift of the papal fiefs of Parma and Piacenza to the king.[48] Not even Guicciardini was privy to these negotiations and he worried, with reason, that Clement VII was about to stir up the Habsburg–Valois hornet's nest again by making an alliance that would break the terms of the league he had joined at Bologna; 'may it please God to enlighten his holiness so that we will not have to witness the ruin of the world again,' he wrote to a colleague.[49]

While the talks went on behind closed doors, the two courts hunted, jousted, partied and played. The gathering in Marseilles was an impressive one. A French chronicler judged that there was 'not a single nobleman in France' who had not travelled to Marseilles.[50] Diplomats from all the major European states were present with their entourages. The Venetian ambassador was angry about the way in which the summit had been delayed because he had only brought summer clothes with him; as it was now October, he had to buy new outfits and complained bitterly that the furriers in Marseilles were taking advantage of this predicament – which was shared by many lords and ambassadors – by charging double the usual price for their furs.[51] Italian and French culture were also on show. Clement VII and Cardinal Ippolito were leading patrons of music: the cardinal, who was a keen huntsman and jouster, also enjoyed the theatre and poetry. His court, which included many literary figures, was one of the most glittering in Rome. A skilled composer and musician himself, he played not only the lute with skill, but also the viol, the flute and, most unusually, drums and castanets, 'barbarous instruments that provoke the soul to war'.[52] Even Paolo Giovio managed to indulge his passion for history at an audience with Francis I, who answered his questions on the events of the Battle of Pavia of 1525 when the king was captured and then imprisoned at Madrid.[53]

Caterina made her entry into Marseilles on 23 October, riding a chestnut horse caparisoned in cloth of gold, surrounded by her ladies and twelve young girls dressed in the Italian style, all escorted by an entourage of cardinals together with the papal guard.[54] She was received by Clement VII and knelt to kiss his feet before being presented to Francis I, who, characteristically intolerant of the formalities of courtly ritual, embraced her with affection. He presented her to her future husband, Henri, the first meeting between the couple, and after being presented to the other princes Caterina was escorted to the queen's apartments to meet Queen Eleonora and Francis I's daughters. That evening the royal family were guests at a banquet hosted by Cardinal Ippolito, whose household, 'so sumptuously dressed that it rivalled that of the king', included many of his musicians who had accompanied him from Rome.[55] The next day Clement VII held a splendid banquet in her honour followed by a ball at which the king and his court danced late into the night.[56]

On 27 October Francis I went to Clement VII's apartment for the formal signing of the contract outlining the financial arrangements for Caterina's marriage to Henri.[57] The king settled an annual income of 4,500 écus (10,000 livres) on the bride and gave her personal use of the royal château at Gien. Clement VII for his part gave Caterina a dowry of 100,000 scudi to which lawyer Guicciardini, after checking and revising the clauses of the contract over the past week, judiciously added another 30,000 scudi to cover the reversal of Caterina's rights to Medici property in Italy, a move designed to allay the emperor's worries that Francis I might claim the right to the duchy of Urbino.[58] The money raised by Filippo Strozzi to pay the dowry was the largest single loan the banker made to Clement VII and there were precise terms specified for its settlement.[59] It was a huge financial risk for Strozzi: the loan was guaranteed on papal income from various sources, notably ecclesiastical revenues and a raft of new taxes the pope was to impose in the Papal States. The pope had promised to repay the monies in a series of five instalments, with a final payment due on the eve of All Saints, 31 October 1534. The first instalment was made on signature of the marriage contract and Clement duly paid Strozzi using cash stored in the strong-boxes brought from Rome to fund expenses at Marseilles.

The wedding itself took place on 28 October, with the nuptial mass celebrated by Clement VII. Caterina wore a robe of gold brocade, sparkling with pearls and diamonds, a surcoat lined with ermine and a ducal coronet on her head.[60] That evening the pope hosted the wedding feast, followed by masques and dancing, after which the young couple, both fourteen years old, were escorted to their sumptuous nuptial chamber with its lavishly gilded bed. Clement VII seems to have backed down from his earlier insistence that he must witness the consummation in person and left Francis I to do the honours: the king judged that 'each had shown valour in the joust'.[61]

The summit came to a close with the traditional exchange of gifts and favours. Renaissance gift-giving was a complex transaction with multiple levels of meaning, of which one of the least important was the monetary value of the gift. It was not considered appropriate to offer cash for favours, but it was perfectly acceptable to offer a present and expect a gesture in return. Moreover, it was also acceptable to recycle a gift, a process that could even add to the cachet. While in Marseilles, Francis I gave Cardinal Ippolito a tame lion that he had been given by the Turkish corsair Barbarossa! More conventionally, the king gave Clement a tapestry of *The Last Supper* and granted pensions to several papal courtiers, including Paolo Giovio.[62]

For his part Clement VII gave the king a unicorn horn, a

curio much prized in sixteenth-century Europe (actually a narwhal tusk) and one of the most expensive artworks made in Renaissance Italy, a rock crystal casket engraved by the Italian sculptor Valerio Belli with scenes of the life of Christ that cost over 2,000 scudi. On All Saints' Day (1 November), after celebrating papal mass in the palace chapel, he gave a public benediction and offered absolution to some 10,000 people who had gathered in the cathedral in Marseilles that day.[63] On 7 November he gave red hats to four French nobles. Charles V attempted to block this conspicuous favour to Francis I on the grounds that the creation of cardinals could only take place in Rome, but the pope went ahead.[64] Two of the new cardinals were favourites of the king: Jean le Veneur, bishop of Lisieux, a royal councillor and Grand Almoner of France; and Claude de Longwy, bishop of Langres, who had undertaken many diplomatic missions on behalf of Francis. The third, Philippe de la Chambre, was a Benedictine monk who seems to have been chosen because of his links to Caterina: he was half-brother to her uncle, the duke of Albany. The fourth red hat was an unusually indulgent favour on the part of the pope: it went to Odet de Châtillon, a youth aged just sixteen who was Montmorency's nephew but who held no religious position whatsoever – however, he was to play a significant role in Caterina's future.

The summit meeting ended on 12 September when Francis I left Marseilles for Avignon and Clement VII set sail for Rome aboard the French fleet commanded once again by Caterina's uncle, the duke of Albany. On this occasion Guicciardini chose the overland option and must have been relieved that he had done so when news arrived that the fleet had run into storms and the ship carrying all his possessions was missing.[65] For Caterina, whom we must now call Catherine, it was the start of a new life.

Dauphine
1533–1547

Catherine was now the duchess of Orléans. Her new identity was French; she signed her letters 'Caterine', dropping her Italian name. The letters themselves were now all written in French, even to Italian recipients such as her Medici and Strozzi cousins or the abbess of the Murate. Language was the most obvious change but not the only one. The French currency was different, so was the system of weights and measures. Even the calendar year had a different rhythm: New Year's Day, for example, in France was Easter Day – in Rome it fell on 1 January; in Florence it was 25 March, the Feast of the Annunciation. Everything was new: the etiquette of a royal court, its daily routine, the courtiers, the gossip, the fashions, the food and table manners. Little in her upbringing had prepared her for this dramatic change but, with a characteristic sense of duty, she worked hard to adapt to her new life.

Catherine had joined the royal court at the height of its Renaissance fame. 'He who has not seen the French court has no idea of its grandeur,' the Mantuan ambassador instructed his prince.[1] Widely recognized as the most glamorous of its kind in Europe, it was famous for its sumptuous palaces and châteaux, ostentatious ceremonial, splendid entertainments and extravagant clothes – as one contemporary aptly put it, Francis I's courtiers 'wore their mills, forests and meadows on their backs'.[2] Catherine's father-in-law was a powerful character, tall, attractive, cultured, clever and oozing self-confidence. It was fortunate for her that, from the beginning, he showed himself to be very fond of his Italian daughter-in-law. The marriage itself, however, was not popular: the Venetian ambassador claimed it was 'disliked by the French who all thought that the king had been duped by the pope'.[3] Certainly the anticipated political benefits were not forthcoming.

When Clement VII returned to Rome from Marseilles in early December 1533 the Milanese ambassador thought he looked so well that it appeared as if he had been on holiday.[4] Six months later he was fatally ill: the rumour-mongers in Rome claimed he had been poisoned in France; others accused the Florentines. Whatever the cause, his condition continued to deteriorate and he died on 25 September 1534. The election of Cardinal Alessandro Farnese as Paul III on 13 October brought a dramatic change to the political map of Europe. The new pope was a tough old politician; he had been a cardinal for over forty years, time enough to amass a decent fortune and father several children. It was a disaster for Filippo Strozzi: Paul III refused to repay his predecessor's debts, leaving the banker in severe financial straits. It was also a shock for Francis I. Less than a year after the wedding, the king's hopes of reviving his claims to Milan and Naples were again in shreds. Not only had he lost his papal ally, he was without part of his daughter-in-law's dowry. Worse, it was soon clear that Paul III intended to pursue a pro-imperial policy to further his own priorities: the reform of abuses in the Church to stem the tide of Protestantism, which was spreading rapidly in the empire, and, perhaps most importantly, the promotion of his family, the Farnese.

Charles V himself showed an unusual interest in the impact that the death of Clement VII was having on the future of Catherine's marriage. On 7 November, while the conclave was still in progress, he instructed his ambassador to 'send me news about the duchess of Orléans, what ladies she has with her and whether she is held in the same favour, esteem and respect as she was when the pope was alive'.[5] If Charles had hoped that Catherine was to be repudiated, he was disappointed. It seems the duchess was more popular than the emperor had anticipated. Certainly that was the Venetian envoy's conclusion: her marriage may have been unpopular 'but she is very obedient and the king, her husband, the dauphin and their siblings evidently love her greatly'.[6]

Life at Francis I's court revolved around his principal pleasures: women and hunting. While he enjoyed the refined art of falconry, he much preferred the more aggressive and dangerous pursuit of stags, boar and other large beasts, as did his sons, particularly Catherine's husband, Henri. The Venetian ambassador claimed that Francis spent 150,000 scudi a year on hunting – salaries for his huntsmen and the staff in charge of his kennels and mews, as well as his dogs, falcons, horses, spears, nets and so on – and that this was three times the sum he spent on his lavish banquets, masked balls and other revelries.[7] Although the royal accounts show that this figure was a wild exaggeration, it did make the point of the central importance that Francis I placed on the sport.[8] Indeed, he seized every possible opportunity to hunt, which also provided a perfect excuse to avoid tedious encounters with foreign ambassadors. He would often disappear for days at a time to hunt in private with his favourite courtiers and his 'little band' of women, presided over by his mistress Anne d'Heilly de Pisseleu, duchess of Étampes. It was a far cry from the papal court in Rome.

Hunting was a popular sport among the elite ladies at the courts of northern Europe, their skills enhanced by the use of the new side-saddle. This was not introduced to France by

Catherine, as is sometimes claimed, but was already in use at the imperial court at Brussels where another enthusiast, Mary of Hungary, ruled as governor of the Netherlands for her brother Charles V. She not only used the side-saddle but was nicknamed 'the male huntress' for her controversial habit of dressing as a man and riding astride her mount.[9] Their sister Eleanor, who was Francis I's queen and also enjoyed the sport, was nicknamed 'Atalanta' after the legendary huntress of Greek mythology.[10]

Queen Eleanor was Francis I's second wife. His first, Claude, had borne him seven children before dying in 1524 aged just twenty-four. Five of their babies had survived into adulthood: the dauphin François, aged sixteen in 1534; Catherine's husband, Henri, duke of Orléans, now fifteen; Madeleine, a year younger; Charles, duke of Angoulême, aged twelve; and little Marguerite, just eleven, who would become one of Catherine's closest friends. Francis's betrothal to Charles V's sister Eleanor had been arranged to cement the terms of the Treaty of Cambrai (1529), by which Francis promised to abandon his claims to Milan and Naples. When Eleanor crossed the Franco-Spanish border at Bayonne the following year, she brought with her the young princes François and Henri, who had spent the past four years in Madrid as hostages for their father's good behaviour.

Queen Eleanor was above all a political bride. Educated, cultured and musical, she presented the image of a dutiful wife and one of her assets was to provide Francis I with a private line of access to Charles V, enabling him to circumvent the more official diplomatic channels. Moreover, with three healthy sons to guarantee the succession, he did not require her to take on the task of child-bearing. He made no secret of preferring the company of Madame d'Étampes, who had become his mistress around 1526 at the age of just eighteen. Remarkably, as we shall see, far from becoming bitter rivals both queen and mistress played the courtly game with polished elegance, each respecting the other's position as first and second queen – in public at least. It was a lesson Catherine would not forget.

This show of amity was less visible among Francis I's courtiers whose competitive pursuit of royal favour was an open, and often vicious, quest for power. The Bourbon family, France's premier dynasty styled 'princes of the blood', was in disgrace after Duke Charles III, who had been *Grand Constable de France*, the most prestigious position at Francis I's court and head of his armies, defected to Charles V's camp in 1523. He was killed four years later leading the mutinous imperial army in the bloody Sack of Rome, and his title passed to the cadet branch of the family from which Catherine herself was descended. Rising up the social hierarchy were two other figures: Claude of Guise and Anne de Montmorency. Claude, second son of the duke of Lorraine, had been rewarded for his loyal service on the battlefields of northern France and during Francis's captivity in Spain with the title of duke of Guise. He was also Master of the Hunt (*Grand Veneur*) but he was perhaps too dour and uxorious for Francis's tastes and did not belong to the king's inner circle of favourites.[11] His children were still young but his brother Jean had benefited from royal favour. Jean, evidently much more fun than Claude, shared the king's fondness for gambling as well as hunting and women.[12] A member of the king's privy council (*conseil du roi*), he had been destined for a Church career from an early age, becoming bishop of Metz at the age of two. He received his red hat in 1518, one of the many favours done by Leo X for the king that year, not least the marriage of Catherine's parents.

Anne de Montmorency was the most important figure at Francis I's court. A year or so older than the king, he belonged to the minor nobility but had been a close companion of the king since childhood. He fought with Francis at Pavia, where he too was captured, and was rewarded for his loyalty in 1526 with the prestigious position of *Grand Maître de France* (major-domo), in charge of the royal household.

His family also benefited: although his own sons were too young at this stage, he used his influence to gain places at court for his three nephews, the eldest of whom received his red hat from Clement VII on the occasion of Catherine's marriage. The shifting rivalries that developed over the next decades between these three houses – Bourbon, Guise and Montmorency – would profoundly impact French politics and the course of Catherine's own life.

It is important to remember that Catherine was not an outsider – as she is often depicted – but belonged to the French noble elite. Francis I himself designated her mother as his blood relative on her parents' marriage contract.[13] She was cousin to the dukes of Bourbon and Guise and, as the sole heir to her maternal family, she owned large estates in southern France. Moreover, there were large numbers of other Italians at Francis I's court. The king was a fan of all things Italian. He spoke the language fluently, having been taught it by his mother, Louise of Savoy. He employed Italian painters and sculptors on his artistic projects, and prized his Italian horses and hunting dogs, many of which were presents from the dukes of Ferrara and Mantua. Italians served as captains and soldiers in his army; others held positions in the royal household as valets, squires, doctors and musicians.[14] Francis even appointed a Milanese nobleman to another of the great offices of state, *Grand Écuyer* (master of the horse).[15] There were also the embassies sent to France by all the major Italian powers as well as several semi-permanent guests, notably Ippolito d'Este, brother of the duke of Ferrara, who spent thirteen years at the French court.

Catherine's first years in France saw her own personal links to Italy diminish. In August 1535, less than a year after the death of her 'uncle' Clement VII, her cousin Ippolito died very suddenly after contracting a fever. He was only twenty-five years old and though it was rumoured that he had been poisoned by Duke Alessandro's agents, the cause of death was probably malaria. Alessandro himself was assassinated in January 1537 and the duchy was seized by Maria Salviati's son, Cosimo. The assassin, a distant cousin, fled to Venice and the protection of Catherine's uncle Filippo Strozzi, who had certainly given his tacit approval to the enterprise, if not his concrete support.

The young duchess seems to have adapted with ease to the peripatetic pattern of life at the French court. Francis I rarely stayed long in one place. He spent his year travelling around the kingdom from battlefield to battlefield to face Charles V's armies as the Habsburg–Valois struggle continued to divide Europe; hunting whenever possible, he hosted summit meetings with foreign rulers and staged lavish entertainments to celebrate the feasts and rituals of court life. The court on the move must have been an impressive sight, as indeed it was intended to be: the size of one's entourage was a visible statement of prestige in Renaissance Europe. Francis I's court included 10–15,000 riders and some estimates put the figure as high as 22,500, the size of a large town in those days.[16]

The *Hôtel du roi*, the king's personal household, numbered 622 persons in 1535: his valets, barbers, doctors, stewards and squires, the confessors, preachers and musicians of the royal chapel, as well as the chefs, pastry cooks and turn-spits who created the elaborate dishes for his dining table.[17] Queen Eleanor had her own household of *filles* and *dames d'honneur* (maids of honour and ladies-in-waiting), many of whom were Spanish, as well as staff to serve in her chamber, chapel and kitchen, numbering some 298 persons in all.[18] The dauphin and his brothers each had their own house-hold, while Madeleine, Marguerite and Catherine shared one between them. Similarly, the nobles and cardinals at court travelled with their own entourages of personal attend-ants, as did guests and ambassadors. Also in the cavalcade were the horses, dogs and falcons, as well as hundreds of pack mules laden with furniture, rolls of tapestries and wall hangings, chests of clothes, cooking utensils and all the court paraphernalia. Finally, there were the merchants and craftsmen who held the royal warrant, such as tapestry makers, tailors, goldsmiths or suppliers of luxury goods, numbering 160 under Francis I; and, of course, the so-called *filles de joie* ('joy girls').[19]

Wherever possible the court lodged in the castles, hunting lodges and other royal residences scattered across France. In Paris the king resided at the Louvre, a medieval palace situated inside the city walls and the only one of his residences not set in extensive hunting grounds. There were also the grand castles built by Francis's predecessors west of the capital at Saint-Germain-en-Laye, to the north-east at Vincennes and Compiègne and in the Loire Valley at Amboise and Blois. Francis I, a major patron of Renaissance architecture, improved and enlarged several of these medieval structures, adding new wings at both Saint-Germain and Blois, the latter ornamented with a magnificent spiral staircase.

Francis also built his own hunting lodges, many of which were small and very private, and known as *maisons de plaisance* (houses of pleasure).[20] Chambord and Chenonceau, which he acquired from a bankrupt tax collector, were in the Loire Valley but the others were all in the Île-de-France: Saint-Maur, Charleval, Villers-Cotterêts, Challuau, which he gave to Madame d'Étampes, La Muette in the forest at Saint-Germain and, famously, Fontainebleau (see below). Also, to provide an escape from government business at the Louvre, he enclosed the Bois du Boulogne, just 4 miles to the west of Paris, and built a lodge for 'pleasure and relaxation'.[21] Known as the château of Madrid, it was inspired by a villa that Francis had seen during his captivity in Spain, though the wags at court quipped it got its name because the king could be as invisible there as he had been when a prisoner of Charles V.[22]

In the absence of a convenient royal residence, the court might lodge in an abbey or in the palaces and castles of senior courtiers, such as Montmorency's châteaux at Écouen or Chantilly. In smaller towns the task of finding accommodation for everyone must have been a logistical nightmare for the servants assigned to this unenviable job. On one occasion, when Francis was hunting in the forest of Crécy, the Mantuan ambassador was shocked to find him in a village 'with only six or eight poor houses and his majesty is lodged in a stable'; 'the queen has only a tiny room' and Catherine shared a room with the princess Marguerite.[23]

The royal residences were, by and large, considerably more comfortable. In most of them the king occupied a suite of four rooms: a reception room, a bedroom, a cabinet or private office, where he worked with his secretaries, and a wardrobe for his clothes chests. The queen had a similar suite adjoining her husband, which also included her own private chapel. The other apartments were not so spacious, just two or three small rooms, and few had lavatories: courtiers had servants to empty their commodes and the staff used the communal privies. The number of apartments varied. Saint-Germain was exceptional with eighty sets of rooms: the king and queen on the second floor, together with their favoured courtiers and guests, and the nurseries of the royal children on the floor above.[24] Even a small set of rooms on the least prestigious ground floor of a royal residence was a conspicuous sign of favour. Important figures were accommodated close to the king wherever possible. At Saint-Germain, as in the other major palaces, Francis I's suite of rooms was flanked by the apartments of Queen Eleanor and Montmorency while Madame d'Étampes occupied a suite directly below that of the queen, and connected to the king's rooms by a private staircase.[25] Less favoured courtiers and guests, along with the diplomatic corps, were lodged in inns or private houses nearby, while sleeping quarters for the servants were even less salubrious: the royal valets slept in the king's wardrobe, the maids of honour shared a dormitory, the kitchen staff slept on the floor and the stable boys were lodged with their horses.

The routine of royal life was also a novelty for Catherine. The king's day started with his formal *lever*, an all-male affair that took place in the presence of his senior courtiers and chamber staff; an invitation to attend was considered a mark of favour. On the days when he was not hunting Francis I would spend several hours in his cabinet, holding private meetings and dictating letters to his secretaries. Mid-morning he would leave his apartments and, escorted by his courtiers through the halls of whichever residence they were in, proceed to the chapel for mass. His chapel choir contained all three male voices as well as boy sopranos for singing polyphonic music, high fashion at the courts of sixteenth-century Europe. Mass was an important event, and one that he rarely missed. On the occasion when he had to lodge in the stables at Crécy, the servants arranged a space for his 'chapel'; even when he was ill he attended mass, though he did avoid the palaver of the royal progress through the palace.[26]

The queen followed a similar morning routine with her own *lever*, which was attended by courtiers and guests, both male and female, but she celebrated her daily mass in the privacy of her own chapel. After mass came the main meal of the day, another public affair for both king and queen. The queen, who reportedly kept 'Spanish hours' and dined very late, was accompanied by her senior *dames d'honneur*.[27] The king usually dined alone at his table, though occasionally guests might be given the honour of dining with him. Surrounded by his courtiers, and entertained by his musicians, he was formally served by his personal carver, his cupbearer and a procession of stewards and pages.

In the afternoon Francis I devoted himself to fun in the company of the ladies. At Saint-Germain-en-Laye there was an animal pit where they could watch fights between the wild beasts from the royal menagerie; 'most exciting was a battle between lions, bears, tigers and two ferocious bulls,' reported the Mantuan ambassador, 'it was the best fun in all the world'.[28] Then, as now, exercise in the fresh air such as riding was highly recommended by the medical profession as good for the health. Francis I was keen on carriage riding and was thrilled to receive one, painted turquoise and ornamented with gilded fleurs-de-lys, from the duke of Mantua, which he raced in the royal parks.[29] Real tennis,* a demanding sport played in a three-dimensional court with a hard ball – not lawn tennis, our gentler version of the game – was in high fashion at the French court, with players and also with gamblers betting on the outcome of the matches. Catherine's husband, Henri, was so good at this game that, according to the Venetian ambassador, he rarely lost a match.[30] Indeed, the dauphin was keen on all sports and excelled at wrestling. It was said that he could joust for two or three hours without tiring; 'he looks as if he is all muscle'. Catherine herself enjoyed pall-mall,† a game played with a mallet and ball that was more cerebral than physically taxing; she also enjoyed archery and owned an elegant gilded rosewood crossbow.[31]

Among the less energetic court pastimes were flirtation or a gentle stroll to gossip with friends in the elegant gardens of the royal residences. Card games were popular, especially with gamblers, as were board games. Catherine owned a backgammon set, a set of draughts made of ivory and ebony, and two boards, one of rosewood and the other covered in mother-of-pearl.[32] One afternoon she joined Francis, Madame d'Étampes and Henri on a surprise visit to the workshop of the Italian goldsmith Benvenuto Cellini, who was working on a figure of Jupiter for one of a set of candlesticks ordered by the king for his dining table.[33] She did not, however, accompany the king on

---

*   Real tennis developed out of the boisterous ball games popular in the Middle Ages to become a formal game with formal rules played exclusively by royalty and the nobility. Francis I had purpose-built courts for this sport at all his major residences.

†   Pall-mall, another sport that evolved out of the anarchic medieval ball games, is thought to have developed in Naples but quickly spread to France, where it was particularly popular at court. It is the precursor to croquet, golf and even, on a smaller scale, billiards.

the occasion when he took Cardinal Jean of Lorraine, Ippolito d'Este and Montmorency to his mistress's apartments, where they found her sitting in the bath with his teenage daughter Marguerite and three *filles d'honneur*, all bare-breasted, and 'they spent a long time joking with the ladies'.[34]

In the evening there was supper, often followed by dancing; on other evenings there were informal gatherings in the royal apartments to which favoured courtiers and guests were invited. The first night Ippolito d'Este spent at the French court in April 1536 he dined with Montmorency 'and afterwards we went to the king who was spending the evening very domestically' in the company of Queen Eleanor, dauphin François, Henri, Catherine, Madeleine and Marguerite, as well as other senior courtiers 'and we stayed until after midnight', no doubt enjoying music, board games and gossip, that indispensable staple of court life.[35]

Despite the setback of Clement VII's untimely death, Francis I was not deterred from continuing his struggle with Charles V for Milan, far from it. There was a brief pause in hostilities in 1535 when the emperor sailed across the Mediterranean with his armada to launch an attack on the Turks in North Africa and defeated Barbarossa at Tunis. Following the advice of Montmorency, the king agreed not to take advantage of the emperor's absence, but the situation changed dramatically that autumn when Francesco II Sforza, the duke of Milan, died unexpectedly on 1 November. The emperor immediately claimed the title and backed this up with a show of force in the duchy. Francis responded by invading Savoy, a move calculated to annoy Charles V, and his troops swarmed across the Alps in February to take Turin the following month.

Francis I moved the court to Lyons, from where he could oversee the mustering of the army and indulge his passion for hunting. He spent much of the spring and early summer of

1536 chasing stags and boar in the surrounding hills – and avoiding the hordes of diplomats sent by Paul III, who wanted an end to the fighting. By mid-summer the queen and her ladies were back in Lyons, gripped by the gossip from England that Henry VIII had arrested his queen Anne Boleyn on a charge of adultery and then executed her for treason. The pope's attempts to mediate between the rivals proved fruitless and in July Charles V launched a two-pronged attack on Francis I, seizing the counties of Artois and Saint-Pol in northeastern France and invading Provence in the south. The court left Lyons for Valence to be closer to the army camp which Montmorency pitched at Avignon. With the imperial troops marching along on the narrow coastal road between the Alpes-Maritimes and the Mediterranean, the French decided to burn all crops, poison wells and destroy everything edible between Nice and Avignon. A nightmare for the region's inhabitants, but it was a highly successful tactic from a military point of view: starved by famine and decimated by dysentery or plague, some 8,000 imperial soldiers died and the rest quickly retreated back to Italy.[36]

Catherine's life changed abruptly and irrevocably that summer when the dauphin died suddenly in Tournon-sur-Rhône, just north of Valence, on 10 August after drinking a glass of cold water following an energetic game of tennis. The eighteen-year-old almost certainly died of natural causes but the court seethed with rumours of poison. Chief among the suspects was the emperor and his agents but there were some who accused Henri and Catherine on the grounds that they were the persons who stood to benefit most from the death. In the end the dauphin's Italian secretary, Sebastiano de Montecuculli, who had given his master the glass of water, was charged with the murder and executed in public in Lyons on 7 October, his limbs brutally torn from his body by horses (*écartèlement*).

At the age of just seventeen and still childless after three years of marriage, Catherine was now the future queen of

France and the highest ranking lady at court after Queen
Eleanor herself. We have no first-hand knowledge of her reaction to this dramatic change in status – indeed, few of her
letters survive from this period in her life. There is a story,
often repeated, that she offered to retire to a convent so that
Henri could marry someone more suitable, but Francis I
refused the gesture, saying, 'since God wants you to be my
daughter-in-law and the wife of the dauphin, I do not want
it otherwise'. The story, however, is a myth that was invented
later, as we shall see, for quite another reason.[37]

Far from being repudiated by Francis, she continued to
be a favourite with the king; and she evidently adored him.
Catherine was not conventionally pretty but, according to a
Venetian diplomat, she was kind, modest and intelligent.[38]
One particular fan of hers, Pierre de Bourdeille, abbé of
Brantôme, described her as 'very good company and of merry
humour, enjoying all honourable exercises like dancing in
which she had great grace and majesty'.[39] Francis I liked the
company of lively women, especially those who enjoyed the
chase, as Catherine evidently did: according to Brantôme,
'one of her greatest pleasures was to ride far and fast'.[40] The
Venetian ambassador was astonished at her recklessness: 'what
is unusual is that she enjoys hunting [and] unbelievably, goes
after stags in the forest where the trees and boughs make
it very dangerous for anyone who is not an accomplished
rider'.[41] She became part of the select circle of ladies, headed
by Madame d'Étampes, who went out hunting with the king
and she became close to many of his favourites, notably his
sister, Marguerite, queen of Navarre, and his daughter, also
Marguerite. The Florentine ambassador reported an occasion
when her horse took off in fright and they 'collided with a
cottage roof, which was very low, and the shock was so great
that her saddle-bow broke and she was thrown off, badly
bruised on her right-hand-side'.[42] The king, apparently, 'put
her to bed and nursed her very affectionately'; he also went
out of his way to groom her for her future role.

✤

Francis I left Lyons with his entourage soon after the execution of Montecuculli and rode north slowly towards Paris. Catherine's new status was evident in the grander apartments allocated to her on the journey and, the most visible sign of her new status, her own household. The court was lodged at the medieval castle of Loches, just south of Tours, in the middle of November when an incident occurred that served as a sharp reminder that she could lose her new status as suddenly as she had acquired it. 'Yesterday the king was hunting wild boar in the nets with the king of Scotland and many others including myself,' Ippolito d'Este informed his brother, when a huge boar escaped and charged directly at the dauphin, who managed to wound the animal in the shoulder but failed to kill it.[43] Henri 'was forced to take some six steps back but fell over and the boar rushed past him at great speed, chased by the dogs; it was a very dangerous moment but thank God no one was injured'.

With the fighting season over for the year, the court concentrated on pleasure. After Loches they travelled up the Loire, spending a few nights each at Amboise, Blois and Orléans, reaching Fontainebleau, where they celebrated Christmas, and arrived at Paris on 31 December. Although Francis I had announced publicly his intention of making the capital his 'customary residence', in fact he was not there very often, though he did spend more time in Paris than anywhere else. On average he spent six weeks a year at the Louvre, compared to four weeks at Saint-Germain-en-Laye, four weeks at his favourite château of Fontainebleau, just fifteen nights at Amboise and eleven at Blois.[44] Paris was impressive by any standards: with a population of over 300,000, it was easily the largest city in Europe. The Venetian ambassador was astounded by its magnificence, describing it as 'the most beautiful, the grandest, the richest and most populous city, the only one in my opinion that can be compared to Venice' – high praise indeed

– and he went on to describe the streets lined with expensive shops, the 'infinite' number of wealthy merchants, the university teeming with an 'incredible' number of students and the 'marvellous' abundance of foodstuffs.[45]

It was traditional for Francis I to spend at least part of the annual holiday season, which lasted from Christmas to the beginning of Lent, at the Louvre. Although there was no hunting park, the palace boasted lists for jousting and two tennis courts. However, the accommodation cannot have been very comfortable in this cramped medieval fortress, particularly as Francis's builders were busy converting it into a grand Renaissance palace with elegant *all'antica* courtyards to replace the great keep. On this occasion there were grand celebrations for the wedding of the king's daughter Madeleine to James V of Scotland, which took place in Notre-Dame on 1 January 1537. This was Catherine's debut as dauphine in the French capital. As second lady of the realm, she had a prominent position in the procession directly behind Queen Eleanor and the king, who led the bride into the church. The nuptial mass was followed by a banquet and dancing, followed by two weeks of jousting competitions in the grand court of the Louvre.

The French court celebrated the Feast of Epiphany (6 January), or Twelfth Night, by choosing one of the queen's *filles d'honneur* to take her place for the day. The 'election', which was held on the eve of the feast, traditionally involved a cake in which a bean had been baked; whoever got the bean became Queen of the Bean and, at the king's expense, was given all the outward signs of royalty. Dressed in superbly regal outfits, she took the queen's place at the dinner table, escorted to her seat by Francis himself, and served with all the grand ceremonial normally due to the queen. On this occasion, dinner was followed by a masked ball at which Montmorency, Marguerite of Navarre and her husband Henri II d'Albret, accompanied by several other courtiers, followed the theme of misrule by all appearing as 'servants' dressed in the same livery.[46]

In late January, once the jousting was over, the court left Paris for Saint-Germain-en-Laye, some 20 miles away, to enjoy the excellent hunting in the surrounding forests. This imposing medieval fortress, set in the middle of a vast park, gave Francis I more privacy than the Louvre. On one visit he left the queen and the court in Paris, and 'ordered his staff not to lodge anyone closer than Paris' except the servants of those who were with him; when the court was present, he would disappear with his favourites to La Muette, his small lodge deep inside the woods.[47] In addition to the hunting, there were other amenities: formal gardens and fountains, a menagerie, a tilting yard, jousting lists and a tennis court. Francis substantially rebuilt the château, adding a great ballroom to the castle as well as a new wing, built around a lower court, to provide more apartments and offices. It offered considerably more spacious accommodation than the Louvre – there was even a workshop for the royal clockmaker.[48]

By early March the court had moved on to Compiègne, some 90 miles north-east of Paris, spending a few days hunting at Francis's new château at Villers-Cotterêts on the way. It was now the beginning of the fighting season and the king's primary objective for 1537 was to retake Artois and Saint-Pol, the two counties on the Flemish border that Charles V had seized the previous summer. The invasion of Artois started easily enough but came to a halt at Hesdin where Anne de Montmorency, Francis's general in command of the army, laid siege to the castle. With the king at the army camp were his two sons, the dauphin and Charles, who had inherited his brother's title of duke of Orléans, both of whom took an active part in the fighting. The dauphin evidently relished the danger: when presented with a magnificent suit of jousting armour by the ambassador of Ferrara, he asked if he could have a battle suit as well.[49] With the siege underway, Queen Eleanor, Catherine, her sisters-in-law Madeleine, the new queen of Scotland, Marguerite and Marguerite of Navarre all moved to Amiens to be closer to the action. Hesdin fell on 13

April and the next day the king visited the victorious camp; a
few days later 'the ladies arrived for two nights before returning to Amiens' while the king and the army advanced towards
Pernes.[50]

Although the campaign had not been entirely successful,
Francis I left Picardy in the middle of May and rode south to
Fontainebleau where he intended to spend a few days before
travelling down to Lyons to join the rest of his army in Savoy,
guarding the Italian frontier. Unfortunately fighting broke
out again in the north in mid-June so Montmorency and the
dauphin, recently promoted to lieutenant-general, were sent
back to Amiens. Ippolito d'Este reported their departure on 14
June complaining that 'they have left the court very empty'.[51]
The king himself was ill and though initially it was not thought
to be serious, his condition worsened. In early August he was
considered too ill to be told the tragic news that his daughter
Madeleine, who had sailed from France in mid-May, had died
from tuberculosis just six weeks after landing at Leith.[52]

There were worse places to spend the summer months than
Fontainebleau, a rural retreat in the Seine Valley, some 35
miles south-east of Paris, set amid forests teeming with game.
A royal hunting lodge since the twelfth century, it had been
a favourite haunt of many medieval kings, but it was Francis
I who transformed the modest structure into a grand palace,
designed for luxury and above all for the display of royal prestige. Francis was inordinately proud of it and enjoyed taking
visitors on a tour of its treasures. The papal legate reported
that when he told the king that this was his first visit, Francis
I insisted on 'showing me a beautiful loggia decorated with
stuccoes, paintings and sculptures ... and explaining the
stories behind the pictures'.[53] This was the famous gallery,
the so-called *Galerie François Ier* with its intricate carved wood-
work, painted panels and stucco sculptures representing the
exploits of the gods and goddesses of classical mythology. The
gallery was also liberally studded with the royal fleurs-de-lys
and Francis's personal emblem, the salamander.

Work on the gallery was well underway that summer of 1537 and it was conspicuously Italianate in style. An enthusiastic patron of Italian Renaissance art, Francis I commissioned three Italian craftsmen to take charge of the decoration: Rosso Fiorentino, a Florentine painter who had trained in Rome; Francesco Primaticcio, a stucco expert who had been recommended to the king by Federigo Gonzaga, now the duke of Mantua; and Scibec da Carpi, who was responsible for the elaborate inlaid dado panels and coffered ceiling. Primaticcio also decorated apartments at the château for Francis, Queen Eleanor and Madame d'Étampes, and probably designed the marvellous Italianate rustic grotto in the gardens (*Jardin des Pins*). He also painted the murals that decorated the luxurious *all'antica* baths, where Francis I displayed his collection of Italian art, which included works by Raphael and Leonardo's *Mona Lisa*. Francis, following the Italian fashion for antiquities and keen to amass his own collection, sent Primaticcio to Rome to buy items and to make moulds of the famous sculptures of antiquity on display in Rome, such as the *Laocoön* and the *Apollo Belvedere* in the Vatican, and the great horse from the statue of Emperor Marcus Aurelius on the Capitol.[54] The moulds were shipped back to France where they were cast in bronze – in those days, an astonishingly expensive procedure – and put on display in the gallery.

Prior to her marriage Catherine had lived mainly in the male-dominated world of the papal court or the patriarchal society of Florence, where men not only did the voting but also the shopping; at the convent of the Murate, by contrast, she had seen at first hand how women negotiated power in an exclusively female context. Life at the French court was not so strictly gendered and she must have been pleasantly surprised to discover what role women played there. Francis substantially increased the number of women at court: under Louis XII the queen's *dames* and *filles d'honneur* numbered fifty-three; Queen Eleanor had almost double that number.[55] 'A court without ladies is a garden without lovely flowers,' he is reputed to have said, and took an unusual interest in how they looked.[56] Federigo Gonzaga wrote to his mother, Isabella d'Este, with a request from Francis for a 'doll dressed in your style of shirt, sleeves, undergarments and outer garments, dresses and hairstyle', so that the king could have similar outfits made for his ladies.[57] On another occasion he spent over 2,000 écus (4,756 livres) on lengths of purple and crimson velvet and white taffeta to make dresses for twenty-two ladies, including Catherine and his daughters Madeleine and Marguerite: the cost of each dress was the equivalent of one year's wages for a skilled craftsmen working on his projects.[58]

Francis evidently valued his ladies for more than their beauty. Attitudes to women of the elite had changed since the Middle Ages and this change was visible on the chessboard, a game popular with both men and women at the French court. The 'queen' in the medieval game had been an insignificant piece; by the end of the fifteenth century, however, she had become all-powerful in the game, outmanoeuvring the men as she moved boldly in all directions across the board.[59] In fact, as a contemporary explained, the queen piece ought to be termed 'lady' (*dame*) because 'nothing has so much authority over kings as do ladies, as [the kings] are not ashamed to show themselves as their servants; I do not mean those to whom they are married but those with whom they are in love'.[60] Besides their role as passive actors in royal display and ceremonial, and their value as political pawns, Francis's ladies were skilled in the art of conversation and played active roles in the literary, musical and religious life of the court. Above all, they acted as mediators and diplomats, negotiating marriages, for example, or settling private disputes, to provide a more peaceful and creative counterpart to the aggression and violence of male leadership.

The women of Francis I's court were a highly educated elite

– indeed, sometimes better educated than their men. Thanks to the determination of his mother, Louise of Savoy, his sister, Marguerite of Navarre, had received an extensive intellectual education in the humanist culture of the Italian courts. She was the author of several comedies that were performed by the *dames d'honneur* and wrote a collection of stories, the *Heptameron*, inspired by the fourteenth-century Italian classic, the *Decameron* by Giovanni Boccaccio.[61] Evidently Catherine was also involved in this last project: as the queen explained in her prologue, she and the dauphine 'together with several others of the court, determined to do like Boccaccio with, however, one exception – they would not write any story that was not true'.[62]

Italian literature was popular at Francis I's court. The humanist Gabriel Cesano reportedly gave daily readings of Dante to Catherine and her sister- and brother-in-law Marguerite and Charles.[63] In 1537 Francis commissioned a French translation of Baldassare Castiglione's *Il Cortegiano*, a series of discussions on the behaviour of the ideal courtier, which emphasized the civilizing influence of the women of the noble elite. Catherine owned a copy of the book, in Italian: one of the characters in it was her own great-uncle Giuliano de' Medici, though one imagines she disagreed with his assertion that riding was an unsuitable recreation for a lady of noble birth.[64] It is likely that Marguerite of Navarre, who was twenty-seven years older than Catherine, took the young girl under her wing and encouraged her to continue her education. According to the Florentine ambassador, the dauphine 'to the great astonishment of the court, applies herself to her studies, including Greek'.[65] Her knowledge of history and geography was exceptional and the poet Pierre de Ronsard praised her understanding of mathematics, painting, science and music.[66]

Noblewomen in Renaissance France seem to have been freer than elsewhere to discuss the new ideas that characterized this innovative period, especially in the field of religion.[67] Inspired by Christian humanists like Erasmus who called for the reform of abuses in the Church and a return to the simplicity of Christ and his Apostles, they preferred to dedicate their lives to piety and prayer rather than the pomp and ritual associated with Rome. Now that this reform movement had split the Church into two separate faiths, many of its ideas were perceived as heresy. One of Marguerite of Navarre's religious poems, *Miroir de l'âme pécheresse* (Mirror of the Sinful Soul) was blacklisted in 1533 by the theologians of the Sorbonne.[68] The following year saw the Affair of the Placards, when Protestant notices appeared on the streets of Paris attacking the Catholic doctrine of the mass and provoked riots across the city. Francis I ordered a crackdown on the new religion, but Protestantism continued to spread, fuelled by the missionaries who swarmed out of Geneva after 1536 when John Calvin reformed the city and made it the capital of the new faith.

Strikingly, Francis I did not attempt to suppress the new ideas at court, where they were championed by Marguerite of Navarre and several other important women: Louise de Montmorency, sister of *grand maître* Montmorency and senior *dame d'honneur* to Queen Eleanor, for example, or Jacqueline de Longwy, who was one of the queen's *filles d'honneur* until her marriage to Louis II of Bourbon, duke of Montpensier in 1538, when she was promoted to *dame*, and would become a confidante of Catherine in years to come. Other key supporters were the king's mistress Madame d'Étampes, whose sister actually converted to the new religion; and Cardinal Jean of Lorraine, who was one of several French prelates who belonged to the evangelical wing of the Church. While all remained Catholics, at this stage at least, they continued to use their privileged positions to protect those accused of heresy.

Nor were Protestant works banned at the French court, as they were elsewhere in France. The reputation of Francis's court as a stronghold of Protestant ideas was evident in a Catholic tract that praised Queen Eleanor as another Judith, the biblical heroine who infiltrated the enemy camp.[69] Francis's court poet was the Protestant Clément Marot, who was also Marguerite's secretary and took refuge in Navarre when he was declared a heretic after the Affair of the Placards. Marot, whose patrons also included the cardinal of Lorraine, was commissioned by Calvin to translate the Psalms into French, so that they could be sung more easily. Francis, despite the fact that this work transgressed the ban on all translations of the Bible imposed by the Catholic Church, asked him to present a copy of it to Charles V when the emperor visited France in 1539.[70] Even Queen Eleanor asked her sister Mary of Hungary to send six French bibles from Antwerp, where the translations were more freely available.[71]

The court had remained at Fontainebleau throughout the summer of 1537 while Francis I was ill and it was not until the autumn that he had recovered enough to restart his punishing schedule on the roads. He arrived in Grenoble on 20 October and crossed the Alps into Piedmont to make an official visit to his new territory now that Montmorency and the dauphin, with the army reinforced by the troops from Picardy, had secured the garrisons. By the middle of December they were back in France and spent Christmas and Epiphany with the court at Montpellier. Francis I rewarded Montmorency for his loyal service with the highest honour he could bestow by making him *Grand Constable de France*. Montmorency was now not only the head of Francis's household but also the highest ranking officer in the army and, significantly, the senior noble in the realm after the king himself.

The ceremony took place on 11 February 1538 in the Bourbon castle at Moulins, a choice heavy with symbolism – the castle had belonged to the last, traitorous, holder of the title, Charles III. The court assembled in the great hall where, the Ferrarese ambassador complained, they were kept waiting for rather a long time for it to begin.[72] 'Finally,' he wrote, 'the

door opened', and the procession entered the great hall, led
by the heralds, the nobles of the court, a squire carrying the
great sword that would become Montmorency's badge of
office, and an usher with the sceptre. The king, who would
bestow the sword on his new constable in person, followed,
dressed in black velvet embroidered with silver, followed by
Cardinal Jean of Lorraine and the two royal princes, the queen
of Navarre and Montmorency, who wore a fur-lined coat of
deep red velvet. 'Lastly came the dauphine and madame
Marguerite', though the ambassador did not describe her
clothes in the same detail as those of the men. 'The queen was
not there, I don't know why,' he concluded, though it seems
likely that she thought it inappropriate for her to attend this
ceremony to honour the man whose achievements on the
battlefield were her brother's losses.

Both Francis I and Charles V had begun to feel the financial
impact of their bellicose policies. War was a very costly business – the 1537 campaign alone had cost Francis 2,500,000
écus (5,500,000 livres) – and with the threat of bankruptcy
looming, both were coaxed into putting aside their personal
animosities to begin peace negotiations.[73] Having agreed to
have Paul III as mediator, they travelled to Nice in May 1538
to meet the pope for the conference. Inevitably it was fraught
with difficulties that started with the problems associated
with housing these dignitaries. The duke of Savoy refused
to consign the keys of the castle at Nice to Paul III's captain-
general, his unsavoury son Pier Luigi Farnese, so the pope,
who arrived by sea on 17 May, was obliged to lodge in the
Franciscan convent. Charles V, who had arrived a week earlier,
refused to come ashore and remained aboard his galley
anchored off Villefranche for the duration of the summit.
Francis I, who had fallen ill in April after a month's hunting in
the hills around Lyons, used this as an excuse for a delay and
did not arrive until 30 May.

The congress at Nice was the first time for many centuries that Europe's three most powerful rulers – the pope, the

emperor and the king of France – had met together. For the next few weeks they were engaged in an intricate diplomatic dance, complicated by the fact that Francis I and Charles V both refused to meet each other in person. First, Paul III held separate audiences with envoys from each side – Francis I was represented by Montmorency and Cardinal Jean of Lorraine – before chairing a meeting between the four envoys over lunch on 31 May. Then Francis I met the imperial envoys, while his own were rowed out to the imperial galley to talk with Charles V. Finally, the two rivals each had their own audience with the pope. The atmosphere certainly lightened as the summit progressed. According to Nicolò Tiepolo, the Venetian envoy to the summit, the 'slander, harsh words and accusations' that had been traded to show the distrust and loathing between Francis and Charles 'has improved over the days'.[74] In the end they agreed to a ten-year truce, signed on 18 June 1538, to end seventeen years of almost continuous warfare between the rivals, which had started back in 1521 when the imperial army first ousted the French from Milan. Francis I promised to respect the emperor's rights in the disputed provinces on his north-eastern border while Charles V promised to install the king's second son Charles as duke of Milan, with one of the emperor's nieces, the daughters of Ferdinand of Austria, as bride.

The two rivals may have refused to meet but their courts had no such misgivings: this summit was the social event of the decade, the excuse for endless visits, banquets, balls and hunting expeditions. The French, according to the Mantuan ambassador, were 'more magnificent' than usual, 'especially on account of the pomp brought by the ladies who have left no ornament behind in order to present themselves most honourably as much by their clothes as their jewellery and gold'.[75]

Catherine also played her part in the diplomatic game. Taking advantage of the close relationship between Queen Eleanor and Charles V, Francis sent his wife to visit her brother on board the imperial galley on several occasions. After one visit Charles V sent a courtier to his sister with presents for 'the queen and for all the ladies who had visited him with the cardinal of Lorraine and Montmorency'.[76] We can assume that Catherine was one of these ladies who were given jewellery, while the envoys were given 'large and very beautiful gold Flemish cups' decorated with sapphires for Cardinal Jean and rubies for Montmorency. We do not know if she was with Eleanor on another visit that nearly ended in disaster when a wooden pier broke, throwing the queen and her ladies into the sea – fortunately the water was not deep enough to cause serious harm.[77] But Catherine definitely accompanied the queen on a later occasion when Eleanor stayed on the galley 'to sup with [the emperor] and she slept there with her daughter, the dauphine'.[78] Was this part of Francis's plans to groom Catherine for her future role as queen, or was it so that he could have a reliable report on what was said between the emperor and his sister? Perhaps it was both.

One result of the conversations between Eleanor and her brother was that Charles V agreed to meet Francis I in person after the conference closed. When the two men finally met at Aigues-Mortes on 14 July, both broke protocol by making unprecedented gestures of trust: Francis I boarded the imperial galley without an armed escort, while Charles V, coming ashore onto French territory the following day, knelt in front of the dauphin, offering his apologies for the way Henri had been treated while a hostage in Spain. Both men, despite their old enmity, were doing their diplomatic best to appear close friends.

The new rapport was visible that October when Mary of Hungary, Charles V's other sister and his governor in the Netherlands, was Francis I's guest at the royal castle in Compiègne. He staged a splendid ceremony for her entry into the city and entertained her lavishly for eight days of banquets, masques, dances and hunting parties. It was well known that Mary's passion for the chase matched that of the king himself; she reputedly 'preferred to wield pike and sword rather than needle and scissors'.[79] Francis and Mary signed a treaty agreeing to respect each other's borders and there were further signs of the new rapport at the celebrations for Twelfth Night the following January when, as the Mantuan ambassador noted, the clothes that Francis I ordered for the Queen of the Bean were conspicuously Flemish in style.[80] Moreover, when news arrived of the tragic death of the empress the following May after giving birth to a stillborn son, Francis held grandiose obsequies at Notre-Dame in Paris in her honour.

Perhaps the most astonishing sight, and one that provided visible proof of the diplomatic truce between the rivals, occurred in December 1539 when Charles V himself crossed the frontier into France to be welcomed as a guest of the king. There were practical reasons behind the visit: there had been riots in Ghent against taxes and the emperor needed to consult Mary of Hungary urgently. The cross-country journey would certainly have been preferable to battling the late autumnal storms in the Bay of Biscay or the Channel – and quicker than taking a sea and land route via Italy. For Francis I, however, it was an ideal opportunity not only to trumpet the new peace but also to put on a spectacular display of French cultural supremacy.

Charles V crossed the frontier near Bayonne, where he was met on 27 November by the dauphin, the duke of Orléans and Montmorency. Francis I, who had intended to receive Charles in person, was unwell, too ill to travel that far. The king gave orders for elaborate entries to be staged at each town en route celebrating the new Franco-imperial alliance – and the emperor reportedly gave lavish gifts of 'diamonds, rubies, little crucifixes and other things' to the owners of the places he lodged en route so that 'at each lodging he gave not less than 500 scudi'.[81] At Poitiers the decorations included an *all'antica* fountain ornamented with figures representing France and Germany, as well as a statue of Peace, clad in cloth of gold with her two nipples spouting wine, one red and the other white.[82]

Francis I finally met Charles V on 12 December at Loches, where the two men spent several days hunting – Francis in a litter – before sampling the game in the forests around Chenonceau, Amboise and Blois. At Amboise the emperor had a narrow escape from a fire which broke out while he was riding his horse up a ramp inside a tower, filling it with smoke; fortunately no one was hurt.[83] At Blois he was courteously received by the king and escorted to the foot of the ceremonial staircase where Queen Eleanor and Catherine waited with the rest of the ladies.[84] For the emperor's formal entry into Orléans Francis put on a display of his military might with 20,000 troops and 2,392 arquebusiers firing volleys of artillery.[85] The theme at Fontainebleau a few days later was more rustic, with dancing satyrs, nymphs and other woodland deities greeting the emperor. The château, where the court celebrated Christmas, was ornamented with a triumphal arch decorated with statues of Francis I and Charles V, accompanied by Peace and Concord.[86] Montmorency vacated his usual apartments adjoining those of the king so that the two rulers could talk in private: on Christmas Day 'both majesties were alone for a good two hours walking in a gallery which caused many to complain,' reported the ambassador of Ferrara.[87] After several days of hunting, banquets, balls, masques, the court and guests boarded the royal barge, which was equipped with every luxury including fireplaces to keep out the bitter cold, for the journey to Paris.

The emperor made his official entry into Paris on 1 January 1540, riding through streets lavishly decked for the occasion with triumphal arches crowned with imperial eagles. At Francis's personal request the rich decorations were, unusually, ornamented with only Charles V's coats-of-arms and devices, not those of the king.[88] The procession, led by some 350 soldiers in various royal liveries, included civic dignitaries, courtiers and cardinals; then the constable carrying his ceremonial sword in front of Charles V, who was escorted by the dauphin and Charles, duke of Orléans. Greeted by loud salvoes of artillery fired from the cannon at the Bastille, the cavalcade crossed the Seine onto the Île-de-la-Cité and made its way to Notre-Dame, where the emperor prayed, and finally arrived at the Palais de Paris,* the residence of medieval kings. Here he was officially greeted by Francis I standing at the foot of the grand ceremonial staircase, a signal mark of honour that the French monarch only accorded to the pope and the kings of England and Spain.[89] At the banquet that followed Francis I and his guest ate at the same table in a hall hung with costly tapestries depicting the *Acts of the Apostles*, a set made from the original cartoons designed for Leo X by Raphael, which Francis I had recently commissioned from the same Flemish weavers.

For the next five days Charles V and his entourage were guests in sumptuously decorated apartments at the Louvre, where a huge gilded statue of Vulcan brandishing a flaming torch had been erected in the courtyard. He was entertained with jousts, tournaments and other military games; he reported that he had been 'hunting and hawking' by day, 'whirling and dancing' every night.[90] The court then moved to Montmorency's château at Chantilly, no doubt for more hunting and hawking, and finally to Saint-Quentin, where Charles V took his formal leave of the king on 20 January and continued his journey to Brussels. From a political point of view the meeting ended in stalemate. The two men had agreed not to discuss the issue of Milan in any depth, and Francis had to be content with verbal assurances from the emperor that he would cede the duchy to Francis's second son, Charles of Orléans, very soon.

⚜

---

* The palace was destroyed by a fire in 1871 and rebuilt; it is now the Palais de Justice.

It was now 1540 and it was evident at court that Catherine's marriage was in trouble. Although the couple performed their public duties together, it was clear that in private all was not well. That year would see the seventh anniversary of her wedding in Marseilles and there was still no sign of a child. Her failure to get pregnant was a cause for serious concern, especially after 1537 when Henri gave proof of his own ability to sire children after the daughter of one of his grooms gave birth to a baby girl and he admitted paternity. Soon after this he had begun a more serious relationship with Diane de Poitiers, widow of the grand seneschal of Normandy, a woman who was twenty years his senior. Coincidentally, she was one of Catherine's many cousins at court. There were certainly three of them in this marriage. The dauphin was not an easy personality, perhaps traumatized by being sent to Spain a few weeks before his seventh birthday and spending four long years as a hostage for his father's good behaviour. He was certainly addicted to danger and, unlike his father, not a social animal. 'By nature he is gloomy and taciturn and rarely laughs; indeed I have been assured by several courtiers that they have never once heard him do so,' recorded the Venetian ambassador.[91] It seems Diane was able to give him the security and reassurance he badly needed.

Despite her childless state and the inevitable calls for the marriage to be dissolved, Catherine remained in favour with Francis I. She was obedient to her father-in-law and a dutiful, loving wife to Henri, despite the attentions he lavished on Diane. Like his father, Henri was very public in his devotion to his mistress. At a masque held during Carnival in February 1541 the Ferrarese ambassador recorded that the dauphin appeared 'dressed in the guise of Diana with four nymphs, leading dogs and carrying hunting spears'.[92] Cross-dressing was part of the fun of entertainments at the French court, as indeed were more esoteric costumes. The king and Cardinal Jean of Lorraine appeared at the same masque 'dressed in silk cloth of gold sewn to resemble bark with their heads and hands covered in ivy to look like a tree trunk that has been thrown out'. The following year Henri again appeared as Diana – on this occasion the king and the cardinal disguised themselves as bears and prawns.[93] Though Henri's behaviour must have been distressing to her, Catherine kept her feelings to herself. Francis I was more public in his disapproval of the affair. Not only did he take a dim view of the way Diane dominated his son, he took Catherine's side on the issue, thus souring relations with his son. As Henri wrote later to Diane, 'I never thought it possible that I would lose the good grace of the king by staying close to you'.[94]

The rift between Francis I and his heir had important ramifications, not least the king's now obvious preference for his younger son Charles, duke of Orléans. As boys the competitive nature of the brothers had been channelled into sport, with the princes regularly captaining opposing teams for the jousting tournaments or mock battles that were the staples of court celebrations. Catherine must have been present at many of these shows: on one occasion she watched them playing *palla al calzo*, an early form of football, with Henri captain of a team of Frenchmen against Charles and his men, who were all Italians (on this occasion the French won).[95] But the rivalry between the brothers now began to take on more serious overtones, exacerbated by the plots and intrigues of the two royal mistresses, who detested each other. Their relative ages did not help: Diane de Poitiers was forty-one years old in 1540, nine years older than Madame d'Étampes and only five years younger than the king. Nor was the situation improved by Henri, who refused stubbornly to defer to Madame d'Étampes, exacerbating the poor relations with his father.

However, Francis I was still the king and one of the first indications that his mistress had the upper hand over her rival was the downfall of Montmorency. The diplomatic truce between Francis I and Charles V over Christmas broke down in the summer of 1540 when the emperor appeared to backtrack over his promise to hand over Milan. The king blamed

Montmorency, who had advised him that it would be possible
to negotiate with Charles V and acquire the rights to Milan
by diplomacy rather than by war. Just how over-optimistic
Montmorency had been became clear that October when
the emperor invested his own son Philip as duke of Milan.
Over the following year Montmorency was slowly stripped of
his privileges and titles, though Francis could not remove him
from the position of *Grand Constable de France*, as this was an
appointment for life The most telling sign of his loss of favour
was that he was no longer lodged in the suite of rooms adjoining those of the king; indeed, he retired from court entirely.

The influence of Madame d'Étampes attracted international attention. Mary of Hungary's ambassador informed
her in May 1541 that 'no member of the [privy] council dares
speak to the king about matters small or large without her
approval'.[96] Charles V even contemplated using the difficulties that had arisen between the king and the dauphin to
force Francis to abdicate in favour of Henri, and did what he
could to stir up trouble between the two princes. Significantly,
Francis I's old advisers, Montmorency and Cardinal Jean of
Lorraine, were replaced by close allies of the king's mistress,
Claude d'Annebault and Cardinal François de Tournon. When
the admiral of France died in June 1543, Annebault was promoted to this prestigious position, while his brother Jacques
was made a cardinal by Paul III on the king's recommendation.
Madame d'Étampes was 'more in favour than ever,' reported
the Ferrarese ambassador in code that December, 'Monsieur
d'Annebault is the most important man and he and the cardinal of Tournon are in charge of everything'.[97]

Factional rivalries at court were nothing new. Inevitably
the rift between the king and his heir, and their mistresses,
was reflected in the divided loyalties among the scheming
courtiers. One faction gathered around Francis I, Madame
d'Étampes and Charles of Orléans; others preferred to back
Henri, who would be their future king. His allies included
Montmorency, who had taken considerable trouble to

cultivate the friendship of the dauphin in the years following the death of his elder brother, and had become a mentor to the insecure prince. Another was the young François of Guise, eldest son of Duke Claude, the same age as Henri and a close friend since childhood. Catherine herself remained neutral, determined to show herself both as obedient daughter-in-law to the king and as dutiful wife to Henri. She continued to correspond with Montmorency during his years of absence from court, affectionately addressing him as 'my godfather', *mon conpère* (her spelling of *compère*).

More damaging – and this *was* new – these political rivalries were beginning to acquire a religious dimension. Relations between Catholics and Protestants across Europe deteriorated dramatically in 1541 after the failure of the imperial diet of Regensburg and the disgrace of Paul III's moderate legate who had worked hard for reconciliation between the two faiths. It was a triumph for the hardliners on both sides, who were irrevocably opposed to compromise. This would be the last attempt by Rome to negotiate a peaceful solution to the problem: henceforth, the two religions were at war. Madame d'Étampes, like Marguerite of Navarre, was sympathetic towards the Protestant cause (and would later convert to it); Henri and Diane de Poitiers were firmly opposed.

In the aftermath of Montmorency's downfall in 1541, Francis I had abandoned the diplomatic approach to resolving his conflict with Charles V and returned to the battlefield. With Paul III openly supporting the emperor, he was in need of allies of his own. One target was Florence where Cosimo de' Medici had succeeded as duke with the support of the emperor, their alliance cemented by Cosimo's marriage to Eleonora of Toledo, daughter of the imperial viceroy of Naples. Francis offered support, military and financial, to the group of exiles, led by Filippo Strozzi, who were plotting the overthrow of the

new duke and a return to the republican constitution, but this
project failed after Strozzi and the exiles were resoundingly
defeated by Cosimo at the Battle of Montemerlo in 1537.
Strozzi had been humiliatingly paraded through the streets
of Florence and cast into prison, where he committed suicide
the following year. His four sons escaped to Lyons, where the
family bank was still in business, and sought the protection of
their cousin Catherine. Robert was made *chevalier d'honneur*,
head of Catherine's household, and the other brothers took
positions in the French military.[98] Piero in particular became a
favourite at the French court: a keen sportsman, he was one of
the Italians playing on the football team captained by Charles
of Orléans and reportedly played cards every day with Madame
d'Étampes.[99] Catherine herself, however, did not take sides:
she was not only Strozzi's niece, she was also Cosimo's cousin
and, although they did not always agree, the correspondence
continued.

Although Francis I failed to tempt Cosimo I away from
Charles V, he was more successful with the emperor's
enemies, the German Protestant princes and the Ottoman
Sultan Suleiman. Evidently religious scruples mattered little
to the king in his struggle against the emperor. In July 1542 he
declared war on Charles V on two fronts, sending the dauphin
south and his other son Orléans to Luxembourg. Orléans had
a run of successes in the north but the dauphin was unable to
secure a victory at Perpignan, exacerbating the already tense
relationship between the brothers. The following year Francis
I faced a coalition of Charles V and Henry VIII, whose armies
mounted a joint attack along the Flemish border and the
Channel coast. Francis retaliated with a move designed deliberately to infuriate the emperor as well as Paul III and the
rest of Christian Europe by signing an alliance with Suleiman;
in the process he also angered his own subjects by forcibly
evacuating the port of Toulon on the Mediterranean coast,
declaring it a Muslim town, so that Barbarossa's fleet could
winter there in safety.

There was better news for Francis I closer to home. During June 1543 the court was gripped by rumours that Catherine was finally pregnant. Unlikely as it seemed, ten long years after their wedding Henri had finally been persuaded to do his duty in the marital bed. We can assume that Diane de Poitiers had something to do with this: she was approaching the age of fifty, too old to bear children, and Henri needed a male heir. On 30 June, Ippolito d'Este – now the cardinal of Ferrara, thanks to Francis I – sent some surprisingly detailed information on the subject to his brother Duke Ercole: that the court had departed from Villers-Cotterêts, leaving the dauphine behind as 'it is said that she is pregnant and that on 24th of this month it was two months and five days since she had her regular period'.[100] Further bulletins followed over the summer months and on 6 September the cardinal confirmed the hopes of the French royal family: 'the latest news of Madama Delfina's pregnancy is that she has felt the baby move, so it is now taken for certain.'[101]

The infant François was born at Fontainebleau on 19 January 1544 in the presence of the king. Birth in royal circles was a public affair: Catherine was in labour the whole day and the baby was born at sunset, Francis informed the papal ambassador.[102] In February, writing to her cousin Cosimo I to offer her condolences on the recent death of his mother, Maria Salviati, in whose care she had spent the last year before her marriage, she added, 'you should have heard from Jehan Baptiste my major-domo that I am almost recovered from my confinement; both son and mother are well, thanks to our Lord'.[103] She also wrote a heartfelt letter of thanks to the abbess of the Murate 'for your prayers to God and the Virgin of the Conception on my behalf'.[104]

The baby was christened at the château on 10 February, carried from his mother's apartments to the chapel accompanied by a great procession. As was customary, neither

Catherine nor Henri took part but prominent at the front were many 'favourites of the dauphin', followed by the king, the papal legate, the cardinals of Lorraine and Ferrara, and the Venetian ambassador, who, with the legate, had been given the honour of holding the infant over the font; then came the ladies, led by Queen Eleanor 'followed very closely by Madame d'Étampes', the king's daughter Marguerite and his sister, Marguerite of Navarre, and 'infinite numbers of other ladies who were all so richly dressed in jewels, cloth of gold and gold embroidery that it was an astonishing sight'.[105]

With the christening over it was time for Francis I to get back on the road for the beginning of the fighting season. In April his army won a hard-fought and bloody victory over an imperial force at Ceresole, near Turin, but it was countered the following month by Charles V and his ally Henry VIII, who launched a double assault in the north of France, with the emperor invading from Flanders and Henry attacking the Channel ports. By late summer the English had taken Boulogne and Charles V in person was marching through Champagne towards Paris. Once again lack of funds on both sides forced them to the negotiating table and they signed a peace treaty at Crépy on 18 September. This time Francis was able to extract a significant concession from the emperor: the treaty was to be guaranteed by the marriage of the duke of Orléans either to Charles's daughter Maria with the Netherlands as her dowry, or to his niece Anna, in which case the dowry was to be Milan. Moreover, the emperor was to make his choice within four months.

In celebration of the new entente Francis sent Queen Eleanor with all her *dames d'honneur* on an official visit in October to her sister Mary of Hungary in Brussels, escorted by the duke of Orléans. Although this gesture did not carry quite the same political weight as a formal visit of his own to meet Charles V, who was also in the city, it was nevertheless highly significant. Also significant was the honour paid to Madame d'Étampes, who rode beside the queen on the journey across

France.[106] In Brussels the ladies were treated to hunting expeditions, tournaments, masques and other entertainments, and throughout the festivities, no doubt at Eleanor's request, Charles V treated Francis I's mistress with the respect due to a second queen and notably ignored protocol by sitting between her and Eleanor at the grand state banquet. Francis sent his queen a personal letter of thanks for this exceptional courtesy – and the lesson in how the mistress–wife dynamic could work was one that was not lost on Catherine.

The new peace between Francis I and Charles V was, however, not universally popular, especially with the dauphin and his faction at court. Madame d'Étampes had encouraged the king to sign the treaty but Henri was firmly opposed to it and went so far as to challenge its legitimacy. His failure at Perpignan still rankled and peace denied him the chance of making his own name on the battlefield. His jealousy of the duke of Orléans was becoming increasingly divisive at court. The king, despite the poor relations between him and the dauphin, was conspicuously generous to Catherine. When he presented the customary gifts to all the court ladies on 1 January 1545, it was Catherine who received the most valuable gift – a diamond and a ruby worth 10,000 écus.[107]

However, in Brussels Charles V continued to procrastinate over the issue of a bride and dowry for the duke of Orléans. The duke himself tried to pre-empt the issue by appearing in public with his royal coat-of-arms quartered with those of Milan, and it was not until April, six months after signing the treaty, that Charles announced his decision: Orléans's bride was indeed to be Anna of Austria and the dowry Milan. 'Here at court the joy of everyone at having the duchy of Milan is quite incredible,' reported the Ferrarese ambassador on 6 April, 'and all they can talk about is going to Italy.'[108] The Florentine ambassador, he continued, had heard from Catherine herself 'that she had been with the king and Madame d'Étampes planning their journey to Italy and that his majesty said he wanted to go to Milan, Ferrara and Venice and that when the dauphine had suggested he should also go to Florence, he had replied "yes, yes!"'. But the tour never took place: on 9 September 1545 the duke of Orléans died very suddenly at the age of just twenty-three. Francis was devastated by the personal loss but also by the political tragedy of the death of 'he by whom Christendom might have remained in perpetual repose and quietude; he would have nourished peace and tranquillity among the princes'.[109] For Henri there was relief at being back in his father's favour. Francis was a pragmatist and invited the dauphin to sit on the privy council and take his share in the business of government, but the dauphin refused, preferring to wait.

That summer Catherine became pregnant again and gave birth to a daughter, Elisabeth, at Fontainebleau on 2 April 1546 – in the old-style documents the date appears as 1545 but Easter was unusually late, so that year, 1546, did not begin until 25 April. Francis hosted particularly elaborate festivities for the baby's christening which took place on 4 July in the chapel at the château, followed by a great banquet and ball which both took place in one of the courtyards. This space had been transformed into a luxurious setting, with a ceiling of 'blue cloth studded with gold stars' and the walls hung with lengths of green velvet sewn with gold fleurs-de-lys, cloth of gold, tapestries and other costly hangings.[110] The Ferrarese ambassador was particularly impressed by the magnificent display of 'great gold vases, wine coolers, basins, ewers, large goblets, most studded with gems, and many other gold items, two-thirds of which, at least, were pure gold'.[111] He also sent the duke a long account of the day's festivities, which were evidently equally grand: 'the salads were carried in on gilded platters by forty of his majesty's pages'. Catherine, he wrote, watched the christening from a window in the chapel but there is no mention of her attending the evening party. However, two days later the ambassador reported that she had watched her husband leading one of the teams in the tournament held in honour of the christening 'dressed in a dress of silver brocade ornamented with elaborate gold embroidery and pearls, and many jewels on her head and chest'.[112]

A month later Catherine was a guest at the splendid banquet hosted by the cardinal of Ferrara for Francis I at the Italianate villa, or pleasure palace, known as Le Grand Ferrare that he had built in the grounds of Fontainebleau. After the feasting was over the company, which also included the dauphin, Madame d'Étampes and Diane de Poitiers, the cardinal of Lorraine and the cardinal of Tournon, watched Henri and a troop of riders playing various games and larking about, which was 'much enjoyed by everyone and the greatest joy was to see his Most Christian majesty so well'.[113] On the surface the court continued to hunt and feast as normal but behind the scenes the animosities were intensifying, between Francis I and his heir, between their two mistresses and between their respective bands of loyal courtiers.

The situation was exacerbated by Francis I's declining health. That January he had been severely ill with an abscess 'in his lower parts', a painful condition that had been troubling him on and off for the past five years: his doctors had diagnosed syphilis, though modern medical opinion is divided on the issue.[114] Whatever the cause, he was well enough in February to go hunting, albeit in a litter, but he was able to leave this behind by the summer. That autumn he was in excellent health, according to the English ambassador, but after some weeks of energetic hunting in February he fell ill again. This time it proved fatal and he died on 31 March. In his last words to the dauphin he warned his son of the dangers of being too much under the influence of another person, as he himself had been with his mistress.

4

Queen
1547–1559

The official entry of Henry II (as we must now call him) and his queen into Lyons in September 1548 is well known to art historians for the scholarly recreation of ancient Roman temples, columns, triumphal arches and an amphitheatre erected in the city for the occasion. There was even an obelisk, painted to imitate old marble complete with cracks through which weeds were growing, a reminder that Lyons (*Lugdunum*) had once been the capital of the Roman province of Gaul.[1] Many of the ephemeral structures were ornamented with the king's personal cipher of the letters H and D – it could stand for Henry II (*Henri Deuxième*) but, as the gossips at court were quick to note, the letters were also the initials of the king and his mistress Diane de Poitiers.[2] More strikingly, they would also have noticed that his entourage was dressed in her black and white livery, and guessed at the symbolism of the tableau of Diana, which showed the chaste huntress of Roman mythology leading a mechanical lion on a leash of the same colours.[3] Since his accession the image of Diana had taken on a new importance for the lovers. The king adopted the crescent moon, one of Diana's emblems, to symbolize his increasing (*croissant*) power, while Diane even persuaded one Venetian envoy that their relationship was purely platonic, though few at court shared this view.

Much had changed in the eighteen months since Francis I's death. Madame d'Étampes was no longer at court; her property and jewels, including a diamond worth 50,000 écus, were now in the possession of the new royal mistress.[4] Henry II lavished favours on Diane: he gave her the beautiful château of Chenonceau in the Loire Valley and, more importantly, the title of duchess of Valentinois, making her the senior lady at court after the queen and the royal princesses. His obsession with Diane was abundantly evident to all. Less interested in the intricacies of politics and public affairs than his father, he stopped giving audiences after the midday meal and went directly to her apartments where, according to the imperial ambassador, he sat in her lap, played the cittern and fondled her breasts while telling her the details of that morning's government business and asking those favourites present to admire her beauty.[5]

Just as Francis I's mistress had done before, Diane de Poitiers adeptly exploited her position to establish her own network of clients and enrich her family – her letters show her creepily subservient to those with influence but a bully to minor officialdom.[6] It was not long before she had the power to control access to the king; and she frequently reminded the recipients of her letters of this fact to bolster her authority. While Catherine held the title of queen, it was evident that her rival occupied the post.

Catherine kept her own counsel, behaved with every courtesy and never complained, though she later told a friend, 'if I was polite to Madame de Valentinois, it was for the king's sake yet I always told him that it was against my will, for no wife who loves her husband has ever loved his whore; such a woman deserves no other name, though it is an ugly word for us to use'.[7] It was in this context that the apocryphal story emerged at court of how Francis I had refused to allow her to

enter a convent to enable the dauphin to remarry and have
children, by telling her that 'God wants you to be my daughter-in-law and the wife of the dauphin': it was proof of her
self-sacrificing, dutiful and obedient nature.[8] But Catherine
did undermine the duchess's position in more subtle ways, not
least reinterpreting the ambiguous HD cipher to read HC and
using it to mark ownership of the books in her library.[9]

Henry II continued to wage war against his father's old
enemy Charles V. His implacable dislike of the emperor,
which must have had its origins in the unpleasant years he
spent as a hostage in Spain, took on a more political and
religious hue. Within days of his accession he announced that
work was to stop on all but the most important of Francis I's
architectural projects, notably, the Louvre, Saint-Germain and
Fontainebleau: the new king 'only wants to build fortresses
on his borders,' reported the Ferrarese ambassador.[10] Charles
V, however, was preoccupied with a challenge to his imperial
authority. In April 1547 he won a resounding victory over a
Protestant army at Mühlberg, a triumph he achieved with the
assistance of several German Protestant princes who agreed to
support his campaign in return for a promise that he would
institute religious toleration across the empire. Charles V kept
his promise with the edict *Interim* (1548) that made significant
concessions to Protestants but it also brought him into direct
conflict with Paul III and an increasingly intolerant Catholic
Church that would not countenance any form of compromise
with the Protestants.

Henry lost no time in capitalizing on the breakdown of
Charles V's hitherto close relations with Rome: an alliance
with Paul III was his chance to re-establish French interests in
Italy. In September 1547 the pope's son Pier Luigi Farnese was
assassinated on the orders of the imperial governor of Milan,
whose soldiers seized control of the Farnese duchy of Parma

and Piacenza. Although Pier Luigi's heir, Ottavio Farnese, was Charles V's son-in-law, the emperor refused to recognize his rights and Paul III called on his new ally for help; judiciously, Henry II chose not to fight but to make a very public show of strength by travelling to Italy in person at the head of his army in the summer of 1548. One repercussion of this decision was the postponement of Catherine's coronation, as well as the formal entry of both king and queen into Paris – his own coronation had taken place at Rheims in July 1547 – but he appointed her as regent during his absence and left her with the court at Mâcon. Very few of her letters survive for this period and none give any indication of her first experience of power. Nor did it last long: Henry was away less than three months, and rejoined the court in Lyons in September when the king and queen made their ceremonial entries into the city.

The ritual of a triumphal entry dated back to the Middle Ages and was given to newly crowned kings in the major towns and cities of the realm, the grandest taking place at Paris, Lyons and Rouen. The honour was also granted to queens, who made their own entries on a separate day, and it could also be granted to visiting princes and to the governors appointed by the king to take charge of the various provinces of the realm. The entry followed a broadly standard format. On his arrival at the city gate, the king was met by civic dignitaries, who handed him the keys to the city and gave an official speech of welcome, the *harangue*, usually read by the mayor. After these formalities came the procession itself, a noisy, colourful affair. Accompanied by the deafening roar of salvoes of artillery, trumpet fanfares and the peal of church bells, the cavalcade made its way slowly through streets hung with tapestries and greenery, and ornamented with columns, statues and triumphal arches.

The parade included armed soldiers and archers; civic officials, guildsmen and other citizens, often in large numbers and all in their best clothes, followed by churchmen in their

formal robes; and the royal party, all dressed in conspicuously expensive outfits and mounted on superbly caparisoned
chargers. Finally came the king himself riding under a ceremonial canopy, deliberately redolent of the canopy held over
the Eucharist in the annual processions to celebrate the Feast
of Corpus Christi. Designed to give visual expression to the
king's role as God's anointed, it also symbolized his formal
title of 'Most Christian King' by which French monarchs had
been known since the Middle Ages. The choice of the four
men to carry the canopy was a crucial matter of protocol and
personal ambition of those involved.

Henry II made his entry into Lyons on 23 September, followed a day later by Catherine, with the mechanical lion now
tastefully displaying a heart decorated with her coat-of-arms.
Reflecting the cosmopolitan character of France's second city,
the parade included Milanese, Genoese and imperial trades-
men, and especially the Florentines, who had a long tradition
of association with the commercial and cultural life of Lyons.
The court spent the next week in Lyons as guests of Cardinal
Ippolito d'Este, who was archbishop of Lyons, and he entertained them in royal fashion: the Ferrarese ambassador Giulio
Alvarotti estimated that the cardinal spent 10,000 scudi on
the festivities.[11] Among the entertainments were a battle on
the River Saône between galleys manned by 'Roman' sailors
and a gladiatorial contest that Henry particularly enjoyed.[12]

The cardinal's most ambitious project was the reconstruction of a classical theatre at his palace, probably designed
by Sebastiano Serlio, where he staged a performance of *La
Calandria*, a comedy by Cardinal Bibbiena, who had been a
close adviser of Catherine's great-uncle Leo X.[13] It was the
first occasion that a modern Italian comedy was performed
in France with a cast of Italian actors; and there is evidence
that it was Henry II who requested it in Catherine's honour.[14]
There were conspicuous references to the queen in the decoration of the room itself. The backdrop was painted with a
perspective view of Florence and the statues placed along the

walls portrayed the city's great poets and soldiers, including Catherine's father. Cosimo I was conspicuous by his absence, a gesture of solidarity with Catherine's Strozzi cousins and with the large numbers of Florentine exiles living in Lyons.

On 20 October the court was at Moulins to celebrate the wedding of the daughter of Catherine's friend and mentor Marguerite of Navarre to Antoine, duke of Bourbon. It was a prestigious union: the bride, Jeanne d'Albret, was Henry's first cousin while the groom was 'first prince of the blood', next in line to the throne after the dauphin, a sickly child in poor health. So it was surprising that it was celebrated with none of the usual pomp and show. Indeed, it had been arranged in a hurry: the Spanish ambassador reported that there had not been time 'to organize the usual festivities'.[15] In fact it was Henry who had forced the marriage on the king and queen of Navarre, his aunt and uncle, after discovering from his spies that they were negotiating with Charles V to betroth their daughter to the emperor's heir Philip.[16] Jeanne and Antoine, who could now look forward to the certainty of a royal title on the death of his father-in-law, together with their son Henri (born 1553) were to play significant roles in Catherine's story – and that of France. For the present, however, Catherine's sympathies were with her old friend, who attended the wedding with reluctance. 'I feel for you in your trouble,' Catherine told her, 'as I always knew you felt for me in mine.'[17] It was to be one of their last meetings: Marguerite, who had been made very unwelcome at her nephew's court, spent most of her time in Navarre, where she died in December 1549.

Catherine's coronation finally took place on 10 June 1549 at Saint-Denis. It was less formal than Henry's coronation, the *sacre*, which was designed to affirm the king's spiritual as well as his political authority and was more akin to a consecration. As queen-consort Catherine was subservient to the crown and her coronation displayed the dignity of the monarchy in the royal procession, which saw Diane de Poitiers walking among the princesses of the blood, and in Catherine's magnificent clothes, a sleeveless surcoat of ermine with a velvet mantle, underneath embroidered with gilded fleurs-de-lys.[18]

Henry made his formal entry into Paris on 16 June, an event in which Catherine could not participate, to the roar of salvoes from 350 pieces of artillery, accompanied by 11,000 Parisians, including the chancellor with his seal, government officials, guildsmen and clergy, preceding the king's entourage.[19] Catherine made her own entry two days later in a litter borne by two mules, a practice that dated back to the fourteenth century.[20] Like the king, she was granted the honour of a canopy, which was carried by the members of the city's guilds, and she was accompanied by cardinals, ambassadors and all the court ladies.[21] The ever-observant Alvarotti sent home a long description of the queen's entry, in which he himself had taken part: indeed, as he admitted with some pride, the first of the ambassadors in the cavalcade.[22] 'I won't give you the precise details of the ceremony and order of the entry of the most serene queen, because it was the same as that which preceded the king,' he wrote, 'down to the queen's three pages.' Catherine herself rode 'in an open litter with Madame Marguerite beside her on foot and her majesty was dressed in a royal mantle of red velvet covered with golden fleurs-de-lys', followed by the princesses of the blood and, of course, Madame de Valentinois.

Catherine's accession as queen brought dramatic changes to her daily routine. For a start she moved into the queen's apartments in the royal residences and they were considerably more spacious than those she had occupied as dauphine. At Saint-Germain, for example, where her apartment was on the second floor, her superb reception room was large enough to need two fireplaces and had six windows, three on either side of the room, giving views over both the courtyard and the forest.[23] Opening off one end of the reception room was her private chapel, also with its own fireplace and a door that led into the king's apartments; at the other end was her bedroom, with two windows and a single fireplace, and several smaller rooms, beyond one of which was a lavatory that she blocked up to provide more space, though perhaps also because of the smell.[24] Although only half the size of the reception room, her bedroom was still grand: it was 70 square metres, slightly smaller than that of the king which covered 100 metres.[25] It was not a private space but played an important role in the public ceremonial which delineated the queen's day. Catherine's daily routine had become considerably more formal since her accession. She held her own *lever* and *coucher* ceremonies in public; her daughter's memoirs recalled how her mother insisted that she must attend both rituals.[26] Her bedroom was also the setting for other rituals of court life, not least the election of the Queen of the Bean at Epiphany.[27]

Interestingly, Catherine felt the need for her own, more private space; certainly the effort of being polite to Madame de Valentinois and her set must have been wearing. During her years as queen she acquired three properties, all near royal residences: Chaumont, in the Loire Valley, close to Blois and Amboise; Mi-Voie at Fontainebleau; and Montceaux, not far from Villers-Cotterêts. She acquired Chaumont, a medieval castle, in 1550 but we know little about her activities there. Three years later she spent some 500 écus (1,150 livres) on the purchase of Mi-Voie, a smallholding comprising a farmhouse, garden, barns, a stable and 5–6 acres of land in a secluded spot between the château and the nearby village of Avon.[28] Again, there is no evidence of any building here at this stage, suggesting that its role was as a private retreat. She was given Montceaux in 1556 as a gift from Henry II and here she did start building, though it is not clear whether the château was begun by the king before 1556 or by her after that date.[29] The architect Philibert Delorme recorded that he had worked on the pall-mall court for the queen.[30] He also designed a garden building for Catherine at Montceaux* – half grotto, half pavilion – which was inspired by the grotto built by the cardinal of Lorraine for his château at Meudon (*c.*1555).[31]

Catherine's need for her own space might well have been a reaction to the massive changes that had taken place at court since Henry II became king. All his father's favourites had gone and in their place was an inner circle of advisers: Diane de Poitiers, of course, Anne de Montmorency, Jacques d'Albon de Saint-André and the two sons of Duke Claude of Guise, François and Charles. It was no surprise that Henry should restore the constable to royal favour. He reinstated his faithful mentor in the important post of *Grand Maître de France* and as governor of Languedoc, honouring him with the title of duke and paying him some 100,000 écus to cover the income he was owed as constable for his six years of exile.[32] Montmorency's nephews too benefited: François d'Andelot and Gaspard de Coligny were both given army commands, while Coligny was promoted to admiral of France in 1552. Saint-André, who had been one of Henry's companions since they were boys and had served as his equerry since 1532, was now promoted to the prestigious position of *Premier Gentilhomme de la Chambre* (first gentleman of the bedchamber).[33] He was made a marshal of France and, after the death of his father in 1549, appointed as governor of Lyons, Auvergne and Bourbonnais.

Thanks to Henry II's favour, the Guise brothers too moved dramatically up the social ladder. François, who would become duke of Guise on the death of his father in 1550, was made governor of Normandy and the Dauphiné, and the king also arranged a royal bride for him. In September 1548 he was betrothed to Anna d'Este, the daughter of Duke Ercole and Renée of France, younger daughter of Louis XII. His brother Charles, meanwhile, who had been appointed archbishop of Rheims in 1538 at the age of thirteen, received a cardinal's

---

* The château of Montceaux ceased to be a royal residence in the mid-seventeenth century and now lies in ruins.

hat on 27 July 1547, just four months after Henry's accession (he inherited the title of cardinal of Lorraine after the death of his uncle Jean in May 1550). Their younger brothers also benefited: Claude was married to one of Diane de Poitiers' daughters, while Louis became bishop of Albi and received his red hat in 1555. The family further strengthened its position in the summer of 1548 when Henry agreed to the betrothal of their six-year-old niece Mary Stuart – better known to us as Mary, Queen of Scots – to the dauphin. That December in Paris the king and the court celebrated the wedding of François and Anna in truly regal fashion, a telling contrast to the modest festivities Henry staged for the wedding of Jeanne d'Albret and Antoine of Bourbon just two months earlier. This time the king hosted a royal banquet as well as 'tournaments, jousting and other festivities to honour this marriage more than that of any other prince for a long time'.[34]

Henry II's palace revolution had a visible impact on life at court: when the cardinal of Ferrara hosted a banquet for the king in November 1547 the guests comprised 'all the house of Guise, men and women, and Madama [Diane de Poitiers] together with her daughters'.[35] It could also be seen in the allocation of apartments at Saint-Germain.[36] Montmorency was back in the suite next to that of the king on the second floor, the rooms he had occupied before falling out with Francis I; his wife had her own suite of rooms on the first floor directly below, while their children (they had a total of twelve) were lodged on the ground floor. Most of the favourites were on the first floor, not least Diane de Poitiers, who had moved into the suite which had been occupied by Madame d'Étampes; the Guise brothers, Cardinal Charles and François, whose duchess had the adjoining suite; and Saint-André, whose rooms were linked to the king's apartment above by a private staircase.

The personnel may have changed but the royal routine remained much the same: the *lever*, followed by meetings, mass, dinner, afternoons spent relaxing, riding or playing tennis, followed by supper and the formal *coucher* at the end

of the day. Seasoned observers might have noticed that the
court was less informal than it had been under Francis I, less
fun and with a greater emphasis on ceremonial. The Venetian
ambassador, for example, was surprised to find that new regulations meant that he now had to be formally escorted into
the presence of the king.[37] Henry II also made changes to
the layout of the royal apartments, further distancing himself
from his public by the addition of an extra room between
the reception room and the bedroom: the so-called ante-
chamber (Italian *anticamera*). This was a standard feature in
Italian palaces of the period and seems to have been popular-
ized in France by the cardinal of Ferrara, who included one
in the villa Le Grand Ferrare that he built in the grounds at
Fontainebleau (begun 1541).[38]

The court also maintained the itinerant lifestyle it had
enjoyed under Francis I. Under Henry II it spent most of the
year at the royal residences of the Louvre, Saint-Germain and
Fontainebleau, though, unlike his father, the king evidently
preferred Villers-Cotterêts and the castle at Compiègne to the
Loire châteaux at Blois and Amboise.[39] Henry was not a builder
like his father, though he did continue to embellish the royal
residences. He completed the ballroom at Fontainebleau
and added a superb one at the Louvre, known as the Salle
des Caryatids after the classically inspired statues by Jean
Goujon that supported the gallery. At Saint-Germain he built
the Château Neuf, a theatre designed by Philibert Delorme
and perhaps inspired by the ruins of Emperor Hadrian's villa
at Tivoli, which provided a large space for court festivities.[40]
Delorme, who spent several years in Italy studying the architectural remains of antiquity, also designed Francis I's tomb in
Saint-Denis and a chapel at Villers-Cotterêts. Like his father,
Henry II was a fan of Italian *all'antica* culture: in addition to
his interest in classical theatre, he also employed Italian artists,
musicians and dancing masters, as well as Italians to instruct
his sons in the arts of swordsmanship.[41]

Delorme's major project was the rebuilding of Diane de

Poitiers' château at Anet, the estate to the west of Paris that she had inherited from her husband after his death in 1531. It was a sign of her influence over the king that the court regularly spent time there. Although Diane was the patron of this ambitious project, the money to pay for it came directly from the royal coffers. It was regal and grand, and filled with imagery relating to the goddess Diana. Prominently displayed on the entrance portal was Cellini's bronze relief of a nymph, originally intended for Fontainebleau but requisitioned for Anet and renamed for Diane; surmounting the portal was the huge statue of a stag, emblem of Diana. In the gardens was a fountain of Diana,* ornamented with a beautiful statue of the goddess embracing her stag, while inside the reception rooms were hung with tapestries depicting her story.

As queen there was much for Catherine to enjoy: besides the grandeur and the ritual, she also had the best seats in the house for the tournaments, mock battles, theatrical performances and the other entertainments that formed such an important part of court life. Poets wrote sonnets in praise of her and she was the dedicatee of choice for authors in search of patronage at court: among the works she received was a genealogy of her French forebears and another of her Medici ancestors, this last written by a Florentine in search of employment in France.[42] Above all, she could indulge her taste for expensive clothes and jewels. She was, after all, expected to look regal and the monetary value of what she wore was a direct statement of the wealth of the French crown. Significantly, Henry II excluded the queen and her ladies from the sumptuary laws that listed what could and could not be worn by different classes of his subjects.[43]

The new queen evidently had a taste for quality and bought

---

*   The statue of Diana is now in the Louvre.

expensive fabrics imported from Italy: on one occasion Catherine asked a courtier travelling to Italy to buy her 'cloth of gold, silks and other clothes'.[44] She also had style: when the duke of Ferrara asked his ambassador for advice about his daughter Anna's clothes for her wedding to François of Guise, Alvarotti 'immediately went to the queen's tailor, who is the best at court'.[45] According to the ledgers that survive for the years 1556–7, Catherine's wardrobe expenses amounted to over 12,000 écus (28,167 livres); Henry's, by contrast, came to just 9,000 écus (21,047 livres).[46] The Venetian ambassador reported that she dressed 'in a most superb fashion, so that the dress she wears one day is not seen again for many months; her headdress includes many valuable jewels and is made of velvet, like her sleeves, as all French noble ladies wear', adding that 'she lives honourably and keeps an excellent table'.[47]

Catherine had rather less freedom of movement when it came to appointing the two senior figures in her household, who were both chosen by Henry II and his mistress. One of their close allies, Jean d'Albon de Saint-André was appointed as her *chevalier d'honneur* to run her household. He was the father of Henry's favourite, Jacques; and when Jean died in 1549 he was replaced by Joachim de Chabannes, baron de Curton, whose friendship with Henry also predated the king's accession. The other key post, senior *dame d'honneur*, was given to Françoise de Brézé, the daughter of Diane de Poitiers, who was now expected to take charge of the other ladies-in-waiting, supervise the manufacture of Catherine's clothes and accompany the queen on all public occasions.[48] Catherine had the faces of many of these ladies, and the gentlemen at court, recorded for posterity in drawings similar in style to those of her children.[49] Mostly crayon drawings, sketches rather than oil paintings, they emphasized the personalities and facial expressions of the sitters rather than their rank, and this stimulated a fashion at court for amassing for collections of these portraits. During her reign as queen she is thought to have commissioned portraits of forty-three ladies and seventy-five gentlemen; her collection of 551 drawings was listed among her possessions after her death.[50]

Catherine's court was suitably regal in both size and quality. She had her own chambermaids, pages, hairdressers, doctors and secretaries; her own chapel with nine singers and two boy sopranos; her own stables, sommeliers and chefs.[51] In 1547 her household numbered 291 persons and it expanded over the years to reach 405 by 1554.[52] Several Florentines held positions in her household: Giovanni Battista Benciveni served over the years as her chaplain, almoner and librarian; her dresser was Maddalena Bonaiuti, whose husband, Luigi Alamanni, served as her major-domo (*maître d'hôtel*). Alamanni's real talent was as a poet and one of his comedies, *Flora*, was performed at Fontainebleau for Carnival in 1555. Above all Catherine was surrounded with elegant, educated ladies chosen for their noble French birth, and their ability to dance, sing and act.[53] For Brantôme her court was 'a true worldly paradise, a school of honesty and virtue, and an ornament of France'.[54]

Catherine's prestige at court rose significantly as she bore Henry four sons: an heir and three spares. Evidently she was far from barren: over the twelve years 1544–56 she gave birth to a total of ten children, seven of whom survived into adulthood – no wonder she rewarded her midwives with a velvet collar and a gold chain in recognition of their services.[55] She must have been a month or so pregnant when Francis died at the end of March 1547, for her third child, Claude, was born at Fontainebleau on 12 November, a sister for the dauphin François, then almost four years old, and the two-and-a-half-year-old Elisabeth. Despite Henry's behaviour, Catherine continued to behave as a loyal, loving wife – indeed, there seems little doubt that she genuinely loved her husband. In April 1548, when the court was on the road north from Fontainebleau towards the Cistercian abbey of Vauluisant, near Troyes, she was suddenly taken ill and had to make an unplanned halt in the tiny town of Noyen-sur-Seine. As Cardinal Ippolito d'Este informed his brother, 'the king, when he heard what had happened, returned here yesterday and in truth it is known that the presence of his majesty has helped a great deal because, although she has a troublesome illness that is not without some danger, nevertheless her condition began to improve immediately'.[56]

A month later Catherine was pregnant again and gave birth to a son, Louis, at Saint-Germain on 3 February 1549. The king of Portugal sent her 'a most beautiful collar of jewels' but sadly the little boy died before his second birthday.[57] Two more boys followed: Charles-Maximilien (Charles), born on 27 June 1550, and Edouard-Alexandre (Henri), born on 20 September 1551. When the latter was christened in December ambassador Alvarotti was unusually curt in his letter to Duke Ercole, merely reporting that the ceremony had been performed by the cardinal of Bourbon: 'I have not written any more details of this christening because I have described so many others that there is nothing more to say as they are all the same.'[58] Catherine had another daughter, Marguerite, on 14 May 1553 and a son, Hercule (François), on 18 March 1555. Finally, aged thirty-seven, she went into labour for the last time and on 24 June 1556 gave birth to twin daughters. The experience nearly killed her: Victoire lay dead in her womb for six hours and the surviving baby's leg had to be broken to save Catherine's life; little Jeanne died seven weeks later.[59]

One of the disadvantages of being queen was the separation, often for long periods, from the royal children. Excused the discomfort and upheaval of the peripatetic court, they spent much of their time at the royal castles in the Loire Valley or at Saint-Germain, where the third floor of the castle was used for the royal nursery.[60] They were left in the care of their own household, headed by the *gouverneur des enfants de France* (governor of the children of France), Jean de Humières, who had served in that role since Henry was a boy, and his wife, Françoise de Contay, as *gouvernante* (governess). Catherine's sadness at having to hand over her children to the care of others was evident in March 1548 when she relinquished that of her four-month-old daughter Claude to the Humièreses at Saint-Germain. 'I am glad to hear news of my son and my daughter [François and Elisabeth] and that they are well,' she wrote from Fontainebleau; she added, rather poignantly, 'I think that at this hour my daughter [Claude] will have arrived at Saint-Germain, and I beg you to let me know how she is and to send me news as often as you can.'[61]

In early September 1548 there was another addition to the royal nursery. Earlier that summer negotiations had been finalised for the betrothal of the dauphin, now four years old, to Mary Stuart, niece of the Guise brothers, who had inherited the Scottish throne when she was just six days old. On 7 August the five-year-old queen boarded a French royal galley at Dumbarton and sailed south to be brought up with Henry and Catherine's children: at Saint-Germain she was given a suite of rooms adjoining those of her future husband.[62] Travelling in her entourage was her governess Janet Stuart, Lady Fleming, who attracted the attentions of Henry II – like Madame de Valentinois, she was considerably older than the king – and, while his mistress was laid up with a broken leg, they had an affair. In April 1551 Lady Fleming gave birth to a son, whom the king recognized as his own but, to avoid trouble, he had the baby's mother removed from court and sent back to Scotland – the boy was named Henri and given the title of duke of Angoulême. It was one of the few occasions when Catherine overtly sided with her rival. As she wrote to the duchess of Guise, Lady Fleming had left 'without presenting herself at the least to madame de Valentinois, or to myself'.[63]

Catherine's relations with her husband's mistress were not easy. It must have been distressing for Catherine to discover that she was expected to give way to Diane de Poitiers in the upbringing of her own children. It was the duchess who took charge of sending Humières instructions from Henry II – she addressed the governor as 'my ally' – regarding wet nurses, diet and the importance of fresh air as well as their education.[64] Indeed, the royal mistress was so prominent in the lives of the royal infants that one physician dedicated his translation of a treatise on menstruation to her, praising 'her care not only for their conception and birth but also to have them nourished by wet nurses who are strong, healthy and well-complexioned'.[65]

Catherine had to ask Humières and his wife for news of her children. 'You have given me great pleasure in sending news of my children and I am glad to hear they are well,' she wrote to Humières from Villers-Cotterêts in July 1547, asking him: 'I beg you to write to me as often as you can about their health.'[66] He must have done as she asked because a fortnight later she wrote again, this time from Compiègne: 'I see from your letters that my children are now at L'Isle Adam', a castle on an island in the River Oise, north of Paris, and offering advice about their accommodation in the summer heat: 'it seems to me that they would be better lodged in the pavil- ion rather than the château because it is beside the water'.[67] However, there seems to have been some disagreement between Catherine's wishes and those of the king, or Diane de Poitiers, regarding this issue or another, because ten days later, still at Compiègne, Catherine wrote, 'I have received the letter you sent me and it seems to me that it would be better to obey the king's orders'.[68]

The same pattern emerged on another occasion when there was a dispute about the health of the eleven-month-old Charles. Diane de Poitiers wrote to Françoise de Contay to voice her concern over the quality of the milk the wet nurse was feeding the baby and this letter was followed a few days later by one from the king himself.[69] Madame de Contay then wrote to Catherine to ask her opinion and she replied that she believed the wet nurse 'to be honest and healthy'.[70] Evidently there must have been another row in the royal apartments because three days later Catherine wrote to the governess again, this time to say that 'the king is sending Monsieur d'Andelot to you to tell you what he wants to be done about the milk for my son'.[71] Catherine remained obedient and loyal to her husband, but it must have been humiliating all the same to have her own wishes countermanded.

For us, one of the bonuses of Catherine's enforced separation from her children was a series of portraits that she commissioned of the little princes and princesses, which was to lead to similar portraits of the men and women at court. Importantly, these were not formal painted pictures, but quick sketches in crayon designed to capture the day-to-day progress of her children as they grew up – in much the same way as we take photographs with a camera. In 1547 she asked Humières to allow a painter access to the nurseries and was very satisfied with the results.[72] Two years later she wrote to Humières from Compiègne, thanking him for 'the portrait of the dauphin which you have just sent me', and asked him to arrange for two more portraits of her sons, 'and also I beg you to send me pictures of my other children as soon as the painter can send them and to send news of my little daughter', who had been ill.[73] In 1552 she asked Françoise de Contay to organize another set of portraits of 'all my said children, both sons and daughters, including the queen of Scotland, just as they are with nothing missing from their faces'.[74]

Outside the cloistered world of the French court the Protestant Reformation continued its relentless march across northern Europe. Charles V had been obliged to compromise in 1548 in order to maintain his authority in the empire by making important concessions to the new religion. Henry II, by contrast, was robustly opposed to any such gesture, and certainly not those granted by the emperor that included the marriage of priests and communion in both kinds – the Catholic Church allowed the laity to take only the bread at communion, reserving the wine for priests alone. Moreover, he refused to take part in the general council on Church reform that Julius III had reconvened at Trent in 1551, not least because it had the support of Charles V. He did accept the need for reform, however, and announced he would hold a national Gallican council to appease the moderate wing of the Church in France. He celebrated the oath he swore at his coronation in 1547 to uphold the Catholic faith by executing fourteen heretics and then set up a special court to hear heresy trials; it was known as the *Chambre ardente*, or burning chamber, because of the severity of its sentences. Four years later, in June 1551, he issued the Edict of Châteaubriant, which imposed harsh penalties on all those found guilty of heresy, barred Protestants from public office and ordered the provincial *parlements* to institute regular checks on the religious beliefs of their officials.

Despite these draconian measures to curb the spread of Protestantism in France, Henry II took a pragmatic view of the new religion in his search for allies in his fight against Charles V. During the autumn of 1551 he negotiated an alliance with several German Protestant princes, unhappy at the emperor's policy on religion. Once the fighting season opened the following year he launched an attack on Metz, Toul and Verdun; by June all three cities had fallen to the king's army. The campaign was a triumphant success and owed much to the military skills of Montmorency, marshal Saint-André, François of Guise (now duke of Guise since the death of his father in 1550) and Antoine of Bourbon (who would have to wait until May 1555 to become king of Navarre). And the new duke of Guise became a national hero after he successfully defended Metz from Charles V's counter-attack and forced the emperor to withdraw at the beginning of January 1553.

Catherine, who was appointed regent in Henry's absence from court, was closely involved in the war on France's north-eastern frontier, which continued on and off for the next few years with no decisive result. With the army camped at Metz in the spring of 1552, she moved to Châlons-en-Champagne, 80 miles or so to the west, and, rather conspicuously, insisted

on wearing mourning. According to the Venetian ambassador, 'when the king is in camp, she dresses in black, as do
all her court, and she urges everyone to pray piously for the
happiness and prosperity of the absent king'.[75] However,
much to her annoyance, her authority in the king's council
was circumscribed by two men: chancellor Jean Bertrand,
who owed his appointment to Diane de Poitiers, and admiral
Claude d'Annebault, one of Francis I's close advisers recalled
by Henry II for his experience in raising troops. 'The queen
wanted to see the terms of the power you had left for her,'
Annebault informed the king, but 'she did not seem satisfied'; she evidently expected the same freedom of movement
that her father-in-law had granted his mother, Louise of Savoy,
during his own absences.[76]

Several letters survive from her terms as regent that give
some idea of her duties: she was involved with provisioning the
camp and gave audiences to foreign ambassadors, attended
meetings of the king's council and, on occasion, dealt directly
with the Paris *parlement*. In April 1552 she wrote to the cardinal of Bourbon, younger brother of Antoine, to inform him
that news had reached her in Chalôns of 'some preachers in
Paris who, among other things, are talking of affairs of state
to rouse the people to mutiny, which we must guard against,
even more than fire or the plague'; in particular she drew his
attention to a Franciscan who preached at Notre-Dame against
'the king's campaign, and the alliance he has made with the
German princes', which she considered treasonable.[77]

The following month the diplomatic corps were ordered
to join the court. The English ambassador, William Pickering,
was not happy, writing from Metz that 'the ambassadors are
uncourteously commanded ... to depart the camp and are
henceforth addressed to the queen and council at Chalôns
in all their masters' affairs'.[78] That month Henry asked her
to arrange for supplies of corn, flour and wine to be sent to
the camp.[79] Catherine took her role seriously: 'I am losing no
time in learning about the position and responsibilities of a

military contractor,' she informed Montmorency, 'and I am becoming a past mistress at it.'[80]

Catherine evidently worried about her husband and wrote kind, reassuring letters to the duchesses of Montmorency and Guise, assuming they, too, were concerned about their own spouses. She also wrote regularly to Montmorency himself asking for news of the king, confiding her own fears about his health: in June 1552, for example, she worried about 'the troublesome and dangerous fever that is around this year'.[81] Montmorency for his part warned Catherine not 'to enter into any expense ... without first letting [the king] know and learning his wishes'.[82] The letters reveal how freely and confidently Catherine offered her opinions to Henry though she always qualified them with the assurance that she will 'gladly' help the king do whatever he deemed necessary.[83] 'You know better than I do' is a recurring phrase in her letters to him, and she invariably signed them 'your most humble and most obedient wife.' She also frequently apologized in case her letters were too long, which suggests that Henry's attention span was limited.

The French army was also fighting in Italy, where Henry II's anti-imperial policy inevitably drew him into conflict with Charles V, but this campaign proved less successful. Paul III had died in November 1549 without securing his family's hold on the duchy of Parma and Piacenza, and his successor, Julius III, supported the emperor's refusal to recognize Ottavio Farnese as duke. Henry's relations with the new pope were not helped by his stubborn refusal to attend the Council of Trent and his insistence on the independence of the Church in France. Offering his support to the Farnese, he took advantage of Charles V's preoccupation with a rebellion in the empire to persuade Julius III to agree to the restoration of the duchy to Ottavio Farnese.

With the papal–imperial alliance dismantled by the truce signed by Henry II and Julius III at Parma (29 April 1552), the Sienese took the opportunity to ask for the king's help and his troops marched south to force out the garrison that Charles V had stationed in the city. Henry installed the cardinal of Ferrara as his governor in Siena and appointed Piero Strozzi as his lieutenant-general in Italy. Behind this move was an ambitious plan to force a coup against Cosimo I, the pro-imperial duke of Florence. It had the support of the large Florentine community in France which raised large sums of money for the campaign: even Catherine herself mortgaged some of her estates to help the cause.[84] Despite the planning, the coup backfired. With the assistance of Charles V, Cosimo defeated the French at the Battle of Marciano in August 1554 and seized Siena, which now became part of the Florentine duchy, ending that proud city's 400-year tradition of republican rule.

Relations between Catherine and her cousin Cosimo I were frosty. Although she had known him since she was a child, she was far closer to her Strozzi cousins. Nevertheless, Catherine and Cosimo had been in correspondence for many years – until 1553. That January she asked Cosimo to allow her chaplain Giovanni Battista Bencivenni to become a prebendary 'in the church of San Lorenzo in Florence, founded by our house of Medici', even though he was resident in France.[85] In September, in reply to a letter from Cosimo announcing the betrothal of his daughter Isabella, she thanked him for the news and admitted to having 'a singular affection for my paternal house'; but it would be some time before Catherine wrote to her cousin again.[86]

By contrast, she maintained close links with the enemies of Cosimo's regime, the so-called exiles (*fuorusciti*), especially her four Strozzi cousins, Piero and his brothers Leone, Roberto and Lorenzo. Piero had long been a favourite with Henry, who appointed him to the prestigious position of marshal of France in 1544. When he was wounded later that year in the Battle of Marciano, there was some reluctance to tell Catherine the news because she was pregnant.[87] Roberto Strozzi, who had served as Catherine's *chevalier d'honneur* while she was dauphine, had moved back to Rome, where his bank performed an important role in financing Henry II's military campaigns in Italy, while his daughters were placed as maids of honour in Catherine's court.[88] Leone Strozzi was reputedly a daring naval commander, but also a troublemaker: when he murdered one of his servants, whom he suspected of planning his own demise, Catherine used all her influence to have him exonerated.[89] After a brief period of disgrace, he fought with his brother during the war in Tuscany but died at Porto Ercole in June 1544. The youngest brother, Lorenzo, was persuaded to abandon his plans for a military career in 1547 in favour of the Church. Soon after Henry's accession he was appointed bishop of Béziers and acquired several valuable benefices, including the abbey of Saint-Victor at Marseilles; he was made a cardinal, thanks to the influence of Catherine, in 1557.

Almost imperceptibly at first, the political landscape of Europe began to change as it moved towards an upheaval of seismic proportions. In England the Protestant Edward VI died in 1553 to be succeeded by his half-sister Mary, who lost no time in returning the kingdom to the Catholic faith, suppressing the new religion with brutality and burning its bishops at the stake. Charles V was equally prompt in negotiating the betrothal of his son Philip to the new queen, who was his first cousin, and the wedding took place on 25 July 1554 in the august surroundings of Winchester Cathedral. A year later, on 23 May 1555, the hard-line wing of the Catholic Church scored a major victory with the election of the authoritarian Inquisitor-General Gianpietro Carafa as Paul IV. That September the German Protestants celebrated their own victory at the Diet of Augsburg when they were granted freedom of worship in the empire. The following January saw a more dramatic event when Charles V, worn out by work, abdicated and retired to the monastery of Yuste in Spain, where he died on 21 September 1558. He divided his vast realm between his brother and his son: Ferdinand became emperor and ruler of the ancestral Habsburg territories in Austria, while Philip, already titular king of England, now took over power in Spain, the Netherlands, Naples, Milan and the colonies in the Americas.

Charles V's dreams of a united Anglo–Netherlandish state under the Spanish crown were short-lived: Mary I died in November 1558 and was succeeded by her half-sister, Elizabeth. One of Philip II's first acts was to sign the Truce of Vaucelles (February 1556) with Henry II, agreeing to suspend warfare for a period of five years, but all too soon it proved illusory. By September Henry II and Philip II were at war in Italy but this time the French, led by the duke of Guise, failed to make any impact on the army of Don Fernando Alvarez de Toledo, duke of Alba and the Spanish viceroy in Naples. There was a much worse defeat for the French the following year, 1557: on 10 August the French army under the command of Montmorency was routed at Saint-Quentin.

Some 2,500 French troops were killed and 7,000 men were taken prisoner, among them Montmorency himself and two of his nephews, admiral Coligny and colonel-general d'Andelot, as well as marshal Saint-André.[90] Catherine, who was at Compiègne less than 40 miles away, made a hasty retreat with the court back to the safety of Saint-Germain. It was fortunate for the king that Philip II chose not to seize the advantage. On 13 August, at Henry's request, Catherine asked the *parlement* in Paris for money to raise 10,000 troops to defend the kingdom. She arrived at the city hall at the head of a delegation of her ladies, including Henry's sister Marguerite, all wearing black, and successfully petitioned the members for the funds, for which she thanked them profusely, apparently with tears in her eyes.[91]

The battle was also to have significant political ramifications at the French court. In particular, it provided the duke of Guise and his brother Cardinal Charles with the opportunity to establish themselves firmly at the heart of Henry's regime at the expense of their rival Montmorency. With Montmorency in prison, Henry II needed their support and they were happy to oblige. Duke François, recalled from Italy, and Cardinal Charles effectively took over the roles of constable and *grand maître*, though the king refused all requests to make the appointments official. The duke did much to restore the honour of the French crown, first by capturing Calais from the English in December and then the following June defeating an imperial army at Thionville, where one of those killed was Piero Strozzi.

The Guise brothers reaped royal favours at the expense of the imprisoned Montmorency and his nephews. On 24 April 1558 their niece Mary Stuart married the dauphin in Notre-Dame in a magnificent ceremony organized by Duke François in his role as acting *grand maître*.[92] It was the duke who proudly carried Montmorency's sword of office in the procession; and at the wedding banquet that evening the poet Ronsard read an epic poem in praise of the Guise family. The only member of the Montmorency clan at the top table was Odet de Châtillon, who was seated with the other French cardinals. And there was another marriage between the two clans in January 1559 when Duke Charles III of Lorraine, cousin of François and Charles, married Henry's second daughter, Claude of France, though the couple – the groom was only fourteen, the bride just eleven – were too young for the union it to be consummated.

Along with the rise of the Guise family, there was another factor threatening the stability of the French court: the new religion. Despite Henry II's legislation Protestantism was spreading rapidly across France by the mid-1550s, to the extent that the king asked Paul IV for permission to establish an inquisition in France, along the model of the Spanish Inquisition, and in April 1557 the pope appointed three cardinals – Lorraine, Bourbon and Châtillon – as inquisitors for France. Three months later Henry issued the Edict of

Compiègne ordering tougher punishments for heresy, including the death penalty.[93] But opposition to both measures among the moderates in the *parlement* of Paris delayed their implementation and Protestantism continued to spread. In the summer of 1557 Henry himself survived an assassination attempt by a clerk who claimed he had been sent by God to kill the king.

Alarmingly, the new ideas were spreading among the aristocracy. In September 1557 in Paris a demonstration by Sorbonne students, who were protesting about a clandestine service taking place in a house on the rue Saint-Jacques, turned violent and the police arrested several members of the congregation, including thirty-seven women, most of whom came from noble families.[94] By the following May Parisian Protestants were confident enough to gather en masse to sing psalms in the Pré-aux-Clercs, a meadow across the River Seine from the Louvre. One of those present was Antoine of Bourbon, king of Navarre and first prince of the blood, who was in Paris for the dauphin's wedding.[95] Antoine and his wife, Jeanne d'Albret, who were co-rulers of Navarre, had been prime targets of Calvin's missionaries and Protestantism had made significant inroads in the kingdom of Navarre. Both king and queen were sympathetic to the cause, regularly attended Protestant services and travelled with their own personal Protestant preacher, an ex-monk, though neither had as yet converted. Calvin, who was in direct communication with Antoine, was doing all he could to persuade him to do so: what a coup it would have been to have the first prince of the blood as the political figurehead of the Protestant movement.

Others at court did convert, in growing numbers after 1555, a year that saw Protestant churches being established in Paris, Meaux, Angers and other towns in the realm.[96] Families and allies were split over the issue. Antoine's youngest brother, Louis, prince of Condé, converted after visiting Geneva and hearing a sermon, though the middle brother, the cardinal of Bourbon, did not.[97] Similarly, two of Montmorency's three nephews, Gaspard de Coligny and François d'Andelot, converted in the 1550s but not the third, Cardinal Châtillon. Their mother, Montmorency's sister, died in 1547 refusing the last rites of the Catholic Church. D'Andelot converted in the mid-1550s and it was he who had organized the meeting at the Pré-aux-Clercs, for which he was arrested by the authorities. Admiral Coligny reputedly converted after spending his time in prison after the defeat at Saint-Quentin studying the Bible. Another convert was the son of Françoise de Brézé, Catherine's *dame d'honneur* who was the daughter of Diane de Poitiers and, like her mother a staunch Catholic, though he kept his beliefs a secret from his mother and grandmother.[98] Even among those who remained Catholic, there was widespread support among the nobility for compromise with the Protestants. As obedient wife and loyal subject, Catherine was careful not to oppose her husband's wishes but many of her close confidantes were interested in the new ideas. Both her sister-in-law Marguerite and Jacqueline de Longwy, duchess of Montpensier, were sympathizers, while several of her ladies were arrested in the rue Saint-Jacques protest.[99] Moreover, outside the confines of the royal court, populist preachers, Catholic and Protestant alike, had begun to fan the flames of religious hatred with their sermons.

The escalating costs of the wars between Henry II and Philip II threatened the economies of both realms with bankruptcy. Guise's campaign in Italy alone had cost Henry II over 750,000 écus (1.8 million livres).[100] From his prison Montmorency urged Henry to sue for peace and the king, acting on his mentor's advice, announced his intention of opening negotiations with the Spanish. Much to the fury of the Guise brothers, it was evident that the king had not abandoned his constable, who returned to court in December 1558 and was reinstated in all his offices. Montmorency was also the leader of the delegation negotiating with the Spanish, along with marshal Saint-André and two others, who would later become close advisers to Catherine: Jean de Morvillier, bishop of Orléans, and Claude de L'Aubespine, a young secretary of state.[101]

Negotiating the treaty was complicated, to say the least. One of the few issues on which both monarchs were agreed was that Protestantism was a heresy that had to be exterminated, with violence if necessary. Talks opened at Cateau-Cambrésis in October 1558 and were not concluded until April the following year. One of the stumbling blocks was the enormous sum demanded by Philip II as part of the peace settlement, which the constable, with the vocal support of Diane de Poitiers, urged a reluctant Henry to accept. Another complication was agreeing on the various marriages which would be needed to cement the terms of the peace. Philip II wanted to marry Elizabeth I of England so that he could regain his title of king which he had lost when Mary I died in 1557; according to the English ambassador, Montmorency was overheard wishing that Catherine was dead so that Henry could marry the new queen, though both these schemes came to an abrupt end when Elizabeth established herself as head of the Church in England and granted Protestants freedom of worship.[102] Another proposal was a union between Philip II's heir Don Carlos and Henry's daughter Elisabeth but there were questions about the mental instability of the Spanish prince.

In the end it was decided that Philip II himself would marry Henry's daughter. Catherine, apparently to squash rumours that Elisabeth was too young, measured the thirteen-year-old's height with a gold chain and then presented the chain to Philip's jester.[103] The negotiators arranged another marriage as further cement for the alliance between Henry's sister Marguerite and Philip's first cousin Emanuele Filiberto of Savoy, the victorious commander of the imperial troops at Saint-Quentin – the problem here was age rather than youth: Marguerite was thirty-six years old, five years older than her

husband and perhaps too old to bear children. In addition
to a royal bride, Emanuele Filiberto was rewarded with the
return of his duchy of Savoy, which had been occupied by the
French since 1536. The treaty was signed on 3 April 1559 and
when the news that the long years of war had come to an end
was published in Paris four days later, the city erupted with joy.
'When the peace was announced here there were great celebrations with salvoes of artillery, the ringing of church bells
and lots of fireworks,' reported the Mantuan ambassador.[104]

However, the treaty met with mixed reactions at court, where
many considered Henry's decision to cede all his Italian territories in the interests of peace to be unfavourable to France
and a victory for Philip II. Ludovico Gonzaga informed his
brother, the duke of Mantua, that 'in my opinion the peace is
the work of the constable: he has given Piedmont to the duke
of Savoy to give him influence here in France in order to get
the better of the Guise family, and this is secret'.[105] Strong-
willed as ever, Henry ignored the objections to the treaty
voiced by many among his courtiers and concentrated instead
on dealing with the economic and religious troubles afflicting
his kingdom. On 2 June he announced what was effectively
a declaration of war on the Protestants, ordering his governors and *parlements* throughout the realm 'to proceed with the
expulsion, punishment and discipline of all said heretics'.[106]
He also began planning for the magnificent festivities for the
two weddings which were to take place in Paris that summer to
celebrate the end of war and the benefits of peace.

Widow
1559–1560

On Wednesday 14 June, Catherine stood at the head of an impressive array of royal ladies who had gathered in the ballroom at the Louvre to witness the signing of the marriage contract between her daughter Elisabeth and the king of Spain or, to give him his courtesy title, the Catholic king.* The Mantuan ambassador listed them in order of precedence: the Most Christian Queen (Catherine), the Queen-Dauphine (Mary, Queen of Scots), the Catholic Queen (Elisabeth, about to become the new queen of Spain), Madame of Lorraine (Catherine's second daughter, Claude, married to Duke Charles III of Lorraine), Marguerite (the youngest of the princesses, just six years old) and Madame of Savoy (the king's sister Marguerite, soon to be the bride of Duke Emanuele Filiberto of Savoy).[1] Together they represented the new political order in Europe created by the alliance signed that spring between the great Catholic powers of France and Spain, together with Scotland, Lorraine

---

* The titles of 'Catholic King and Queen' were first granted to Ferdinand II and Isabella of Spain by Pope Alexander VI in 1499, a counterpart to the French honorific 'Most Christian King'.

and Savoy, that was designed to bring an end to the wars that had dominated the French court for the last fifty years.

The wedding between Elisabeth and Philip II took place in grand style on Thursday 22 June in the magnificent setting of Notre-Dame, with Don Fernando Alvarez de Toledo, the duke of Alba, acting as proxy for the Catholic king. It was followed by the usual round of banquets and balls and on the following Wednesday, 28 June, the marriage contract between Marguerite and Emanuele Filiberto was formally signed. That day was the first of five days of jousting which took place in the lists that had been specially set up along the rue Saint-Antoine, by the fortress of the Bastille and the sprawling medieval palace of the Tournelles.* Henry II, a fearsome opponent in the lists, led the challengers, who included the dauphin and the dukes of Lorraine and Guise. Catherine sat in the place of honour in the stands, which were hung with costly materials displaying the arms of France, Spain and Savoy, surrounded by her daughters and the ladies of the court including, of course, Diane de Poitiers, and those male members of the court not taking part in the tournament, such as the cardinal of Lorraine. Among the foreign guests were the duke of Alba and two senior members of Philip II's court in Brussels, Prince William of Orange and the count of Egmont. One notable absentee was Antoine of Bourbon, king of Navarre and the senior prince of the blood, who was preoccupied with business in his own realm.

On the afternoon of the third day of the jousting Henry entered the lists wearing the colours of his mistress and riding a horse called *Malheureux* (Unfortunate), which he had just received as a present from his new brother-in-law, the duke of Savoy.[2] It was hot – unbearably so inside the heavy steel jousting armour – and Catherine tried to bring the day's competition to an early end but Henry insisted on fighting his

* The palace of the Tournelles was located north of the present-day Place des Vosges.

last challenger, Gabriel de Lorges, count of Montgomery and captain of the king's Scots guards. From her ringside seat she watched in horror as the two riders crashed into each other with such force that their lances were shattered. Henry fell heavily, splinters from Montgomery's lance protruding from the visor of his helmet. When the helmet was removed, there was blood everywhere. He was carried into the Tournelles, where Catherine kept vigil by his bedside, and excluded Diane de Poitiers from the palace. The doctors, who included Ambrose Paré and Andreas Vesalius, two of the most cele-brated medical minds of the era, removed five large splinters from the king's eye and after a few days he had rallied suffi-ciently to ask for musicians. On 3 July he was well enough to dictate two letters and to order the festivities to restart, but the following day his fever returned.[3] As his condition deterior-ated, Marguerite and Emanuele Filiberto were married in a quiet ceremony on 9 July, and the following day Henry died.

Catherine was devastated. As queen her favourite emblem had been a rainbow but she now added less joyful items to her devices: teardrops, a cracked mirror, a scythe and a broken lance, the latter inscribed with the motto 'tears from this, from this anguish' or, more elegantly in Latin, *lacrymae hinc, hinc dolor*.[4] She went into deep mourning, not only dressing in black but also wearing a black veil, which was the colour preferred by Italian widows rather than the white headwear that was more common in France.[5] When the Venetian ambassador went to offer his condolences he was struck by the decor of her bedchamber, where the bed, the walls, even the floor were all covered with black cloth.[6] She commemorated the anniversary of his death every year on 10 July and wore black for the rest of her life.

Black may have been plain but it could also be elegant and expensive: Catherine invariably chose the best quality materials, often exquisitely embroidered and expensively ornamented with pearls, silver and precious materials, with a pretty white collar or ruff showing at the neck. The inventory of her possessions taken at her death (1589) included fifteen of the dolls used at the time as fashion plates, six of which were specified as wearing black and might well have been models for her own outfits.[7] Among the bed hangings there was a surprising quantity made of black velvet: one particularly lavish set was embroidered with pearls, gold and silver, and 'spangled in crescents and suns'.[8]

Catherine's role at court had changed abruptly from reigning queen to grieving widow; she was also now the queen mother and, until the new king, Francis II, produced sons of his own, mother of the three princes next in line to the throne. Her eldest daughters Claude and Elisabeth were married but the other four children – Charles (aged nine), Henri (seven), Marguerite (six) and François (four) – were still much in need of parental care. By all accounts she lavished love on her children; she no longer had to share the role of mother with Diane de Poitiers. The Spanish ambassador, Thomas de Perrenot de Chantonnay, who was not one of her fans, reported in early August 1559 that she was an exemplary mother.[9]

It was characteristic of Catherine that she did not neglect her duties and replied to the many letters of condolence she had received from friends and foes alike. On 8 August, for example, she wrote to Charles V's daughter (Joanna, princess of Portugal), to Philip II's fourteen-year-old son (Don Carlos) and to her cousin Cosimo I, whom she thanked for 'much comfort in my cruel affliction'.[10] To Elizabeth I of England she sent thanks for 'the wise and prudent consolation that you gave us in our misfortune'.[11] What is striking about all these letters is the very personal nature of her grief. Overwhelmed by her own loss, she had not, as yet, started to consider what the impact of Henry's death might have in the political sphere, where it left a huge vacuum at the heart of power.

Henry II had possessed all the attributes expected of a leader in those days: adult and male, he was tall and well-built, with a strong personality and a reputation for bravery on the battlefield matching that in the lists. The fifteen-year-old Francis had neither the physical presence of his father, nor the charisma of his grandfather. Describing the boy a few years earlier, the Venetian ambassador had noted that 'he speaks little, is somewhat irritable and lacks strength, however he does prefer physical exercise to the study of literature'.[12] The envoy also noted how dependent he was on two women: his mother, Catherine, and his wife, Mary Stuart, the niece of the duke of Guise and the cardinal of Lorraine. It was thanks to Mary's influence that the Guise brothers had been able to groom the impressionable dauphin to gain influence with him; for his part the new king worshipped his uncles.

In her misery Catherine was totally unprepared for the *coup d'état* engineered by the duke and the cardinal. Although neither mentally nor physically robust, Francis II was legally old enough to rule (the age of majority in France was fourteen) and the brothers lost no time in exploiting their influence over the new king to seize the reins of power. They were a formidable pair: Duke François, who was forty years old – the same age as Catherine – was a military hero, whose skills were better suited to the battlefield than the subtleties of debate in the council chamber, but Cardinal Charles, six years younger, was an intellectual and a born politician. And behind them was a family bound by unusually strong bonds of loyalty, whose mottos were 'All for one' and 'One for all'* (*Toutes pour une* and *Une pour toutes*).[13]

Even as Henry II lay dying in the royal bedchamber in the palace of the Tournelles his senior courtiers were jostling for position. Montmorency, hoping to curb the power of the

---

* The motto 'All for one and one for all' was later adopted by Alexandre Dumas as the rousing cry of the Three Musketeers in his novel *Les Trois Mousquetaires*, published in 1844.

Guise brothers, urged the king of Navarre to leave immediately for Paris in order to assert his authority as senior prince of the blood in this national emergency. But Navarre was slow to act: the moment passed and the Guise brothers were quick to seize the advantage. They knew that once the king was dead Montmorency would be preoccupied – one of the duties of the *grand maître* was to organize the mourning rituals. These took place at the Tournelles where, as senior members of the late king's household, the constable and Jacques de Saint-André would have to spend the next eleven days performing their last official duties to Henry by serving lunch and dinner to his effigy with the same ceremonial as if he were alive – the food was later distributed to the poor.

Within hours of the king's death on 10 July Francis II, Mary and Catherine were moved into the Louvre, where they were surrounded by Guise loyalists. Two days later the Venetian ambassador Giovanni Michiel reported that the king had placed the duke of Guise in command of the army and the cardinal was to take charge of all state business.[14] Montmorency's star was 'diminishing openly', Michiel said, and he had been removed from the prestigious suite of rooms adjoining the royal apartments. He lost his position of *grand maître*, though he remained constable of France and retired from court to his château at Chantilly. The official duties of grand master continued to be performed by the duke of Guise though he was still not formally invested with the title, aware that they needed to disguise their blatant pursuit of power. The truth was highly visible in the Louvre, where the duke moved into Montmorency's suite of rooms next to the king and the cardinal settled into the apartment that had belonged to Diane de Poitiers.[15]

The Guise brothers also took steps to consolidate their control of the organs of power through which the French crown exercised its authority.[16] The most important of these was the king's council (*conseil du roi*) whose members were chosen by the king – and could be dismissed by him at will – from among the royal princes and princes of the blood as well as cardinals, bishops, officers of the royal household, lawyers or marshals of the army. As early as 16 July, ambassador Michiel reported that the dukes of Lorraine and Savoy had been given places on the new council, and that it was rumoured that Montmorency's nephew Cardinal Châtillon was to lose his seat.[17] Another man out of a job was Jean Bertrand, who had owed his promotion to the post of Keeper of the Seals (*garde des sceaux*) to Diane de Poitiers, allowing him to act as chancellor in place of François Olivier. The Guise brothers recalled Olivier from retirement: as the post of chancellor was legally a lifetime appointment, they would have to wait before they could appoint their own candidate to this key government post.

The role of the chancellor (*chancelier*) was not unlike that of a prime minister and it usually carried a seat in the king's council.[18] Like the positions of constable and *grand maître*, this was one of the *Grand Officiers de la couronne* (great officers of the crown) and an appointment for life. It was his department, the chancery, that took charge of drawing up legislation proposed by the council, which he then formally approved with his official seal. The legislation was then presented to the *parlements* for ratification: the most important *parlement* was that of Paris, which had jurisdiction over two-thirds of France, but there were similar institutions in Toulouse, Bordeaux, Rouen, Aix-en-Provence, Grenoble and Dijon. Not only were the *parlements* the royal courts of justice, they also played an important role in the domestic administration of the realm, with the power to fix prices, taxes or wages and to oversee the upkeep of roads and bridges. Most importantly, they could – and did – refuse to pass laws deemed unacceptable by a majority of their members and exercised the same authority over papal bulls, though in the last resort the king could force them to adopt the legislation in a process known as a *lit de justice* ('bed of justice') which entailed a formal sitting of the *parlement* of Paris presided over by the king himself.

✤

Catherine's position in the new regime was somewhat ambiguous. For a start, it was the French custom for a widowed queen to spend the forty days following her husband's death in deep mourning, secluded in the chamber in which he had died. She had broken with this custom – and she would later order the destruction of the Tournelles. It is not clear whether the move to the Louvre was her own choice, though she had certainly not been kidnapped by the Guise brothers and excluded absolutely from power, as some believed. According to an announcement by Francis II – read, the Guise brothers – Catherine was to be a prominent figure in the new regime: on 12 July ambassador Michiel reported that she would 'not only participate in but superintend everything, and that all matters shall be referred to her'.[19] Four days later he wrote that the duke of Guise and the cardinal of Lorraine met every morning in the king's chamber or in that of the queen mother, whose apartment was below that of her son and connected to it by a private staircase, and 'they discuss privately all matters of the greatest importance without communicating their deliberations to others'.[20]

By the end of the month Catherine was evidently involved in the day-to-day government of the state though her main role was to give credibility to the Guise regime. As ambassador Michiel wrote on 30 July, 'all decisions are made in the afternoon in the presence of the queen mother'.[21] He then added a very revealing point: when unpopular decisions had to be made 'the Guise brothers always tell the injured parties that it is the will of the queen mother, from which the king cannot dissent'. So Catherine's role was not so much a leader as a shield with which the cardinal and the duke could deflect attention from their own ambitions.

Lorraine himself was more truthful when he explained somewhat smugly to Ippolito d'Este, cardinal of Ferrara, in late August why he was unable to attend the conclave that was about to open in Rome: 'I would willingly have made the journey to be with you,' he wrote, 'but the king has done me the honour of putting me in charge of his affairs, with which I am fully occupied, and his majesty has not given me leave to go.'[22] It was a claim he would not have made to that cardinal, who had many friends at the French court, not least Catherine herself, if she had actually been in charge. Moreover, when Ferrara wrote a letter on 25 December to inform France of the election of Pius IV, he did not address it to the king, or to the queen mother, but, tellingly, to Cardinal Charles and Duke François.

On 21 August Catherine finished her forty days of deep mourning and was seen in public for the first time since the jousting accident that killed her husband. After attending mass in memory of the dead king, Michiel reported that she 'went out accompanied by her daughters with all the princesses and ladies of the court, everybody being much distressed and the queen's tears in chapel were never ceasing'.[23] Michiel added that 'her majesty has now left off deep mourning and will wear what is usually worn by widows'. Her new status was amply evident in the domestic context at court. She was no longer the senior lady at court – that position now belonged to her daughter-in-law, the sixteen-year-old Mary Stuart – but there is no evidence that she had any difficulty adapting to her loss of status.

As queen mother Catherine had to relinquish her grand apartments at the royal châteaux to the new queen, Mary, and accept a smaller household which was reduced from 400 to 278 persons.[24] The loss of the royal suite was not always a disadvantage: at Fontainebleau, for example, she exchanged the queen's suite overlooking the Cour Ovale for the grand set of rooms that Henry had built for his own use in the quieter pavilion beyond the gallery.[25] She was also given a generous allowance from the royal coffers amounting to some 30,000 écus (72,000 livres) and acquired two royal châteaux for her own use: Villers-Cotterêts and Chenonceau, which she exchanged with Diane de Poitiers for her own estate at Chaumont, a generous arrangement as Chaumont was more valuable in terms of income, though Chenonceau was undeniably more beautiful and would become one of Catherine's favourite residences.[26]

There was much in favour of her new position, not least the freedom to make her own appointments to the two senior positions in her household. She appointed Antoine de Crussol, vicomte d'Uzès, as her new *chevalier d'honneur*: he was the husband of one of her close confidantes, Louise de Clermont, and Catherine later rewarded them both by raising their title to a duchy. Another close friend, Jacqueline de Longwy, wife of Louis II of Bourbon, duke of Montpensier, became her senior *dame d'honneur* to replace Diane de Poitiers' daughter Françoise de Brézé; however, Catherine was not vindictive and Diane's daughter was still one of the ladies of her household in the 1560s.[27] She also promoted another *dame d'honneur*, Catherine de Pierrevive, Madame du Perron, to the post of *gouvernante* to her son Charles, the dauphin until François and Mary had a son. From a Piedmontese family resident in Lyons, Madame du Perron was a lively, educated woman and married to the Florentine banker Antonio Gondi, another member of the Italian community in Lyons, whose business profits had enabled him to buy the lordship of Perron.[28]

Above all, Catherine celebrated her husband's life in art and architecture. On 14 November 1559 she wrote to Michelangelo, with a reminder that the Medici family had been among his most generous patrons, offering him the commission for a life-size bronze equestrian monument to Henry II which she wanted to erect in the courtyard of her palace, or at least a design which could be cast by a bronze specialist.[29] It was an unusual for Catherine to choose an Italian for such a prominent project: she preferred French architects and artists, or at least Italians who had established reputations at the French court. Perhaps it was the family connection that she valued: in any event Michelangelo turned the offer down on the grounds that he was too old (he was seventy-nine) but recommended a fellow Florentine, Daniele da Volterra, who accepted it. The following year her cousin Roberto Strozzi, acting as her agent, signed a contract with Daniele to complete the statue in two years and Catherine sent 6,000 scudi to the Strozzi bank in Rome to cover initial costs. The project soon ran into difficulties: Daniele was a slow worker and had other commissions as well, so that by the time he died in 1566 only the horse had been successfully cast and the figure of the king was never completed.*

Her other two projects to commemorate her husband were part of the traditional funeral monuments for the kings of France. It was the custom for their hearts to be buried separately from the body, which was interred at Saint-Denis, and Catherine erected Henry II's heart monument in the Orléans chapel in the Parisian monastery of the Célestins.[30] Some 10 feet high, it consisted of three distinct pieces: a marble pedestal carved by Domenico Fiorentino, one of the stucco experts learning their craft at Fontainebleau under Primaticcio; a statue of the Three Graces by the French sculptor Germain Pilon; and on top the bronze urn containing the king's heart.[†] It was a conspicuously expensive project, its cost increased by the use of white marble from Carrara.[31] The choice of these pagan figures from classical mythology to stand guard over the heart of a Most Christian King was not as surprising as it might seem. Medieval theologians had established links between the graces and the three Christian virtues of Faith, Hope and Charity, a connection that was made explicit in an inscription on the wall of the chapel in the Célestins.[32] The inscription

---

* The horse was finally shipped to France in 1622 and used by Cardinal Richelieu for the equestrian monument to Louis XIII erected in the Place Royale (now Place des Vosges).

† The monument is now on display at the Louvre with a modern copy of the urn which was melted down during the French Revolution.

also makes clear that Catherine hoped her own heart would be placed in the urn after her death to reunite her with her husband.[33]

More explicitly, Catherine was portrayed with her husband in the elaborate tomb she commissioned for Henry II at Saint-Denis, where his predecessors were traditionally buried with their queens. The project might have been traditional in format, but it was very ambitious in scale. Catherine's initial project was for a grandiose rotunda to be attached to the north transept of the royal abbey, circular in plan and crowned by a majestic dome, to contain the tomb and those of their four sons.[34] Sadly, the chapel project ran into difficulties and was never completed* and the tomb was placed in the basilica. Elegantly classical in style, it was designed by Primaticcio and ornamented with statues by Germain Pilon. Following the pattern for royal tombs established by Louis XII with his queen Anne of Brittany and Francis I with Claude of France, it featured figures of the king and queen (*priants*) kneeling in prayer[†] on top of a temple structure in which their naked corpses (*gisants*) were on display. Henry's body was arched in agony, deliberately reminiscent of the dead Christ, and the initial design for Catherine's *gisant* showed a wasted old woman, but in the end she decided to replace this with the body of a young woman, as she had been at her husband's death.[35]

The completed tomb was conspicuously expensive. The temple structure itself was carved in various types of marble, the white again probably imported at considerable cost from Carrara.[36] However, in a break with royal tradition, Catherine chose to have both the *priants* and *gisants* cast in bronze as well as the four statues of the cardinal virtues of classical antiquity

* The unfinished building was demolished in the early eighteenth century.
† The original prayer desks were melted down during the French Revolution.

(Justice, Prudence, Fortitude and Temperance) which stood at the corners of the tomb. Overall there was little Christian content in the ornamentation of the tomb, though there were reliefs of the three theological virtues (Faith, Hope and Charity) on the base. It is thought that this is why, twenty years later, it was decided to install another monument in the basilica displaying the recumbent figures of Henry and Catherine lying side by side in their robes of state, in similar fashion to their medieval predecessors.[37]

Even before Francis II had been crowned, enemies of the Guises had begun to voice their opposition to the coup in public, while insisting on their loyalty to the young king. Gathering behind the Bourbon brothers – Antoine, the king of Navarre, Louis, prince of Condé, and Charles, cardinal of Bourbon – they argued that excluding the senior princes of the blood from their rightful position as advisers to the young king was a serious breach of the constitution. Pamphlets supporting their cause insisted that the princes of the blood outranked the Guise family – and that Catherine should be excluded from any direct role in government because she was a foreigner and a woman.[38] The Guise brothers defended their position: the king was of age, they argued, with the right to select his own advisers and had chosen the Guise brothers and his mother. The difficulty, apparent to both sides, was how to persuade Navarre to assert his rank as senior prince of the blood and take over as the leader of the opposition. And they were not the only ones trying to hijack Navarre for their cause: there is evidence that in Geneva John Calvin was planning his own coup to put Navarre in charge of Francis II's government though he would not take any important steps in this direction until the king committed himself to the new religion – Navarre, typically, continued to vacillate over his conversion.[39]

The court was still at the Louvre when news arrived that the king of Navarre, who was travelling north for Francis II's coronation, had been joined at the Bourbon stronghold of Vendôme just north of Blois by Condé and Montmorency's three nephews, Cardinal de Châtillon, admiral Coligny and François d'Andelot; Montmorency himself had sent his secretary to report on the meeting.[40] With so many of their enemies only a few days' ride away, the Guise brothers were alarmed enough to move Francis II, Mary and Catherine to the castle at Saint-Germain. On 2 August ambassador Michiel reported that Navarre had asked to know why such 'a good and loyal servant' as Montmorency had been deprived of his offices and asked for him to be reinstated.[41] The result of the Vendôme meeting was the decision to exclude the Guise brothers from government by persuading Francis II and Catherine to head a coalition of the Bourbon princes with Montmorency and his nephews instead. This coalition would have the added advantage of uniting the moderates on both sides of the religious divide and allowing freedom of worship for Protestants in France.[42]

Catherine, who must have been aware of the animosity between the factions, feared the situation would turn violent. Michiel's letter of 2 August also reported how she, 'with many tears and crying almost the whole time', had begged Navarre's cousin, the prince of La Roche-sur-Yon, not to join the rebellion against the new regime and so add civil war to the kingdom's other woes. The English ambassador reported that when Navarre and the other princes of the blood arrived at Saint-Germain on 18 August they were 'well received by his majesty and greatly honoured by the Guises, who treat him with the utmost respect'.[43] It was not until Francis II's coronation on 18 September that the Guise brothers' intention became clear. In early September the court left Saint-Germain for Rheims – Catherine's spirits had recovered enough for her to write to the French ambassador in London to tell him that she was sending one of her squires to England 'to buy half a dozen *guilledins*', a type of English gelding, and asked him to help the squire find 'the most beautiful and best' horses there.[44]

After the ceremony, which the princes of the blood and the constable had the right to attend, the Guise brothers revealed their true plans and stripped their rivals of their political roles. Condé was replaced as governor of Picardy by a Guise loyalist, while the duke of Guise was formally appointed to the post of *grand maître* in Montmorency's place. The problem of what to do about Navarre was kicked into the long grass. He, together with his brother the cardinal and his cousin, the prince of La Roche-sur-Yon, were given the prestigious though politically meaningless command of the escort which would accompany the queen of Spain south to her new home; a long journey that would keep them away from court, and away from their supporters there, for several months.

The autumn must have been a sad time for Catherine. The loss of her husband was now compounded by the departure of her daughter Elisabeth for Spain, with her close friend Louise de Clermont in the queen's retinue, and that of her sister-in-law and close friend Marguerite, who left court to take up her new role as duchess of Savoy. From Rheims the court travelled to Bar-le-Duc and spent the next few weeks hunting on the various Guise estates. Catherine wrote to Montmorency, still her *compère*, in mid-October to thank him for asking for her news, that her health was good and that she was looking forward to hearing from him.[45] A month later Elisabeth set off with Navarre on the first stage of her journey to Spain, accompanied briefly by the court. In late November Catherine wrote again to the constable with the news that 'we leave tomorrow to escort my daughter to Verteuil-sur-Charente, though the king and myself only go as far as Châtellerault'.[46] She added 'Madame of Savoy is leaving also, which makes me very unhappy'. The Guise brothers, however, were delighted to have got rid of Navarre so easily: they had won the first battle, though not yet the war.

High on the Guise agenda were plans to stem the spread of Protestantism in France, which had been one of Henry II's priorities in the wake of the signing of the Treaty of Cateau-Cambrésis the previous April. More explicitly, the king had agreed with Philip II on the need to exterminate the new religion, much to the approval of the pope. Many of the French court, however, were sympathetic to the Protestant cause: it is thought that a majority of the political elite at this stage wanted a moderate solution between the hardliners in Geneva and Rome.[47] As many of these moderates, Protestants and Catholics alike, opposed the Guise regime and lined up behind the Bourbon princes, the political rivalries that had split the court under Francis I and Henry II now took on a more menacing tone as their personal animosities merged with the religious divide.

In September 1559 the Guise brothers had attempted to stem the tide of the new religion in urban populations with the Edict of Villers-Cotterêts that banned Protestant worship in towns and cities. The edict ordered the demolition of houses where meetings had taken place, the imposition of the death penalty on those attending meetings and promised offers of financial rewards to anyone who informed on unlawful assemblies. Landlords were required to check on the religious beliefs of their tenants; other checks were made to ensure all citizens attended mass on Sundays.[48] However, the edict was not strictly enforced. Many members of the *parlements* were converts or sympathizers; and the Paris *parlement* authorized just seventeen executions between July and the end of January 1560.[49] When the aldermen of Metz showed some reluctance to introduce the harsh measures contained in the edict, the cardinal of Lorraine warned them not to delay its implementation or they would 'soon be threatened by ruin and perdition, letting you judge if a town where there is a diversity of religion can long remain united'.[50] The aldermen also approached Catherine, asking her to intercede with the king. She, significantly, did not see the issue in terms of religion, but, rather, in terms of loyalty to the crown and advised them 'to do as my lord and son asks of you'.[51]

Fundamental to the debate was the visceral emotion of fear. For Catholics, Protestantism represented a profound threat to what they saw as the established social order, one that attacked the very foundations of their society and their lives. Rumours in Paris that December that the Protestants were planning to attack the church of Saint-Médard led to violent riots – and then to warnings that they were planning to torch the entire city.[52] The atmosphere was particularly tense in the capital that month, where Anne du Bourg, a prominent Protestant judge and member of the *parlement*, was on trial. He had been imprisoned in the Bastille since his arrest in the summer, shortly before Henry's death, for questioning why a man should be burned at the stake for believing in Christ while adulterers went free, an accusation that the king had taken as a personal insult. The situation escalated dramatically when the member of the *parlement* Antoine Minard, who had been vociferous in his condemnation of the judge, was shot and killed. More anti-Protestant violence followed, such that the men who had been guarding du Bourg were now obliged to protect him from the Catholic mob. Catherine was asked to intervene on his behalf, but she was unable to stop him being sentenced to death and burned at the stake on 23 December.

The king of Navarre continued to prevaricate over whether to take on the leadership of the anti-Guise faction, and whether to convert to Protestantism, with alarming results. His supporters, frustrated by his refusal to make any sort of commitment to a political leadership role, took matters into their own hands. In January or early February 1560, they began plotting to kidnap the king and form a new government in his name which would introduce freedom of worship for both religions; the cardinal of Lorraine and the duke of Guise were to be arrested and killed if they offered any resistance.

Significantly none of the key figures in the anti-Guise faction
– neither Navarre, nor his brother Condé, nor Montmorency
and his nephews – can be definitively associated with the
plot – though rumours abounded. The plotters themselves,
all members of the lesser nobility, were led by Jean du Barry,
seigneur of La Renaudie. Evidently the grander nobles were
reluctant to mount an open challenge to the Guise regime,
though many scholars suspect that Condé was involved behind
the scenes, a silent contributor.

The court was at Blois in the middle of February when
details of the plot were leaked to the Guise brothers by one of
the cardinal of Lorraine's army of spies. Their first response
was to move the king, queen and queen mother to the château
of Amboise, which was considered more secure. A week later,
on 2 March, they issued a royal edict offering an amnesty for
'crimes' of heresy and ordered Protestants to be released
from prison. It was widely believed that Catherine herself was
responsible for this olive branch designed to appease the plotters, but the attempt failed. All remained quiet on 6 March,
the date the coup was supposed to take place, and four days
later the king went hunting.[53] But a week later there were
reports of men gathering in the woods around the castle and
the duke of Guise ordered the royal troops to kill the rebels.
The result was the savage slaughter of several hundred men,
many of them starving soldiers who had been refused arrears
of pay due to them, as one of the measures imposed by the
Guise regime to cut back on public expenditure, and had
been promised cash by La Renaudie for participating in the
coup.[54] La Renaudie himself was killed, and his corpse was
strung up at the entrance to the château. Catherine herself,
appalled at the violence of the suppression, pleaded for the
life of one of the captains, to no effect.[55]

In the aftermath of the failed plot the Guise brothers took
steps to strengthen their hold on power. Duke François was
appointed lieutenant-general to take command of the army
and in April, after the death of chancellor Olivier, they were

able to put their own appointee into this important position. The new chancellor, who had a seat on the king's council, was Michel de L'Hospital, a humanist-educated lawyer and member of the *parlement* of Paris, who served as chancellor to Marguerite, duchess of Savoy, and owed much of his career to the patronage of the cardinal of Lorraine. Like Lorraine the new chancellor held moderate views on reform, preferring persuasion to coercion, though perhaps the less cerebral Duke François preferred the latter course. It was Lorraine's belief that the wholesale reform of abuses in the Church would encourage all but the most rabid Protestants back into the fold and, in an attempt to diffuse the volatile situation, drew up plans for a national council to institute reforms to the French Church, asking Pius IV to appoint Cardinal Tournon as legate to oversee the project. It was unfortunate that this move horrified both the pope and Philip II in equal measure. The pope feared that Lorraine's plans would trigger the split of the French Church from Rome just as Henry VIII had separated the English Church from papal authority in the 1530s. For Philip II the issue was more political: he required his subjects to adopt the Catholic faith as a sign of their loyalty to Spain and insisted that Protestantism was not only heresy but also a treasonable offence.

The conspiracy of Amboise marked the moment at which Catherine herself began to play an increasingly important role on the political stage: her influence had grown to the extent that the Guise brothers asked their niece Queen Mary to behave submissively towards her mother-in-law.[56] Catherine was firmly on the moderate side of the religious debate. Although she remained a Catholic throughout her life, she was sympathetic to the Protestant cause; apparently she even allowed her children to say their prayers in French, despite the Catholic insistence on the use of Latin.[57] Many of her ladies-in-waiting were also sympathizers; some were widely believed to be secret converts, notably Louise de Clermont, wife of her *chevalier d'honneur*, and Jacqueline de Longwy, her *dame d'honneur*. In early 1560 she made a point of welcoming Renée of France, royal princess and mother-in-law to the duke of Guise, who had been obliged to leave Ferrara after the death of her husband, Duke Ercole, because of her Protestant sympathies. More publicly, that spring Catherine's influence could be seen behind the Edict of Romorantin, issued in May, which made a distinction between the political crime of treason and the religious issue of belief by requiring all charges of heresy to be tried in the ecclesiastical courts and banning the *parlements* from 'any cognisance of the crime of heresy'.[58]

It is at this point that Catherine begins to emerge as her own person, unhampered by the need to be dutiful to her husband. Treatises of the period – written by men – invariably describe widowhood as a terrible disaster for a woman but this was not always the case, particularly of those belonging to the political elite. 'To be out of the domination of a husband seems to them paradise,' wrote Brantôme, 'they can pursue their pleasures and enjoy companions who will do as they wish; they remain widows in order to keep their grandeur, dignity, possessions, titles and good treatment.'[59] Widowhood evidently suited Catherine. It gave her the opportunity to exercise some control over her own life; it also enabled her to play a significant role in the political debate.

In the longer term the events at Amboise heralded the outbreak of sectarian violence, an ominous sign of what was to come. The pamphlet war conducted by the pro- and anti-Guise factions the previous summer had focused on that family's constitutional rights to power; twelve months later it was religion that held the centre stage. Anger at the brutal execution of many Protestants involved in the conspiracy had provoked a wave of anti-Catholic demonstrations in Provence, Dauphiné and Guyenne in which, for the first time, iconoclastic rioters vented their anger on Catholics by stripping churches of the altarpieces, statues, relics and other symbols of their faith. There were reports from Jeanne d'Albret's court at Nérac that Protestants were openly practising their religion in the city, where 'the streets resound to the chanting of the Psalms'; and that Calvin's right-hand man Théodore de Bèze was expected to arrive there very soon.[60] Particularly distressing for the Guises, and the French court as a whole, was the news which arrived from Edinburgh in August that the Catholic regime in Scotland had been overthrown by a new Protestant government and a reformed 'Confession of Faith' drawn up by the theologian John Knox, who had signed an alliance with its Protestant neighbour, England.

From this point onwards it is often difficult to perceive the 'truth' through the murk engendered by propaganda campaigns launched later in the century by both sides, each determined to rewrite history to suit its own agenda. Take for example the two interpretations of the Guise regime that was to emerge. For the Protestants the brothers embarked on a series of aggressive measures designed to wipe out the new religion and, as a result, were responsible for the devastating series of civil wars that broke out in 1562. For the Catholics the brothers were heroes for the ruthless way they attempted to extirpate the heresy of Protestantism. In the summer of 1560, however, the issue was not so black and white; and it was the moderates not the hardliners who held the upper hand.

In a further attempt to deal with the crisis Catherine and the Guise brothers called both sides to an Assembly of Notables, a non-representative body whose delegates were chosen by the king from among his subjects. With only a consultative role, it could be summoned as needed by the crown: in this case its aim was to restore order in the kingdom by uniting the court behind the young king. It was typical of Catherine that she was committed to solving problems through compromise not through confrontation; she preferred the more subtle art of negotiation to the masculine weapons of violence and war. Among those invited were princes of the blood, other nobles,

royal councillors and senior officers of state. Catherine sent
personal letters to several prominent figures. She wrote to
Montmorency's wife urging her to persuade her husband to
attend; to her *compère* Montmorency himself she sent a short
note, 'hoping to see you soon'.[61] She sent a longer letter to
the king of Navarre, whom she addressed as 'my brother',
describing her sadness at 'this poor realm, afflicted by such
calamities, one on top of another' and of the 'present need
to assemble all those who have the honour to be part of [the
king's] council.[62] Montmorency did attend the Fontainebleau
assembly, with an escort of 800 men, but both Navarre and his
brother Condé declined the invitation.[63]

The assembly opened on 21 August to a carefully choreographed agenda designed to concentrate on the issues in
general and avoid direct confrontation between the parties.
Catherine made the opening address, urging the delegates to
unite behind her young son. In another speech the bishop
of Valence, Jean de Monluc, said that Protestants who were
loyal to the king should not be punished for their beliefs and
commended Catherine's refusal to endorse the violence with
which the Amboise conspiracy had been suppressed. The
cardinal of Lorraine spoke of his plans for a national council
which he hoped would bring many back into the Catholic
fold. But the conciliatory mood changed dramatically when
admiral Coligny insisted on interrupting proceedings to argue
that peace would be best achieved by allowing the two religions to coexist, and he presented the king with a petition
signed by 50,000 people in support of a policy of freedom
of worship.[64] The Guise brothers responded, each after his
fashion. The duke retorted angrily that Coligny should leave
matters of religion to the Church; the cardinal, ever the politician, explained that it was indeed illegal for the royal courts
to punish Protestants – that should be left to the bishops –
but it was impossible to sanction freedom of worship because
the king would be 'perpetually damned' if he showed his
'approval of idolatry'.[65] The one issue on which all sides were

agreed was the decision to delay making any decisions until a meeting of the Estates-General* that Francis II was to convene in December.

Coligny's challenge ignited the spark that fused the political and religious divisions at court: this was no longer simply a factional struggle for control of a weak king but an ideological conflict between the two religions. His speech also laid bare the vast gulf between moderates like Catherine or L'Hospital and those like the duke of Guise who preferred a less pragmatic approach. Moreover, Condé's absence from the assembly had stoked the rumour mill at court and accusations that the prince was complicit in the Amboise plot; and the Guise brothers added fuel with talk of intercepted letters proving his guilt. Ambassador Chantonnay reported to Philip II that large amounts of money were being raised 'whether for men or for other causes but, according to letters which have been intercepted, it has been discovered that over 100,000 écus have been sent from Paris and it is believed that this sum was collected by the Protestant churches'.[66]

By the end of August the Guise brothers were no longer talking of rumours but of actual plots against them, and of their plans to destroy or at least discredit both the princes of the blood. They claimed to have amassed enough evidence to blame Navarre and Condé for the conspiracy at Amboise and for the violence it had generated. They even had letters apparently implicating Condé in a plot to foment an uprising in Lyons, France's second largest city. It seems that the tougher approach of the duke of Guise was about to replace the silver-tongued diplomacy of the cardinal. In early September, soon after the assembly at Fontainebleau had closed, they sent Cardinal Bourbon to Nérac to persuade his brothers to return

---

*   This was a consultative body attended by delegates elected from each of the three estates: the clergy, the nobility and the third estate, which comprised everyone else, from wealthy mercantile bourgeoisie to the peasantry.

to court, which they did. Guise and Lorraine now moved the
court to Orléans in preparation for the meeting of the Estates-
General and watched, with some alarm, as Navarre and Condé
travelled north, their journey increasingly resembling a royal
progress as large crowds, including many Protestants, gathered to welcome them in towns along the route and hail
Navarre as their leader.

Catherine's worries that autumn centred on her daughter Elisabeth. In August one of the queen's *dames d'honneur*
informed Catherine that her daughter's periods 'have come
on very well since being here' and expressed the hope that the
fifteen-year-old would soon be pregnant.[67] In late September,
Sébastien de L'Aubespine, bishop of Limoges and the French
ambassador in Spain, sent news of rumours at the Spanish
court that the young queen was indeed pregnant. 'I am very
afraid that it will come to nothing,' she replied to Limoges, but
if Elisabeth was pregnant then it was important for her to take
plenty of exercise 'provided it is not violent'.[68] It seems it was
a false alarm, more wishful thinking: a week later Catherine
wrote to her friend Louise de Clermont, one of Elisabeth's
ladies, with just a brief sentence to thank her for news that
Elisabeth was well and asking her 'to tell me immediately
when her period comes' before going on to more mundane
matters, such as the gloves and silk stockings which Louise
had sent but had not yet arrived, as the man who was bringing
them from Spain had fallen ill on the way back.[69]

Navarre and Condé arrived at court at Orléans on 30 October
where events were about to spiral out of control in a way that
no one, neither the Guise brothers nor the king and least of all
Catherine herself, could have predicted. Francis II's reception
of the two princes that day was deliberately cool: Navarre he
greeted without enthusiasm and openly accused Condé of
being complicit in the conspiracy of Amboise. Within hours

Condé was under arrest; we do not know what Catherine felt about this plan to destroy, or at least to discredit, the Bourbon princes but there were reports that she wept as Condé was led away to prison and that when his wife was arrested as well she did what she could to ensure her prompt release.[70] Navarre remained at court, not actually under arrest but his movements were so closely monitored that the English ambassador reported that he was as much a prisoner as his brother.[71]

Condé's trial opened on 13 November, a Wednesday, before a special tribunal assembled for the purpose, consisting of chancellor L'Hospital and four members of the *parlement* of Paris. The prince insisted on his innocence and argued that the charges against him had been invented by the Guise brothers but his demand for a fair trial by his peers was denied. On the Saturday Francis II was out hunting in the woods around Orléans when he suddenly collapsed with a violent headache; the following day he developed earache and a high fever. As November drew to a close the news from both the trial and the sickbed was ominous. On 26 November, Condé was found guilty and condemned to death. Although L'Hospital and one of the other judges were able, briefly, to delay matters by 'forgetting' to sign the document authorizing the execution, it was finally fixed for 10 December. Inside the palace the king's condition, which had been diagnosed as an ulcer in his ear, was worsening day by day. At the end of November Catherine wrote of 'the troubles and afflictions which it pleases God to send me' in a letter to her sister-in-law Marguerite of Savoy and 'my unhappiness at seeing the king my son with such an extreme pain in his head'.[72]

On 5 December Francis II died. He was only sixteen years old and had been king for just sixteen months; the new king was his ten-year-old brother Charles IX, who was yet to reach his majority. The following day Catherine attended a meeting of the king's council at which it was announced that she had been put in charge of the government 'in consideration of her great virtues, prudence and wise conduct', with Navarre acting as her chief adviser.[73] Six days later, thanks to the support of L'Hospital, the appointment was confirmed by the *parlement* of Paris without any objections. Catherine's political skills had matured considerably since the death of her husband. Once it became clear that Francis was dying and that the new king would need a regent, she took steps to ensure that this role was not exercised by the Guise brothers.

Confusingly, there were two different French traditions regarding this role: the male choice, a man of royal rank, an uncle perhaps or the senior prince of the blood; or a woman such as the king's mother or his sister. One particularly prominent example of a female regent was Blanche of Castile, who had taken on the role in 1226 for her twelve-year-old son Louis IX, who was later canonized for his role in the crusades and venerated in France as the ideal Christian king. In this instance both Catherine and Antoine of Bourbon had a claim to the position and at the council meeting on 6 December she made it clear that she was taking on the role. Three days before Francis died she held a meeting with Navarre in the presence of the Guise brothers and accused him of treason, in particular with collaboration in the conspiracy of Amboise. Navarre insisted on his loyalty to the crown and offered to waive his rights to the regency as proof.[74] Catherine accepted his gesture but it soon became clear that she had offered Navarre other inducements, which were less acceptable to Guise and Lorraine. Foremost among these was the release of Condé; Navarre was also made a member of the king's council as Catherine's chief councillor; and she gave him the post of lieutenant-general, thus removing the duke of Guise as head of the army. Finally, in a move which was to have a significant impact in years to come, she agreed to the betrothal of Navarre's young son Henri to Catherine's youngest daughter, Marguerite: the two children were only seven years old, so it would be some time before they could be married.

The Guise brothers were furious. During a meeting of the

king's council on 8 December there was a bitter row between the duke and admiral Coligny over plans to allow Protestants to gather together. It was only the solemnity of the occasion that stopped Guise, so he claimed, from stabbing the ad-miral.[75] When the Estates-General opened at Orléans on 13 December the nature of the new regime was visible for all to see: Catherine was seated next to her son Charles IX with Navarre on a dais below, flanked by constable Montmorency and chancellor L'Hospital. Two weeks later the political land-scape changed in dramatic fashion when Jeanne d'Albret, the queen of Navarre, publicly converted to Protestantism on Christmas Day. It was a move that was to have significant repercussions.

Catherine had seized power; not only had she outwitted the Guise brothers, she had also deftly outmanoeuvred Navarre. A letter she wrote to ambassador Limoges in early January tells us something about her state of mind at this critical point in her life. It was a long missive and the first half was devoted to her worries about her daughter Elisabeth, who was suffer-ing from chickenpox, asking for his advice about whether she should send a doctor from France, and discussing all possible side effects of which she thought 'stomach flux is the most dangerous'.[76] She then went on to state business: 'for the rest I notify you that, at the end of the Estates-General, the govern-ment and administration of the person of the king my son and of the kingdom was confirmed to me'. It was as if she had not quite grasped the enormity of her achievement.

6

Regent
1561–1563

Catherine was now the ruler of one of the most power-ful countries in Europe. As acting head of state she chaired the king's council and took charge of both domestic and foreign policy. She opened and replied to all diplomatic correspondence; appointed men to the high offices of state, governorships of the provinces and important Church benefices; and gave orders to the secretaries of state. Her authority was embodied in the seal she commissioned depicting herself enthroned in majesty with the sceptre in her right hand.[1] But she was not greedy for power, a charge later made against her by her enemies who claimed she usurped the crown.[2] In fact she went out of her way to emphasize that this did not belong to her: the inscription on the seal read 'Catherine by grace of God, queen of France, mother of the king'. This attitude was evident even in the privacy of her library, where she adopted a new monogram with the initials C (Charles) and K (Catherine) surmounted by a crown.[3] Writing to her daughter Elisabeth she explained that she wanted 'to preserve my authority not for myself but to preserve this realm for the benefit of all your brothers'.[4] Significantly, when the king's council confirmed her appointment as regent, the actual title used was *gouvernante de France*.[5] It was an intriguing choice; 'gouvernante' implied the more feminine tasks of nurture and education, rather than the masculine exercise of power by more forceful means.

Catherine herself was to become highly adept at exploiting the value of propaganda to promote her image. An early example of this was a history of France (*L'Histoire françoyse de nostre temps*) written around 1565–70 by Nicolas Houël, a Parisian apothecary and humanist, and illustrated with twenty-seven lavish designs, attributed to Antoine Caron – these were intended for a cycle of tapestries though, as far as we know, they were never made.[6] The subject of the book was 'the deeds of the great king Francis I, Henry II, Francis II and Charles IX, kings of France', though the episodes chosen by Nicolas Houël came largely from the lives of Francis I and Henry II, and were carefully chosen to justify Catherine's position as regent for her son.

One of the twelve scenes featuring Francis I showed the king among a tableau of his predecessors, an image designed to trace the authority of the Valois dynasty back beyond Charlemagne to Clovis, the first king of the Franks. Three others were devoted to Catherine's marriage in October 1533: the meeting between Francis I and Clement VII; the exchange of gifts between pope and king; and the wedding itself. Among those chosen from Henry II's life were his *sacre* and Catherine's coronation, a scene of the royal couple enthroned and another of the couple with their children. Probably associated with this cycle is a drawing of Parnassus with Apollo and his Muses that symbolized the revival of the arts and letters in France under the Valois monarchs, who appear in profile busts around the scene, including, significantly, one of Catherine herself.

To balance the cycle of the Valois kings that legitimized her position as regent, Catherine defined the nature of this role in a second tapestry cycle, also never realized, based on the life of Artemisia (*Histoire de la Royne Arthémise*). There is evidence that the book, another collaboration between Houël and Caron, was commissioned by the queen mother herself.[7]

While it was relatively simple for a king to find an image to exploit from among the pantheon of classical deities, the options for a female ruler were more limited. Catherine's choice was unusual, but well suited to her purpose. Artemisia was the widow of King Mausolus, ruler of the ancient kingdom of Caria (in what is now south-western Turkey), whose untimely death left her as regent for their young son. As Houël wrote in his introduction to the work, a copy of which he presented to Catherine and which remained in her private library: 'she who reads it will derive great profit for it will teach how a queen should govern a kingdom.'[8]

Houël drew the obvious parallels between Artemisia and Catherine, embellishing the story with inventions to forge closer links between the two royal widows.[9] Both, for example, built monuments to their husbands, though even the ambitious scale of Catherine's grandiose funeral chapel for Henry II in Saint-Denis could not compete with the Mausoleum of Halicarnassus, which was one of the seven wonders of the ancient world. Other tasks included the education of their sons, which included finding masters to teach them swordplay and horsemanship, as well as their own involvement in government. Personalizing the cycle, the decorative borders of the scenes displayed Catherine's monograms, her mottos and, in particular, the images such as the broken mirror and the scythe that she had chosen to mark her widowhood.[10]

There were other, more subtle, messages in the two cycles. One of the Artemisia tapestries showed Catherine seated at a table discussing the plans for the mausoleum with her architects. An image commonly used by male patrons at the time, it was rare among their female counterparts and underlined Catherine's active involvement with the design of her projects. In the background of the scene is an avenue of palm trees, a motif that also occurs in the Valois cycle where Henry and Catherine were depicted with their children under an arch created by two intertwined palms.[11] It was widely believed in the ancient world that the date palm felt sexual desire and could fall in love, thus mating palm trees became symbols for conjugal love and fertility. The choice of Artemisia also gave Catherine a tactful way to undermine her husband's mistress.[12] The Greek goddess of hunting was Artemis, the counterpart of Diana in Roman mythology, who had been the favourite emblem of Diane de Poitiers. Catherine was now able to requisition the image of Diana for herself – and she was certainly more convincing in the role of chaste huntress than her rival.

However, it was not so simple to silence her male opponents at court. As the Guise brothers had discovered during the reign of Francis II, the lack of a strong king on the throne enabled rival factions at court to flourish, each claiming to be acting out of loyalty to the crown. Her efforts to unite the kingdom behind her young son were further hampered by the fact that political rivalries between the Bourbon, Guise and Montmorency families took on a new dimension as the rivals gave their support to opposing sides of the religious divide. She faced a power struggle of enormous complexity, exacerbated by hatred and fear. She had succeeded in extricating the crown from Guise control, but she could not afford to alienate the brothers completely; nor could she afford to alienate Navarre or Montmorency. As she had told her daughter Elisabeth in December 1560: 'God has taken your brother whom I loved as you know, and has left me with three small children and a kingdom which is deeply divided and where there is not a soul I can trust who does not have a particular purpose of his own.'[13]

In fact Catherine was not nearly so isolated as she made out, though admittedly she was right to have doubts about putting her trust in either Navarre or the Guise brothers, who continued to pursue their personal rivalries rather than support the policies of her regime. She surrounded herself with people of moderate views, not least the chancellor Michel de L'Hospital.

She could rely on impartial advice from loyal members of her administration who had gained extensive experience of both home and foreign affairs in the service of Francis I and Henri II, notably Jean de Morvillier, bishop of Orléans, and his nephews, the L'Aubespine brothers, Sébastien, ambassador Limoges, and Claude, one of her private secretaries.

Above all, her household was dominated by men and women sympathetic, in varying degrees, to the Protestant cause, such as Louis de Saint-Gelais de Lansac, the illegitimate son of Francis I and captain of her guard who had helped persuade Navarre to cede her the regency.[14] Her *chevalier d'honneur* Antoine de Crussol was a powerful and respected figure at court, and a member of the king's council, who played a prominent role as intermediary between the factions.[15] Her *dame d'honneur* Jacqueline de Longwy, duchess of Montpensier, was also an avowed moderate, suspected by many Catholics of being a secret convert to the new religion. The Spanish ambassador Chantonnay complained bitterly that all his efforts on behalf of the queen mother to enable her to 'maintain her authority' – in other words, to persuade her away from her moderate policies in favour of those of anti-Protestant Spain – 'have come to nothing thanks to the underhand dealings of madame de Montpensier'.[16] When Jacqueline died in 1561 Catherine appointed another good friend in her place: Philippa de Montespedon was Jacqueline's sister-in-law and held similar views on religion.

As an integral part of her policy Catherine went out of her way to welcome Protestant nobles and their wives at court. She gave Condé and Coligny seats on the king's council and allowed the royal chapel to be used for Protestant services.[17] Coligny arrived at court with his personal Protestant pastor, who conducted services in his apartments which were attended, much to the horror of ambassador Chantonnay, by Catherine and her children, including the king.[18] Indeed, according to Jeanne d'Albret, who arrived at court later that year, Charles IX was confused by the different services and only attended mass 'for the queen my mother's pleasure'.[19] The king of Navarre also attended both Catholic and Protestant services, still reluctant to take on a role as political leader for either side.[20]

At the end of January 1561 Catherine confided her thoughts on the Protestant problem to Limoges, explaining why she thought it 'necessary to change the medication' to deal with the disease.[21] 'For the past twenty or thirty years we have tried cauterization to attack the spread of this illness amongst us and we have seen by experience that this violence does not work and that, thanks to the repressive punishments continually carried out in this kingdom, an infinity of poor people have been converted.' For the present, she continued, it was calm, 'the fires have been put out but the cinders are still hot and the smallest spark could lead to another one, even larger than before'. As we shall see, her preference for seeking a peaceful solution to the religious issue in order to preserve the kingdom from being ripped apart by war was a policy to which she dedicated herself single-mindedly for the rest of her life.

One of Catherine's first acts as regent was to confirm the Edict of Romorantin by ordering the release from prison of those accused of Protestantism and a halt to heresy trials. Her conspicuous show of support for the new religion boosted the cause across France, where it attracted even more converts especially among those who had been reluctant to oppose the crown during the Guise regime. She was also quick to criticize those Catholic preachers who made a public display of their opposition, accusing them of disloyalty to the crown: she complained to the *parlement* of Paris about 'the insolence of some preachers who are not as well-behaved as we would like'.[22]

However, there were signs that her policy was contributing to an increasing polarization of views within the political elite. The duke of Guise made his feelings on the issue abundantly clear that spring when he broke off his daughter's betrothal because his future son-in-law refused to attend mass.[23] On the other side Jeanne d'Albret was not the only prominent convert: another royal supporter was Renée of France, Guise's mother-in-law, whose Protestant sympathies had caused her to leave Ferrara in early 1561 after the death of her husband. Several senior bishops became Protestants; so did Montmorency's nephew, Cardinal Odet de Châtillon, though this remained an open secret so that he could continue to receive the income from his lucrative collection of benefices.

The division between Catholics and Protestants was growing more visible on the European political stage: Protestant regimes now ruled in England and Scotland, while in the empire, where the new religion was recognized in many princely states, Ferdinand I had been obliged to order his heir Maximilian to recant his Protestant views. More threatening to the stability of France, the new religion was gaining ground in the Netherlands, much to the horror of the pope and Philip II, who had begun negotiations with the Guise brothers in an attempt to subvert Catherine's regime. Fortunately for her, thanks to the unofficial private correspondence between the two L'Aubespine brothers, it was possible for her to keep a close eye on the dealings between two of her most influential enemies.[24]

In his report on France in 1561 the Venetian ambassador Giovanni Michiel reported the 'desire that everyone has to see a different regime because of the widespread dislike of the house of Guise'.[25] He had much to say in Catherine's favour: she was 'respected everywhere for her good character, her kindness and modesty; a woman of rare intelligence, and accustomed to managing affairs, especially affairs of state'.[26] He also expressed surprise that she 'was thought to be timid but in fact has great courage ... and conducts herself not like a woman but like the bravest of men with long experience of the business of government'. He was rather less complimentary about her personal habits: 'she is a woman who likes her comforts and lives in a disorderly fashion, eating and drinking too much though she remedies this with exercise', listing walking, riding and hunting as her recreations of choice.

Another leisure activity, not mentioned by Michiel, was Catherine's growing passion for architecture and gardens. In early February 1561 the court moved to Fontainebleau, south-east of Paris, where it remained for several months; her regime was markedly less nomadic than those of her predecessors, its travels dictated by political necessity rather than a desire for the excitement of chasing game, or imperial armies. That spring she renovated the queen's garden (*jardin de la Reine*), dividing the space into four parterres embellished with sculpture. At the centre stood the antique statue of Diana the huntress,* a gift from Paul IV to Henry II and now symbol of Catherine's new image as Artemis/Artemisia.[27] Around the sides she placed several of the bronze copies of the famous Vatican antiquities, cast by Primaticcio for Francis I in the 1540s, notably the *Laocoön*, the *Tiber* and the *Cleopatra*, an appropriate choice for the queen mother.[28] She also built an elegant wooden pergola there, a colonnaded walkway some 40 metres in length, ornamented with statues of ancient gods and goddesses.[29]

Ambassador Michiel made no mention of her other project at Fontainebleau: the renovation of the farm of Mi-Voie with stalls for a dairy herd that she bought in 1553. Planting the gardens with fruit trees and herbs, she added the *Laiterie*, a dairy designed by Primaticcio which was connected to the house by another stylish walkway.[30] Scholars make much of the links between this project and the dairy farm at Poggio a Caiano, near Florence, where Catherine's great-grandfather Lorenzo *il Magnifico* built his famous villa; but they miss the point that the fashion for these farms had

---

*   Now in the Louvre.

already been brought to France by other patrons.[31] They also miss the point that Lorenzo's dairy was not part of the villa complex: by contrast, Catherine's dairy was the focal point of her project, and it was designed not for cows, nor for cheese-making, but as a fashionably rustic setting for court ceremonial, an elegant room where she could receive visitors, host meetings and hold receptions. Decorated with paintings, gilded stuccoes and grotesques, the room was deliberately redolent of the rural villas described in the literature of ancient Rome such as the so-called *Amaltheum* in the garden of Cicero's friend Atticus. Named after the sanctuary where the nymph Amalthea nourished the baby Jupiter with goat's milk, it was an apt metaphor for Catherine's role as regent.

Early in 1561 the rivalry between Navarre and the duke of Guise broke out into open hostility. After one particularly public row Navarre tried to persuade Catherine to remove the Guise brothers from court altogether but she refused and attempted to negotiate a settlement between the men. That March she wrote to Limoges to say that her efforts 'to pacify and appease the divisions that exist between these princes' had been successful and that Navarre and Guise 'are reconciled and promise friendship'.[32] But the peace did not last long and by the end of the month the Guise brothers had left court as a protest against Catherine's policy of toleration, which they feared masked a pro-Protestant, and therefore anti-Catholic, agenda.

It must have come as a shock to Catherine in early April when Guise made peace with his other rival at court, Montmorency. The two men took communion in public together to celebrate the end of their feud and, united by their dislike of her policies, announced that they, together with Saint-André, had formed a triumvirate with the stated aim of defending the Catholic faith against what they saw as the dangerous threat posed by Protestantism. They made it clear that they wanted to eradicate the new religion; and they planned the elimination of its leaders, not least Guise's particular enemy, Condé.[33] Acting through ambassador Chantonnay, the triumvirate opened negotiations with Philip II to form an alliance, key to which was the ambitious plan to persuade the king of Navarre, first prince of the blood, to become the figurehead for their cause. But Navarre was reluctant to become involved with the political complexities of factional rivalries: in the absence of his wife, he was enjoying himself in the less demanding pleasures of the flesh with Catherine's *dames d'honneur*.

Faced with such powerful opposition to her policies, Catherine concentrated on organizing shows of loyalty to the crown for the *sacre* of Charles IX at Rheims and his formal entry into Paris, originally planned for the spring of 1561. Ambassador Michiel had mixed feelings about the ten-year-old Charles: at one level he 'was everything you could want in a king regarding intelligence, spirit, kindness, generosity and courage'; he was also good-looking and had 'very beautiful eyes, like those of his father' but he was not strong, with a pallid complexion and a poor appetite.[34] In late March, Catherine informed the *parlement* that she intended 'to make the entry of the king my son into Paris on 10 June', warning that it would be 'necessary for you to change rooms for a time so that preparations can be made' at the Palais du Paris, the city hall.[35] A week later, on 2 April, she told the *grand écuyer* (master of the stables) that 'we have decided to hold the coronation next month, a date recommended by an infinity of good servants', one of whom, it appears, was an astrologer – astrologers were ubiquitous at the courts of sixteenth-century Europe, and made a handsome profit from their predictions.[36] She also issued an order in the king's name which she hoped would prove popular, lifting the sumptuary regulations 'for the days that we make our entry into the city of Rheims for our *sacre* and that of our entry that we hope to make into our city of Paris and for these three days only we allow the use of all types of clothes'.[37]

The court left Fontainebleau in early May to travel north to Rheims for the ceremony, which took place on 15 May, the Feast of the Ascension. It was a daunting ritual for the boy, who was still a month short of his eleventh birthday. Much of the ceremony was designed to emphasize the sacerdotal nature of kingship: he was expected to lie prostrate on the cold stone floor before the altar in the cathedral for half an hour; then he was anointed with holy oil and took communion in both kinds, a privilege normally granted only to priests. As the new Most Christian King, he swore to defend the Catholic religion from heresy. It was all too much for him and he burst into tears during the ceremony.[38]

Charles IX's coronation was performed by the cardinal of Lorraine as archbishop of Rheims and it was accompanied by a new ceremony known as 'the sleeping king', probably instigated by Catherine herself.[39] At previous coronations the king had been formally greeted in his bedchamber by two bishops who then escorted him to the cathedral. On this occasion the ritual was made more explicit by the ceremonial 'waking' of the king, a task performed by the ten-year-old Henri, eldest son of the duke of Guise. Moreover, the escorting of the king to the cathedral was no longer performed by just two bishops but by the twelve peers of the realm who had been selected to represent the nobility at the *sacre*. The peers – six lay, six ecclesiastic – included Henri, duke of Orléans, next in line to the throne, the king of Navarre, constable Montmorency and marshal Saint-André as well as the cardinal of Lorraine and the duke of Guise with their two younger brothers, Claude, duke d'Aumale, and Louis, cardinal of Guise. Although the Guise family had left court in March in protest at Catherine's toleration of Protestantism, this was an invitation they could not refuse. Their appearance at such an important event, acting in concert with their rivals, was a rare and unprecedented show of solidarity, choreographed by Catherine to force the warring factions to give the impression at least of a united front.

However, Catherine found it impossible to repeat this show of solidarity, as she had hoped to do, on the more public occasion of Charles IX's entry into Paris. With incidents of religious violence rising alarmingly in the capital, the king's security could not be guaranteed and the entry was cancelled. Moreover, Catherine was obliged to recall the Guise brothers to court, the cardinal to the king's council and the duke to restore order in the capital with his troops. However, she did not abandon her policy of conciliation. In early June the court moved to Saint-Germain-en-Laye, where political events would keep it for the next nine months. Later that month she assembled a committee of princes, privy councillors and members of the *parlement* who held a series of meetings, chaired by chancellor L'Hospital, to discuss the situation. Despite exhaustive talks, the committee remained evenly divided: the vote over whether to allow Protestants freedom of worship failed by just three votes.[40] At the end of July, acting on the advice of the committee, Catherine issued an edict that was carefully worded to appease both sides: although it did not legalize Protestant assemblies, it did repeal the death penalty for heresy and banned both sides from carrying weapons.

Inevitably the edict met with opposition in Rome, where Pius IV wanted support for his own council with its exclusively Catholic agenda for reform which was about to open at Trent (a north Italian city high in the mountains by the border with the empire). The bull summoning delegates to Trent, issued in late November 1560, had arrived in France in the middle of the crisis following the death of Francis II but so far Catherine had resisted papal pressure to comply. Like many moderate French Catholics, she still believed that a national council for the reform of the Church in France, at which members of both religions would participate, was the best way to bring 'the pacification of the troubles and the union of our people under the same religion', as she explained to Bernardin Bochetel, her ambassador in Vienna.[41] But the situation was tricky: both the papal nuncio and the Spanish ambassador Chantonnay warned her against any sort of compromise. In the middle of June she asked Limoges to explain her actions to Philip II: the situation in France was entirely different from Spain where Protestantism was uncommon; 'here it is so entrenched that it is impossible to eliminate it without resorting to the remedy of a national council'.[42]

In the end she was able to come to an agreement with Pius IV, who persuaded her to drop the idea of a national council in favour of a more informal colloquy at which Catholics and Protestants could discuss their religious differences. Pius IV, a moderate at heart who had voiced his opinion that compromise with Protestantism was still a possibility during the recent conclave, agreed to Catherine's choice of Ippolito d'Este, the cardinal of Ferrara, as legate to France for the occasion.[43] Ferrara had a long association with the French court; a favourite with both Francis I and Henry II, he was also one of the richest benefice holders in the kingdom; perhaps most importantly, as Catherine knew, he belonged to the moderate wing of the Church.[44] On 25 July, much to the horror of the hard-line Catholics, she agreed to open the colloquy to all who wished to attend, Catholic or Protestant, and issued safe-conduct passes for those travelling from Geneva to Poissy, where the colloquy was to be held.

Leading the Protestant delegation was Théodore de Bèze, a Frenchman by birth – his brother was a member of the *parlement* of Paris – and a formidable theologian who would become Calvin's successor in Geneva. Catherine greeted him warmly when he arrived at Saint-Germain on 23 August and gave him permission to preach in the castle. The Protestant presence was further boosted a week later with the arrival of Jeanne d'Albret, whose journey from Navarre had turned into a triumphant progress as crowds gathered along the route to greet the woman they hailed as the darling of the Protestant cause. She, too, was welcomed by Catherine, who hosted a banquet in her honour that evening, seating the queen on her right and Jeanne's seven-year-old son Henri next to his betrothed, princess Marguerite.[45]

Not all were so welcoming as Catherine. Bèze and his colleagues had to be housed 'for their safety in a house outside the château belonging to Cardinal Châtillon', as he recorded.[46] The Protestant sermons inside the walls of Saint-Germain prompted ambassador Chantonnay to complain that they might as well be in Geneva.[47] Chantonnay, who bullied Catherine with threats of a Spanish invasion if she persisted in her pro-Protestant policies, was not alone in wanting the colloquy to fail; the triumvirate, too, was spreading rumours of trouble ahead. A few days after Bèze's arrival the duke of Guise and constable Montmorency came to Catherine's rooms at midnight with reports that the Catholics had begun to arm themselves in preparation for war. 'This poor queen,' secretary L'Aubespine confided to his brother Limoges at the end of August; he was particularly angry at the way she was treated by the Spanish envoy, 'with no consideration for the pain she endures, behaving and living amid such a harassment as there is here at present'.[48]

The colloquy itself opened on 9 September 1561 in the Dominican convent at Poissy, conveniently close to Saint-Germain with a refectory large enough to seat the delegates. A contemporary engraving showed the attendees arranged around a square with Charles IX and Catherine at the top, seated on a raised platform flanked by Henri, duke of Orléans and Marguerite – one wonders what those two children, aged ten and eight respectively, made of the proceedings – with the king and queen of Navarre and other courtiers behind them. Along the other sides of the square were the twenty-four Protestant delegates led by Bèze, six French cardinals and over forty bishops (including sympathizers as well as converts to the new faith), theologians, canon lawyers, chancellor L'Hospital and, seated at a separate table in the centre, the two secretaries of state recording the proceedings in their ledgers.

Among the first to speak was Bèze, who ended his outline
of the tenets of the Protestant faith by addressing the controversial issue of the Eucharist, the most important of the issues
dividing the two religions. For Protestants the bread and
wine served at communion merely represented the body and
blood of Christ, and both were offered to all attending their
services. Catholics, by contrast, believed that the bread and
wine had been transformed into the actual body and blood
of Christ by the miracle of transubstantiation, and restricted
the wine in the chalice to priests. Bèze horrified many in the
refectory when he announced that 'the body of Christ is as far
from bread and wine as heaven is from earth'. The word 'blas-
phemer' buzzed around the room and the elderly Cardinal
Tournon was heard to say to Catherine: 'is it possible that your
majesty can tolerate such a sacrilege?'[49]

At the second session the cardinal of Lorraine gave a measured response to Bèze's speech, defending the Catholic
doctrine of transubstantiation, but others were not so
restrained and soon both sides were hurling insults at each
other. Diego Lainez, the hard-line general of the Jesuit order,
who had travelled from Rome with the cardinal of Ferrara,
gave a speech that was particularly distressing to Catherine.
Accusing Protestants of being 'serpents, wolves in sheep's
clothing, and foxes', he insisted they were 'spreading venom',
and warned his audience to beware of their 'falsehoods and
lies'.[50] Bèze described the address as 'a collection of insults
and slander which lasted for almost an hour'.[51] The Jesuit
criticized Catherine for holding the colloquy at all, insisting
that she should have submitted to the authority of the Council
of Trent, and he reduced her to tears by warning her that if
Protestantism were not destroyed in France she would lose the
kingdom.[52]

The vitriol evident in Lainez's speech should have served as
a warning to Catherine and other moderates that the extremists on both sides had become so entrenched that any kind
of reconciliation was now impossible. But she continued to

misunderstand the mindset of the fanatic for whom the concepts of compromise and toleration were anathema. Her error of judgement was evident in late October during an audience with the cardinal of Ferrara in her rooms at Saint-Germain when they were interrupted by the royal children, who paraded through the room dressed as churchmen – Charles IX wearing a bishop's mitre and Henri of Navarre in the red robes and hat of a cardinal.[53] Catherine and the legate both roared with laughter at the joke but others at court were not so amused. Pius IV's ambassador, newly arrived from Rome, and the ever-vigilant Chantonnay were quick to report the story to their masters as convincing evidence that Catherine was about to convert to Protestantism.[54] Religious attitudes had changed dramatically over the past two decades: in 1539 when Cardinal Jean of Lorraine attended a masked ball dressed as a satyr and danced with topless nymphs, there was no outcry – on the contrary, the Mantuan ambassador had been hugely amused.[55] In the fraught religious atmosphere of the early 1560s, however, such behaviour was heresy to doctrinaire Catholics.

Nevertheless, Catherine persisted in her hopes for a negotiated settlement between the two religions. In November she, together with the queen of Navarre, persuaded the cardinal of Ferrara to listen to a Protestant sermon, an event that caused outrage in Rome. Pius IV chided his legate not, significantly, for attending the sermon; 'but it would have been better if you had done it more privately, and known to few, and that it had not become such a public scandal'.[56] Tellingly, at the end of the letter the pope added the sombre words, 'it seems to us that this tolerant approach is no longer possible'. Catherine, however, continued doggedly to seek a compromise solution.

By the autumn of 1561 the Protestant movement was gaining strength across France. Bèze himself officiated in public over a Calvinist wedding service uniting two noble families; and the choice of date, 29 September, enabled Condé, Coligny and other Protestant nobles to avoid attending the annual mass celebrating the royal chivalric order of St Michael.[57] Even in staunchly Catholic Paris a printed edition of the speech Bèze gave at the recent colloquy was selling surprisingly well.[58] He was a popular figure and Catherine gave him permission to remain in France with a guarantee of his safety.[59] When he held a service at Saint-Germain on 1 December as many as 700 people took communion; the service he held in Paris a few weeks later attracted a congregation of 6,000.[60] Disgusted at Catherine's support for the new religion, the Guise brothers left court in late October, while her daughter Elisabeth wrote from Spain to warn her that if she did not ally with Philip II against the Protestants then he would take up arms with the French Catholics against her.[61] But Catherine was not cowed by the threat: in November she asked ambassador Limoges to intervene on behalf of two Breton sailors who had been arrested in Seville on a charge of heresy; 'it is not reasonable to use this accusation of religion to imprison our subjects', she told him.[62]

On the streets of Paris the Catholic mob attempted to disrupt Protestant services; Protestants responded by looting Catholic churches. As the propaganda war heated up, religious violence was fuelled by the spread of fake news. There were rumours that the Protestant prayer meetings were in fact vile orgies, even that the attendees were cutting off the ears of the faithful.[63] For their part the Protestants accused the cardinal of Lorraine of acquiring the blood of innocent children to feed to Francis II during his final illness.[64] Alarming reports reached Catherine at Saint-Germain from across the south of France. In Montpellier all sixty churches and convents were looted and 150 monks and priests murdered; at Nîmes there was a public bonfire of relics. In Lyons the iconoclastic rioting was recorded by one artist in a painting that showed soldiers stripping banners, statues and crucifixes from the city's churches, their carts piled high with booty.[65]

Catherine's response to what was becoming a dangerous situation was to redouble her efforts to find a peaceful solution. In early January 1562 she assembled another meeting to discuss the issue and the delegates, chosen for their moderate views, were warned by chancellor L'Hospital that their mission was to restore order not to make judgements about the two rival religions.[66] They decided – by twenty-seven votes to twenty-two – against allowing Protestants to have their own churches but they did agree that Protestant services should be made legal. The discussions were formalized in the edict which Catherine issued on 17 January, the so-called Edict of January.* A landmark in the history of Christianity, it was the first step on the road to the co-existence of the two religions. For the first time the crown had recognized the rights of Protestants to worship in peace, though their services had to be held during daylight hours and they were banned from taking place inside the walls of a town. The edict also signalled the end of Catherine's belief in the possibility of reconciling Protestants to the old religion through reform of abuses in the Church; from now onwards, her goal was toleration of the new religion.

Unsurprisingly, the *parlement* of Paris refused to register the edict. Six days after issuing it Catherine had to remind them that 'prompt publication is necessary in order to deal with the troubles and rebellions in this kingdom'.[67] Three weeks later she wrote again to ask why it was still not recognized and urged them 'to proceed with the reading, publication and registration of the said edict'.[68] But the *parlement* continued to prevaricate and only passed the necessary measures on 6 March. Even then it was with the greatest reluctance: 'due to the pressing urgency of circumstances, obeying the royal will but without approbation of the new religion' was the terse

---

*   This is also known as the Edict of Toleration or the Edict of Saint-Germain.

codicil they added at the end of the edict.[69] By then, however, events had begun to spiral out of control.

Catherine was well aware that her edict would attract controversy, though she refused to repeal the legislation as the triumvirate demanded. Instead, she took measures to reassure her Catholic subjects. She made a point of attending mass in public every day with her children and, to underline her loyalty to Rome, finally consented to Pius IV's demand for her to send a delegation to the Council of Trent. She appointed more conservative tutors for Charles IX and his siblings; her ladies were banned from attending Protestant services and were required to go to mass. She limited the Protestant presence at court. Condé and Coligny left Saint-Germain in February though Jeanne d'Albret remained; she and Catherine apparently went shopping together in Paris in mid-February, 'disguised as bourgeois ladies'.[70]

At the same time Catherine also took steps to reconcile the two religions. That February 1562 she held a series of bilateral meetings, presided over by cardinals Ferrara, Châtillon and Tournon, designed to stress what the faiths had in common by debating the less controversial issues that divided them.[71] In theory it was a good idea; in practice, however, less so. One of these topics was the role of religious art and Ferrara sent a lengthy report of this meeting to Rome: the queen mother, he insisted, 'wanted to know the different opinions of everyone'.[72] Nobody disputed the verse in the Bible (Exodus 20:4) which banned 'graven images'; the difficulty was its interpretation. For Catholics the role of religious art in the veneration of God had been redefined and legitimized in the eighth century by the Council of Nicaea (AD 787). Protestants, however, insisted on the authority of the Bible above that of Church tradition and, though they had no problem with these images as educative tools, they objected to their use as objects of devotion. The two sides remained as far apart as ever.

Moreover, Catherine's efforts to prove her Catholic credentials were not enough for the hardliners whose doubts about her commitment to Rome continued to grow as she insisted on tolerating the new religion. It should be said that the hardliners suspected all moderates as guilty of heresy, claiming that their attendance at mass was merely a cloak to disguise their real beliefs. They dubbed the practice 'the chancellor's mass', named for their chief suspect, Michel de L'Hospital, whom they held in particular odium; 'God save us from the chancellor's mass' was their catchphrase.[73] That spring the *parlement* of Paris conducted an investigation into the chancellor's beliefs which, the optimistic ambassador Chantonnay assured Philip II, would result in his dismissal.[74] Catherine was robust in her defence of L'Hospital, a lifelong Catholic: as Chantonnay reported, when she heard these rumours she just 'laughed and said that her chancellor was the best man in the world'.[75]

The triumvirate – Montmorency, Guise and Saint-André – with their allies continued to undermine Catherine's position. One of their schemes was to kidnap Henri of Orléans, the king's younger brother, to provide a figurehead for their cause, but this proved difficult. More realistically, their hopes for a leader rested on the king of Navarre, who, although not yet fully committed to the Catholic cause, showed signs of doing so: they did persuade him to speak out against the edict, leaving Catherine in the uncomfortable position of having her policies opposed by her lieutenant-general. Meanwhile, incidents of religious violence were on the rise in the capital. In late February, Catherine summoned marshal François de Montmorency, the constable's eldest son who was governor of Paris and the Île-de-France, to Saint-Germain to discuss the issue. 'Having heard of the disorders happening recently in Paris, I urgently need to speak to you to decide what to do to preserve peace and tranquillity and to stop the people from rioting,' she wrote on 24 February 1562, asking him to be at Saint-Germain 'at eight or nine hours tomorrow morning'.[76] It was decided, probably at this meeting, to ask the duke of Guise to return to court to restore order. Three days later the duke set out from the Guise château at Joinville to ride to Paris, with an escort of 200 soldiers armed with swords, daggers and arquebuses.

It was Lent and the following day Guise decided to hear mass at Wassy, a small town in the family demesne but, significantly, one which had become a hotbed of Protestantism.[77] It was a provocative decision, and probably deliberately so; certainly its repercussions were momentous. Finding a group of Protestants attending a sermon in a barn near the church, he and his men attacked the worshippers, killing some fifty of them and wounding another two hundred. Seen through the prism of religious hatred, the event was viewed in sharply different lights: for Protestants it was a massacre of innocent men, women and children; for Catholics it was the break-up of an illegal meeting that contravened the law by meeting inside town walls. The duke himself, who owned the barn, was shocked that his vassals had dared to stage such a blatant challenge to his seigniorial authority. In the broader historical context, the killings that morning at Wassy marked the start of the religious wars that were to engulf France for almost four decades and fuel sectarian violence across northern Europe.

Meanwhile, the triumvirate's campaign for the soul of the king of Navarre was on the verge of success. Philip II had agreed to consider the king's claim to the southern part of Navarre[*] on condition that he abandoned his Protestant sympathies and forced his wife to do likewise. Unsurprisingly Antoine was unable to make his headstrong queen obey his orders and the issue became critical in early March on the occasion of the baptism of Chantonnay's son. Catherine, using the occasion

---

[*]   This was Haute Navarre, which had been conquered by Spain and was the southern section of the kingdom.

to grant favours to Philip II's envoy, agreed to allow the christening to take place at Saint-Germain and, as a signal honour, to allow Charles IX to act as godfather to the boy together with the king of Navarre. However, Jeanne d'Albret refused to attend the ceremony on 5 March and, moreover, insisted that her son Henri, now eight years old, would also not be in the royal chapel. Navarre was furious; and so was Chantonnay, who demanded that the queen must be expelled from court.[78] Navarre, very publicly siding with the Catholics, ordered his wife to leave court and took custody of Henri – he also dismissed the boy's Protestant teachers and replaced them with a team of more orthodox tutors. Jeanne bade a tearful farewell to her eight-year-old son, begging him not to abandon his Protestant beliefs, making him promise never to attend mass: with a show of the stubbornness that would be a hallmark of his character, the boy managed to keep his promise for four months before submitting to his father's authority.[79]

Catherine was more concerned with Guise's behaviour: she had been appalled by the massacre at Wassy and anxious about its repercussions, especially since Bèze, fearful that Guise was planning a wider conflict, was writing to Protestant churches in the south calling for men and arms to defend the cause. Catherine summoned Guise to court to explain his behaviour.[80] She had moved from Saint-Germain the day after the christening, stopping off briefly at Montceaux so that she could show the cardinal of Ferrara her work at the villa, before settling at Fontainebleau where she planned to spend the next few months. Guise, however, deliberately and arrogantly disobeyed her order; instead he rode directly to Paris and entered the capital with an escort of 3,000 men. He was given a triumphant welcome, hailed as a hero by the Catholic mob and greeted by the mayor, who offered him 20,000 men and 2,000,000 écus to pacify the rest of the kingdom in the same manner.[81] The entry marked the moment at which the Guise family took over leadership of the Catholic cause, a role they celebrated by commissioning a plaque of *The Triumph of*

the Eucharist and of the Catholic Faith. This expensive enamel
featured Antoinette of Bourbon, dowager duchess of Guise,
with her sons: prominent in the relief were Duke François
and Cardinal Charles, who held the text of the speech he had
given at Poissy in defence of the Eucharist; and above them
their mother, brandishing the chalice aloft from her seat in a
chariot, the wheels of which were crushing piles of corpses.[82]

Guise's entry into Paris on 16 March 1562 also marked
another important event: riding prominently with the duke
and his fellow triumvirs, Montmorency and Saint-André, was
the king of Navarre. The cardinal of Ferrara reported that one
of his men had seen him 'today in Paris accompanied by a
great entourage of the principal promoters of the Catholic
religion riding with him to the church; and when they came
out they all dined together at the house of the constable
where there was much joy'.[83] 'He wanted,' the cardinal continued, 'the whole world to know of his wish to be Catholic.' The
senior prince of the blood had finally added his royal kudos
to the Catholic cause.

Navarre's decision changed much at court. At a personal
level it marked the parting of the ways between himself and
his brother Condé; they were now on opposite sides, each
bestowing the legitimacy of royal blood to their followers.
The atmosphere of Catholic triumphalism in the aftermath
of Guise's entry made Paris unsafe for Condé; he left on 23
March for Meaux, where he was joined by Bèze and the other
Protestant leaders, to begin raising an army to defeat the
troops being mustered by the triumvirs. Above all, Navarre's
decision deprived Catherine of much of her authority as
regent and made her powerless to prevent war. Between 16
and 26 March she wrote four letters to Condé, begging him to
disarm and put a halt to a war that would be 'the ruin of the
kingdom'.[84] At the end of the month, however, she was made

uncomfortably aware of her lack of authority: on 27 March, Montmorency and Guise arrived at Fontainebleau with an escort of 1,000 troops to force her and the young king to return to Paris.

The spark had been lit: the war which Catherine had dreaded, and tried so hard to avoid, was now inevitable. On 2 April, Condé and an army of 2,000 men seized Orléans, the ancient capital of France; six days later he issued a manifesto 'to show the reasons' why he had been 'forced to undertake the defence of the authority of the king, of the government of the queen and of the peace of this realm'.[85] He urged the implementation of the Edict of January, allowing Protestants the freedom to worship according to their faith, and justified taking up arms by accusing 'the lord of Guise, the constable and Saint-André ... of seizing the persons of the king, the queen mother and the duke of Orléans' and keeping them captive in Paris.[86] It was 'the most damaging, miserable and shameful thing that has ever happened in this kingdom'. The triumvirate responded by declaring that neither the king nor the queen mother were being held prisoners; on the contrary, they insisted, Catherine and Charles were at liberty in Paris, the capital of the kingdom – where, unspoken of course, they were giving royal legitimacy to the Catholic cause.[87]

During the next three months much of France outside the Île-de-France and the north-east, where the Guise family remained dominant, fell to the Protestant army. Some places surrendered peacefully, others were only captured after a struggle; the savagery on both sides was appalling. In Sens, Catholics massacred Protestants in huge numbers, throwing their bodies into the River Yonne to float downstream into the Seine for all to see. Astutely, the Protestants concentrated their firepower on the towns and cities along the banks of France's largest rivers – the Seine, the Loire, the Rhône and the Garonne – in order to gain control of the main arteries of trade and communications. Rouen, near the mouth of the

Seine, fell on 15 April to the Protestants, who proceeded to force Catholics out of the city and destroy all their churches. Along the Channel coast Le Havre, Caen and Dieppe fell; further south they took La Rochelle, Poitiers and Bourges, which was brutally sacked by Protestant troops who pillaged the city's churches of their treasures. La Charité-sur-Loire, Blois, Tours and Angers on the Loire were all taken. France's second city Lyons, at the confluence of the Rhône and Saône rivers, fell on 29–30 April, followed by Grenoble and much of the Dauphiné. By the summer the Protestants held almost all of south-western France, including Nîmes and Montpellier, though Toulouse and Bordeaux, both seats of provincial *parlements*, held out against the Protestant onslaught.

Inundated with reports of orgies of killing and looting from across France, Catherine watched with horror as the violence put an end to her efforts to maintain peace: as she explained to Limoges in early April, 'in the end it did not please Our Lord that this should work'.[88] She blamed the Protestants for starting the war, telling the ambassador of her shock at how they took 'the honour of God as a pretext and cloak for one of the most miserable and damaging ventures that was ever undertaken in this realm'; she even wondered, naively, whether Condé, of whom she was fond, was being held in Orléans against his will. Despite her anger, however, she resolutely refused to take sides. This decision put her in an ambiguous position and one that was exploited by both sides. On the one hand she was in charge of the regime whose army was fighting Protestantism and, as such, was required to take decisions regarding the conduct of the war from the Catholic standpoint: she corresponded with the governor of the Dauphiné, for example, about munitions, promising to send him artillery as soon as possible.[89] On the other hand, although she was legally obliged to accept that the royal army was under Catholic control, she infuriated Catholics by insistence that both Condé and Guise must disarm their troops. 'God grant they will be prepared to believe and obey her,' secretary L'Aubespine wrote; there was little trust between the two sides.[90]

These were busy months for Catherine. From her desk at court she wrote copious letters: over half her correspondence in May was directed to provincial *parlements* and governors. She insisted on viewing the war as a political not a religious issue, urging both sides to remember the loyalty they owed the crown. In a letter to the *parlement* of Rouen, for example, she urged them 'to lay down arms and render obedience to the king my lord and son' by returning the government of the city 'to what it was before these troubles and disorders'.[91] Above all, she was determined to stop the war and opened negotiations with the Protestants in Orléans. Initially they were conducted by the city's bishop, Jean de Morvillier, who went on several missions to talk to the rebels. On 2 May she held an audience in her garden at the Louvre to hear how Morvillier and secretary L'Aubespine had fared on their recent mission and invited Navarre, Montmorency and chancellor L'Hospital to attend the meeting.[92] In particular they discussed the demands Condé had made before he would agree to any truce: first, that the Catholic army was to be disarmed and, second, that the Edict of January must be enforced.

A week or so later, to demonstrate to Condé that she was not being held captive in Paris, Catherine moved to her château at Montceaux and decided, remarkably, to lead the negotiations in person.[93] Aware of the fragility of her position, she was careful to give visible proof of her Catholic faith and on 28 May she attended celebrations for the feast of Corpus Domini at Meaux, a hotbed of Protestant defiance. Returning to Paris, she left the king and the court at the château of Vincennes, and travelled south for her first meeting with Condé, which was to take place on 5 June at Toury, a small town between Orléans and Étampes, where she was staying. Catherine arrived at Toury escorted by 200 cavalry and 300 foot soldiers but Condé failed to turn up; as the cardinal of Ferrara reported to Rome, he 'gave the excuse that the queen's entourage was too large' and his advisers 'feared some violence was planned towards the prince'.[94] A few days later, with an escort of just 100 horsemen, she had better luck and met Condé in person at Angerville, another town in the neighbourhood. But this meeting, too, was inconclusive: Condé refused to dismount and although the two 'spoke for three-quarters of an hour, exchanging the usual compliments, when Catherine started to discuss the situation, the prince curtly refused to negotiate'.[95]

Catherine blamed herself for the failure of the talks. As she explained to ambassador Bochetel on 16 June, she had undertaken the task of mediation 'between the two armies in hopes that, if I could speak directly to my cousin, the prince of Condé, I would be able to persuade him to accept a reasonable offer', but Condé had been deaf to her proposals so, 'as my presence is not helping the advancement of this affair, I am returning to join the king my son', in the hope of 'doing what I can to arrange a general peace'.[96] Perhaps this was a bargaining tool: if so it was effective. After a few days in Paris, Catherine returned to the negotiating table and further meetings with Condé took place at Artenay, Beaugency and Talcy; but the prince stubbornly refused to give way on his central demand of allowing Protestants the freedom of worship they had been guaranteed in the Edict of January. And the Catholic leadership remained equally stubborn in its refusal to accept this condition.

In addition to her difficulties with Condé, Catherine found her way blocked by another contentious issue: money. Waging war was an expensive business: in the 1560s the royal army ate up half the annual revenues of the crown, a situation that was exacerbated by the huge debts inherited from the wars with Charles V.[97] She raised funds from her cousin Cosimo I and from bankers in Genoa, but she needed far more than they offered.[98] Indeed, with both sides seeking funds from friendly foreign powers – the Catholics from Rome and Spain, the Protestants from German princes and England – the conflict began to take on an international dimension. It briefly threatened to become a European war in May when it emerged that Cosimo I was negotiating a league with Pius IV and Philip II to crush the rebellion in France; fortunately for Catherine, the pope refused to commit himself to bloodshed on this scale. Instead he offered her money – 100,000 scudi as a present and another 100,000 scudi as a loan – but there were strict conditions attached: she must agree to end all negotiations with the Protestants unless they renounced their beliefs; she must cancel all edicts she had passed in their favour; and, most offensive of all, she was 'to exile from court all those suspected of heresy, in particular the chancellor'.[99]

The cardinal of Ferrara, who had had the unenviable job of relaying Pius IV's terms to Catherine, warned they would be 'impossible to carry out, especially given the character of the queen'.[100] He was proved right: Catherine was appalled at this blatant attempt to undermine her authority and wreck her efforts to negotiate a truce. As the cardinal reported to Rome, she was adamantly opposed to the removal from court of anyone suspected of Protestant leanings. Moreover, regarding the demand for her to exile her chancellor, 'she, more angrily than before, replied that all these things were inventions by selfish persons and that she refused absolutely to be guided by the interests of others'. In the end Pius IV backed down. Acting on the advice of the cardinal, he accepted Catherine's refusal to exile L'Hospital or any other suspected heretic from court and that she would not take active steps to outlaw Protestantism; in return she agreed to fulfil her earlier promise to send French bishops and theologians to the Council of Trent. The delegation, which included over seventy men, finally left Paris on 19 September with the cardinal of Lorraine at its head.

By the autumn of 1562 the war was beginning to turn in favour of the royal army, which had been reinforced in

August. At the beginning of the month it had numbered some 17,000 infantry and 5,200 cavalry; over the next few weeks 4,000 soldiers arrived from Spain, 5,500 from Germany and 3,000 from Italy, as well as the sum of 280,000 écus, mainly from Florence and Venice.[101] The results were immediate: in the south the Spanish troops under the command of Blaise de Lasseran-Massencôme, seigneur of Monluc, conducted a vicious campaign in Guyenne to retake Agen, Bergerac, Lectoure and several other towns. Monluc, the brother of Jean, the moderate bishop of Valence, was notorious for the savagery with which he treated his Protestant foes: 'one could follow my trail,' he bragged in his memoirs, 'by the corpses hanging from the trees along the road.'[102]

By the end of August, Poitiers, Troyes and Tours had all been retaken and Catherine was at the army camp at Lazeny with the king, to witness the recapture of Bourges, and they made their ceremonial entry into the city on 1 September. The following day she sent a report of the event to Jean Ebrard, seigneur of Saint-Sulpice, who had replaced Limoges earlier in the year as ambassador to Philip II: 'the king my son and myself, accompanied by the king of Navarre and all the nobles, attended mass in the great church and had mass said at all the other churches in the city'.[103] Less welcome was the news that Le Havre had been taken by the English thanks to Condé, who had just signed a treaty with Elizabeth I giving the port to the English queen in return for a large loan.

Catherine returned to Paris briefly before setting out for Rouen, where Navarre was leading an assault on this Protestant stronghold with an army of over 30,000 men. On 29 September she was at Gaillon, staying in the luxurious Italianate château some 20 miles south of Rouen built as a summer residence by an earlier bishop of the city, and on 1 October she arrived at the army camp: Guise apparently warned her that it was dangerous; 'my courage is as great as yours,' she retorted.[104] A few days later she informed the duke of Montpensier that the fortress on the hill of Sainte-Catherine on the south-eastern edge of the city had fallen, that some '300–400 men were killed' and that she expected Rouen itself to fall within days.[105] She was still at the camp on 15 October when Navarre was wounded in the left shoulder by an arquebus shot during an attack on the city: as she told Anna d'Este later that day, it was hoped the wound was not too serious.[106] Her real reason for writing to the duchess was kindly and sympathetic: 'I wanted to send you word to reassure you that your husband is very well and, God be thanked, was not hurt even though he was standing next to Navarre.'

Over the next few days Navarre's wound continued to heal, though these reports seem to have been deliberately over-optimistic: an English diplomat voiced concern that the doctors had been unable to locate the bullet, which was not a good sign.[107] Montmorency took over command of the army and Rouen finally capitulated on 26 October, but Navarre's condition began to deteriorate. On 7 November Catherine despatched an envoy on a peace mission to Condé in Orléans: 'I beg you to hurry over your journey,' she urged him in a postscript written in her own hand, 'because I fear that God unfortunately intends to take the king of Navarre.'[108] Three days later she was at Saint-Germain and on 17 November she was back at the château of Vincennes when news arrived that Navarre was dead. His heir was his son Henri, who was a month short of his ninth birthday. Catherine generously ensured that the boy was allowed to return to his mother, Jeanne d'Albret, and for his Catholic tutors to be replaced with the Protestants who had been sacked by the late king that spring.[109]

The Catholic celebrations of the victory at Rouen were considerably muted by the news of Navarre's death; and they were interrupted suddenly in early December with the dramatic news that Condé had left Orléans with a Protestant army intending to march on Paris. The duke of Guise, who had remained in Rouen with the army, reacted with characteristic decisiveness and immediately left to intercept the Protestants before Condé could reach the capital. The two

armies – 20,000 Catholics and 13,000 Protestants – met at
Dreux on 19 December 1562 and the Catholics, with their
larger force, won the day. However, the victory was marred by
disappointment: although the Catholics had captured Condé,
Montmorency had also been taken prisoner, while Saint-
Andre had died in the fighting; and the Protestant army, led
by admiral Coligny, managed to escape safely back to its head-
quarters at Orléans.

Despite the setbacks the duke of Guise, now in command of
the royal army, decided to seize the advantage and launch an
attack on Orléans itself. Catherine and the court moved south
from Paris to be close to the action, first to Chartres and then
to Blois, where she was based until late January 1563. Once
again she was busy with munitions: on 8 February she sent a
courier to Paris to Artus de Cossé, the official in charge of the
royal treasury (*surintendant des finances*), to alert him that ten
cannons were urgently needed, with all their supplies, as there
were only 4,000 balls and 40,000 pounds of gunpowder left.[110]
She also sent instructions that the guns were to be sent by river
to Montargis, for which he needed to arrange for horses to
pull the barges, and he was to act 'with all possible speed, and
do not lose even a single quarter of an hour,' she insisted. The
treasurer was prompt in relaying his excuses that her request
was impossible; Catherine thanked him and forwarded his
letter to the duke of Guise.[111]

A week after this incident, on 18 February, Guise was shot
in his right shoulder by an assassin who had been lying in wait
for him as he rode home to his lodgings. The following day
Catherine, who was at Blois, wrote to Guise's younger brother
Cardinal Louis with the information that the shot had passed
through the duke's shoulder: 'the surgeons do not think it is
mortal, which gives me some comfort, and it has not touched
the bone, nor entered the chest cavity'.[112] Six days later he
was dead. His assassin was Jean Poltrot de Méré, a member of
the minor nobility and a Protestant; under torture he admitted that admiral Coligny had been the leader of the plot to

eliminate Guise but he later retracted this confession. For his part Coligny too denied any complicity though he did admit that the death of his great rival was a welcome relief. Later Catherine herself would be blamed for Guise's death; however, although she too might have been relieved, there is no real evidence to suggest she was guilty. For Guise's grieving widow, Anna d'Este, Coligny was to blame for her husband's murder and she made sure that her thirteen-year-old son Henri, the new duke, understood that it would be his duty to avenge his father's murder. It was a mission that would have terrible consequences.

The anger felt by many Catholics at the death of their hero was evident in the particularly vicious execution of Poltrot de Méré in the Place de Grève in Paris on 18 March. Watched by huge cheering crowds, he was mutilated with red-hot pincers, drawn and quartered, pulled apart by four horses.[113] The following day the same crowds turned out for the duke's funeral, which was staged by the *parlement* with Catherine's approval. It was an exceptionally grand affair, with the mayor, aldermen, merchants, shopkeepers and some 12,000 men of the city's militia all taking part in the procession.[114]

That same day, 19 March 1563, Catherine issued the Edict of Amboise, bringing an end to the war. Negotiations had started within days of the duke's death and Catherine arranged for Montmorency and Condé to be released from prison in early March so that they could join her and the other nobles conducting the peace talks. Once again she was warned by Pius IV and Philip II not to make any concessions to the Protestants; once again she ignored them. The war might have been won by the Catholics in the north of the kingdom but the south was now largely Protestant. With neither side able to claim a decisive victory, the resulting Edict of Amboise was inevitably a compromise. Like the Edict of January, it too guaranteed freedom of worship to Protestants, though with some limitations. They were only permitted to worship in those towns and cities where the new religion was already established; and they were banned from practising their faith in Paris as well as in any place where the court was resident. Nobles, however, were given much more freedom: they were allowed to worship as they wished in their own homes and could grant the same rights to the inhabitants on their estates.

Catherine had achieved her goal of bringing the war to an end, but she was aware that this was, at best, a tenuous victory. That autumn Lansac, riding through southern France on a mission for her, wrote from Bordeaux that he had passed 'many churches, monasteries and houses in ruins' along the road, especially in Montpellier and Carcassonne, and warned her of the 'distrust, rancour and hatred' that existed between the members of the two religions.[115] Nevertheless she remained determined to promote her tolerant agenda as the only means of maintaining the hard-won peace and uniting the realm behind the crown.

7

Grand Tour
1563–1566

Catherine decided that her best chance of persuading the reluctant to accept the policy of toleration enshrined in the Edict of Amboise would be to make a very public display of the crown's commitment to it. With this in mind, early in 1563 she announced that the king and court would undertake a grand tour covering over 3,000 miles through Champagne, Lorraine, Burgundy, Dauphiné, Provence, Languedoc, Guyenne, Navarre, Angoulême, Anjou, Brittany, Touraine and the Auvergne. The presence of the court would be a visible statement of the power and prestige of the monarchy while towns and cities across the realm would have the chance to celebrate their loyalty in splendid entries. The scheme was imaginative as well as ambitious. The itinerary included both Catholic and Protestant towns, especially those that had suffered during the war, and, in a conspicuous show of her personal commitment to the edict, she insisted on hearing complaints from each side in person. To balance her tolerance of the new ideas, and to dispel rumours proliferating in the provinces that the royal family had converted, she made a point of attending mass with her children in public at every place they visited and taking part in the major feasts of the Catholic calendar, notably the public processions to

celebrate Maundy Thursday and Corpus Christi. To pacify
those Catholics who accused Charles IX of breaking his coronation oath to uphold the faith, she planned a more specific
programme of religious duties for the king tailored to the
celebration of local patron saints and to the rites associated
with the sacerdotal role of the French crown, such as touching
for scrofula.*

Prominent on the tour was Charles IX's device of two
intertwined columns, Justice and Piety, emphasizing that
obedience to the crown meant obedience to its laws, civil and
religious. 'One of the main reasons that has led the king my
son to undertake this journey,' she told admiral Coligny, 'is so
that he may make his will known more clearly in the places he
visits and no one may henceforth use pretexts for contraven-
ing the edicts.'[1] Catherine wanted Charles to attend each of
the provincial *parlements* on the tour and, to make this possible, declared his majority before the *parlement* at Rouen in
1563 – she had argued in council that although her son had
not reached his fourteenth birthday, he had entered his fourteenth year. It was a shrewd move: the monarch's personal
appearance would carry far more weight in the *parlements* than
her own as regent. At Rouen that month, addressing his first
parlement, the young king was explicit: 'we intend, desire and
command,' he said, 'that all our subjects observe and maintain completely and perfectly the declaration we made last
March regarding the pacification of the said troubles, on pain
of imprisonment and confiscation of property.'[2]

The tour would prove an important rite of passage for
Catherine – a point that is often ignored by her biographers.
For the next two years she would pass through all the major
cities of the realm, as well as countless towns and villages,
much of the time in the public eye. It would bring her into

---

*   Scrofula, also known as the king's evil, was tuberculosis of the
lymph nodes in the neck, caught from unpasteurized milk, which often
resulted in unsightly swellings or hideous suppurating sores.

direct contact with ordinary people, their hopes and fears; above all it would enhance her understanding of the difficulties involved in bringing peace to France.

✤

Catherine was now forty-four years old, in robust health and, despite the trials of the past few years, still cheerful and optimistic. Writing in 1563 the Venetian ambassador Marcantonio Barbaro thought 'her figure is still young and pleasing, and her countenance is graceful and amiable'.[3] He listed her main occupations as 'peace, hunting and hard work' – a curious combination, but one that rings true – and judged her to be both 'shrewd and wise'. He was impressed by her political skills: 'she is a deft, clever negotiator, and steadfast in bearing the misfortunes that have befallen this kingdom in matters of religion'. Certainly the events of the past four years had honed her talents. That July the French won an impressive victory against the English at Le Havre, 'by the grace of God,' as she explained to Bernardin Bochetel, her agent in Vienna, 'and contrary to the expectations of many'.[4] Even the poets celebrated this moment of national triumph that briefly united the French against an old enemy: 'we have a king in a queen' as one put it.[5]

The peace signed at Amboise gave Catherine valuable breathing space. The deaths of Navarre, Saint-André and Guise had weakened the opposition; moreover, the influence of the Guise family was further diminished by Lorraine's absence at the Council of Trent. This new balance of power enabled her to gain control of the king's council: over the years 1563–67 she had the votes of six Protestants and some twenty moderates against just sixteen Catholic extremists.[6] Moreover, she again had the support of constable Montmorency: although one of her fiercest critics, he was unfailingly loyal to the crown and his vote was guaranteed by his animosity towards the Guise family, who persisted in accusing his nephew Coligny of complicity in the duke of Guise's assassination. As he explained, he intended to support Coligny's bid to be declared innocent of the murder and, significantly, 'to do everything possible to keep the Guise family out of power'.[7]

The Guises' animosity towards Coligny continued to fester. In January 1564 they made a formal request for the admiral to stand trial for the duke's murder but, to their fury, Charles IX suspended the case for three years. Catherine was delighted with the verdict and her son's behaviour: as she told the duchess of Savoy, 'the king my son on his own initiative, with no one telling him what to do, has put a halt to the proceedings' – evidently Charles was continuing his mother's policy of avoiding confrontation between the two factions.[8] The Guise family remained out of favour: when the cardinal of Lorraine returned from Italy later that month he received a cool reception; and it was soon evident that his views on religion had changed. Whether motivated by anger at his brother's murder or by his experience at Trent, he had ditched his moderate stance for the hard-line attitude taken by the council.

Lorraine's insistence that the crown must introduce the reforms drawn up at Trent brought him into direct conflict with Catherine and chancellor L'Hospital. Not only did he insist that Protestants be denied the right to worship, he also required the clergy to be granted immunity from taxation and civil law. Catherine refused to implement the measures and she had a powerful ally in the staunchly Catholic *parlement* of Paris, which rarely agreed with her or her chancellor, and now refused to have its role as the senior law court undermined by excluding the clergy from its jurisdiction. Lorraine and L'Hospital argued heatedly over the issue in the king's council, descending to personal insults when the chancellor, who had been the cardinal's protégé, insisted on placing his loyalty to Catherine's policies before the debt he owed to his erstwhile patron.[9] It marked the point at which the Guise family, and the cardinal of Lorraine in particular, turned decisively against any form of compromise.[10]

Opposition to her policies might have lessened at home but Catherine's dealings with European courts remained as taxing as ever. While the edict was broadly welcomed by Elizabeth I and Protestants in the Netherlands, it was condemned by Catholics, especially her son-in-law Philip II. Her preference for the subtleties of diplomacy over the aggression of the battlefield was not always well understood. Although he admired her abilities, ambassador Barbaro described her as 'very Florentine', by which, as a Venetian, he probably meant devious and two-faced.[11] She certainly tailored her justification of the edict to suit her audience. To Bochetel in Vienna she explained that it was not intended 'to establish a new form and exercise of religion in this kingdom but instead to enable, with the least difficulty, the uniting of our people in the one, same holy and Catholic religion'.[12] To an ally of Jeanne d'Albret, however, she described royal policy slightly differently: 'what the king himself does is to let [Protestants] all live in freedom of conscience, and in the exercise of their own religion without forcing [the consciences] of anyone.'[13]

An indication of her commitment to religious toleration, and of the importance she attached to foreign affairs, Catherine significantly increased France's diplomatic presence abroad.[14] She doubled the number of posts, with permanent embassies at Venice and Rome and non-resident envoys at other Italian courts. She infuriated Philip II by sending an envoy to the Turkish court at Constantinople; and her decision to establish contacts with Protestant rulers did little to endear her to her son-in-law.[15] She refused to close the resident embassy in England, sent diplomats to the Swiss cantons, Catholic and Protestant alike, and to both sides in the Netherlands: Philip II's governor at Brussels and the Dutch Protestants at The Hague. In another foreign policy initiative, she asked her envoys at Madrid and Vienna to invite Philip II and Ferdinand I to meet her during the grand tour with a view to establishing a new Habsburg–Valois entente, like that negotiated by Henry II in 1559, secured with another set of marriages between the dynasties. She had a favourable response from the emperor; as she told the duchess of Savoy, he had agreed to the marriage of 'my daughter [Marguerite] and his eldest grandson [Rudolf] and of the king my son and one of his granddaughters', though neither ruler would commit themselves to a face-to-face meeting.[16]

Catherine was hoping to meet Philip II and her daughter Elisabeth at Bayonne, but he was evasive; since Amboise, he had been keeping a close watch on his mother-in-law. In early 1564 he appointed a new ambassador, Francisco d'Alava, with instructions to report all her dealings with Protestants in Germany, England and the Netherlands as well as keeping a watchful eye on the state of the true religion in France.[17] He also instructed Alava to make it known at court that Spain backed the Guise family's position in the vendetta against Coligny; and he was to tell Montmorency, Coligny's uncle, of the king's 'astonishment that, under his direction, religious affairs were in such a bad state that threatened ruin' in France.

While Catherine remained the power behind the throne – and would do for many years to come – her term as regent had ended. In a conspicuous statement that she was no longer acting as head of state, she made plans to set up her own official residence at the Tuileries, which had been built by Francis I for his mother on the site of the medieval tile works (or *tuileries*) outside the city walls. Since the building was too dated – and too modest – for Catherine's tastes, she acquired several adjacent properties in order to create a much grander palace.* She had her own ideas about the design which she discussed with the architect Philibert Delorme: typically, she required grandeur and one of her requirements was for a splendid ballroom covering 750 square metres.[18] As Delorme recorded in his treatise on architecture:

* The original plans for Catherine's palace were superseded later in the sixteenth century with more ambitious projects; it was destroyed in a fire in 1871.

In Paris her majesty the queen, wanting to take the trouble, with a singular pleasure, of ordering the distribution of her palace for the apartments and places for the reception rooms, antechambers, chambers, cabinets and galleries, and gave me the measurements of lengths and widths which I executed in this palace following the wishes of her majesty.[19]

While some scholars argue that the design of the palace, which was built around a large square courtyard, is based on Italian prototypes, the ornamentation was explicitly French.[20] Delorme claimed, with some pride, to have invented a 'French order' for the palace, articulating the garden loggia at the rear of the palace with Ionic columns, the appropriate order for a queen, but decorating their shafts with horizontal bands of intricately carved masonry.[21] The gardens themselves were more explicitly Italian and Catherine employed a Florentine gardener, Bernardo Carnesecchi, to take charge of them: in 1565 he was paid some 1,800 écus (4,500 livres) for 'past services rendered to the queen and which he continues to render in her gardens at the Tuileries at Paris'.[22]

The tour officially started on 24 January 1564 when the court left Paris, leaving marshal Montmorency, who was governor of the city, to take charge of the capital during the king's absence. Catherine and her children went first to the château of Saint-Maur-des-Fossés,* a day's ride from Paris. Another of her favourite residences, this elegant Italianate villa in the idyllic valley of the Marne had been built by Delorme for Cardinal Jean du Bellay in the mid-1540s. Set in a large hunting park, its spacious gardens were ornamented with antique statues acquired by the cardinal during his time in Rome. Du Bellay's

---

* The château was destroyed during the French Revolution.

secretary, the satirical writer François Rabelais, described Saint-Maur as 'a paradise of health, enjoyment, calm, comfort and delight, offering all the honest pleasures of the farm and the rustic life'.[23] Francis I had been a guest here on several occasions and it is likely that Catherine had been part of the royal party.[24] She certainly liked the villa enough to buy it from the cardinal's heirs in January 1563 and probably one of her motives for stopping here on her way to Fontainebleau was to make plans for its enlargement. Among the additions she commissioned from Delorme were a set of apartments for herself and a pall-mall court, a sport she much enjoyed.[25]

After a week relaxing at Saint-Maur, the family left for Fontainebleau where they celebrated Carnival with 'jousts, tournaments and balls, hunts, comedies, banquets and masques', reported the Venetian ambassador.[26] The festivities that year were particularly lavish, a reflection of Catherine's desire to give visual expression to the new era of peace, and began in earnest on Sunday 6 February with a week of entertainments hosted by various courtiers: constable Montmorency hosted a banquet while Cardinal Bourbon entertained his guests to a feast and a tournament.[27] The last three days of Carnival were reserved for the royal family: Sunday 13 February was the Queen's Day, Catherine's party; on the Monday it was the turn of the king's younger brother Henri, who put on a banquet and a splendid fencing competition; and finally on Shrove Tuesday Charles IX staged a spectacular mock battle between his knights and the giants, dwarves and devils guarding an enchanted castle.[28]

Catherine's festivities started with a banquet in the *Laiterie*, the ornamental dairy she had built in the gardens, followed by masques in the ballroom acted by the king, his brothers 'and all the young princes and lords of the court'.[29] Particularly notable was the 'Bergerie' (literally, the sheepfold), a pastoral comedy composed for the occasion by Pierre de Ronsard with the leading parts designed for the royal children:[30] 'Carlin' for the thirteen-year-old Charles IX; 'Orléantin'

for his brother Henri, aged twelve; 'Margot' for their sister
Marguerite, aged ten; and 'Angelot' for the eight-year-old
François. Significantly, there were parts for the young nobles
whose fathers had died in the war: 'Navarrin' for Henri of
Navarre, the ten-year-old son of Antoine of Bourbon, whose
mother was the Protestant queen of Navarre, Jeanne d'Albret;
and 'Guisin' for the thirteen-year-old Henri, the new duke
of Guise; and Catherine was the shepherdess (*bergère*). The
play made explicit references to recent events, in particular to her hopes for reconciliation between Protestants and
Catholics. In one speech 'Orléantin' praised his mother's
role as peace-maker, 'une Catherine' who, with the help of
'un Bourbon' – code for Condé – had brought an end to the
sufferings of war; 'if we see a return of the Golden Age, it is
due to the favour of Catherine'.[31]

Ash Wednesday, 16 February, saw a more sombre atmosphere at court. The crowds who gathered in the great hall
on Sunday listened to the cardinal of Lorraine, who, with his
customary eloquence, delivered a sermon to a congregation
from both sides of the religious divide. Among those present
with the king and Catherine were the Spanish ambassadors,
Chantonnay and Alava, as well as the Protestants Condé and
ex-cardinal Odet de Châtillon, who had finally lost his red hat,
and his benefices, after being found guilty of heresy by the
Inquisition in Rome. Noticing that several Protestants refused
to kneel during the service, the king was obliged to order
them to do so.[32] It was an appropriate gesture to mark the
start of the grand tour that, now that the worst of the winter
weather was over, could start in earnest.

While Catherine devised the route, Montmorency took charge
of the logistics of moving the court across France, a daunting
task for the seventy-year-old constable who was responsible for
arranging accommodation and food, and for ensuring the

safety of the royal family. Thanks to the diary of a certain Abel Jouan, a servant in the royal household, we are remarkably well-informed about the tour. In his *Recueil et discours du voyage du roy Charles IX* (published in Paris in 1566) he recorded the day-to-day progress of the tour, where the court dined and slept, and the distances covered each day; occasionally he added some local detail, though sadly there are few references to the dishes served at the royal dining table.

The court left Fontainebleau on 13 March and the next day Charles IX made his entry into Sens, where hundreds of Protestants had been massacred during the war. After three nights there they moved on to Troyes, the capital of Champagne and seat of the provincial *parlement*. This was a Guise stronghold – the governor of the province was the young duke Henri, who had inherited this position from his father. The triumphal arch welcoming Charles at the entrance gate was embellished with statues of Charlemagne flanked by Victory and Fame, proclaiming him as heir to this famous king of the Franks and the first Holy Roman Emperor.[33] It also carried a significant subtext: the Guise family too claimed descent from this hero, and thus kinship to the king, enabling them to boast their superiority over Montmorency and add yet another edge to the feud between the houses.[34]

They spent a month at Troyes, where they were joined by envoys from Elizabeth I to finalize a treaty which both sides had been struggling to negotiate since the battle for Le Havre the previous summer and which Catherine now managed to settle at very little cost to France.[35] There were problems, too, with the edict in this staunchly Catholic city: as Théodore de Bèze commented, 'the seed' of the new religion 'fell on hard ground'.[36] With the city's councillors insisting that it was contrary to Charles IX's coronation oath to uphold the Catholic faith, the king threatened them with dismissal unless they adopted the new code.[37] To appease Catholic sensitivities, Catherine took care to make very public statements of belief during this important period in the Church calendar. On 25

March, the Feast of the Annunciation, Charles touched 200 men and women for scrofula.[38] The next week was Holy Week: on Maundy Thursday, in a ritual enacted by rulers across Catholic Europe, he washed paupers' feet and served them lunch; on Easter Day, Catherine and her son attended mass in the cathedral. She also urged the court to go to confession and take communion in the hope that moderates suspected of Protestantism would show their faith by receiving the sacrament; Protestants like Condé and Andelot insisted on taking communion in their own manner.

The court left Troyes on 16 April, a Sunday, travelling north-east to Bar-le-Duc, one of the few private stops on the tour. Here Catherine was the guest of her daughter Claude and son-in-law Charles III, duke of Lorraine, for the christening of her first grandson. The journey was slow, deliberately so. Instead of the direct route, she spent a fortnight taking her message of toleration to as many places as possible in Champagne, where opposition to the edict was widespread. Jouan recorded the names of the places where the royal entourage stopped: Saint-Sépulcre, 'a little village' where they spent that Sunday night; Arcis-sur-Aube, 'a beautiful village with a castle', where they slept on Monday; Écury-sur-Coole, 'a poor village', where they spent Tuesday night; then a five-day break at the fortified city of Châlons-en-Champagne, before May, 'a pretty little house' where they slept on 26 April; Vitry-le-François, 'a small town' the following night; Bignicourt, another 'poor village', where they lunched on 29 April; and so on to the border with Lorraine.[39]

Their arrival in these places must have been a thrilling sight. Heralded by the blare of trumpets, colourful banners waving, armed soldiers, over 8,000 horses and as many as 15,000 people, the royal cavalcade was several miles long. Catherine herself travelled mostly in a coach pulled by six horses; she had a smaller carriage for rougher terrain and mounts if she wanted exercise. Riding with her were her courtiers, servants and even her dwarves; the king and his siblings too travelled with tutors, domestic servants, and their dwarves.[40] Also on the tour was the king's council, with chancellor L'Hospital and the secretaries of state to ensure the smooth running of government; the diplomatic corps assiduously keeping abreast of developments, though only Alava and the papal nuncio lasted the entire tour; and various nobles who joined the cavalcade at different stages along its route. All brought their own servants, a veritable army of valets, squires, pages, flunkeys, doctors, barbers, tailors, cooks and kitchen boys, as well as vast numbers of stable boys to take charge of all the horses and pack mules laden with the chests of clothes, armour, tapestries, bedding and cooking pots.

After a week at Bar-le-Duc the court took to the road again on 9 May and rode south to Langres, where Catherine had planned a ceremony designed to associate Charles IX with the legacy of his grandfather. The city possessed the so-called relic of the Holy Children: Shadrach, Meshach and Abednego, the three princes of Judea who were cast into a fiery furnace for refusing to worship the golden statue of king Nebuchadnezzar.[41] Francis I had promised a reliquary for the relic, but it had not materialized and Charles took this opportunity to present the cathedral with a silver one, lavishly studded with precious stones and enamel.

On 19 May, Catherine and the king arrived at Dijon, capital of Burgundy, where they were received by Gaspard de Saulx, seigneur of Tavannes and lieutenant-general in the province, and lodged at the Chartreuse de Champmol outside the walls while preparations for the entry were finalized.[42] Tavannes was a fierce opponent of Protestantism, as was the city itself, and the *parlement* had yet to register the edict. The first of the provincial *parlements* on the tour, Dijon was also the first test of Catherine's plans to enforce the edict and L'Hospital assiduously checked documents relating to all recent lawsuits to ensure they complied with the new orders.[43] The king attended the *parlement* in person on 24 May, repeating the speech he had made in Rouen requiring its members to obey their sovereign, though it took over a month before they reluctantly bowed to royal pressure and voted through the measures.[44]

The royal visit was overshadowed by scandal when Isabelle de Limeuil, one of Catherine's maids of honour, gave birth to a son in the queen mother's own apartments. This was a thrill for the gossips at court, and fuel for Catherine's enemies who claimed that these *filles d'honneur* were nothing more than a 'flying squad' of pretty girls, recruited by Catherine for their looks and trained by her to spy on those men she suspected of plotting against her and then to seduce them in order to extract their secrets.[45] In Isabelle's case, it was widely rumoured that the father of the child was Condé, who denied all rumours of paternity. He had left the court abruptly at Bar-le-Duc when news arrived that his wife was seriously ill – she died on 23 July. Isabelle herself had to leave court but later Catherine arranged a marriage for her with a wealthy Italian banker.[46]

The court left Dijon on 27 May and Catherine was able to exchange the discomforts of the road for the luxury of a river barge and a leisurely voyage down the Saône to Chalon-sur-Saône and then Mâcon, where they stayed for five days. This city staged an impressive display of civic pride, with young girls dressed in blue as nymphs of the Saône and the Mâconnais hills, though it took eighteen years to finish paying off the loan needed to finance it.[47] They were still at Mâcon for the Feast of Corpus Christi, taking part in the procession to celebrate the Eucharist, the issue that had created a chasm between the two religions. The divisions were amply evident in the streets: while Catholics proclaimed the importance of the feast by decorating their houses with flowers and greenery, and cheering the procession as it passed, Protestants signified their hostility with silent, shuttered windows. But when the royal procession passed the house where Jeanne d'Albret, queen of Navarre, and her household were lodged, her staff broke the silence, shouting their insults in a very vocal manner.[48]

On 9 June, Catherine and her children reboarded their barge for the voyage to Lyons, dropping anchor at Île-Barbe just north of the city the next day. This was an important stop on the tour for several reasons: Lyons was, as we have seen, France's second city, a cosmopolitan centre of banking and commerce with a large Italian population. Within easy reach of Geneva, it had been targeted by Calvin and was now a Protestant stronghold. Here the security of the royal family was an issue: Montmorency garrisoned troops in the city and passed orders banning Protestants from preaching during the royal visit and from holding meetings in their chapel beside the Franciscan convent of Saint-Bonaventure. This did not stop Jeanne d'Albret from attending a sermon with her son, much to Catherine's fury, who insisted that Henri, who was the senior prince of the blood and a close companion of the king, must return to court.[49]

Charles IX made his entry into Lyons on 13 June, splendidly dressed in costly green velvet, escorted by his brother Henri in crimson velvet and Henri of Navarre in crimson cloth of gold. The three boys rode in regal splendour through the city to the usual clamour of salvoes of artillery, blaring trumpets and noisy church bells.[50] The streets, shaded with cloth hangings as protection from the summer sun, were decorated with triumphal arches and other *all'antica* structures proclaiming the fame of Lyons as a seat of learning, a second Parnassus where Apollo and the Muses celebrated peace after the horrors of war: Catherine herself was shown suckling the young Hercules, an appropriate image for her role as queen mother.[51] Unlike many other places, the inhabitants of Lyons were making serious efforts to co-exist: merchants, evidently, were prepared to accept compromise, especially if war threatened their profits. Children from both religions took part in a parade in front of their sovereign, though the Catholics identified themselves with a cross on their cap badges.[52] As Catherine wrote to Saint-Sulpice in Spain, 'everything here is as obedient as we could desire'.[53]

Their stay in Lyons was cut short when plague broke out in the poorer quarters of the city and Catherine also had to cancel plans to attend the *parlement* at Grenoble, capital of the Dauphiné, as the disease was also spreading there – the outbreak would kill 25,000 people.[54] So, after a few days at Crémieu in the hills east of Lyons, the court travelled south and arrived at Roussillon on 17 July. They spent a month at this small town perched high on a ridge above the Rhône, with Catherine and her children lodged at the spacious Italianate villa built by Cardinal de Tournon nearby. It must have been a welcome relief from the summer heat, and there was excellent hunting to be had in the surrounding hills.

All spring Catherine had been corresponding with Saint-Sulpice and Bochetel to set a date for her meetings with Philip II and Ferdinand I to discuss an entente between the two dynasties and the marital alliances to guarantee it, but she had encountered several setbacks. In April she told Bochetel that she would be happy to meet the emperor or his son 'at any time and any place he chooses', but nothing had been arranged and news now arrived from Vienna that Ferdinand I had died suddenly on 25 July.[55] Philip II was also proving difficult to pin down and she was now waiting to hear from secretary L'Aubespine, whom she had sent to Saint-Sulpice in Spain to ascertain whether or not the king intended to travel to Bayonne, and whether he would give Elisabeth permission to meet her mother.[56]

Catherine's quest for partners for her children is often ignored by scholars or slated as a mother's frivolous preoccupation. In fact, this quest was a key tool in her foreign policy, as indeed it was at all the courts of sixteenth-century Europe. It had been the basis of her own marriage and that of her parents; and it was exactly what her husband had done to secure the Treaty of Cateau-Cambrésis in 1559. There were plenty of eligible princes and princesses: Catherine had three sons and a daughter; Maximilian II had two daughters and several sisters to wed; and Philip II had a son, a widowed sister and a nephew. Among the options under consideration by Catherine were unions between Charles IX and Maximilian's daughter Elisabeth; her daughter Marguerite with Don Carlos, Philip II's heir, though there were issues with this prince who had behavioural problems; another option for Marguerite was the king's nephew, the ten-year-old Sebastian, king of Portugal. There was also the Protestant queen of England: Elizabeth I would provide a valuable wild card in the negotiations.

A more pressing problem facing Catherine that summer was the embarrassing refusal of many nobles to observe the ban on Protestant worship at court and she was obliged to issue orders repeating the embargo; in compensation she increased the fines levied on those who prevented Protestants from worshipping within the rules of the edict. Most exasperating was the problem of Jeanne d'Albret, who flatly refused to comply with her orders. In the end Jeanne was allowed to leave court on the condition that her son Henri remained, but Catherine continued to support her cousin's right to choose her faith, even after she was condemned as a heretic by Pius IV the following month and ordered to appear before the Inquisition in Rome; if she failed to do so then Henri would be declared illegitimate and deprived of his inheritance so that Pius could 'give her kingdom to whomever he pleases'.[57] Catherine retorted that Navarre was under the protection of the French crown and the pope was usurping the king's authority. Jeanne was grateful to Catherine: 'I can never sufficiently acknowledge this most recent favour ... and I put myself wholly under the wing of your powerful protection.'[58]

Catherine and the court left Roussillon on 15 August and a week later arrived at Valence, where they stayed twelve nights. Despite the peace, the religious violence had not abated. Catholics continued to vent their anger against what they saw as the defilement of their faith, while Protestants objected to being forced to observe Catholic feasts and fasts. The Protestant inhabitants of one town had sought an audience with Catherine in Roussillon to complain of the savage massacre of a family whose corpses were then left as food for pigs.[59] In Valence she received a group of Protestants from Bordeaux who wanted to be exempt from paying into church collections and from the obligation to hang tapestries from their houses for the street processions on Catholic feast days.[60]

Catherine had personal worries as well. She was still at Valence in late August when news arrived from Spain that Elisabeth had given birth to stillborn twin girls, and that she now had puerperal fever.[61] Fortunately she recovered quickly but a few weeks later Charles IX caught a chill while out hunting and it was ten days before they could continue. Although weak, he was well enough by 24 September to make his entry into Avignon, a city dominated by the vast medieval palace which had been the seat of the papacy for most of the fourteenth century; it now provided ample space to accommodate the court. Jouan thought it 'extremely magnificent'; he also reported a storm in Avignon with wind 'so strong that it threw stones the size of walnuts into men's faces.[62] They left Avignon on 16 October and after a brief stop at Saint-Rémy reached Salon-de-Provence, where Catherine visited the astrologer Nostradamus to ask for her children's horoscopes. Charles, she was told, would live as long as Montmorency: 'I pray to God this is true,' she informed the elderly constable.[63] The prophecy came true though not in the way she had anticipated: Montmorency died three years later though Charles only lived for another seven. More convincing was the prediction that Henri of Navarre would become king of France.[64]

On 19 October they arrived at Aix, where Catherine had to deal with another hard-line Catholic *parlement* that had refused to publish the edict and barred anyone suspected of heresy from attending. Nor were the city's Protestants free to worship and they complained bitterly to Catherine. Faced with such blatant opposition to the authority of the crown, she suspended the *parlement* and replaced it with a new body that would implement the terms of the edict. Again, she balanced this pro-Protestant gesture with a statement of her own faith: the royal family made a very public pilgrimage to Saint-Maximine, a 'beautiful little town with a lovely abbey', as Jouan commented, where Mary Magdalen was buried, and climbed up into the hills to visit the cave where the Magdalen had prayed.[65]

At Brignolles on 25 October Jouan noted that Charles IX spent an enjoyable evening watching 'very pretty girls dressed in taffeta, some in green and some in white, performing Provençal dances' in the town square. Three days later, at the small medieval town of Hyères on the Mediterranean coast, he was excited to see 'a great abundance of oranges, palms and peppers and other trees'. Catherine liked Hyères enough to plan a villa and gardens planted with these exotic trees: over 8,000 écus (20,000 livres) were raised to fund the project, in part by taxing the inhabitants of Hyères, but it was never completed.[66] They celebrated the Feast of All Saints at Hyères on 1 November and left the following day for Toulon, Aubagne and Marseilles, where the king made his formal entry on 6 November. Much of his stay at the port involved the navy: he celebrated mass on board a new galley, which he named *Charlotte-Catherine*, and took part in a mock battle with his attendants all dressed as Turks, much to the horror of ambassador Alava; but a trip to the island of If, a barren rock off the coast where Francis I had built a castle, had to be cancelled because of storms.[67]

Leaving Marseilles on 13 November, they crossed the marshes of the Camargue and three days later reached Arles on the Provence–Languedoc border. It was Catherine's intention to spend only a few days here, but it was over three weeks before they could cross the Rhône, swollen by unusually high floodwaters. While her sons spent their time hunting, Catherine indulged her interest in the ancient world. Arles had been a famous cultural centre in the late Roman Empire and still boasted a theatre, aqueduct, baths, a bridge and the ruins of an amphitheatre, where the court was entertained by bullfights. Catherine acquired eight porphyry columns from the church of Saint-Honorat though unfortunately the barge carrying them up the Rhône sank.[68] A keen collector of antique marbles, she preferred architectural pieces to figure sculpture; she was particularly fond of porphyry, a rare and expensive purple stone[69] which, significantly, in the ancient Roman Empire had been reserved exclusively for imperial projects.

Catherine used the delay at Arles to catch up on business. There were worries about the escalating costs of the tour and rumours reached her that Philip II was having doubts about allowing his wife to travel to Bayonne.[70] A legate arrived from the pope to order the French crown to implement the reforms of the Council of Trent, which Catherine resolutely refused to do. She also listened to the grievances of the citizens of Arles who were divided over the issue of permitting Protestant worship.[71] There were requests from other towns asking her to intervene in religious disputes; and letters from admiral Coligny objecting to the ill-treatment suffered by Protestants at the hands of Catholics.[72]

They finally left Arles on 7 December, travelling upstream to Tarascon where they could cross the swollen river – it took three days for the great cavalcade to reach the other bank in safety.[73] They were now in Languedoc, a province where Protestantism had made considerable headway and which had suffered some of the worst atrocities of the war as the Catholic army fought to regain territory. On 12 December they stopped at the château of Catherine's *chevalier d'honneur* Antoine de Crussol for lunch, 'a beautiful collation of sweetmeats', and admired the massive ancient Roman aqueduct known as the Pont du Gard before the royal entry into Nîmes late that after-noon.[74] The city, which had remained Protestant, gave the royal family a memorable welcome with ingenious machines that included a mountain that opened and a huge crocodile as well as wine fountains and fireworks.[75]

After two nights at Nîmes they moved south to Montpellier, covering 70 miles in just three days. A university town with a famous faculty of medicine, Montpellier had been a thriving centre of Protestantism but, unlike Nîmes, had been retaken by the Catholics after a relentless artillery bombardment led by the governor of Languedoc, Henri de Montmorency, count of Damville and the constable's second son. Unlike his more moderate brother, the governor of Paris, Damville had acquired a reputation as a merciless enemy of the new religion and Catherine had to listen to many complaints about him during her visit. The delay at Arles had made it impossible for the court to reach Narbonne, where Catherine had planned to spend Christmas, and they celebrated it here. She ordered the entire city to take part in a procession, led by the king himself, to mass on the Feast of St Stephen (Boxing Day) or risk a fine of the substantial sum of 40 écus (100 livres).[76] Her attempt to enforce religious unity was further undermined when several Protestants refused to remove their hats during the service.

They left Montpellier on 30 December and, with brief stops at Agde and Béziers, arrived at Narbonne, which had remained Catholic throughout the war, in time for Epiphany, one of the favourite feasts at the French court. With the weather worsening, they arrived at Carcassonne on 12 January 1565, a city where Catholics had inflicted savagery on a terrible scale; there were even rumours of them skinning Protestants alive and eating their livers.[77] The court lodged in the huge citadel, built by the Romans to protect their trade route between the Atlantic and the Mediterranean, which towered over the medieval town on the banks of the River Aude below. The next day they awoke to find that it had snowed so heavily in the night that they were cut off; worse, all the decorations prepared for the royal entry, which should have taken place that day, were ruined and many triumphal arches had collapsed under the weight of the snow.[78] The weather was so bad that it was not until 26 January, when the roads had cleared, that they could leave; Jouan recorded that Charles IX – now aged fourteen – and his brothers amused themselves by building a snow castle in the citadel's courtyard.

The next stop was Toulouse, capital of Languedoc. Charles IX's entry on 1 February was a splendid affair. Appropriately for this centre founded by Emperor Augustus, the triumphal arches along the route proclaimed him as heir to that emperor and also to two others: the pagan but virtuous Trajan and Constantine, whose Edict of Milan (AD 313) established Christianity in the Roman Empire. There was the usual noisy accompaniment of trumpets, church bells and artillery salvoes but the gunners were somewhat over-enthusiastic and, after four men were accidentally killed, the king ordered the firing to cease.[79] The procession through streets hung with costly tapestries began with companies of arquebusiers and pikemen and included one hundred little children dressed in white taffeta; fifty young men in white satin doublets and black velvet cloaks riding great chargers; Toulouse's nobility in expensive black velvet coats, her merchants in all their finery; and members of the *parlement* in their red robes, who escorted the king under his crimson-and-gold canopy.

The court spent six weeks at Toulouse, where Catherine, lodged in rooms in the archbishop's palace by the cathedral, had a welcome break from the rigours of the road. It was Carnival and although her mornings were occupied with meetings, letter writing and other business, afternoons and evenings were filled with parties, banquets and dancing. Lent started on 7 March (Ash Wednesday), which Catholics would mark by giving up meat, though their diet in Toulouse was far from plain: a feast of freshwater fish, such as pike, carp, lampreys, salmon, trout, gurnet, shad, turtle, frogs and snails, as well as salt cod, pickled herrings and other preserved fish.[80] Protestants, by contrast, did not fast during Lent, nor indeed on Fridays as was the rule in Catholic Europe, rejecting these dietary laws as superstition.

Toulouse was a Catholic city and its Protestant population had been decimated during the war by the commander of the royal army, Blaise de Monluc. Catherine must have been dismayed by reports of the reign of terror he conducted with governor Damville, brutally massacring Protestants across southern France; he had further incurred her wrath by urging Philip II to allow him to seize Navarre from Jeanne d'Albret. In Toulouse Monluc had publicly executed over two hundred Protestants and expelled twenty-two members of the *parlement* on suspicion of heresy: their expulsion was visible in the gaps on the walls of the city hall where their portraits had been removed.[81] Not surprisingly the Catholic *parlement* had refused to introduce the edict, despite several requests from Catherine reminding them of their duty. She was to have to make several difficult decisions during her stay.

On 5 February, Charles IX attended the *parlement* in person to berate its members for 'the disobedience that you demonstrate towards your king'; as at Dijon, they reluctantly voted to register the edict.[82] Catherine made a point of demonstrating her commitment to toleration. She held audiences for Protestants complaining bitterly about Monluc and Damville and received a petition, with 300 signatures, asking for permission to allow Protestant preachers in the city, which she granted. The *parlement* was ordered to reinstate those twenty-two members who had been expelled for their faith and for their portraits to be repainted.[83] Alava complained in disgust to Philip II about the numbers of heretics it now contained.[84] He must have been shocked when Catherine granted the Protestants permission to ignore the Lent fast, overturning a ban on the consumption of meat until after Easter on the grounds that this went against the edict and that fasting was a matter of personal conscience.[85]

As she had done elsewhere, Catherine made efforts to appease Toulouse's Catholics, who were not happy with her favourable treatment of Protestants, admitting thirty citizens into the prestigious order of St Michael.[86] To mark Quadragesima, the first Sunday in Lent, she arranged for Henri and Marguerite to be confirmed by Cardinal Armagnac, archbishop of Toulouse – confirmation was an important sacrament for Catholics that conferred the grace of God on the recipient; for Protestants it was merely a formal pledge. This ceremony was also given greater local significance with a formal procession of the relics of St Saturnin (Sernin), the first bishop of Toulouse (died AD 257), whose tomb was in the basilica of Saint-Sernin, an important site on the pilgrimage route through France to Santiago de Compostela.

In Toulouse rumours reached Catherine of trouble in Paris. It appeared that marshal Montmorency had angered Catholics the previous summer by installing new artillery at the Bastille: he insisted that this was to improve the city's defences but they, already suspicious that he was a closet Protestant, worried that the guns would be turned against them.[87] While Catherine was at Arles she had warned him of rumours that firearms were being smuggled into the capital and matters came to a head in January when the cardinal of Lorraine entered Paris with his nephew Henri and an armed guard of fifty men, in blatant contravention of the marshal's ban on weapons in the city.[88] Montmorency's troops broke up the illegal demonstration; the cardinal avoided arrest by hiding in a rope-maker's yard, but the situation threatened to escalate when Coligny, the marshal's cousin, began to assemble his own men.[89] Catherine ordered both sides to leave Paris: Coligny obeyed but Lorraine did not. However, the Guises' bid for power had failed and the rivals reverted to bickering about the relative status of their houses. Catherine continued to worry about the marshal's safety, voicing her concerns about his bodyguard; 'if you find you are in need of a larger number than the fifteen arquebusiers on foot that you have chosen, and instead want twenty-five of them, mounted', then the necessary papers could be organised, and he was not to worry about the cost, 'because it is for your security'.[90]

Not all Catherine's letters to the marshal related to security in the capital: he was also in charge of building infrastructure projects associated with her new palace at the Tuileries, which included the layout of a new road, wharves on the riverbank and a drain.[91] Other letters include requests for luxury items needed on the tour, such as bales of gold and silver cloth as well as crimson wall hangings ornamented with fleurs-de-lys.[92] Writing from Toulouse in February 1565, Catherine also asked him to arrange for the transport of 'some precious furnishings' and a quantity of gilded silver dishes, plates and other items for her sideboard which were to be sent directly to Bayonne under armed guard of 'fifteen to twenty men'.[93]

News from Spain about the meeting at Bayonne added to Catherine's worries. Saint-Sulpice informed her in February that Philip II had agreed to the summit and given Elisabeth permission to travel to France but letters between the king and Chantonnay, his ambassador in Vienna, reveal that he had no intention of going to Bayonne.[94] In March another letter from Saint-Sulpice warned her that the king threatened to cancel his wife's visit to Bayonne because of rumours, leaked to him by Alava, that both Jeanne d'Albret and Condé would be there and 'he does not wish her to meet with rebels and fomenters of sedition'.[95] Moreover, the king insisted, if the prince of Condé and the queen of Navarre were at Bayonne when Elisabeth arrived, then he expected his wife 'to turn right round and go home'. Philip particularly disliked the queen of Navarre and refused to recognize her title, insisting that she had lost her rights to it by leaving the Catholic faith – insultingly, he referred to her as the duchess of Vendôme, the title she had acquired on her marriage to Antoine of Bourbon.

Catherine bowed to pressure, promising her son-in-law that

neither Jeanne nor Condé would be at Bayonne. Perhaps her desire to see her daughter again clouded her usually astute political judgement, but this was a mistake. As Saint-Sulpice presciently warned her, banning Protestant leaders from the summit would cause much anger.[96] Worse news was to come: not only had Philip outwitted her over the issue of Protestant leaders, the seasoned diplomat he was intending to send to Bayonne had been replaced by a very different character: Don Fernando Alvarez de Toledo, duke of Alba, a soldier with a long history of loyal service to the Spanish crown and, critically, a man who shared his master's hard-line views on religious orthodoxy, notably the need to exterminate the heresy of Protestantism by force.

The court left Toulouse on 19 March and the next day arrived at Montauban, a Protestant town that had suffered cruelly at the hands of Monluc. Keen to display its loyalty to the crown, the aldermen had deliberately petitioned Catherine to be included in the itinerary and they welcomed Charles IX by kneeling before him in a gesture of obedience to beg him to confirm their rights and privileges. Interestingly, instead of the mythological themes chosen by most centres for the royal entry, Montauban hailed Charles as heir to two biblical kings, decorating their triumphal arches with stories of the wise Solomon and Josiah, a devout ruler noted for the zeal with which he rooted out idolatry, who was a particular hero to Protestants. After a night at Montauban, where Catherine acquired several antique jasper columns for her marble collection, they stopped at Moissac and Lamagistère on the Garonne, 'where there were just three poor houses', according to Jouan.[97] Their next stop was Agen, where the king celebrated the Feast of the Annunciation by performing the scrofula ceremony and attended the christening of Monluc's baby daughter, another Charlotte-Catherine.[98]

The next day they began a leisurely cruise of 80 miles down the Garonne to Bordeaux, where they made their entry on 9 April, sailing into the port with an escort of seven galleys. The

entry had a distinctly maritime theme, with artillery salvoes
fired from gunships and the triumphal arches along the route
decorated with Neptune and his trident, as well as figures representing the Garonne and the Dordogne, the two rivers that
flow into the Gironde estuary sheltering Bordeaux from the
sea. Bordeaux had been a thriving port since Roman times,
a safe harbour for ships sailing between the Mediterranean
and northern Europe and, more recently, across the Atlantic.
The capital of Guyenne, the city had its own *parlement* and,
although largely Catholic, a vocal Protestant minority: Alava
claimed to have met one parish priest there who complained
that two-thirds of his flock were heretics.[99] Like Toulouse,
Bordeaux was yet to register the Edict of Amboise and on 12
April Charles IX, Catherine and the privy council attended the
parlement to chastise it for disobedience and 'the contempt in
which you hold the king and his ordinances which you neither
fear nor obey'.[100] They remained in Bordeaux for Easter on
22 April and, in a now familiar pattern, the royal family were
assiduous in their public observance of the Catholic rites and
ceremonies of Holy Week.

On 3 May the court set out from Bordeaux on the final
leg of the arduous journey to Bayonne. Saint-Sulpice had confirmed that Philip II had accepted Catherine's assurances that
neither Condé nor Jeanne d'Albret, the 'fomenters of sedition', were expected; no doubt he had verified this from the
more clandestine sources he had at his disposal – the Guise
family among others. On 7 May they crossed the border into
Navarre and spent five days at Mont-de-Marsan, where the
Friday feast for the Catholic guests on 10 May included fresh
salmon, trout, sole, skate, sturgeon, cod and carp, but also –
a sign that they were far south – new broad beans, peas and
artichokes, the latter a particular favourite with Catherine.[101]
The next day at Tartas news arrived that the queen of Spain,
although delayed by rumours of plague, was definitely en
route. On 28 May the court halted at Dax, a town Jouan
described as 'a very beautiful spa with a great abundance of

hot water springs', though Catherine was not to enjoy them.[102] The next day she rode on to Bayonne to check arrangements, and was observed attending mass in the cathedral on 31 May, the Feast of the Ascension.

Bayonne was a frontier stronghold, fortified and compact. Accommodation was limited and much of the court had to be lodged some distance away, to the fury of diplomats who would be hampered in their search for first-hand gossip.[103] On the Feast of Pentecost (10 June), Charles IX attended mass in the cathedral and performed the scrofula ceremony; three days later the royal family, escorted by two regiments, left Bayonne for Saint-Jean-de-Luz, where they spent the night, and the next morning rode down to the River Bidassoa, the frontier between France and Spain, to welcome Elisabeth and the duke of Alba. They had a long wait in the stifling midday heat: it was not until late afternoon that a salvo of artillery announced the queen's arrival. Charles formally greeted his sister and escorted her to the bank where light refreshments were laid out – 'hams, tongues, salami, pies of all sorts of fruits, salads, sweetmeats and a great abundance of good wine'.[104] The next day, 15 June, in the cool of the evening, Elisabeth made her entry into Bayonne through streets lit with torches, mounted on a horse whose trappings were valued by Jouan at the huge sum of 400,000 ducats.[105]

The ten-day extravaganza of feasting, competitions and ceremonies that Catherine staged for her guests at Bayonne displayed her growing talent for devising the allegorical entertainments combining dance, music and poetry that were to become the standard feature of the festivals, known as 'magnificences', with which she promoted her political agenda.[106] For Brantôme, these glittering events showed 'that the realm was not so completely ruined and poverty-stricken by the recent wars as they thought'.[107] Above all, they showcased the superiority of French culture and gave visible expression to her desire to restore the immense prestige that France had enjoyed during the reign of Francis I, an era which, in her own more troubled times, was seen as a golden age of peace and prosperity. Although criticized by Catholics and Protestants alike for her excessive use of public funds, there can be little doubt that the entertainments at Bayonne were a cultural tour de force. 'France was all the more feared and esteemed,' wrote Brantôme, 'whether through the sight of such wealth and richness, or through that of the prowess of her gentlemen, so brave and skilled at arms.'[108]

The festivities began on Tuesday 19 June with the 'prowess of the brave gentlemen', a series of tilting competitions and, in a conspicuous display of the authority of the crown, the knights who took part did homage to Charles IX in the costumes of knights and savages from across history – Troy, Rome, Greece, Albania, Scotland and Turkey as well as France and Spain.[109] Catherine watched the spectacle with her Spanish guests in the royal box, which had been specially decorated for the occasion with tapestries of the Triumphs of Scipio Africanus, including marvellous scenes of Hannibal's army fighting with elephants. This famous set[*] of twenty-two pieces, glittering with gold and silver thread, had been woven in Brussels for Francis I at the enormous cost of 22,000 écus (50,000 livres).[110] The tapestries were a key part of his propaganda campaign to promote the Valois dynasty as heirs to the emperors of ancient Rome.[111] In Bayonne they carried a more pertinent message: like Scipio's victory over the Carthaginian Empire in Spain, France, too, could triumph in the Iberian peninsula.[112] According to Brantôme, 'the Spanish lords and ladies greatly admired [the set] never having seen anything like it in the possession of their king'.[113] Brantôme was

---

[*]   The tapestries were destroyed on Napoleon's orders in 1796 to extract the gold and silver thread which was used to mint much-needed money.

unaware that Philip II did in fact own a set of these tapestries inherited from his aunt, who had them woven from the same cartoons, though her set, which had only seven pieces, was considerably inferior.[114]

Over the following days Catherine staged a series of entertainments, each with its own theme. On the second day this was the nature of Charles IX's rule: the guests watched him and his knights besiege an enchanted castle, fighting the devils and giants who guarded its entrance in order to rescue Peace from the clutches of an evil wizard.[115] The message was clear: under the rule of the Most Christian King 'Christianity flourished as never before'. She celebrated the king's Catholic faith with a procession for Corpus Christi, after which Charles was invested by the duke of Alba with the insignia of a knight of the Golden Fleece. Another day saw a Battle of Love and Virtue 'fought' by two teams of knights led by Charles and his brother Henri, an elaborately choreographed equestrian ballet accompanied by the spectacles of horse-drawn floats and a dramatic fireworks display.[116] A landmark in the history of dance, this is widely considered to be the first performance of a *ballet de cour*, a genre that was to become a staple in the 'magnificences' devised by Catherine for her court festivals.

Particularly impressive was the day on the River Adour. The guests boarded a boat designed to resemble a castle and watched various spectacles on the water including a battle against a monstrous sea creature that lasted half an hour.[117] It was followed by the arrival of Neptune, riding on his conch shell chariot drawn by sea horses, to give the king a trident which had the power to move rocks – read, political obstacles.[118] The guests then landed on an island in the river for a banquet in an artfully constructed 'rustic glade', where they were entertained by a ballet celebrating the different provinces of France.[119] The feast was served 'by great lords and ladies dressed as shepherds and shepherdesses', with nymphs singing verses celebrating peace between France and Spain.[120] The sight of Catholic and Protestant 'lords and ladies' acting in concert also carried a clear message: 'between shepherds there will be no discord', as the nymphs sang. Catherine's own position was eloquently visible: she sat at a table with her children and Henri of Navarre as Mother of the Gods, presiding over the 'deities'. 'Take note that all these inventions came from no other devising and brain than that of the queen,' wrote Brantôme, 'for she was mistress and inventor of everything; she had such faculty that whatever magnificences were done at court, hers surpassed all others.'[121]

After the festivities at Bayonne were over, one of Catherine's secretaries commented, no doubt somewhat jaded by the surfeit of parties, that there had been 'feasts, fighting and ten thousand sorts of entertainments and pretty things'. What of her political ambitions?[122] Despite the pastoral island banquet celebrating peace between France and Spain, in reality nothing had been negotiated. Alba's instructions from Philip II had focused on the religious issue: he was to force promises from Catherine that she would ban all Protestant worship in France, expel all preachers or order their execution, require all office holders to take an oath of loyalty to the Catholic Church and implement, immediately, the reforms codified by the Council of Trent. He refused to discuss the alliance and marriages; nor would he discuss other issues dividing the two nations such as French Protestants settling in the Spanish colony of Florida or French support for the Turks in the Mediterranean. Again and again he returned to the issue of religion – a favourite theme was to insist on the sacking of chancellor L'Hospital. A soldier of the black and white school, intolerant of the nuances of the diplomatic world, Alba was, of course, following Philip II's coercive agenda to the letter. Moreover, it must have been a great disappointment not to have the support of Elisabeth, who had wholly adopted the hard-line views of her husband and urged her mother to do the same.

Catherine was tough but it cannot have been easy dealing with a bully like Alba; nor with Alava, whose attitude towards her was condescending in the extreme. 'I can see clearly,' the ambassador informed Philip II, 'that the queen mother is very perplexed; sometimes she says one thing and the next the complete opposite.'[123] Although men routinely dismissed women of the period as stupid, emotional and indecisive, it is vital to note that Catherine was far from 'perplexed'. She knew what she wanted to achieve: she was fully committed to implementing the edict and, if her travels through France had taught her anything, it was that any attempt to crush Protestantism by force would irreparably break up the kingdom. In response to Alba's strident demands she made general and vague promises to take steps to remedy the religious situation.

The secrecy surrounding the summit has made it difficult to ascertain what actually happened; confusingly, three reports reveal different versions of events.[124] Alba informed Philip II that Catherine had refused to comply with the king's orders to eradicate the new religion; the king himself wrote to Cardinal Francisco Pacheco in Rome that she had agreed to 'remedy the matter of religion' and to implement the Tridentine reforms, a formula no doubt designed to appeal to the papal court.[125] Cardinal Granvelle, an imperial councillor and brother to Chantonnay, was more convincing: he judged that she had agreed to deal with the religious situation, 'to do marvels, though with the proviso that she would avoid anything that could cause the renewal of hostilities'.[126] He continued, less convincingly: 'I believe her so thoroughly persuaded by the idea that, in entertaining these two parties, she has found the means of consolidating her authority in that kingdom, that I believe she will follow this course; from this surely the result will be the ruin of religion and her son's authority.'

Unfortunately, far from being the peace-making initiative she had planned, the summit had the disastrous result of inflaming hard-line positions on both sides of the religious divide. Alba's presence at Bayonne gave the Catholic nobility – Cardinal Bourbon, Monluc and the duke of Montpensier, for example – the opportunity to establish more personal ties with Spain. Alba himself reported to Philip II on 15 July that among the topics they had discussed was the assassination of Condé, Coligny, d'Andelot, Coligny's brother-in-law François III, count of La Rochefoucauld, and other Protestant leaders.[127] Worse, as Saint-Sulpice had warned her, the exclusion of Protestants from the summit sparked the fear that Catherine herself had done a deal with Alba and had turned against them. In truth she had been thoroughly outmanoeuvred by her son-in-law: by banning the queen of Navarre and Condé from attending the summit he had effectively guaranteed that the Protestants would suspect a plot against them, which, as we will see, was to have serious consequences.

Catherine and Charles left Bayonne for Saint-Jean-de-Luz on 2 July to escort Elisabeth and the duke of Alba to the frontier, where 'the farewells of the queen, the queen mother and the king were very distressing', reported ambassador Alava to Philip II, 'the tears fell in floods'.[128] A week later they were back on the road in horrendous conditions with a heatwave that caused both men and horses to die of sunstroke: Jouan reported that it was so hot that they decided to travel at night.[129] They had a brief respite at Dax, where they spent three days – with Cardinal Bourbon uncomfortably lodged with a married priest because of the shortage of accommodation.[130] After another ten gruelling days the cavalcade reached Nérac on 28 July, where they spent four days as guests of Jeanne d'Albret. The royal château, with its spacious gardens, must have been a welcome relief from the sweltering heat. No doubt, too, the two women had long talks about the Bayonne summit. Whatever the wording of her promise to Alba a month earlier, this visit was the clearest possible indication of Catherine's rejection of Philip II's policy of elimination and of her own stubborn commitment to religious toleration – though it should be said that she failed to persuade the queen to do likewise and allow Catholics the freedom of worship in Navarre.

The heatwave seems not to have abated: after leaving Nérac on 1 August they continued to travel at night and over the next fortnight they covered 125 miles, rarely stopping longer than a single day in one place. They reached Angoulême on 13 August and the pace now slowed. After five nights at Angoulême, they rested for three nights at Jarnac and ten days at Cognac, the birthplace of Francis I, which they reached on 21 August. Here the court could relax: in a letter to Anna d'Este, a rare glimpse into her private thoughts, Catherine informed the duchess that the family were well: 'God be thanked we are all in good health and all the rumours to the contrary are untrue.' Cognac, she said, was 'a most beautiful place' and she loved 'the beautiful parks where one can take walks or go hunting'.[131] She also confided her optimistic belief that peace was a very real possibility, priding herself that she had seen 'Protestants and Catholics dancing together' at Bayonne.

The cavalcade left Cognac on 1 September, spending that night at Saintes, and two days later were given a warm welcome at Marennes, a Protestant town in the salt marshes south of La Rochelle, described by Jouan as a 'beautiful, large village'.[132] They visited Brouage, a new port on the marshes, where the locals gathered to greet Charles IX with a display of artillery followed by lunch and a mock sea battle; unfortunately two people were killed by the guns and one of the galleys caught fire. Marennes's Catholics had been looking forward to the royal visit with much excitement and the following day a large crowd gathered – Jouan estimated 800 or 900 people – at the church of Saint-Pierre-de-Sales where they had been given special dispensation by the king to celebrate Easter – despite the date – with confession and communion according to the rites of their faith.[133] Charles IX also presided over the baptism of hundreds of children, who were named Charles, Charlotte, Catherine or Marguerite, in honour of himself, his mother and his sister.[134]

They left Marennes the next day and, after stops at Saintes and Saint-Jean-d'Angely, arrived at the abbey on the outskirts of La Rochelle, where they made their entry the following day, 14 September. A centre of maritime trade and an important naval port, La Rochelle had a long tradition of political independence that had fostered the growth of Protestantism in the city. Thirteen Catholic priests had been cruelly murdered during the war and violent iconoclastic riots had denuded the churches of altarpieces and statues, destroying much of the city's medieval heritage. It was this history of Protestant aggression that persuaded Montmorency to take steps to ensure the safety of the royal party and issue an order that all the artillery pieces on the city walls were to be moved out to nearby fields for the duration of the visit.[135] The precautions may have been unnecessary: as in many other Protestant centres, the inhabitants of La Rochelle were keen to display their loyalty to their monarch, though the choice of scenes of the Labours of Hercules to decorate the triumphal arches erected for the entry suggested they were aware of the scale of the religious difficulties faced by the crown.

Although Nantes, the next major city on their tour, was only 85 miles to the north, Catherine chose to make a wide detour inland to visit the towns and villages of Poitou and Anjou.[136] They left La Rochelle on 18 September and rode north-east via Niort and Parthenay to Thouars, where they stayed with Louis III de La Trémoïlle, constable Montmorency's son-in-law; they attended the christening of their host's daughter, who was named Charlotte-Catherine, and enjoyed watching the locals perform the dances of Poitou. After a brief stop at Loudon, they reached Champigny-sur-Veude on 27 September, a beautiful castle belonging to the duke of Montpensier, where they spent four nights and celebrated Michaelmas. After a night at the abbey of Fontrevaud they turned west and, keeping to the south bank of the Loire, reached what Jouan described as 'the lovely little château' at Brézé on 3 October. Their route now took them to Martigné-Briand, Brissac-Quince and Gonnord, where they spent two nights as guests of Artus de Cossé, *surintendant des finances*; after stops at Chemillé and Jallais, they reached Beaupreau on 9 October, where Charles of Bourbon, prince of La Roche-sur-Yon and husband of Catherine's senior *dame d'honneur*, was suddenly taken ill and died the next day. Worried that the illness might be contagious, Catherine insisted on dining al fresco in the castle's park and spent the night at the nearby abbey of La Regrippière.

Two days later they were lodged in an abbey just outside Nantes, where Charles IX made his entry on 12 October. Situated at the mouth of the Loire, Nantes was another Protestant stronghold, like La Rochelle: it, too, had a long tradition of political independence and had only become part of France in 1532 with Francis I's marriage to Claude, heiress to her mother's title of duchess of Brittany. The court spent three days at the port, performing official duties and enjoying entertainments, which included lively local dancing, and on 16 October arrived at Châteaubriant, a fortified medieval town belonging to Montmorency, where they spent the next three weeks. There was much excitement on 20 October when news arrived that the Turks had abandoned their siege of Malta, with a loss of 38,000 men, Jouan reported, a victory the court celebrated with fireworks.[137]

Catherine's original plan had been to continue north to Rennes, the capital of Brittany, where the king was to address *parlement*, but she had received disturbing news that religious violence had broken out in Tours and other places nearby. As she explained to secretary L'Aubespine, the information was 'so inconsistent between one side and the other that it is impossible to find out the truth and yet it is certain that the trouble proceeds from one of the two factions'.[138] As a result she decided to cancel the visit to Rennes and return to the Loire Valley so, after celebrating the Feast of All Saints, they left Châteaubriant for Angers, where Charles IX made his entry on 6 November. Here she boarded a boat to travel up the Loire to Tours, where she spent ten days attending to grievances, and, after a welcome visit to her château at Chenonceau and a brief stop at the royal castle at Blois, Catherine set out for Moulins, some 132 miles to the south-east, covering the distance in just eight days.

The court spent Christmas 1565 at Moulins and remained there to celebrate New Year in advance of an Assembly of Notables which had been summoned to discuss plans for government reform early in 1566. A small town on the River Allier and capital of the Bourbonnais, Moulins was part of the Bourbon patrimony of Henri of Navarre, and dominated by the great Bourbon castle set in lovely parks and gardens with groves of orange trees, fountains, a maze and an aviary as well as lists for jousting. That December the nobility gathered at court in large numbers for the festivities. Friends and foes alike, all the key players in the enmities dividing the court were together again after an absence of almost two years, notably the feuding Montmorency and Guise clans, as well as many Protestants and sympathizers, including Jeanne d'Albret and her son Henri, Renée of France, the prince of Condé and his bride, as well as admiral Coligny and his brother d'Andelot, the constable's nephews. Ambassador Alava noted with alarm the presence of 6,000 Protestants at court that Christmas.[139]

The festivities that year had a particular significance. On 5 January, Catherine wrote to marshal Montmorency, signing her letter, as she invariably did, with the location and date on which it had been written.[140] She was using the new style of calendar, beginning the year on 1 January, as in Rome, rather than on Easter Day, which had been the custom in France. She had ordered this change back in January 1564, but it had proved unpopular and, inevitably, it had taken much persuasion for the conservative *parlement* in Paris to register it.

On 24 January, Catherine and Charles IX opened the Assembly of Notables, which proceeded to discuss chancellor

L'Hospital's plans to reassert the authority of the crown over the *parlements* by reforming the judicial system of the kingdom to put a stop to abuses like nepotism and bribery which had become widespread. In his speech to the assembly L'Hospital explained: in order 'that everything should be restored to the good old ways of justice, all means should be sought to remove avarice, ambition, theft and malice'.[141] The reforms, which ran to eighty-six articles and re-established royal authority over law and order, were ratified in February 1566 by Charles IX, his mother, Catherine, and his heir Henri, now fourteen and old enough to take part in government, as well as a long list of powerful figures in the realm, Catholic and Protestant, led by prince of the blood Condé: cardinals Bourbon, Lorraine and Guise, as well as ex-cardinal Châtillon, recently married to his mistress; the dukes of Montpensier, Nemours and Nevers; constable Montmorency, chancellor L'Hospital, the marshals of France and admiral Coligny.

The gathering of so many important figures provided Catherine with a public platform to announce the investiture of her two younger sons as royal dukes: Henri was given the title of duke of Anjou, while François, a few weeks short of his eleventh birthday, became duke of Alençon. It also gave her an opportunity to encourage the healing of the rifts at court, in particular to reconcile the Guise and Montmorency families. One of the first acts of the assembly was to declare Coligny innocent of all charges relating to the assassination of the duke of Guise. Despite the eloquence of his address urging members of the king's council to find Coligny guilty, the cardinal's motion was heavily defeated. Then, in March, Lorraine quarrelled violently with L'Hospital during a meeting of the king's council at which the cardinal accused the chancellor of overstepping his authority. The accusation was true, but Lorraine's arrogant assumption that L'Hospital should now be sacked backfired: when the cardinal announced his refusal to attend further meetings of the council if the chancellor was present, L'Hospital retorted that his presence was not

necessary and Lorraine was forced to leave.[142] Catherine and
her moderates were again in control of the council and the
Guise family faced an uncertain future: their desire to avenge
Duke François's murder was to provoke civil war – it was a
decision that would have terrible results.[143]

Catherine and the king left Moulins on Saturday 23 March,
heading south on the final leg of their grand tour. They spent
Sunday night at Varennes, where they celebrated the Feast
of the Annunciation the following day. On the Wednesday,
Charles IX made his formal entry into Vichy, after which
the cavalcade crossed into the Auvergne and the Limagne,
large parts of which belonged to Catherine herself, inherited
from her mother.[144] Their next stop was Clermont-Ferrand:*
as countess of Clermont, she had been adept at using her
position to grant privileges to encourage trade, and on this
occasion the city was rewarded for its 'obedience and loyalty'
by the grant of the same tax exemptions as those given to
other provincial capitals.[145] After Clermont the court moved
on to Riom and then north to Cosne d'Allier, where they celebrated Palm Sunday (7 April); on Wednesday they arrived at
La-Charité-sur-Loire, where they spent five days celebrating
the events of Holy Week and Easter. Over the next fortnight
they travelled briskly, visiting Auxerre (18 April), Sens (20
April) and Montceaux (24 April), where they spent five days,
and on 1 May, after an absence of two years and three months,
Catherine and the court were once again back in Paris.

After a few days in the capital Catherine left for her château
at Saint-Maur, where she spent the next six weeks, a long and
welcome rest after the rigours of the tour. In public at least,
she was confident that it had been a success. In mid-May she
wrote to her new ambassador in Spain, Raymond de Beccarie,
baron of Fourquevaux, who had taken over from Saint-Sulpice
in 1565: 'in answer to what you wrote about the misfortunes

---

* In the sixteenth century the city of Clermont and the nearby town
of Montferrand were separate centres.

that [Alba] predicts will result from the diversity of religion in this realm, I believe truly that there are those here who are very upset to see so much pacification here', adding that she hoped 'the troubles which have lasted too long, will soon be at an end'.[146]

Fourquevaux was busy not only furnishing Catherine with news about the political situation in Spain; one of her preoccupations that summer was the progress of her daughter's pregnancy. With the birth imminent, her letters to Fourquevaux were filled with advice and 'recipes she might need' for him to pass on to the French doctor in Elisabeth's household.[147] Evidently this man and the medics attached to the Spanish court disagreed about how to treat the queen. Catherine believed that it was important for her to take daily exercise, but the Spanish insisted on Elisabeth being as inactive as possible, preferably in bed. Fourquevaux, who respected Catherine's superior knowledge in these matters, welcomed her interference and was disappointed that 'these Spanish doctors' refused to follow her advice. Fortunately, all went well and Elisabeth gave birth to a daughter, Isabella,* on 12 August.

Catherine might well have reflected with satisfaction that, although the tour had not been a complete success, the Edict of Amboise had been registered in the provincial *parlements* and she saw signs that her policy of pursuing religious toleration remained on track. But there were ominous signs of change on the wider international stage which would have serious implications for France's internal affairs. In Rome a new pope had been elected in January 1566. Pius IV's successor, Pius V, was a Dominican friar who had risen through the ranks to the post of Inquisitor General. Devout and austere, he wore a hair shirt under his papal robes and was unwavering

---

* Isabella would marry her Habsburg cousin Albert of Austria after he renounced his cardinal's hat; known as the Archdukes, they were appointed rulers of the Netherlands by Isabella's father in 1598.

in his hostility to Protestantism. That summer he bombarded
Catherine with bulls ordering her to accept the decrees of the
Council of Trent and to take other steps designed to eliminate
the new religion in France.[148] Pius V's more robust approach
was echoed in Brussels. That summer anti-Catholic fervour
across the Netherlands saw rioting mobs strip churches of
their religious ornaments after Philip II's governor refused to
repeal a raft of laws aimed at the repression of the new religion. In response to this attack on his authority, Philip planned
to crush the rebellion by force and asked Catherine for permission to allow his army to march to Brussels via France, a
request she refused.

In France the immediate impact of the so-called 'iconoclastic fury' was to increase support for the ultra-Catholic cause
and thus make Catherine's policy of toleration harder to
enforce. It also strengthened the anti-Protestant position of
the cardinal of Lorraine, who had already used his immense
wealth – he was easily the richest member of the College of
Cardinals – to establish himself as an influential force at the
papal court. Catherine must have seen, with some trepida-
tion, how he was using his authority to gain influence at the
French court. Most ominous was the growing suspicion among
Protestants, who had been among her staunchest supporters
until excluded from the talks at Bayonne, that they could not
trust her efforts at reconciliation – but that was something that
she refused to believe.

8

Civil War
1567–1571

Catherine was in Picardy on 4 September 1567 when she was warned of a plot to kidnap the king. 'We have been advised that men have begun to gather in large numbers, as many as 1,200 to 1,500 horses around Montargis and Châtillon,' she wrote to Artus de Cossé, recently promoted to the rank of marshal of France; 'I beg you to find out and let me know the truth.'[1] Montargis and Châtillon were both Protestant strongholds: the former the castle of Renée of France, the latter the family seat of the Châtillon brothers. All remained peaceful, however, and a fortnight later she was able to reassure ambassador Fourquevaux from her château of Montceaux that it had been a storm in a teacup.[2] But the rumours persisted and late on 24 September, a Wednesday, news arrived at Montceaux that a large Protestant force had been seen at Rozay-en-Brie, just 20 miles away.

On Friday, with a band of Swiss mercenaries on the royal payroll summoned from their barracks at Château-Thierry, Catherine and Charles IX moved to the nearby city of Meaux which Montmorency and L'Hospital considered safe; the cardinal of Lorraine, by contrast, urged her to leave immediately for Paris. Both the constable and the chancellor warned her against this move, which they considered to be provocatively anti-Protestant: 'to go to Paris would risk war', counselled Montmorency, while L'Hospital thought it 'would betray the crown and make pacification impossible'.[3] But Charles was determined to leave and on Sunday they left for the capital.

Catherine was furious with the Protestant rebels; and it is important to underline here that it was not their religious beliefs to which she objected but their act of disloyalty to the crown, which in her eyes was treason. 'You will have heard from the letter my son has sent you of the state of affairs here and of the disgraceful attempt,' she informed Fourquevaux a few days later; 'you can imagine the vexation with which I have to see this kingdom return to the troubles and misfortunes from which by God's grace I have taken such pains to deliver it'.[4] In her anger, she seems to have been unaware that the sight of the royal family, forced to flee from rebellious Protestants in fear of their lives, with a bodyguard of foreign mercenaries to protect them from danger, was powerful propaganda for the ultra-Catholic cause. Montmorency and L'Hospital were to be proved right.

That the attack so nearly succeeded was at least partly Catherine's fault. Blind to the warning signs that had been evident all year, she had been caught by surprise – the event is known as the 'Surprise de Meaux'. An early alarm had been Jeanne d'Albret's escape from court with her son Henri in February after Catherine had expressly refused to give her permission to travel to Navarre. Ambassador Alava informed Philip II that the duchess of Vendôme, as he titled Jeanne, intended 'to fool the king and his mother' and that Catherine was 'very much surprised' by the news.[5] That spring and summer the rumour mill at court seethed with reports of plots to kill Condé, Coligny, d'Andelot, La Rochefoucauld and other figures in the Protestant leadership, one of many signs of a deepening of the rift between the two religions.

1. Jean Clouet, *Francis I*, *c.*1535 (Paris, Musée du Louvre). Catherine's father-in-law was one of her most loyal supporters.

2. François Clouet, *Francis, duke of Guise*, *c.*1547 (Chantilly, Musée Condé). Brave and skilful on the battlefield, he was a powerful figure at court until his assassination aged forty-two.

3. Fontainebleau, château, Galerie François Ier, begun *c.*1528. Glittering and expensive, this gallery provided a fitting image for the most magnificent court in Europe.

4. François Clouet, *Cardinal Charles of Lorraine c.*1550 (Chantilly, Musée Condé). An intellectual and a born politician, he was one of Catherine's most formidable opponents.

5. François Clouet, *Anne de Montmorency, c.*1540 (Chantilly, Musée Condé). Soldier, statesman and unswervingly loyal to the crown, he was an important figure in Catherine's life.

6. François Clouet, *Marguerite of France, queen of Navarre, c.*1561 (Chantilly, Musée Condé). A charming portrait of Catherine's eight-year-old daughter, though she was to cause much trouble later.

7. After François Clouet, *Catherine de' Medici, c.*1556 (Versailles, Musée National). As queen, Catherine could indulge her love of expensive clothes and jewels.

8. François Clouet, *Diane de Poitiers*, *c.*1555 (Chantilly, Musée Condé). Henry II's mistress and twenty years his senior, her influence was the cause of much heartache for Catherine.

9. Workshop of François Clouet, *Henry II*, *c.*1555 (New York, Metropolitan Museum of Art). Brave on the battlefield and jousting ring, he possessed the ideal qualities of a king.

10. The joust in which Montgomery wounded Henri II, from Jean Perrissin and Jacques Tortorel, *Premier volume*, 1569–70 (Paris, Bibliothèque Nationale).

11. *Water Festival at Fontainebleau.* Drawing by Antoine Caron (Edinburgh, National Gallery of Scotland). Catherine's love of spectacle inspired the lavish festivals she staged to promote her political agenda.

12. The Château of Chenonceau, begun in 1514, was one of Catherine's favourite residences. She embellished it with a gallery (1570), designed by Jean Bullant, set on a bridge over the River Cher.

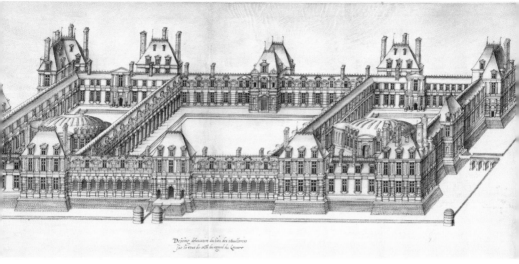

13. Paris, palace of the Tuileries. Engraving by Jacques I Androuet du Cerceau, *Les plus excellents bastiments de France* (1576–9).

14. Oval dish with fishes and snakes, *c.*1875 by Barbizet & fils after Bernard Palissy. Palissy's imaginative ceramics still inspire potters today.

15. François Clouet, *Charles IX*, 1569 (Vienna, Kunsthistorisches Museum). This regal portrait promised much but sadly Catherine's second son died of tuberculosis in 1574, a month before his twenty-fourth birthday.

16. François Clouet, *Gaspard de Coligny*, *c.*1565–70 (St Louis, Art Museum). It was the failed attempt to assassinate this Protestant leader that triggered the St Bartholomew's Day Massacre.

17. After François Clouet, *Catherine de' Medici*, *c.*1580 (Baltimore, Walters Art Museum). Catherine around her sixtieth birthday, still in mourning for the husband she lost over twenty years earlier.

18. François Dubois, *The Massacre of St Bartholomew's Day*, 1572–84 (Lausanne, Musée des Beaux-Arts). An imaginative recreation that accused Catherine of instigating the massacre, showing her gloating over Protestant corpses.

19. Unknown artist, *Nicolas de Neufville, seigneur de Villeroy, c.*1575 (Paris, Musée du Louvre). One of the hard-working royal secretaries and a trusted ally of Catherine.

20. François Quesnel, *Henry, duke of Guise, c.*1585 (Paris, Musée Carnavalet). He became duke of Guise at the age of eleven after the assassination of his father.

21. Unknown artist, *Ball at the Court of Henry III*, 1582 (Paris, Musée du Louvre). An image that gives an insight into the uneasy relations between the Guise family and Henry III.

22. Estienne Dumoustier, *Henry III*, *c.*1585 (Paris, Bibliothèque Nationale). The third of Catherine's sons to inherit the French throne, and the last king of the Valois dynasty.

23. Unknown artist, *Henry, king of Navarre*, *c.*1575 (Pau, Musée National). As senior prince of the blood, he was Henry III's legitimate heir after the king's assassination in 1589.

24. *Mascarade à l'éléphant*, Brussels tapestry *c.*1575 (Florence, Galleria degli Uffizi). Catherine commissioned the Valois tapestries to celebrate her achievements and those of her sons, the last Valois kings.

In April the court was at Fontainebleau, where it was entertained by the sight of Henri of Anjou persuading Charles IX to take part in a silly game in which they publicly mocked the new religion by ripping psalm books into tiny pieces and throwing the confetti over each other.[6] Until the king had a legitimate son, the sixteen-year-old Henri was heir to the throne; moreover, unlike the delicate and sickly Charles, he was a dashing young man and popular at court. Thanks to the influence of the cardinal of Lorraine, he was fast becoming the darling of the ultra-Catholics. Lorraine had begun to twist the normal sibling rivalry that existed between the brothers, who were just fifteen months apart, into something more sinister and actively encouraged Henri to abandon Catherine's policy of toleration in favour of his own ultra-Catholic agenda. She must have become aware of Lorraine's intentions because in the summer of 1567 she sent an envoy to England to sound out the possibility of a marriage between Henri and Elizabeth I, a union that would have the advantage of providing a throne for her ambitious second son, but he returned without success.[7]

In early May came news that the duke of Alba had sailed from Spain for Italy to take command of the 10,000 imperial troops stationed at Milan and that Philip II's plan to put down the rebellion in the Netherlands was finally underway. On 18 June, Alba set out on the long march from Lombardy to Brussels, a distance of some 700 miles. By the end of the month they had reached Chambéry, less than 30 miles from Grenoble, capital of Dauphiné, and only 60 miles from Lyons. Philip II's army was the largest in Europe, and the best equipped; its slow march through Savoy and Lorraine, provocatively close to the French frontier, was watched with alarm by the French, Catholic and Protestant alike.

Catherine, too, worried about Alba's intentions. That summer the crown hired 6,000 Swiss mercenaries who were garrisoned at Château-Thierry, a large town in easy reach of the northern frontier, and in early July she set off for Picardy with Charles to make a tour of the defences along the border with the Netherlands. In early July she left Saint-Germain with the king for Compiègne, where they remained a fortnight, and, having heard that Alba had crossed into Spanish territory on 3 August, rode north to Chaulnes, Corbie and Péronne, where they arrived on 21 August, the day before Alba and his army reached Brussels. After visits to Ham, Saint-Quentin and Guise, they reached La Fère, from where Catherine issued orders to marshal Cossé regarding the security of Paris, and complained about the summer heat; to Fourquevaux she mentioned 'the diversity of rumours which change from one hour to the next', with no explanation, and seemed more interested in the progress of her daughter Elisabeth's pregnancy, which was nearing full term.[8] It was not until they reached Marchais on 2 September that she informed Cossé of more specific rumours of Protestant troops gathering in large numbers at Montargis and Châtillon. Cossé evidently replied promptly: on 10 September she thanked him for a letter reassuring her that the rumours were unfounded, and mentioned her intention to arrive at Montceaux the following Monday, 15 September.[9] Two weeks later both Catherine and Charles were in Paris and the country was again at war.

Catherine seems to have been unaware of how Alba's arrival in the Netherlands had affected the Protestant mood. Alba lost little time in starting his campaign against the rebels: on 5 September, just two weeks after his arrival and while Catherine was still in Picardy, he set up a special tribunal to try cases of heresy and sedition, using Catholicism as a weapon to enforce loyalty to the Spanish crown. Four days later he arrested two leaders of the rebellion, counts Egmont and Horne, both Catholics from noble families with long traditions of service to Spain; William of Orange only escaped arrest because he was abroad. Alba's subsequent reign of terror was so brutal that the governor Margaret of Parma, Philip II's aunt, resigned her post in disgust, leaving Alba in control of the army and the government of the province. None of this was reassuring to

French Protestants who had begun to suspect that once he had suppressed the new religion in the Netherlands, Alba's next target would be France.

Nor does Catherine seem to have been aware of how her own actions were being misinterpreted and how her real intentions were in danger of being swallowed up in a storm of rumours that circulated with ever increasing vitriol. It was a problem that would dog her for the rest of her life – and still divides scholars today. Rumours that she had made an alliance with Philip II at Bayonne refused to die down. Why, many Protestants asked, were she and the king so reluctant to disband the 6,000 Swiss mercenaries now that the threat of an invasion by Alba and his army had receded, if they were not planning their own offensive against the new religion? It was widely believed that she intended to meet Philip II in the autumn even though she had asked Fourquevaux in July to inform him that she could not see any point in their meeting: 'it is something that I don't think is useful.'[10]

Protestant suspicions were further aroused when Charles IX sent a troop of soldiers to Paris, 'to safeguard your city', as Catherine told the mayor, in the light of 'these murders and assassinations that are worse than before'.[11] Nor were they reassured when the cardinal of Lorraine was recalled to the king's council in August. According to the English ambassador, this was a decision made by Charles in spite of Catherine's disapproval: she, he reported, was 'nothing pleased knowing [the cardinal's] ambition', but not all believed this; nor did they believe her promise to Condé the following month that, despite rumours to the contrary, she had no intention of revoking the Edict of Amboise.[12]

Suspicions about Catherine's true aims were inflamed by more general rumours at court: that the king's council was planning to arrest Condé and Coligny, for example; or, worse, that the young duke of Guise had been heard to say that he intended to kill Coligny in revenge for the assassination of his father.[13] This context of mistrust and fear of another wave of persecution was what provoked the Protestant leadership to plan to kidnap Catherine and Charles; it was not, despite what many Catholics believed, a plan to murder either of them. Indeed, according to a senior Protestant army captain, François de la Noue, their goal was actually 'to expel the cardinal of Lorraine from the court, who many imagined to be continually pressing the king to ruin all those of the [Protestant] religion'.[14] Like the conspiracy of Amboise in March 1560, the 'Surprise de Meaux' was an attempt to seize the royal family in order to acquire power at court. Condé insisted he was not guilty of treason, but his loyalty to his king did not necessarily extend to the king's councillors, by whom he meant the cardinal of Lorraine.[15] The Venetian ambassador Giovanni Correr was impressed with its organisation: 'it was a remarkable thing that the secret of this conspiracy, of which thousands of men were aware' was not leaked.[16]

The immediate result of the 'Surprise de Meaux' was the outbreak of a second war between the two religions. After the failure of the kidnap attempt, Condé and Coligny pursued their quarry to Paris and set up camp at Saint-Denis, just north of the capital, to begin a blockade of the city. Despite her anger, Catherine's instinct was to open peace negotiations and she offered Condé an amnesty if he would disarm his troops. On 10 October the constable and his son marshal Montmorency with secretary L'Aubespine met the Protestant leadership but the talks ended in failure.[17] Two weeks later she sent the marshal and L'Aubespine to Condé again, this time with Jean de Morvillier, but Condé was no mood to compromise and insisted he would only disband his army if the king's council announced its unequivocal support for the Edict of Amboise, which, of course, Lorraine would not accept.[18]

Catherine was isolated in her search for a peaceful solution. It was not just Condé and Coligny who wanted war; so, too,

did Charles IX, Lorraine and the city of Paris, where anti-Protestant fervour was being whipped up by Catholic preachers.
In the end, she accepted the inevitable and, with the royal
coffers empty, turned her attention to raising money to fund
the fighting. She refused to ally herself with Alba and accept
an offer of 5,000 infantry and 1,500 cavalry which the duke
had promised Lorraine, preferring to turn to her Italian contacts.[19] She asked her cousin Cosimo I, duke of Florence, for
a loan of 200,000 scudi, offering in return an estate in France
as well as a ducal title and an aristocratic wife for Cosimo's
youngest son, Piero.[20] But Cosimo prevaricated, unwilling to
offend either Pius V or Philip II, the two most powerful rulers
in Europe.

There was better news from Fourquevaux in early
November: Elisabeth had given birth to a healthy daughter,
named Catalina* after her mother, and there was no sign of
the puerperal fever that she had suffered after her previous
labour.[21] But in Paris the blockade had started to take effect as
Condé's army, reinforced by German troops sent by Friedrich
III, the Elector Palatine, tightened its grip. With food supplies
dwindling and an angry mob threatening violence, the two
sides met at the Battle of Saint-Denis on 10 November 1567.
The royal army, led by the redoubtable constable who, at the
age of seventy-four, was perhaps too old to be involved in the
fighting, claimed a narrow victory. They had lifted the blockade but lost their leader. Montmorency was shot in the spine
during the fighting: Catherine informed the duke of Savoy
that he was 'badly wounded in the head, the back and face'
and he died two days later.[22] 'If it were not for the misfortune
of the death of Montmorency,' she told Fourquevaux, 'the
battle we fought against those who have taken up arms against
the king my son, we would be much happier.'[23] She ensured

---

* Catalina became duchess of Savoy after marrying her cousin Carlo
Emanuele, the son of Catherine's sister-in-law and friend, Marguerite.

Montmorency was buried with honour after a state funeral at Notre-Dame on 25 November.

Montmorency had been a towering figure, dominating the French political stage with scarcely a break for over four decades, and appointing a successor was no easy task. Catherine decided to leave the office of *Constable de France* vacant to avoid the risk of inflaming court rivalries, but there did need to be a leader of the army and in the end Charles IX gave the post of lieutenant-general to his younger brother Henri of Anjou, who also became the leader of his privy council (*chef de nostre conseil*).[24] For Lorraine, his protégé's appointments were an important coup, though Catherine did manage to curb his influence over her son in military matters: under the cloak of making up for Henri's lack of experience, she appointed three commanders to take charge on the battlefield, carefully picked from each of the rival factions at court: Jacques of Savoy, the duke of Nemours and an ally of the Guise family; the Bourbon duke Louis II of Montpensier; and marshal Cossé for the Montmorency clan.[25] One unfortunate result was that the royal army was severely hampered by disagreements over tactics, though Catherine's own interference probably did not help. She wrote frequently to her son: on 27 November she wrote urging him to listen to 'the advice and opinion' of the commanders; the next day she wrote again asking him 'to reply to the two letters I have sent you yesterday and the day before and send me news of our enemies'.[26]

Peace was now Catherine's priority and in November she started negotiations, but they had to be kept secret. The *parlement* of Paris, vehemently opposed to peace, asked Charles IX the following month to confirm or deny rumours that the talks had begun; he replied that he did not intend to parley with either Condé or his allies.[27] Nevertheless, the Protestants were making significant gains: La Rochelle repulsed an attack by Monluc to force it back to Catholicism, while Blois, Tours and Chartres were all taken early in the new year, 1568. But they lacked the funds to consolidate their gains. In January, Catherine was in Vincennes for talks with ex-cardinal Châtillon, Charles de Téligny, who was Coligny's son-in-law, and François III, count of La Rochefoucauld, the admiral's brother-in-law. As a token of her commitment, she refused to comply with an order from Pius V to arrest Châtillon and send him to the Inquisition in Rome to face charges of heresy.[28] Her efforts to negotiate inevitably aroused Catholic antipathy. After Alava's attempts to bully her into changing course failed, Philip II offered a more powerful bait: in the middle of January a courier arrived from Madrid with an offer of a large sum of money if she stopped negotiating.[29] The Parisians, too, tried to halt the peace process with a bribe of 220,000 écus (600,000 livres) to fund further fighting.[30] Even Charles IX objected: 'you will not force me to make peace', he reputedly insisted to his mother, 'I want to punish my enemies'.[31]

Catherine's letters in early 1568 show how closely she was involved in organizing men and munitions for the royal army. Shortly after returning to Paris from Vincennes at the end of January, she informed Henri that she had 'already sent the foot soldiers that we have drafted and the horses'; and 'about the six cannons, they are loaded onto the boats and ready to leave'.[32] A fortnight later she reported that the money he had asked for was on its way to the camp, along with '100 or 120 horses'.[33] On 21 February she invited Henri to join her for dinner near the capital: 'I am coming tomorrow morning to dine at Villeneuve-Saint-George and will sleep at Melun; and you will find there the king your brother and me and your brother and sister'; she added, 'it is certain the enemy has taken Chartres'.[34]

The capture of Chartres would mark the turning point in the war. With both armies lacking the funds to continue the fight, peace talks began in earnest in late February. Catherine sent three of her trusted courtiers, all moderates – Limoges, Jean de Morvillier and marshal Montmorency – to finalize terms and four days after its signature she wrote a personal

letter thanking them for 'the great care and effort that you
have taken in the service of the king'.[35] The treaty, signed
at Longjumeau on 23 March 1568, reinstated the freedom
of worship that Protestants had been granted in the Edict
of Amboise and, to circumvent opposition in the *parlements*,
it was the crown-appointed provincial governors who were
entrusted with its enforcement. It was a striking contrast to the
Protestant blood bath being conducted by the duke of Alba
over the border in the Netherlands.

It was soon evident that neither side was prepared to
comply with the terms of the treaty. Negotiated by moderates,
it was rejected decisively by ultras on both sides and provoked
riots, massacres and pillage in towns all over the realm. The
Protestants objected to the order to hand back La Rochelle
and the other towns they had seized during the fighting; and
to the demand that Condé's soldiers must 'disarm promptly',
a measure that did not apply to the royal army.[36] Catholic Paris
'accused the king, his mother and his council of being, by this
peace, the cause of the ruin of the true Catholic religion'.[37]
The Catholics were also furious that Condé had been granted
an amnesty for what they insisted was his treachery, and that
the king had agreed to pay the wages of the German troops
who had fought with the Protestant army.

The divisions were equally stark at court, where Catherine
faced serious opposition from the cardinal of Lorraine and
his allies. A devious politician and a thorn in her side for
many decades, he was positioning himself to seize power
again now that the death of Montmorency had removed
his key rival. Catherine called a council meeting for 1 May
to discuss the religious violence erupting across France but
again was too ill herself to attend – indeed, she was confined to her bed for almost the whole month. Inevitably the
meeting split between moderates, led by L'Hospital, and
Lorraine's hardliners: what was significant, however, was that
while Charles IX continued to support the edict, Henri of
Anjou took the opposing side and voted with Lorraine, an

early sign that the cardinal's tactics to divide the brothers had begun to bear fruit. Moreover, Lorraine's ascendancy was mirrored in the collapse of the moderate faction in the council and the declining influence of L'Hospital, who now withdrew from court.

In his determination to block Catherine's agenda Lorraine had no scruples about opposing the crown – treason is the usual word for this contravention of the rule of law. He could count on powerful backers for his plans, notably Philip II and Alba, and the pope in Rome, where he had considerable influence; he could also rely on the city of Paris, with its overwhelmingly Catholic population. The Protestants were fearful of his growing influence, with reason. Just six days after the signing of the treaty, Lorraine and his allies discussed its implications and agreed that once the Protestants had laid down their arms, as ordered, then they would seize Orléans, La Rochelle and other centres of the new religion.[38] Furthermore, in direct contravention of the treaty, they agreed to begin a persecution campaign designed to drive Protestants from the realm.[39] There were anti-Protestant riots in several cities, of which Lorraine was accused of being the instigator.[40] Another move was even more radical. At a council meeting in May, while Catherine was still confined to bed, Lorraine's allies agreed on a more drastic measure, 'to exterminate the chiefs of the said religion', but the plan had to be 'deferred because it had been discovered', presumably leaked to the leaders in question.[41]

One of the difficulties in assessing Lorraine's intentions is the secrecy with which they were surrounded: the cardinal himself insisted that there was no plot, that this was a Protestant fiction invented to damage the Catholic cause. The issue remains controversial today, with scholars as divided in their loyalties as the protagonists themselves were in the sixteenth century. What is certainly true is that Lorraine was increasingly seen by Protestants as the central figure in an international conspiracy to exterminate their faith. Although some scholars have argued to the contrary, there is no evidence that Catherine herself was involved in Lorraine's plots.[42]

It was not until the end of May 1568 that Catherine was well enough to attend council meetings again: according to ambassador Correr, 'politics were suspended during her illness'.[43] Her priority now was to counter the steps that Lorraine had taken in her absence to dismantle the Peace of Longjumeau. One of the first letters she wrote after recovering – dated 24 May while she was still convalescing in bed – was to Coligny reassuring him that Charles IX had no intention of reneging on his promise to enforce the treaty and would punish those who contravened its terms; the king, she told the prince, has 'a great desire to re-establish peace in this realm ... and to administer justice equally to all his subjects'.[44] To Condé she was even more explicit: 'the king's intention is above all to guarantee the edict of pacification and to conserve all his subjects, of whichever religion.'[45] But the task of convincing Protestants of her own commitment to the policy of toleration was one which she was finding increasingly difficult after the collapse of the moderate faction in the privy council and Lorraine's rise to power. In an audience with Correr, she lamented 'the miserable state into which we have fallen' and outlined the problem she had faced with the treaty. 'There are circumstances where one is obliged to do things one does not want to do in order to avoid greater evils.'[46] She also alluded to the increasingly violent atmosphere at court: 'we used to be accustomed to going about in safety throughout the kingdom but now, if we set foot outside, we must be surrounded by guards; in this room where we are there are perhaps men who would like to see us dead and would kill us with their own hands.'

There was little of comfort for Catherine in the news that summer. In the middle of May, Mary Stuart, queen of Scotland

and Lorraine's niece, was forced to flee to England and the protection of her cousin Elizabeth I after many of her court converted to Protestantism. While her cousin remained child-less, Mary was heir to the English throne and her presence in the country soon created another battleground for the two religions. On 5 June, to the horror of Protestants all over Europe, Alba executed Egmont and Horne in the main square in Brussels, along with some sixty rebels. Later that month Protestant troops crossed into France from the Netherlands to join Condé but were routed by the royal army under marshal Cossé. Once again, Catherine deplored this attack on the crown which she perceived as treacherous and wrote to Cossé with instructions: 'regarding the French prisoners, I think some should be executed and the rest sent to the galleys.'[47] Two days later she wrote to admiral Coligny assuring him that it was royal policy to punish 'those who transgress the recent edict, which we wish to be preserved and upheld in full'.[48] Despite her promises, the Protestants were increasingly suspi-cious of her motives, and feared the crown's hostility towards their faith.

One of the few cheering bits of news came from Spain where Elisabeth was pregnant: all was progressing well and there were no apparent problems. But then in July, Charles IX fell ill, so seriously that there must have been moments when Catherine feared for her son's life, and the awful consequences of such a disaster. Fortunately, by the middle of August he had begun to recover and at the end of the month she reported to Fourquevaux that 'he no longer has any fever', news that she asked him to relay to her daughter and son-in-law.[49] But by then yet another political earthquake had shattered the uneasy peace. On 23 August, warned of a plot against them, Condé and Coligny fled to the safety of La Rochelle.

Earlier that month the two men had signed an alliance with William of Orange, the new leader of the rebels in the Netherlands. It was an alliance that would irrevocably link the Protestant struggle in France with the revolt in the Netherlands;

more immediately, it gave the cardinal of Lorraine the excuse he needed to arrest Condé and Coligny. The admiral was staying with the prince at the château of Noyers-sur-Serein in Burgundy where there had already been threats to his life: in July, Catherine wrote to Gaspard de Tavannes, lieutenant-general of the province, asking him to 'punish severely those who are so wicked and inopportune to undertake an attack on his person'.[50] Fortunately Condé and Coligny were warned of Lorraine's plans; the day before they left Noyers, Condé sent a letter to the king insisting that the escape was not an act of rebellion against the crown but it soon began to look exactly like one. As they rode towards La Rochelle, huge numbers of Protestants followed in their wake, including d'Andelot, La Noue, La Rochefoucauld and the other leaders. Ex-cardinal Châtillon escaped across the Channel to England, where Elizabeth I gave him a handsome pension in return for his usefulness as a diplomatic go-between.

Catherine was furious with Condé and Coligny for their disloyalty: 'they have taken up arms again on the pretext that orders were issued to arrest them, such a manifest and overt demonstration of ill will', she told Fourquevaux; 'we have no option but to assemble a large number of troops as quickly as possible to go after them and defeat them before they have a chance of regrouping in order to do worse'.[51] But her anger swiftly abated: once again when faced with a situation that threatened to deteriorate into all-out war, her first instinct was to negotiate: within days of the flight to La Rochelle she offered to meet Condé for talks, though the prince's colleagues advised against this, suspecting a plot.[52]

Then, on 1 September 1568, the king's council issued a proclamation ordering Henri of Anjou to muster troops and put down the rebellion against the crown. It was a covert declaration of war. Catherine's immediate task was to inform the European powers of what had taken place – and reading these letters provides a salutary example of the dangers of taking diplomatic correspondence entirely at face value.

To the Protestant Elizabeth I her message was denial: the English ambassador reported on 4 September that Catherine had assured him that she 'would have no wars' and the king wanted to reconcile his subjects'.[53] The message for the ultra-Catholic Philip II, written just four days later, had an entirely different tone: she asked Fourquevaux to inform the king of her plans to raise an army to attack the rebels 'as soon as possible', to 'fight them and cut them to pieces'.[54] And it was critical for her to placate both Elizabeth I and Philip II if she was to deter them from interfering in France's internal affairs.

With war looming, the biggest headache was the crown's lack of funds. This was something the wily cardinal of Lorraine had foreseen and, exploiting his considerable influence in Rome, he persuaded Pius V to permit the sale of Church property in France in order to raise money to supply much-needed finances for the army. Initially Catherine must have been pleased by the offer but when the bull was published in Rome on 1 August it was evident that the pope had ringfenced the money so that it could only be used in defence of the Catholic Church, more precisely against 'the uprisings of heretical and rebellious Protestants'.[55] Lorraine had no problem with this injunction but, as he correctly anticipated, it was unacceptable to Catherine and to chancellor L'Hospital.

On 19 September the king's council met to agree to the terms of Pius V's loan and the chancellor, who had not been at court since his bruising encounter with Lorraine at the beginning of May, returned to voice his objections to the papal conditions, which he did with considerable force. Lorraine had to be restrained by marshal Montmorency from grabbing L'Hospital by his grey beard: according to the English ambassador, the cardinal 'in great choler' turned to the queen and accused L'Hospital of being 'the cause of the troubles of the realm and that if he were in the hands of the *parlement* his head should tarry on his shoulders twenty-four hours'.[56] The chancellor retorted 'contrariwise that the cardinal had been the original cause of all the mischief and disorder'. It was L'Hospital's final gesture: on 7 October Jean de Morvillier replaced him as Keeper of the Seals, though out of respect he did not lose his title until his death in 1573; nor, as we shall see, did he lose Catherine's support.

Lorraine's domination of the council was confirmed on 28 September 1568 when it issued the ordinances of Saint-Maur, revoking the Peace of Longjumeau: 'we inhibit and forbid' all Protestant worship and exclude Protestants from public office.[57] Although the text states that Charles IX was acting 'on the advice of our most excellent lady and mother, of our said dear and best beloved brothers, of the other princes of our blood ... the lords and the honourable members of our privy council', it seems unlikely that Catherine supported this fervently anti-Protestant measure.

The same day that the ordinances of Saint-Maur were published, Jeanne d'Albret made her entry into La Rochelle with her son Henri of Navarre, now fifteen years old. She had been fortunate to leave her kingdom before the fighting started and had only narrowly avoided capture by Monluc whose troops were guarding all the crossings over the River Garonne.[58] Like Condé, Jeanne insisted that her journey to La Rochelle was not an act of rebellion against the crown; on the contrary, she wrote to Catherine, it was for religious reasons and also in 'the service of my king and the observance of the edict of pacification', as well as her son's status as a Bourbon and the leading prince of the blood.[59]

Early the following month there was worrying news from Spain, where the pregnant Elisabeth had fallen ill. 'Having heard that the queen your wife is unwell,' Catherine wrote to Philip II, offering the diagnosis that her daughter was overeating 'and not taking enough exercise ... I urge your majesty to command her to eat only two meals a day and only to eat bread in between if she cannot wait for dinner or supper'.[60] She was still to learn the awful truth that Elisabeth was already dead, having given birth to a stillborn daughter on 3 October after two days of agonizing stomach pains and vomiting. Fourquevaux wrote to Catherine that day but the letter 'which brought us the unhappy news of the late Catholic queen, my daughter' would not reach Paris until 28 October: she continued, poignantly, 'it was so unexpected, and you can imagine how much I loved her'.[61] Elisabeth was just twenty-three: in her nine years of marriage she had already borne Philip another stillborn son, miscarried twin girls and had two daughters, both of whom would survive into adulthood. For Catherine it was a shattering personal loss; she thanked Anna d'Este, recently remarried to the duke of Nemours, who had visited the grieving Catherine and brought much 'comfort in my afflictions which God sends me'.[62] It was also a political blow for Catherine, breaking the one positive link in her relations with the touchy Philip II.

In addition to her private grief Catherine was fearful for the future. France was again at war. For the rest of the autumn of 1568 Catherine and the court remained within easy reach of the capital, while Henri of Anjou was with the army at its army camp near Poitiers. Unlike previously, there is little evidence in her letters of any involvement in supplying men and munitions; nor did she write as frequently to Anjou, though there are plenty of letters to the duke of Nemours, a Guise ally and one of the men Catherine had appointed to advise her son. In November there was welcome news that the duke of Montpensier had defeated a Protestant army marching up from the south, but he had been unable to follow up with any success in the Midi, which remained predominantly Protestant. The following month William of Orange and his brother Louis of Nassau crossed the borders into France at the head of a Protestant force, but they, too, failed to make any headway and in January Catherine reported that they had been forced to retreat back across the Moselle.[63] As before, with neither side capable of capitalizing on its victories, the result was stalemate.

Over Christmas and New Year there were discussions about the progress of the war that 'provoked such storms in the king's council', according to the Venetian ambassador.[64] On 6 January 1569 Alava reported to Alba that marshal Montmorency and his brother Damville were urging the king to make peace: ever the alarmist, he added 'I do not doubt that their aim is to ally with the prince of Orange and then, afterwards, attack us in Flanders'.[65] The next day he was hanging around the door into the council chamber at Saint-Maur in the hope of picking up gossip when Catherine came out, tearful and distressed: 'I am appalled at the behaviour of the council members, all of whom want me to make peace,' she told him.[66] The implication seems to be that Catherine had abandoned the pro-peace faction and that it was this bloc that now dominated the council; but Alava's account becomes even more confused when apparently she added, 'I do not know who to trust any longer; those who I thought were devoted to the service of the king my son have changed sides and are opposing his wishes.' Whatever the truth – and it may well be that Alava was using the fiction that Catherine was now against peace as a deliberate ploy to increase friction between the religions – there is no other evidence to suggest that she had changed sides. What is certainly true is that the hostility in the council between the moderates and Lorraine's hawks had not abated.

Towards the end of January 1569 the court began a tour of the northern provinces and in late February Catherine fell seriously ill at Metz, where they were forced to remain until she recovered in early April. That month she wrote to her cousin Cosimo I, asking for a favour: 'since it has pleased God that I should recover from the great malady which I have suffered and return me to my pristine health', she wanted to send one of her friars to the church of Santissima Annunziata in Florence and to the shrine of the Virgin at Loreto 'to fulfil the vow that I made during my illness and give thanks to God for my recovery'.[67]

The fighting continued: on the other side of the country the royal army under Anjou, who now had the expert assistance of Gaspard de Tavannes, was getting closer to La Rochelle. On 13 March 1569 the duke won a victory at Jarnac, 50 miles east of the port, and Condé was captured after his horse was killed in the fighting; what followed was not an edifying story in the annals of warfare.[68] One of Anjou's men, no doubt acting on the duke's orders, shot Condé in cold blood and had his body paraded through the streets on a donkey. 'You have won the battle,' Anjou informed Charles IX, 'the prince of Condé is dead, I have seen his body.'[69] Jeanne d'Albret, appalled by Anjou's cruelty, seized the propaganda opportunity it presented to address the defeated troops: the leadership of the Protestant cause was to be shared by two princes of the blood: her own son and her nephew, Condé's heir. It marked the moment when the next generation emerged as leaders on both sides of the religious divide. Confusingly, all four were named Henri. Henri, prince of Condé was sixteen years old, Henri of Navarre a year younger; on the other side, Henri of Anjou was now aged seventeen, while Henri of Guise was eighteen years old, and proving himself a ruthless fighter very much in the mould of his assassinated father.

One of the immediate benefits of the victory at Jarnac was the readiness of Catholic rulers – Pius V, Philip II and Cosimo I – to supply much-needed funds. At the beginning of the war Catherine had asked her cousin for a loan of 100,000 scudi, offering her jewels as security; but the duke insisted on having his own valuation made of the jewellery and she was furious when he informed her that it was significantly lower than her own, and the offer was withdrawn.[70] After Jarnac, however, the duke had a change of heart. When the news of the victory reached Florence on 26 March, Cosimo marked the occasion by attending mass in the city's cathedral to celebrate this 'great rout of the Protestants in France', as a diarist recorded:

'their leader the prince of Condé is dead together with many other nobles and soldiers'.[71] Catherine now heard that he was ready to forward the 100,000 scudi, without any security.[72] There were political reasons behind his new position, not least the pursuit of papal favour.[73] In the aftermath of Jarnac, Pius V had agreed to send aid to France and celebrated the death of Condé as a victory for Catholicism. The pope also urged Charles IX to eliminate the other Protestant leaders of the movement; Alava fuelled the propaganda war by claiming that Catherine was fully in agreement with Spanish and papal policy.[74]

It is unlikely to be a coincidence that, in late May, Coligny and his brother d'Andelot fell seriously ill in mysterious circumstances; though the admiral recovered, d'Andelot died. On 19 May, Catherine informed Fourquevaux that 'we greatly celebrated the news of d'Andelot's death after that of the late Comte de Brissac which I much regretted' – Timoléon de Cossé, count of Brissac and brother of marshal Artus de Cossé, was killed at the siege of Mussidan fighting in the royal army.[75] Ever conscious of treachery towards the crown, she concluded, 'I hope that God will make the others suffer the treatment they deserve'. Inevitably there were accusations that d'Andelot had been poisoned but there is no convincing evidence either way. However, rumours of plots to kill Coligny continued to surface throughout the summer, fuelling fears that there was a plan to exterminate the entire Protestant leadership.

In June, Catherine travelled to Limoges to join Anjou's camp, where she remained for ten days or so, accompanied by a new secretary, Nicolas de Neufville, seigneur of Villeroy. A great admirer of Catherine, and fiercely loyal to her and the crown, he had inherited the post of secretary after the death of his father-in-law, Claude de L'Aubespine, two years earlier.[76] Reporting on Catherine's arrival at the camp, he mentioned she was given lodgings with the Swiss mercenaries, which does not sound very comfortable.[77] Catherine sent lengthy reports back to Charles IX almost every day containing news of the progress of the war against Coligny's troops, which had recently been reinforced by a company of German cavalry (*reiters*) led by the Protestant duke of Zweibrücken. Catherine's tone is unerringly positive and filled with praise for the exceptional quality of the army. On 9 June, for example, she reported that Anjou 'is working as hard as he can, as are all the lords and captains who are with him, to bring about all you desire'.[78] Three days later, she reported that 'all those who are in this army from the highest to the lowest, you have so many men filled with such great affection for you'.[79] She continued her rhapsody: 'since I have been here I have seen your army marching with such speed that, if the *reiters* had attacked … I could have called myself the happiest woman in the world and your brother the most glorious.'

The reality was somewhat less glorious. Charles IX's army was facing considerable problems: the victory at Jarnac (March 1569) had been followed by failure to take either Angoulême or Cognac; indeed, it had been unable to halt the Protestant advance, especially after the arrival of Zweibrücken's *reiters* in early June. Anjou's troops were in no condition to fight. Villeroy recorded his frustration at the quarrelsome relations between the commanders and the absence of strong leadership.[80] Worse, he reported, the army lacked wine, bread and fodder; two cavalry regiments had deserted and many soldiers were dying of hunger and thirst.[81]

The *parlement* in Paris, frustrated by the army's inability to defeat the Protestants in battle, resorted to other tactics. In July 1569 it sacked Coligny from the position of admiral, which was now vacant. Two months later they issued an arrest warrant, offering a reward of 50,000 écus for his capture alive, later amended to 'dead or alive', and his effigy was publicly hanged from a gibbet in the Place de Grève.[82] Unaware that the *parlement* was acting independently of the king, the pope fanned the flames of religious hatred by congratulating Charles IX for getting rid of 'this loathsome and abominable man', urging him to continue the war against heresy.[83] In October the assassins claimed the life of Coligny's lieutenant Artus de Vaudray: significantly, his murderer, Charles de Louviers de Maurevert, had links to the Guise family. By the end of the year even the young Protestant princes, Condé and Navarre, who so far had avoided censure on the grounds that they might be persuaded to convert and thus do more damage to the Protestant cause, had also become targets.

All the senior figures in the Protestant movement were placed under surveillance. Even the old chancellor L'Hospital was threatened and wrote to Catherine asking for her help – something, incidentally, he would never have done if she had become an ally of Pius V, Philip II and Alba. Catherine replied that, on receiving his letter, 'I immediately wrote to my son the duke of Alençon [François], asking him not to send troops to guard your houses nor those of your son-in-law'.[84] On 20 September she wrote again, briefly, to reassure her old ally that she was doing everything she could 'for your peace and welfare'.[85] Further evidence that Catherine had not changed sides comes in a letter dated the following day from Jean de Morvillier to L'Hospital which underlined the queen mother's support for the chancellor: 'she has told me of her great regret that she is aware of many things that are being done to harm you, which she believes comes from those who hate you and from the ambitions of others, but you can rest assured that the king and she will never abandon you.'[86]

The fighting continued. On 7 September, Henry of Guise's successful defence of Poitiers, which had been under siege by Coligny since 24 July, established his reputation as a soldier. The troops promised by Pius V, Philip II and Cosimo I finally arrived to reinforce the royal army and the two sides met again on 3 October 1569 at Moncontour, which was another victory for Henri of Anjou and Tavannes, who would be rewarded with the title of marshal of France. Once again the Catholic world was triumphant. In Rome, Pius V led the celebrations for the deaths of 10,000 Protestants, ordering masses, processions, salvoes of artillery and bonfires as well as the ringing of all the church bells in Rome for three days.[87] Catherine's joy in the victory was maternal, not religious: in a letter to Philip II she crowed, 'my son the duke of Anjou has won another battle against the rebels of the king'.[88]

Behind the celebrations, however, things looked bleak. Secretary Villeroy reported that men were deserting the royal army in droves and, without money and supplies, 'I foresee that this army will gradually disintegrate'.[89] Anjou, who lost his horse during the fighting, was lucky to be rescued by his men and was unhurt. Coligny had been so badly wounded that Louis of Nassau had taken over command of the Protestant forces. Henri of Guise had also been wounded, though less seriously: as Catherine reassured his mother Anna d'Este a week after the battle, 'he has no fever and also the wound just grazed the foot and did not touch the bone'.[90] But the royal army failed to follow up on its victory. Charles IX, who had arrived at camp before the battle, insisted on besieging the fortress of Saint-Jean-d'Angély on the road to La Rochelle, a decision that not only tied up the royal army until early December but also gave Coligny the opportunity to escape south to Montauban, with most of his army intact, enabling him to use the winter to regroup and plan a new offensive for the spring.

By the beginning of November, Catherine was at the camp at Saint-Jean-d'Angély, from where Charles IX wrote, somewhat optimistically, to Fourquevaux that 'the fear my army brings to my enemies and rebels is so great that they have abandoned a large part of the towns they held' and that those inside Saint-Jean-d'Angély, 'which is being furiously battered by artillery, are so frightened that they want to parley'.[91] Catherine also sent the ambassador a short note by the same courier to say, 'everything here is in a good state thanks be to God, as you can see from what the king my son has written'.[92] Catherine's concern, however, was less with the fighting but with the nego-tiations she was now conducting to end the war – which rather gives the lie to Alava's assertion in January that she was set on opposing peace.

In September, soon after the Battle of Moncontour, Catherine had sent an envoy to Jeanne d'Albret in La Rochelle with the message that she was 'well-disposed' to peace and 'promised to obtain favourable terms' if the two sides could agree to parley.[93] In the middle of November the Protestants responded by sending their own agent to negotiate with Charles IX on behalf of Coligny and the two young princes, Henri of Navarre and Henri of Condé. The agent – named in the documents as Mr Nobody (*sieur de Personne*) – was given an audience by the king in his council on 24 November, with Catherine, Henri, cardinals Bourbon and Lorraine, marshal Montmorency, Antoine de Crussol, now duke d'Uzès, the duke of Montpensier, the bishop of Limoges and Jean de Morvillier among those present to hear the agent assure the king that Coligny, Navarre and Condé swore loyalty to the crown, and were earnest in their desire for peace. Catherine sent a brief outline of what had taken place to Fourquevaux a few days later, warning him to be very careful with Philip II: 'above all you must not talk to anyone' about the meeting.[94]

Catherine and Charles IX, for all his bluster, were negotiat-ing from a position of relative weakness. The army may have won victories at Jarnac and Moncontour, but they had been unable to secure a convincing win; moreover, morale was low, the men hungry and ill and deserting in ever larger numbers. Protestant morale, by contrast, was high: they had outman-oeuvred the royal army and their troops were regrouping in the south in preparation for a spring offensive. Their demands were equally bullish, and unwelcome to the other side: their insistence on freedom of worship without restrictions in all France, for example, could not be tolerated in Paris. Less con-troversially, they wanted representation in the king's council and in the judiciary, as well as control of a list of eleven cities, including La Rochelle and Angoulême, from which all foreign troops would be removed.

Negotiations continued erratically into December and Catherine remained with her sons at the army camp into the New Year. In early January 1570 she left for Angers, where she was briefly ill with a 'little fever', but had recovered by the end of the month.[95] The following month the peace negotiations took on more urgency: as Charles IX explained to Fourquevaux on 7 February, the dire state of the kingdom was forcing him to make peace: 'my subjects on both sides do not obey me as they should ... there is no control or military discipline among the gentlemen and soldiers ... the houses of most lords and gentlemen of my realm are ruined or burned ... [and] my finances are exhausted.'[96] There were also rumours that the German Protestant princes were planning to send more troops to reinforce Coligny's army. Catherine added her own voice to that of her son, with a heartfelt plea to the ambassador: 'please make the Catholic king, my good son, believe that extreme necessity has obliged us to take the path of pacification rather than that of force.'[97] Philip II's opposition to any form of reconciliation with the Protestants was well known; the worry was that he might use his own army, conveniently garrisoned in the Netherlands, to force the issue.

Writing from La Rochelle on 10 February, Jeanne d'Albret thanked Catherine for 'the assurance that you are pleased to send me that the king and yourself continue to be willing for peace'.[98] She also warned that Alba and Lorraine were plotting to disrupt the talks; Alba had gone so far as to urge Philip II to invade France in order to halt them.[99] She urged Catherine not to listen to 'those who advise the king to throw us out ... who are disloyal to the crown and want to continue a civil war between the subjects of your majesties until all is ruined'.[100] She also warned Catherine that Lorraine, 'enemy of God, of the king and of his blood, and his loyal supporters', was plotting to eliminate the Protestant leadership: 'I know in

truth that he has sent three men who were easily recogniz-
able, to kill my son, my nephew and the admiral' – Jeanne
did not recognize his demotion by the Catholic *parlement* of
Paris – 'and I do not doubt he has marked me out as well'.
Pius V added his powerful voice to oppose any negotiation,
warning Catherine against 'an accommodation between the
Most Christian King and the abominable heretics'; to Charles
IX he wrote that 'this peace it is said you are negotiating with
the heretics will become the source of the greatest curses for
France'.[101]

The Protestants had used their retreat from Moncontour to
good effect. Having mustered a large force over the winter,
Coligny embarked on a spring offensive and took Languedoc
in March 1570. Catherine was still at Angers on 22 March
when she told Anna d'Este that 'the enemy is approaching
Dauphiné', from where Coligny could advance up the Rhône
Valley.[102] In early April she left Angers for Châteaubriant,
where she received a Protestant delegation with further
offers.[103] Lorraine disliked this Montmorency castle: 'here
we are up to our eyes in filth and cold,' he complained to
his sister-in-law Anna d'Este, envious of her in Paris, 'and the
court is fuller than ever of *broileries* among the ladies'.[104]

After three weeks the court moved north to visit Brittany and
Normandy. From Orbec on 22 June, Catherine wrote urgently
to Henri of Guise asking him to secure towns 'in Champagne
and Burgundy near the route being taken by our enemies'.[105]
A few days earlier Coligny's troops had sacked the medieval
abbey of Cluny and, having defeated the royal army under
marshal Cossé near Autun, took La-Charité-sur-Loire, just 135
miles south of Paris. At Pont-l'Arche on 28 June, Catherine
was able to display her goodwill towards Philip II with a conspicuous favour: his new bride Anna of Austria was on her
way from Vienna to Madrid and, because Turkish pirates had

made the Mediterranean too dangerous, she was sailing from Nijmegen to Santander: Catherine ordered all French ports to give assistance to the Spanish galleys, and do 'all things necessary for her comfort on the voyage to Spain in order to do her all honour ... as befits the grandeur and dignity of the king'.[106]

By early July, Catherine was back at Saint-Germain, from where she ordered Cossé to find out what he could about 'the enemy's plans', but the fighting was about to stop.[107] On 29 July, Coligny's son-in-law Charles de Téligny arrived at Saint-Germain for private discussions with Catherine and her three sons. That day the ex-admiral wrote to Catherine urging her to recognize his loyalty to the crown: 'if your majesty will study all my actions since first she knew me until now, she will admit that I am quite different from the portrait that has been painted of me, I beg you Madame, to believe that you have no more devoted servant than I have been and have wanted to be.'[108]

The negotiations were completed by 5 August when the king's council met to agree to the terms.[109] Two sticking points had both been ceded: the Protestant demand for the crown to pay the *reiters* who had fought with Coligny's army and that all those deprived of government office because of their religion were to be reinstated.[110] However, the crown granted only four of the eleven *places de sûreté*, or surety towns, they had demanded – La Rochelle, Cognac, La Charité-sur-Loire and Montauban – and had refused to allow freedom of worship across France. Instead, they were granted a general amnesty and given freedom of conscience with the proviso that public worship was limited to towns where they had been active before the war; and that the nobility were free to worship according to the rites of the new religion in their own homes but not in Paris or at court. Despite the conditions, however, the Peace of Saint-Germain, signed on 8 August 1570, was an important landmark in the history of Protestants in France. Far more favourable to them than the edicts signed at Amboise (1563) or Longjumeau (1568), it gave them the legal backing to enable them to assimilate themselves into French society from which they had been excluded for so long.

Secretary Villeroy's official minutes of the meeting record Charles IX's words: 'I cannot put an end to the troubles of my realm by force of arms and I have decided to grant to the princes [Navarre and Condé] and the admiral [Coligny] the articles which have just been read.'[111] Catherine's response to the king's statement was a fervent declaration of her long-held desire for peace: 'I am glad that the king my son is now old enough to be better obeyed than in the past; I will help him with my advice and with all my power I will help him observe the articles he has granted, having always wished to see the kingdom restored to the same state as it was during the lives of the kings his predecessors.' The edict was published on 8 August 1570 and registered by the *parlement* of Paris three days later.

The Peace of Saint-Germain was a significant victory for Catherine and the moderates on the council; ultra-Catholics were stunned and many believed that the king and his mother had been deceived by Protestant lies. For his part Pius V urged Lorraine to continue the war: 'there cannot be any peace except one that is fake and counterfeit; under the name of concord is hidden a most insidious trap,' he fulminated; 'make all your efforts to baffle and reverse all these designs on peace and do not permit, in any manner, a coup in France so fatal to the Catholic faith'.[112] But Lorraine was in disgrace and had been excluded from the 5 August meeting: the English envoy commented that Catherine's 'cruel enemy the cardinal of Lorraine is not admitted to the council'.[113] The majority of those present were in favour of the compromise: some, like marshal Montmorency, Limoges, Lansac and Saint-Sulpice, were old allies of Catherine and supporters of her policy of toleration; others feared that continuation of the fighting would result in defeat because of the calamitous state of the royal army, which marshal Cossé warned was in danger of 'disintegrating'.[114]

Lorraine had long been an enemy of Catherine but now he had incurred the wrath of the royal family for his presumption. His first mistake was to suggest a marriage between Henri of Anjou and his niece Mary Stuart, who was not only queen of Scotland but, until Elizabeth I produced an heir, also next in line to the English throne. His plan to unite the French, Scottish and English crowns was ambitious, but nothing compared to the arrogance of his next project: encouraging his nephew Henri of Guise in a flirtation with Catherine's daughter Marguerite. The rumour at court was that the cardinal was planning to betroth the couple, both of whom were seventeen years old, and that if he were not actively encouraging the affair then he at least was turning a blind eye to his nephew's indiscretions.

Anjou was scandalized when he heard what was going on and informed his brother and mother. Catherine was livid and summoned Marguerite to her apartments, where she and Charles IX proceeded to berate her – if we are to believe that gossipmonger Alava, Marguerite's 'clothes were so torn and her hair so dishevelled that it took the queen mother an hour to repair the mess'.[115] The rules governing the behaviour of noble women in the sixteenth century were strict and unforgiving, and breaking the code brought dishonour to the family: women were frequently murdered by their male relations for adulterous behaviour. Catherine's plans for her daughter, a royal princess, did not include the duke of Guise; but the most unfortunate fallout of the affair was the dramatic end to the close friendship that had existed between Anjou and Guise, a split that was to have serious repercussions later.

Catherine's choice of spouses for all four of her unmarried children – Charles, Henri, Marguerite and François – was dictated by her political priorities, the first of which was to establish a Habsburg–Valois entente supported by a web of

marital alliances between the two dynasties. When Marguerite
had been a child there had been talk of a marriage with Henri
of Navarre but this plan had long since been replaced by the
search for a Habsburg husband. In June 1563 the emperor
had agreed in principle to two betrothals: Marguerite to his
grandson Rudolf and Charles to one of his two granddaughters,
Anna or Elisabeth, a choice which Philip II had settled by
insisting that Anna, who was his niece, was to marry his heir
Don Carlos. In January 1568, however, Philip had finally
accepted that Don Carlos's severe mental instability made
him incapable of being king and disinherited his son, locking
him up in a room in the Alcazar palace; the unfortunate
prince died six months later. The situation changed again in
October that year when Elisabeth died in childbirth, leaving
him without a male heir and without a wife; after the death
of all three of his spouses, he was on the marriage market
again. Catherine did contemplate offering Marguerite as a
replacement for Elisabeth, but the king had other ideas.

In March 1569, Philip II informed his close adviser Cardinal
Granvelle that he had three marriages in mind: himself to his
niece Anna of Austria; his two-year-old daughter Isabella to
Charles IX, the girl's uncle; and Marguerite to his fifteen-year-
old nephew Sebastian, king of Portugal, alliances designed
to 'bring peace and universal quiet to all Christendom, hurt
the Turk and extirpate heresies everywhere'.[116] That August,
Catherine wrote to her cousin Cosimo with news 'you will
be very pleased to hear' that betrothals had been arranged
between Marguerite and Sebastian, and between Charles IX
and the emperor's younger sister Elisabeth.[117] For the next few
months Fourquevaux took charge of negotiating the contracts
with Philip II and the imperial ambassador in Spain and,
although there were problems with the Portuguese union,
that of Charles IX and Elisabeth was settled in early 1570. In
late February, Catherine replied to a letter from Fourquevaux
announcing that the contract was now complete, thanking him
for his 'dexterity and judgement' and adding the information

that she had written to the emperor to agree on a date for the wedding.[118]

Despite widespread anger in the Catholic world at the Peace of Saint-Germain, Philip II raised no objections to Charles IX's marriage and relations between Paris and Madrid continued to be friendly at the domestic level. In September, Catherine wrote to Philip to thank him for 'the fine and beautiful horse, the Tiger' which she much appreciated 'for the rarity of this horse but principally I will take care of it and cherish it because it is a present from you'.[119] Four days later she informed Fourquevaux that she was sending 'six horses, the best to be found here' for him to present to the king in her name 'with the most true and gracious words that you think possible.'[120] Later that same day she wrote again to the ambassador with details of more presents which included two small dogs for her young granddaughters Isabella and Catalina, and two lengths of expensive velvet for the duchess of Alba.[121]

The formal betrothal between Charles IX and Elisabeth of Austria was signed on 2 October 1570 and early the following month Catherine and the court travelled to Mézières, where the wedding took place on 26 November. To avoid the risk of bad weather it was decided to delay the coronation of the new queen until the spring and the court spent Christmas and most of January at Villers-Cotterêts. In Paris that winter preparations were underway for the royal entries into the capital, which would follow the coronation. Commissioned by the civic authorities and designed by the court's most eminent humanists and artists, including the poet Ronsard, the sculptor Germain Pilon and the painter Nicolò dell'Abate, the decorations celebrated the peace signed at Saint-Germain the previous August. Relief that the fighting was over and that a workable peace had been negotiated was palpable in the speech Charles IX gave to the *parlement* on 11 March 1571: 'after God I am most obliged to my mother,' he announced, thanking Catherine for the part she had played in ensuring 'that the storms of civil war have not damaged my realm'.[122]

The king's entry, which had taken place five days earlier, reflected his words. At the Porte-Saint-Denis, where the procession entered the city, Charles IX was greeted by a triumphal arch crowned with stucco statues of the mythical founders of the kingdom, the Trojan prince Francion and Pharamond, king of the Franks.[123] At the Pont Notre-Dame linking the right bank of the Seine to the Île-de-la-Cité, a painting was displayed showing two warring hives of bees (read, Catholics and Protestants) pacified by powder dispensed from Heaven, a message that was reinforced by a statue of Mars, god of war, chained to a laurel tree, the symbol of peace.[124] Catherine's role as peacemaker was hailed in a figure of Gallia, the nurturing mother of Gaul, which bore her facial features and brandished a map of the kingdom; the inscription beneath described her as the person 'who has sustained and supported France'.[125] A group of three virtuous widows from the ancient world – Camilla, Lucretia and, Catherine's own inspiration, Artemisia – each carried inscriptions extolling their deeds, which were, nevertheless, inferior to Catherine: 'but greater now is your own glory for, in older years and for your king, you have entered into the very midst of conflicts.'[126]

Elisabeth of Austria's coronation and entry had to be postponed for three weeks because she was ill. It was not until 25 March, the Feast of the Annunciation, that she was formally crowned in the basilica of Saint-Denis, dressed in a velvet cloak lined with ermine and embroidered with gold fleurs-de-lys, and a train over eight yards long.[127] Four days later she made her procession through Paris, where the decorations for the king's entry had been adapted to suit this event, with the newly painted and gilded triumphal arches glittering with wealth.[128] Instead of extolling the peace that had been achieved at home, the emphasis had changed to the international accord between the Valois and Habsburg dynasties. The figures of Francion and Pharamond, for example, now portrayed Pepin, king of the Franks, and his son Charlemagne, the first Holy Roman Emperor, from whom both dynasties could claim descent.[129] The references to Catherine's part in achieving peace, less appropriate to the international theme, were also adapted so that the three virtuous widows now became the Three Graces, a more appropriate image for the new queen.[130] Catherine was visibly present, however, at the banquet in the episcopal palace which followed the procession, where the table was ornamented with huge gilded sugar sculptures depicting the story of Minerva, the chaste and armed Roman goddess of wisdom, as well as the arts, who was identified with the queen mother.[131]

Catherine was now in her late forties, she had settled her son on the throne and, after much effort, finally achieved her goal of peace between the two religions. It gave her more time to devote to her own interests, notably her buildings and gardens: as she wrote to her cousin Cosimo I in October 1571 regarding her plans for a model farm at Saint-Maur, 'we are beginning to hope that the peace will hold', and that this would give her the opportunity to indulge in 'honest pleasures'.[132] Philibert Delorme was full of praise for her in his treatise on architecture published in 1567: 'Madame, I see from day to day the growth in the great pleasure your majesty takes in architecture, and how increasingly your good spirit manifests itself and shines when you yourself take the trouble to make an image and sketch of the buildings that you are pleased to commission.'[133] By all accounts her involvement in her projects was exceptional for the period – indeed, as the architect commented, 'the works of this very excellent and magnanimous princess, most admirable and worthy in her grandeur' represented a scale of architectural patronage such that 'neither king nor prince has done more in this kingdom'.[134] But her importance as a patron is not based solely on the scale of her oeuvre: her projects played a significant role in the development of the French Renaissance.[135]

Despite her Italian background, Catherine chose to display her French loyalties in her buildings. Delorme, who had become her architect after the death of Henry II, fused the language of the Italian Renaissance with local traditions to create a uniquely French style, as demonstrated in his invention of the 'French' column with its ornate horizontal bands of masonry, which he applied to all five classical orders.[136] This emphasis on French identity was part of a wider cultural movement that extended across the arts and found expression in the *Académie de poesie et de musique* (Academy of Poetry and Music), founded with royal backing in 1570 by the poet Jean-Antoine de Baïf and the musician Joachim Thibault de Courville. Delorme's columns must be seen in the context of the new vernacular works inspired by classical precedent, such as Ronsard's epic poem *La Franciade* that traced the descent of the French monarchy from the Trojan prince Francion in deliberate imitation of Virgil's *Aeneid*, the story of another Trojan prince, Aeneas, legendary ancestor of Rome.[137]

In the years following the grand tour work was underway at her Mediterranean villa at Hyères and she contributed funds for the rebuilding of the abbeys of Corbie and for Mont Saint-Michel.[138] At Montceaux she reorganized the layout 'for the comfort of all', as a visitor reported.[139] She commissioned the painter Nicolò dell'Abate for a rustic scene, *The Winnowing of Grain*, to embellish Mi-Voie, her dairy at Fontainebleau.[140] As part of her plans for the model farm at Saint-Maur, she asked Cosimo I for a favour, somewhat outside the grand duke's expertise, 'to send all sorts of people who know how to make all sorts of cheese, milk foods, conserves, cured meats, salads and fruits'.[141] She commissioned Delorme to enlarge the château at Saint-Maur, evidence of her growing taste for pomp and grandeur.[142] After his death in January 1570, she appointed Jean Bullant, who planned even grander designs for its embellishment.[143] Like Delorme, Bullant wrote his own treatise on architecture which showcased his French style, also developed after several years studying classical ruins in Italy, which he had used to impressive effect at Montmorency's châteaux at Écouen and La Fère-en-Tardenois, places where Catherine had been a regular guest and knew well. Interestingly, both architects were Protestants.

Her two most ambitious projects under construction were her palace at the Tuileries and the Valois chapel at Saint-Denis, both in the Paris area where, in contrast to the peripatetic years of the grand tour, she now spent most of her time. Apart from the ten weeks she was at Angers in early 1570 negotiating an end to the war, and her trip to Metz that autumn for the wedding of Charles IX and Elisabeth of Austria, she was based largely in the capital: over the years 1567–71 she stayed 558 nights in Paris, compared to just 91 nights at Fontainebleau, 51 at Saint-Germain or 45 at Saint-Maur.[144] The building sites provided lucrative employment for huge numbers of craftsmen and unskilled labourers of all sorts; and for the carters who transported building materials to the chapel and the palace, notably the marbles which had been brought at huge expense from as far afield as Italy and the Pyrenees. In 1571, for example, the wage bill for the sculptors, stonecutters and polishers at work in Saint-Denis came to some 9,250 écus (25,500 livres). It is an indication of the huge size of the workforce employed there: a skilled stonecutter supplying 'columns, bases, capitals and other pieces of marble' earned 15 livres a month, just 65 écus a year.[145]

Ronsard voiced, though not in public, the widespread disapproval of Catherine's expenditure on these projects, which many thought excessive. 'The queen must stop building,' he wrote in a poem dedicated to the head of the royal treasury; 'her lime is swallowing our wealth ... [while] painters, stonecutters, engravers and carvers suck the treasury dry with their deceits.'[146] He was particularly critical of her palace: 'what use is her Tuileries to us?' Work there, which had started in 1564, had progressed enough by July 1567 for her to tell Anna d'Este of her plans to host a feast there that summer.[147]

The previous year Delorme had drawn up a contract with carpenters for the construction of a huge stable block measuring 60 × 11 metres and included a tilting yard among its amenities; Girolamo Lippomano, the Venetian ambassador, described it as built 'in the manner of a magnificent palace'.[148]

The garden façade, articulated with Delorme's French columns, had been completed when he died in January 1570 and, as with Saint-Maur, Catherine handed the project to Bullant, who drew up new, more elaborate designs for the completion of the palace.[149] The cost of the project was abundantly visible to all in the conspicuously lavish marble decoration. The use of expensive marbles to make mantelpieces, capitals, door frames and other decorative features for palace interiors was common enough in grand residences in both France and Italy but her use of them to embellish the exterior of the Tuileries left observers in little doubt about the high cost of the project.

Catherine had a passion for this expensive stone and amassed a large collection which she kept at a workshop in the palace gardens, conveniently close to the wharf on the Seine: the porphyry she bought from Cardinal du Bellay and the items she picked up on the grand tour, as well as white marble from Grenoble and Italy, black from Dinant, red from Mons and a red-and-grey stone from Rance, near Liège.[150] When she heard of some marbles near Beauvais 'that would be perfect for my building at the Tuileries', she asked a local official to arrange for them to be sent to Paris.[151]

Another example of her love of sumptuous display was her collection of gilded leather wall hangings. Five sets of these costly items, a total of 134 pieces, were listed in the inventory compiled after her death, one of which was probably the gilded set she ordered from Madrid in 1570.[152] In May the following year she thanked ambassador Fourquevaux for his trouble in organizing the transport of the hangings to France; 'they are really beautiful,' she told him as she paid the bill of 112 écus (312 livres) for the muleteers who had brought them to Paris, and generously gave them another 90 écus (250 livres) for the journey home.[153]

Chief among the delights of the Tuileries was its spectacular gardens, one of the grandest in sixteenth-century Europe – as indeed Catherine intended it to be. The Florentine Bernardo Carnesecchi, whom she had invited to Paris in 1564, retained his post as her chief gardener and in 1571 he was assisted by five under-gardeners and nursery men.[154] Inside the palace walls were avenues of sycamores, elms and firs, elegant parterres planted with flowers and fountains that were fed by an aqueduct specially constructed to bring water to the garden.[155] Ambassador Lippomano, describing the place in 1577 when it had had time to mature, thought it 'a beautiful garden, with the trees and plants laid out in an admirable manner, where there is not only a maze but also spinneys, fountains and streams'.[156]

One of the highlights of the Tuileries was a rustic grotto designed and created by the potter Bernard Palissy, who set up his kiln and workshop in the gardens, guarding them with a terracotta watchdog.[157] Palissy was an unusual character: an artisan by training and a self-taught scientist with a passion for natural history, which inspired him to write treatises on subjects as diverse as geology and palaeontology to toxicology; he dedicated his work on gardens to Catherine. An early convert to Protestantism, he was protected from persecution by his first patron, constable Montmorency, and then by Catherine, who appointed him as her 'official designer of rustic figures'. Though frustrated in his search for the secret of Chinese porcelain, he invented his own unique styles of pottery.* Most famous was his 'rustic ware' with its high-relief decoration based on moulds which he took from

---

* Palissy was an important influence on the development of modern ceramics; his pottery was imitated across Europe and inspired English innovations such as Josiah Wedgwood's jasperware and the Palissy ware made by Minton Ltd.

plants, insects and marine life. Other styles included pottery that imitated jasper marble, of which Catherine owned 141 pieces, as well as more conventional dishes displaying stories from classical mythology.[158] The grotto he created for her at the Tuileries must have been an astonishing sight, with water dripping over its walls that were encrusted with fossils, snails, crabs, shrimps, lizards, urchins, eels and turtles set in pebbles, shells, moss, reeds, seaweeds and grasses before it reached the pool below and was sprayed out from a fountain by giant ceramic fish.[159]

While she was in the army camp at Limoges in June 1569 Catherine had written to her son Charles about the impending visit of the Spanish duke of Nájera, urging him 'to make [the duke] understand that you are not a child and welcome him with the majesty and grace of a twenty-year-old king, which is what you are'.[160] However, while she encouraged Charles to take up the royal mantle, she did not retire from her son's court, where her authority was visible long after he ceased being a minor. She influenced appointments to his inner circle: when a new master of the household was needed in 1571, for example, the post went to Antoine de Sarlan, master of her own household.[161] Advancing one's own nominees into positions of power had long been a useful means of acquiring influence, and Catherine exploited it with much success. Among other favourites she promoted were Albert and Pierre Gondi, sons of her close friend Madame du Perron. After a successful military career, and an advantageous marriage which brought him the title of comte de Retz, Albert was nominated as *Premier Gentilhomme de la Chambre*, head of the king's chamber, in 1566 and acted as Charles IX's proxy at his wedding with Elisabeth of Austria. Pierre took the ecclesiastical route and in 1570 became archbishop of Paris and *Grand Aumonier* (almoner) to the new queen.

Catherine seems to have had little difficulty in relinquishing her ceremonial role as first lady to her daughter-in-law, but she was reluctant to give up the perks of the job. Her household, which numbered 334 at this period, was the same size as that of the queen.[162] She avoided moving out of her luxurious apartment at Fontainebleau by having a new set of rooms built for Elisabeth.[163] Above all, she showed no sign of giving up her position at the centre of power. She remained a prominent figure in Charles IX's council and continued to add her own letters to his diplomatic correspondence, reinforcing the widespread belief that her son preferred hunting to the business of government. There was some justification for her lack of faith in his political skills, especially in the summer of 1571 as tensions between Catholics and Protestants escalated alarmingly and threatened the survival of the treaty signed at Saint-Germain the previous year.

Although grateful for the edict's favourable terms, few Protestants were reassured by Charles IX's order requiring government officials across France to implement it; they queried how far the crown would go to enforce the peace in the face of a Catholic majority set against it. Moreover, Protestant rhetoric had begun to turn against the crown: when kings defy God 'they are no longer worthy to be counted as princes', Calvin had argued.[164] To Catholics the treaty was a betrayal: 'we defeated them again and again ... but the edicts are always to their advantage' was Monluc's response, typical of many hardliners.[165] Nor were they reassured by Charles IX's order and made their own plans to counter the Protestant threat, not all of which were on the right side of the law. Rumours of plots to assassinate the Protestant leadership continued to circulate at court; and Catholics across France openly voiced their opposition to crown policy by joining confraternities set up with the explicit aim of exterminating the new religion.[166] Particularly popular were those dedicated to the Holy Ghost which required each member to swear an oath that, when called to do so, they would take up arms in defence of their faith as new crusaders against the infidel – and against the laws of their king.

Catherine's response to the mounting tension was to redouble her efforts to reconcile the two sides though, as we shall see, she was badly hampered by her inability to prevent her actions, which were viewed through the prism of suspicion, from being misinterpreted. Moreover, the political situation had unwelcome ramifications at a personal level. As religious tensions mounted, so too did the increasingly rancorous relations between her sons Charles and Henri. While the king was determined to enforce the Peace of Saint-Germain, his brother overtly proclaimed his anti-Protestant credentials; and the contrast between the sickly king, whose wife showed no signs of pregnancy after nine months of marriage, and the duke, a gallant military hero, spoke volumes.

For the cornerstone of her policy of reconciliation Catherine decided on Protestant marriages for two of her children: Henri to Elizabeth I of England and Marguerite to Henri of Navarre. It was an audacious plan, foolhardy even, and from the first it roused fierce Catholic opposition, not least from Pius V, who was not pleased that negotiations were now broken off for the betrothal of the princess and Philip II's nephew, the king of Portugal. Jeanne d'Albret, too, was against the union but Elizabeth was willing at least to listen to the French proposal, and Catherine inflamed Catholic passions even further by using ex-cardinal Châtillon to act as her go-between at the English court. Henri himself refused to consider the match and made his opposition known publicly in January 1571; nevertheless, Catherine continued to negotiate, ignoring her son's views or, more likely, hoping that she could persuade him to change his mind with the temptation of another crown. In March she wrote to Bertrand de Salignac, marquis of La Mothe-Fénelon, who was her ambassador in England, to inform him 'that everything has changed and that my son infinitely desires to marry the queen of England'.[167] That July she sent Elizabeth two portraits of

Henri, one a full-length figure and the other of his head. As she explained in a letter to the envoy, the first portrait did not look like Henri at all but the second 'is very beautifully and perfectly done'.[168]

That same month Catherine courted more controversy when she and Charles IX met with Louis of Nassau, the leader of a group of Dutch Protestants based at La Rochelle, who had signed an alliance with Elizabeth I to conduct a naval campaign against Spain. They were gaining control of the English Channel, but French support was critical for victory. The talks were supposed to be highly secret. One of the issues under discussion was the partition of the Netherlands between the allies if they successfully liberated the provinces from Spain, which would return Artois and Flanders to France. Despite the secrecy, ambassador Alava heard rumours that 'the king has taken the side of the Protestants completely', as he reported to Philip II, and he warned Catherine that any alliance against the king would lead to war with Spain.[169]

Catherine had been complaining about Alava's behaviour for years. Back in 1567 she asked Fourquevaux to tell Philip II that he was 'impertinent and remote from the bounds of reason'; in February 1571 she cited his capacity for invention, accusing him of misreporting conversations he had had with her and the king.[170] She must have been hugely relieved that summer when Philip II announced that the ambassador was to be replaced. She held her last audience with him in early August and when he left she asked Fourquevaux to convey to Philip her 'great pleasure' at his departure, repeating her complaints that he 'persists daily' in peddling his 'lies and slanders'.[171]

In early September, with Alava's departure imminent and the Guise clan still in disgrace, Catherine made another move to placate the Protestants and invited admiral Coligny to return to court. In spite of a warning from Jeanne d'Albret that he was walking into a trap, Coligny accepted the royal summons and was treated with great respect by both Charles and

Catherine when he arrived at Blois. He was paid over 35,000 écus (100,000 livres) to cover losses he had incurred during the recent war as well as the income due on the benefices of his brother, Odet de Châtillon, who had died in March.[172] As proof of his princely status, the king granted him the privilege of an escort of fifty noblemen and, most importantly, readmitted him to the council. For the Catholic faction this show of Protestant favour was a step too far. Amid rumours of more plots to assassinate him, Coligny left after just five weeks, despite assurances from Catherine and the king that he would have royal protection. Jeanne also received an invitation to come north for discussions about the forthcoming betrothal of her son Henri, but she kept deferring her departure, reluctant to leave the safety of Navarre.

In the hopes of engineering an end to the Coligny–Guise vendetta, Charles IX also invited Henri of Guise and his relatives – though not his uncle the cardinal of Lorraine – to return to court, a move that certainly contributed to Coligny's decision to leave.[173] The Florentine ambassador was scathing about this naive optimism that a meeting between the two sides would solve the vendetta and claimed that things in France were worse than ever. The situation worsened, not helped by the fact that, while Charles IX enjoyed his hunting, Catherine fell seriously ill in late November. The court was rife with rumour and conspiracy: the diplomatic correspondence was filled with reports not only of Guise schemes to assassinate Coligny but also of their plans to seize the throne for Henri of Anjou.[174]

As tensions mounted at court, religious rage fuelled by preachers of both faiths gave rise to mob violence on the streets in towns and cities across France. The king was at Amboise for the Christmas–New Year holiday when trouble erupted in Paris over a Christian cross, erected by the Catholics to mark the site of a house on the rue Saint-Denis that had belonged to two Protestant noblemen, Philippe de Gastines and his son, who were executed for holding religious services there.

However, the Peace of Saint-Germain required the demolition of all monuments commemorating Catholic victories over Protestants and the king asked for this cross to be removed, an order which the city authorities evaded until forced to act; it was taken away during the night of 20 December 1571 and re-erected in the cemetery. The riots that broke out the next day were bad enough for governor Montmorency to be obliged to bring troops into the city to control the rampaging mobs. The unprecedented scale of the violence was a sign of the level of Catholic fury, but it did nothing to change crown policy.

9

St Bartholomew's Day
1572

Catherine was in Paris in August 1572 for the wedding of her daughter Marguerite to Henri of Navarre, which was to be celebrated in the presence of the royal family, princes of the blood and the nobility, Catholic and Protestant, gathering together in the capital for the first time for some years. She had planned a series of splendid 'magnificences' for the occasion, with the expert assistance of the members of Jean-Antoine de Baïf's *Académie de poésie et de musique*, and with her sons Charles, Henri and François as well as Henri of Guise, Henri of Navarre and the groom's cousin Henri of Condé among the performers.

On 20 August, two days after the ceremony itself, the guests assembled in the great hall of the Bourbon palace to watch a masque entitled 'Paradise of Love', a performance that marked a new stage in the development of that distinctively French form of dance, music and poetry known as the *ballet de cour*.[1] Carefully choreographed to express Catherine's hopes for peace and reconciliation between the two faiths, it carried the same political message as the marriage itself. It began with Charles IX, assisted by Anjou and Alençon, defending the castle of Paradise and its nymphs from attack by Navarre and his team of knights, who were all defeated and thrown into Hell, where they were tortured by flames, in the form of dancing demons. Mercury, god of Eloquence and Reason, performed by the famous castrato Étienne le Roy, descended from Heaven with his pupil Cupid, god of Love, to sing and dance with the nymphs, who, in the spirit of reconciliation, persuaded the king to release the knights from their torment. The entertainment finished with a spectacular fireworks display; two days later the celebrations were brought to an abrupt end by a violent event which was to have even bloodier repercussions.

Tensions in Paris, already high after the riots sparked by the removal of the Gastines cross in December, had mounted unchecked through the spring and early summer of 1572.[2] There was anger at the mounting tax burden to pay for the recent war and rising prices had begun to cause real hardship. There was growing resentment at the opulent extravagance of the court and at the excessive profits made from tax-farming by bankers, many of whom were Italians and from families who owed their position to Catherine's favour. She was becoming a figure of hate on the streets; one of her protégés, Pierre Gondi, had been made archbishop of Paris, an unpopular choice in the city, where anti-Italian emotions ran high; one rumour accused them of murdering innocent children to obtain blood to cure Catherine from some malady.

The violence of the Parisian mob was directed above all at Protestants, in flagrant contravention of the edict signed at Saint-Germain. The Catholic preacher Simon Vigor stoked up hatred in his sermons, denouncing the edict: 'this is not peace,' he ranted, 'but blasphemy'.[3] In February the mayor had to order those living or working on the Pont Notre-Dame to stop vandals smearing filth on two houses on the bridge which were rented out to Protestants while Charles IX ordered the *parlement* to be stricter in prosecuting anti-Protestant rioters.[4] Later that month, in his sermon for Ash Wednesday,

Vigor warned his audience against violence, that killing was illegal unless ordered by the king but, ominously, 'if the king ordered [Coligny] killed, it would be wicked not to kill him'.[5]

At court, too, the religious rift was deepening. The rivalry between Charles IX and his popular brother Henri showed no sign of abating; and Henri had begun to make a point of proving his Catholic credentials with ostentatious shows of piety. The Guise–Coligny vendetta continued to divide the court. In late January, amid rumours of a Guise conspiracy to remove Charles from power and place Henri on the throne, Henri of Guise petitioned the king to rescind the declaration of Coligny's innocence which Charles had issued at Moulins in January 1566, and charge the admiral again with the murder of the old duke, a request that was firmly rejected by the king's council at the end of January.[6] Charles then banned the Guise clan from returning to court unless they agreed to end the vendetta, which they refused. He also took steps to protect Coligny, ordering him to stay away from court and offering him protection in case of an attack by Guise and his Catholic supporters.

Above all, Catherine's determination to reconcile Catholics and Protestants by forging links between the faiths caused tensions to escalate further at court, and in Paris where the cornerstone of her policy – Protestant spouses for her son and daughter – was especially unpopular. Although negotiations for the marriage between Henri and Elizabeth I had stalled, that between Marguerite and Henri of Navarre – originally mooted when they were children – was back on the agenda. It was being talked about in the summer of 1571 when several diplomats reported, somewhat ahead of the game, that the betrothal had been formalized. Jeanne d'Albret continued to refuse her consent to the match but Catherine was determined otherwise and, with the help of Albert Gondi, had started to shop for jewels for Marguerite's trousseau; as she informed the king, her daughter 'will be as honourably provided for as her sisters, and with less expense'.[7] It is also possible that one of the reasons for heaping favours on Coligny that autumn was to ensure Protestant support for the project. One envoy reported a meeting between Catherine and Coligny, who explained Jeanne's reasons: she was as suspicious of the crown's motives as he himself had been, to which Catherine replied the queen had 'less reason to be suspicious than you because she cannot believe that the king would be trying to arrange the marriage of his sister and her son only to do him harm'.[8]

Eventually Catherine persuaded Jeanne to give her consent and in February the queen arrived at Blois to negotiate the betrothal. Embarrassingly, after all the work of persuading her to come to court, Catherine was unable to receive her at the castle because of the presence of envoys from Pius V. In the end Jeanne was received by Catherine at Chenonceau and spent a few days there getting to know her prospective daughter-in-law before returning to Tours to await the depart-ure of the envoys. It is an indication of just how desperate Pius V was to stop the marriage that three of his men were at Blois all loudly voicing their opposition. In mid-December he had appointed Cardinal Antonio Maria Salviati, a distant cousin of Catherine's, as nuncio to France with orders to oppose the marriage and complain about the favours being shown to Coligny. Salviati was followed on 7 February by Cardinal Michele Bonelli, the most senior member of the pope's entou-rage, and two days later by Francisco Borgia, head of the Jesuit order, who joined the official envoys at Blois to reinforce Pius V's message.[9] Bonelli, in particular, had arrived at Blois from Lisbon, where he had secured the promise of the Portuguese king to wed Marguerite; he also brought an offer from the pope of 4,000 Spanish troops if Charles IX would call off the wedding and declare war on the Protestants.[10] To no avail: Bonelli and Salviati left on 25 February having failed to secure either objective.

The difficulties surrounding the marriage were many and complex. As Marguerite and Henri were second cousins, the union infringed the laws of consanguinity; but the real hurdle, of course, was religious. Catherine and Charles had asked Pius V for a dispensation, a sign of papal approval that was a political necessity if the marriage were to be recognized by many French Catholics. The pope refused unless Henri converted to Catholicism and threatened to declare him illegitimate and thus ineligible for the throne of Navarre, on the grounds that his mother's marriage was invalid. Catherine asked both Cosimo I and the cardinal of Ferrara to intercede on her behalf, to no avail. Fortunately for her, Pius V died on 1 May and his successor Gregory XIII, elected a fortnight later, chose a less bigoted agenda.

On 2 March the queen of Navarre arrived at Blois, where Charles IX made a point of greeting her warmly in person, for several tough weeks of negotiation. It was five years since Jeanne had last been at court and she was appalled by what she saw. In letters to Henri, who was recuperating from a riding accident, she described her shock at the scheming, intrigues, gossip, decadence and frivolity: it was 'the most vicious and corrupt atmosphere imaginable,' she wrote, 'although I knew it was bad, I find it even worse than I feared'.[11] She was particularly horrified by the lack of piety among the Protestant nobility, adding 'not for anything on earth would I have you come to live here'. Jeanne's letter also conveys the energy and determination with which Catherine refused to contemplate her primary demand, that Marguerite must become a Protestant. Catherine's belief that neither bride nor groom needed to convert posed its own problems: how would Henri behave when the couple were at court, where Protestants were banned from practising their religion; would Marguerite be able to hold mass when she was in Navarre, where Jeanne had 'cleansed her country of all idolatry'?[12] Jeanne was reluctant for the marriage to take place in Paris as was the custom for a royal princess because the capital was notorious for its intolerance towards the new religion.

Above all, there was the minefield of devising the form of

the service itself which had implications for any children of the union: many Catholics did not recognize the legitimacy of offspring born to couples married according to Protestant rites, and vice versa. In the end political priorities won through: in exchange for the wedding taking place in Paris, Catherine and Charles conceded the Protestant requirements for the form of the service and the contract was signed on 11 April, though Jeanne died of tuberculosis on 9 June, before it took place. In view of what happened later, it is worth noting that there was no mention of poison in any of the diplomatic correspondence, though the nuncio celebrated her death as 'a great proof of God's almighty power'.[13] Ten days later, after hearing that Coligny was also ill, he wrote 'it is possible that God will also remove him'.[14] It was a prescient hope.

That spring several events occurred on the international stage that would have important implications for France. On 9 April, Charles IX signed a treaty with Elizabeth I at Blois, both sides agreeing not to assist the other's enemies; although a purely defensive pact, it was viewed with suspicion in Spain. Henri of Anjou having refused to marry a Protestant, Catherine had hopes of a match between her youngest son, François, and Elizabeth to guarantee the pact, but the queen was reluctant to comply – the duke of Alençon was just seventeen, twenty years her junior, and scarred by smallpox. Another event bringing the prospect of war ever closer occurred in early April when news arrived of the capture of the port of Brill at the mouth of the Meuse by the so-called Dutch Sea Beggars (in French, *les gueux de mer*), a motley collection of men, largely Protestant exiles from the Netherlands, based at La Rochelle under the leadership of Louis of Nassau. They had had some success raiding Spanish ships in the Channel, and had seized a large sum of money intended for Alba's army; but their capture of Brill marked the start of a revolt against Philip II's rule in the Netherlands that was to spread rapidly over the coming months. By the end of July the rebels had taken most of the provinces of north and south Holland, including the cities of Haarlem, Leiden, Gouda, Delft, Rotterdam and Dordrecht.

The rebels urgently needed foreign aid to consolidate their position. Elizabeth I was reluctant to get involved, fearing war with Spain and the potential of a Catholic uprising in England that could precipitate the loss of her throne to her cousin Mary Stuart. Instead they looked to France, and to Coligny, who was under an obligation to honour the treaty he had signed with Orange and Nassau in August 1568 and repay them for the help they had given the French Protestants in the recent war. Loyal to the crown, Coligny sought Charles IX's approval for the venture, if not his active involvement. It is unclear exactly what the king promised but Catherine, who was absent from court in April, returned to voice her opposition to the plans, which she worried would provoke war with Spain and destroy her hopes for peace.[15]

Since his marriage Charles IX had begun to act on his own initiative; perhaps the knowledge that his queen was three months pregnant gave a boost to his self-confidence. Despite his mother's opposition he persisted with the project, offering at least covert support to the rebels. In a confidential letter to Nassau, dated 27 April and entrusted to Coligny's son-in-law Téligny, he promised to help liberate the Netherlands from Spanish rule, though with the proviso: 'I am determined to do so as far as the disposition of my affairs permits.'[16] At the same time, he asked Jean de Vivonne, seigneur of Saint-Goard, who had recently replaced Fourquevaux as his ambassador in Spain, to inform Philip II that he did not intend to aid the rebels.[17] A fortnight later he informed his envoy in Constantinople that 'all my thoughts are turned to resisting the might of Spain' and he was equipping ships 'nominally to protect my coasts against the pirates, but in reality to harass the Catholic king and to encourage the *gueux* in the Netherlands to advance'.[18] Nassau, who had been conferring with Charles in Paris, left on 15 May with a small force of Flemish exiles and French Protestants to cross the border and capture Mons, while another force, led by François de La Noue, took Valenciennes. Alba reacted with characteristic vigour, demanding written assurances from Charles IX of his neutrality; he warned the French envoy in Brussels, Claude de Mondoucet, of serious consequences if any of the invaders were found to be French nationals.[19]

Catherine must have been happier at her son's efforts to encourage reconciliation between his Protestant and Catholic subjects. Earlier that month he persuaded Henri of Guise to end his vendetta with Coligny, at least to make a show that their quarrel was over. Coligny returned to court on 6 June in time for the state visit of an embassy from Elizabeth I which was in Paris to ratify the treaty signed at Blois in April – marshal Montmorency crossed the Channel to do the same on behalf of the French crown. Catherine was unwell, and received the envoys 'in a wastecote from her bed'.[20] It was a priority to accommodate Protestant sensitivities: at the official ratification ceremony in the church of Saint-Germain, the English envoys were seated away from the altar in a side chapel though they could evidently hear what was going on: Sir Thomas Smith, one of the envoys, was highly complimentary about the 'very good musick'.[21] The other festivities for the visitors were less contentious: there were fireworks, bonfires and banquets, including one in the garden at the Tuileries, though the sight of more extravagance on the part of the court, and for the entertainment of Protestants, fuelled the unpopularity of the crown in the capital.

Another problem was the Protestant revolt in the Netherlands which needed help and Nassau sent one of his captains, François de Hangest, seigneur of Genlis, for talks with the king. Genlis arrived in Paris on 23 June and three days later the king's council met to discuss Coligny's formal request for French troops to assist the rebels. The council voted overwhelmingly against any form of intervention, though this masked the wide divergence of opinion. The moderates in the council, of which we can assume Catherine was one, might have intervened on behalf of the rebels but feared it would provoke war with Spain; given the strength of the Spanish army, and the weakness of the French, this fear was not unfounded.[22] 'It cannot be denied that the subjects of the Netherlands feel oppressed by the harsh and rigorous treatment by the duke of Alba', Catherine's ally Jean de Morvillier advised, but to risk war with Spain without the full commitment of both Elizabeth I and the German Protestant princes was unwise.[23] For ultra-Catholics, by contrast, it was unthinkable to help the Protestants: the view of the increasingly influential circle around Henri of Anjou. They included several Italians, protégés of Catherine's though they did not share her moderate views, notably Albert Gondi, comte de Retz, who was firmly pro-Spain, as was Ludovico Gonzaga (aka Louis de Gonzague), third son of the duke of Mantua, who had arrived at the French court at the age of ten and, with Catherine's favour, had married Henriette of Clèves, wealthy heiress to the duchy of Nevers.

The situation was not helped by Charles IX's lack of political nous, but he did face a dilemma: to support Coligny and the rebels in the Netherlands was to risk outright war with Spain, a war that he was likely to lose, and, very possibly, his throne as well. A refusal to support the admiral would bring a decisive end to the policy of reconciliation that he and Catherine had been at such pains to promote; and probably Coligny would go to the aid of his allies anyway, which would also lead to war with Spain. In July the talk in Rome was that Charles intended to support Coligny, a rumour the king asked François de Ferrals, his resident at the papal court, to refute. That same day Catherine wrote to Gregory XIII to assure him that her son did not want war with Philip II: 'I have the honour to be the mother of one and the mother-in-law of the other,' she wrote and criticized 'those who want your holiness to believe that the king my son could want to make war against his brother the king of Spain'.[24] She also sent a letter in a similar vein to Saint-Goard in Spain.[25]

Nevertheless, Charles IX did not desist either in his efforts to assist the Protestant rebellion, or in his efforts to deny his involvement. On 12 July, Genlis left Paris for the Netherlands with 4,000 men and 600 cavalry; less than a week later Catherine and Morvillier were proved right when, much to the jubilation of ultra-Catholics across Europe, Genlis was humiliatingly defeated by Alba's troops.[26] In itself this might not have been a problem, as it was evident that Genlis had disobeyed orders; but the Frenchman was also carrying letters implicating the king directly in this strike against Spain and these were confiscated when he was taken prisoner. In public Charles insisted they were forgeries; he wrote to Mondoucet in Brussels admitting that he had given his consent for Genlis's operation, 'nevertheless [you will tell the duke of Alba] these are lies invented to excite his suspicion against me'.[27]

By late July, however, it became clear that Charles IX's priority was the policy of reconciliation enshrined by Catherine in the Peace of Saint-Germain, which was to be guaranteed by the marriage of Marguerite and Henri of Navarre, but they were still waiting for the papal dispensation. In late July the cardinal of Lorraine, who had been in Rome since the conclave in early May, informed Catherine that Gregory XIII was as against the marriage as his predecessor had been: 'the difficulty is in the religion of the king of Navarre' and in the anti-Catholic policies the king was implementing in his realm.[28] Both Catherine and Charles suspected the cardinal of obstructing the process deliberately; the Spanish ambassador in France, Don Diego de Zuñiga, was certain he was doing everything possible to delay the process and therefore the marriage. Given the urgency of the situation, they decided to ignore the lack of a papal dispensation and fixed the date of the wedding for 18 August.

However, in the interests of reconciliation Charles X continued to offer Coligny his covert support for the Netherlands campaign despite a meeting of his council on 9 August which reaffirmed its opposition to any form of intervention on behalf of the Protestant rebels. Zuñiga informed Philip II that the king's support would remain secret, though Elizabeth I's resident in Paris, Sir Francis Walsingham, had a conversation with Coligny in which the admiral confirmed that the king had granted most of his demands.[29] By the middle of August, with the guests assembling in the capital for the wedding, it was clear that Coligny had the king's permission to fight though not in his name; as he informed Orange, he had an army of 12,000 infantry and 3,000 cavalry ready to assist the prince and their departure was fixed for the week beginning 25 August, after the festivities were concluded.[30]

The atmosphere in Paris on the eve of the royal wedding was oppressive. The weather was swelteringly hot and food was getting more expensive: the price of wheat, for example, had risen by 30 per cent since the beginning of July.[31] Jubilation at Genlis's defeat had soon been drowned by rumours that Charles IX had given Coligny permission to wage war against Alba in the Netherlands. The Parisians detested Coligny; they had not forgotten, or forgiven, his siege of the capital in 1567 and were apprehensive about his plans for the 15,000 Protestant soldiers gathering not so far from the capital; and their own governor, marshal Montmorency, had been helping Coligny to muster his troops.[32] Above all, stirred by Vigor's sermons, they disapproved of the forthcoming marriage and the crown's policy of reconciliation.

Catholic fears increased with the news that not one but two interfaith marriages were to be celebrated that month. On 10 August the wedding took place at Blandy-en-Brie between the Protestant prince of the blood Henri of Condé and his first cousin Marie of Clèves, sister of the duchesses of Guise and Nevers. It too went ahead without a papal dispensation despite the close degree of consanguinity and their religious differences. Significantly Charles IX attended the ceremony in person, though few Catholic nobles joined him. A week later the Protestant nobility were in Paris for the royal wedding and rumours spread that they were planning trouble as well as illegally holding their own services in the capital. Simon Vigor reviled Protestants as 'spiritual lepers', warning his audience they risked contamination and urging them to 'exterminate them all'.[33] It was to prove a toxic mix.

The wedding took place on a dais erected at Notre-Dame and was a masterpiece of compromise. To preserve the fiction that negotiations for the dispensation were still ongoing in Rome, and to avoid the untimely arrival of an outright rejection from the pope, which would have seriously complicated the situation, Catherine halted all couriers travelling from Italy from 14 to 18 August.[34] Jeanne d'Albret had agreed that Cardinal Bourbon could conduct the ceremony providing he was dressed in his everyday vestments and not his full cardinal's regalia; Bourbon himself worried that he would be excommunicated for disobeying papal orders and Catherine had to work hard to persuade him to take part.[35] After the wedding he celebrated nuptial mass inside the cathedral but only after Henri of Navarre had left the scene 'in as conspicuous manner as possible in the sight of all'.[36] Parisians were scandalized to see the groom's refusal to attend this key rite, where he was represented by Henri of Anjou.

Over the next few days, while the court enjoyed the parties to celebrate the marriage, Catherine found time to write several letters dealing with affairs of state. On 19 August she wrote to Gregory XIII reassuring him on behalf of herself and the king 'of all the devotion and obedience that you desire of us'; and asked again for the dispensation, repeating her belief 'that this marriage is necessary for the health and repose of this realm'.[37] Two days later she asked La Mothe-Fénelon to arrange a meeting between herself and Elizabeth I to discuss the proposed marriage with François, to take place at sea 'on a beautiful calm day, between Boulogne or Calais and Dover'.[38] The following morning, Friday 22 August, there was a meeting of the king's council, chaired by Henri of Anjou, which neither Catherine nor Charles attended; Coligny was present and walked home afterwards to his lodgings in the rue de Béthisy* nearby. In view of what happened next, one could question why he was on foot and unarmed in a city swarming with people for whom he was a figure of hate. Suddenly a musket shot rang out, fired from an upper window. The sniper missed his target; Coligny, who seems to have unexpectedly bent down at the crucial moment to tie a shoelace, was not hit in the chest but the shot severed a finger of his right hand and wounded his left arm.

Nobody could have anticipated what was to happen next. The failed attempt to assassinate Coligny was the prelude to one of the most shattering events in the history of France.

It was not hard to identify the window from which the sniper had taken aim and two servants arrested in the house revealed that it had been rented by a Guise ally. It later emerged that the would-be assassin was Charles de Louviers, seigneur of Maurevert, who also had links with the Guise family. A page in the household of Henri of Guise's father, he had also been responsible for shooting one of Coligny's lieutenants, Artus de Vaudray, three years earlier. Significantly, from 1573 onwards he received a large annual pension from the duke of over 650 écus (2,000 livres), paid each year on the anniversary of Coligny's death.[39] There is no doubt that the Guise family had wanted to get rid of Coligny ever since the assassination of the old duke in 1563 and while it might have been as

---

* The rue de Béthisy disappeared in 1854 with the building of the rue de Rivoli and the rue du Pont-Neuf.

simple as that, it probably was not: as I shall show below, other explanations were to emerge in the aftermath of the massacre. More importantly at this point, whoever was behind the plot to kill Coligny, the key point is that it failed; and it was this failure that was the essential precursor to what followed. If it had succeeded then it is likely that the rest of the Protestant leadership would have fled the capital to muster troops for another civil war. As one French historian eloquently summarized, 'what happened next has been obscured by controversy and passion'.[40]

There was panic when the news reached the Louvre around midday. Many connected the shooting to the Guise–Coligny vendetta, and Charles IX, writing to La Mothe-Fénelon later that day, referred explicitly to 'the hostility between the house of Coligny and Guise'.[41] Fearful that the attack might lead to reprisals, he took measures to increase security in Paris and, with Catherine, sent letters to his provincial governors asking them to abide by the terms of the Edict of Saint-Germain and to punish all acts of violence against Protestants.[42] That afternoon secretary Villeroy went to Coligny's lodgings, where the admiral had been taken, and reported that the wound was not serious.[43] In a further show of support, the king offered to accommodate Coligny at the Louvre but he refused, so Charles ordered the captain of his guard to arrange protection for the wounded man in case of further violence. Later that day Charles and Catherine also visited Coligny, as did Anjou and other senior courtiers.

During that day Henri of Navarre, Henri of Condé, Charles de Téligny, La Rochefoucauld and other Protestant leaders all sought audiences with Charles IX, demanding that he must punish those responsible. The king agreed to their requests and appointed Christophe de Thou, a lawyer and a leading figure in the *parlement* of Paris, to lead an official inquiry into the matter.[44] However, several diplomats related that the Protestants had acted in a particularly aggressive manner, insisting that they would take matters into their own hands if

Charles did not do as they demanded. It was not the behaviour expected of a subject to his sovereign: as one reported, it was 'an attack on the king's dignity'.[45]

Charles IX summoned his council to discuss the situation, possibly as early as Friday but certainly on Saturday. The records of these meetings, conveniently, have not survived, so what was discussed and who was present remains a matter of speculation. One account mentions a meeting of the king's inner circle, which included Catherine, Henri of Anjou, Henri of Guise, the duke of Nevers, marshal Tavannes, the comte de Retz and René de Birague, who was Keeper of the Seals as well as chancellor in all but name (he would acquire this title in 1573, after the death of Michel de L'Hospital), the majority of whom did not share Catherine's hopes for reconciliation.[46] What we do know from official sources is that late on Saturday evening Charles summoned the mayor of Paris to an audience at which it became clear that he had abandoned Coligny and taken up a very different position. He informed the mayor 'that he had been warned that those of the new religion intended to mount a conspiracy against his majesty and his state and disturb the peace of his subjects and this city of Paris'.[47] The attack, in which Protestant troops would seize the royal family and take control of the Louvre, was planned for the next day, Sunday.[48] He may or may not have told the mayor that he, with the backing of his council, had decided to counter this threat by eliminating not only Coligny but the entire Protestant leadership.

We can only speculate about the arguments that persuaded the king to make such a spectacular U-turn. Was there even a plot? There were rumours in Paris that Protestants were planning reprisals for the attack on Coligny, with the aid of Téligny's 4,000 troops garrisoned outside the capital.[49] How would staunchly Catholic Parisians react if one of their number was charged with the admiral's murder, especially their hero Henri of Guise? Would the king's continued support for the Protestant cause provoke a revolt against the crown?[50] Did the ultra-Catholics in the council, who were determined to change the pro-Protestant direction of crown policy, convince Charles IX of the existence of a plot against the crown to eliminate the new religion? Or perhaps the king's change of heart was brought about by the aggressive and disrespectful behaviour of Coligny's colleagues the previous day. We know that Jean de Morvillier, who was committed to the policy of reconciliation, was horrified by the decision, though his loyalty to the crown obliged him to accept it. He had urged Charles to be sure the crown had proof of the conspiracy before acting and apparently wept when it became clear that a majority of the council would vote for this brutal measure.[51] For Catherine, too, it was her duty to stay loyal to the crown, even though it meant the end of the policy of toleration which she had worked so hard to promote.

The attack on the Protestant leadership, which was to take place early on Sunday morning, was planned meticulously. In his audience with the mayor the previous evening, Charles IX ordered him to set guards at the city gates 'so none might go in or out', to immobilize all boats on the Seine and to arm the city's militia; he also gave orders to the soldiers guarding Coligny's lodging not to resist any royal troops entering the building.[52] Each target was located and assigned to one of the squads of troops led by senior nobles: Henri of Anjou, Henri of Guise, Claude d'Aumale, the duke of Montpensier and Henri of Angoulême, the illegitimate son of Henry II.[53] Before dawn on Sunday the soldiers began their butchery, the attacks co-ordinated by the ringing of the bells of the church of Saint-Germain-l'Auxerrois at 4 a.m. on the king's orders. The honour of killing Coligny was given to Guise's men, who threw the admiral's corpse out of the window onto the rue de Béthisy where it was identified by the duke, while others pursued the admiral's companions attempting to escape; some seventy-two Protestants were murdered, among them Téligny and La Rochefoucauld. Those Protestants with rooms in the Louvre were taken from their beds and butchered by the guards in the courtyard below.[54] The lives of the two young princes of the blood, Navarre and Condé – the bridegrooms – were spared but they were arrested and forced to recant their faith.

What no one seems to have anticipated is how dramatically the violence would spread beyond the premeditated strike planned in the king's council and engulf Paris in an orgy of slaughter and savagery on an unprecedented scale that lasted for three days. Charles tried to stem the violence by ordering everyone off the streets, but the order was ignored, though some Catholic nobles gave shelter to Protestants fleeing from the mob. La Rochefoucauld's son found safety with Louis de Lansac, one of Catherine's courtiers, who would become her *chevalier d'honneur* in 1573.[55] One Protestant who escaped from the city hid with marshal Montmorency at Chantilly.[56] Henri of Guise hid several Protestant children in his house, including the daughter of Michel de L'Hospital.[57] But they were among the lucky few: the Protestant noble who sought sanctuary in Walsingham's house was discovered by the mob and the English ambassador was forced to hand him over to be executed.[58] In a ruthless drive to rid the city of the contamination of the new faith, men, women and children were killed indiscriminately; and not just killed but butchered like animals, their corpses dumped in wells or thrown into the Seine in a ritual of purification that also saw Protestant houses burned to the ground.[59] Coligny's corpse was beheaded and castrated, dragged through the mud and finally hung on the public gibbet at Montfaucon, where it was burned at the stake.

That the general butchery was not part of the plan became clear that Sunday morning when the mayor returned to the Louvre to complain that the royal troops were taking part in the killing.[60] We will never know exactly what sparked off the riots. Perhaps the tocsin rung from Saint-Germain-l'Auxerrois alerted others to join in the killing; perhaps it was Henri of Guise's words to encourage his squad of soldiers on the street outside Coligny's lodgings: 'it is the king's command', he is supposed to have said, words that echoed the sermon given by preacher Vigor just a few months earlier, that it would be wicked not to kill Coligny if the king ordered it.[61] Fuelled by the anti-Protestant sermons of their preachers and boiling with fury at the favour their king was showing to the new religion, the Parisian mob reacted instinctively to the sight of royal troops killing Protestants on the orders of the crown and rampaged through the streets killing anyone known or suspected of Protestant sympathies.

Despite the warning letters sent by Charles IX and Catherine to the provincial governors asking them to take measures to avoid violence, the butchery spread rapidly to towns outside Paris. By sunset on Sunday 24 August the wholesale massacre of Protestants had begun at La Charité-sur-Loire, one of the surety towns given to the Protestants as part of the 1570 peace treaty; by Wednesday it had spread to Meaux, Bourges and Orléans, where as many as 1,500 bodies were thrown into the Loire; by the end of the week the violence had engulfed Angers, Saumur and Lyons; and the killings spread further afield in September and October, to Troyes, Rouen, Bordeaux, Toulouse and Gaillac.[62] Significantly, all had sizeable Protestant minorities and the massacres were Catholic revenge for the harsh treatment dealt out to them by the Protestants who had taken charge of these cities during the first civil war.[63] As in Paris, the butchers thought they were doing the king's bidding, a message opportunely spread by ultra-Catholic nobles to their estates and territories.[64] It is difficult to be certain about how many died. Contemporary accounts invariably exaggerated the figure for political effect: François Hotman, a Protestant lawyer and historian who fled Bourges to escape the massacre, claimed that 50,000 had been killed in the first eight days.[65] Modern scholars have estimated 2,000–3,000 were killed in Paris, with another 3,000–7,000 in the provinces, maybe as many as 10,000 victims in all.[66]

✤

The news of the massacre sent shockwaves across Europe. For Protestants it was a disaster and many feared for the survival of the reformed faith. In the Netherlands it dealt a savage blow to their hopes for their revolt against Spanish rule. In England fears about a Catholic uprising designed to place Mary Stuart on the throne took on a new significance and Elizabeth I had second thoughts about the wisdom of her marriage to Alençon.[67] At the Catholic courts of Europe, by contrast, the news was greeted with jubilation and they celebrated this crushing victory with fireworks, bonfires and, above all, with special masses. Philip II hailed it as 'one of the greatest joys of my entire life' and asked his ambassador to congratulate Catherine on 'the satisfaction which I feel for an act of such value to God and to Christianity'; the ambassador himself, in Paris, celebrated by dressing his servants in bright red cloth.[68] For Alba there was relief at the sudden removal of the threat posed by Coligny's planned invasion of the Netherlands. In Florence the diarist Agostino Lapini recorded on 14 September 'a mass of the Holy Ghost was sung in the cathedral as a sign of the great happiness' at the slaughter.[69]

In Rome the cardinal of Lorraine, who had spent the summer at the papal court, had an audience with Gregory XIII on 2 or 3 September at which, according to the bishop of Imola, 'he asked the pope what news he would most like to hear; and the pope replied "the extermination of the Protestants" and the cardinal replied that that was what had happened'.[70] Lorraine held a service of thanksgiving to celebrate the massacre at San Luigi dei Francesi, the French national church in Rome, which was attended by the pope and thirty-three cardinals.[71] Three months later Gregory commissioned the Florentine artist Giorgio Vasari to paint three frescoes commemorating the event in the Sala Regia: *The Wounding of Coligny*, *The Slaughter of the Protestants* and *Charles IX ratifies the death of Coligny in Parlement*, which carried the eloquent inscription 'the king approves the murder'. This grandiose hall in the Vatican, reserved for the reception of kings and princes, was appropriately decorated with scenes celebrating the supreme authority of the papacy over secular rulers. Vasari's depiction of the massacre made a telling point about Catholic attitudes to the new religion: the royal soldiers were depicted as classical heroes, while their victims were outlandish barbarians, so uncivilized that they even lacked helmets and swords.[72]

In France the mood was sombre. Although many Catholics celebrated their victory, the massacre was a disaster, above all for the policy of reconciliation. The future was uncertain: the nightmare scenarios were an invasion by Alba that would trigger war with Spain or a revolt against the crown itself.[73] The urgent priority was to exculpate the crown of complicity in the massacres taking place across France. The official version coming out of the Louvre was careful to describe what had happened as three separate events: the failed attack on Coligny, which was blamed on one of the admiral's many enemies, such as Henri of Guise and his relatives, or Philip II and the duke of Alba, none of whom had made a secret of their desire to have the admiral killed; the execution of the Protestant leaders, guilty of high treason, for which the king himself took responsibility; and the massacres, a disaster which he had tried hard to stop.

This was the message Charles IX gave when he attended the Paris *parlement* on 26 August, where he also expressly confirmed the Edict of Saint-Germain to make it clear that his actions had not been directed at Protestants in general. The high treason theory was also the explanation given by Catherine and the king to ambassador Walsingham in an audience on 1 September.[74] In early September, Charles IX commissioned a pair of medals to confirm this 'truth', celebrating the failure of the Protestant plot in a depiction of the king as Hercules slaying the many-headed Hydra.[75] Acting on the instructions of his king, the French resident in Basel gave a colourful description of the Protestant leaders gathering at Coligny's bedside on 23 August to plot the assassination of Henri of Guise, 'even if it were at the king's feet', a deliberate act of lese-majesty.[76] A week later, this story developed further: in a letter to Gaspard de Schomberg, his ambassador to the German princes, Charles claimed that Coligny had become 'more powerful and more obeyed by those of the new religion than I was'. [77] As he added, 'I could no longer call myself absolute king.'.[78]

Catherine's letters in the weeks following the massacre show that she, too, was busy transmitting Charles IX's version of events to courts around Europe, and her words were carefully chosen depending on the recipient's religion. Writing to Philip II on 28 August, she thanked God for giving 'the king the means to get rid of those subjects who were rebels to God and to himself', for the benefit 'of all Christianity and to the service and honour and glory of God'.[79] Her words gave the tacit impression that she had cleared up a nest of heretics; to Protestants, by contrast, she was explicit that Charles IX had cleared up a nest of traitors. To Elizabeth I, via ambassador La Mothe-Fénelon, she explained that 'the king my son being well aware from experience and seeing clearly in the papers of the admiral after his death ... that they were planning the establishment of a second king in [my son's] realm and many other evil projects and ideas against him'.[80] She asked the ambassador to stress her message by assuring the queen of her intention 'to maintain with sincerity the edict of pacification and to allow the exercise of the [Protestant] religion in this realm'.

What do we know about Catherine's role in the horrendous chain of events that unfolded in Paris that August? One problem is the glaring lack of official sources: there are no minutes of the meetings of the king's council, for example.

Witness accounts of the events often make only hazy distinctions between fact and rumour, though all agree that Catherine and her sons did visit the wounded Coligny in his lodgings on the afternoon of 22 August. As a leading member of the council we can assume she attended the meetings that took place on Saturday 23 August which resulted in the decision to eliminate the Protestant leadership; and the mayor's account of his meeting with the king lists her as present in the audience chamber at the Louvre late that evening when Charles IX ordered him to lock down the capital. We also know that the king himself publicly took responsibility for the murder of the Protestant leaders when he addressed the Paris *parlement* on 26 August. Official sources may have been largely silent on her role but the diplomatic bags, by contrast, were bursting with information.

Despite Charles IX's determination to present his 'true version' of events, foreign envoys were much more interested in the colourful rumours that were circulating at court. They were quick to conflate all three episodes into a single event: it was easier to cope with the enormity of what had happened by merging them into a single premeditated conspiracy. What is striking is how quickly Catherine herself emerged as its author. The papal nuncio Cardinal Salviati had reported on 22 August that the attack on Coligny had been the work of the Guise family; five days later, however, his finger was pointed at Catherine, who, so he claimed, had planned to kill the admiral because she was insanely jealous of the influence he had over the king.[81] Salviati further claimed that she 'intended not only to revoke the edict but also to restore the Catholic faith'; moreover that she and the king had arranged for the murder of all the Protestant chiefs.[82] The Spanish ambassador Zuñiga too reported this jealousy motive, arguing that she had convinced the king to eliminate all the Protestant leaders after the attempt on Coligny failed.[83]

According to the Venetian ambassador Sigismondo Cavalli, Catherine had persuaded her son to act by convincing him of 'the great opportunity God had given him to free himself from these plagues'.[84] Similarly, an English account in early September stated that Catherine 'with her loving and motherly persuasions began to inform the king that the admiral did hate the king and herself' and that 'the authors of this monstrous bloodshedding' were the queen mother, Anjou, Nevers and Tavannes.[85] More succinctly, the other Venetian envoy Giovanni Michiel informed the doge that she had been motivated by her hatred of Protestantism: 'this entire affair was, from start to finish, her doing – conceived, hatched and conducted by her, with as sole participant, her son Henri of Anjou.'[86]

Catherine's guilt was soon visible in the paintings and prints of the massacre that appeared across Europe. One widely copied painting was a composite scene depicting all three episodes by the Protestant painter François Dubois, an exile who had not witnessed the massacre.[87] The setting was clearly identifiable by Paris's landmarks: the church of the Grands-Augustins and the windmill on Mont Saint-Geneviève on the left bank, and the fortified gatehouse of the Louvre across the Seine, with Coligny's lodgings nearby.[88] In the foreground the admiral's corpse was being thrown out of the window to be identified by Henri of Guise on the street below; there are bands of armed soldiers attacking the Protestant leaders, and Parisians killing men, women and children. In front of the Louvre is the stout figure of Catherine, dressed in her usual black, presiding over a pile of naked corpses.

Catherine's role was confirmed in the pamphlets and histories that appeared in the aftermath of the massacre, as well as in personal memoirs of the events of 22–24 August by Catholics and Protestants alike. Within weeks of the news arriving in Rome, Camillo Capilupi published *Lo stratagema di Carlo IX*, heaping praise on Catherine for the success of her long-planned policy to exterminate Protestantism in France; few followed his example.[89] The Protestant author of *Le tocsin contre les massacreurs* (1577) outlined her evil influence at court and her egotistical ambition for power, likening her to Jezebel, the biblical whore and witch with a taste for cruelty.[90] The owner of a print of Catherine annotated it with 'Thais', 'Medea' and 'Circe', the names of three famous sorceresses of classical antiquity which, the owner pointed out, could all be spelled from the letters of 'Catharine Medices'.[91]

Catherine's own daughter, writing many years after the event, accused her mother of orchestrating the murders though, in Catherine's defence, the relationship between the two of them was to become very difficult in later years.[92] Marshal Tavannes included an account of the events of that August in his memoirs and he, too, incriminated Catherine, blaming her excessive ambition for power and her unreasonable jealousy of Coligny though, once again, this 'witness account' needs to be seen in the context of personal animosity.[93] The memoirs were actually written long after the event by Tavannes's son, who was not a fan of Catherine, nor of Anjou and the Italians, Nevers, Retz and Birague, whom he accused of complicity in the plot. By far the most offensive account was a biography of Catherine, the *Discours merveilleux de la vie, actions et deportemens de le reyne Catherine de Medicis, Royne-mere* (the wondrous discourse of the life, deeds and behaviour of Catherine de' Medici, queen mother), first printed in 1575.[94] Although the first edition seems to have been written by a Catholic, by 1576 it had become a Protestant tract and a bestseller, running into many editions as well as translations into English, German, Latin and other languages.

The *Discours merveilleux* was unprecedented in its vitriol, reviling Catherine as a woman and as a foreigner, consumed by her presumptuous and insatiable ambition for power and prepared to sacrifice anyone who stood in her way.[95] Its prime object was spelled out in the subtext, which was to show 'all the means she used to usurp the government of the kingdom of France and to ruin it'.[96] This 'monstrous woman' was not just Italian, she was Florentine, a term deliberately redolent of the cunning of Machiavelli; moreover, she was a Medici, 'quintessence of Florentine wickedness', a family of corrupt tyrants who cared nothing about committing adultery, incest and murder to get what they wanted; worst of all, a jibe at the family's mercantile origins, they were obsessed with money. Catherine was responsible, so the *Discours merveilleux* claimed, for deviating French politics from its true path. The rivalries that split the court after 1559 were the result of her uncontrolled fury, malicious deceitfulness and love of sowing discord. Her orchestration of the events surrounding the events of 22–24 August, from the murder of Coligny to the massacres, was the culmination of years of diabolical scheming. She murdered her way to power, poisoning Francis I's eldest son, François, in 1536 to become dauphine and queen; then, after the death of her husband Henry II 'for whom she did not cry long', she killed her own sons in pursuit of the throne and used her devious talents to amass power for herself. The book describes how she plotted with her Italian allies at court to poison the Protestant army and, though this failed, she successfully ordered the assassination of Louis of Condé after the Battle of Jarnac. She was even accused of killing the queen of Navarre in June 1572, with a pair of gloves steeped in poison, and then of covering up the crime by refusing to allow an autopsy, though the diplomatic bags at the time carried not a single rumour that Jeanne had died of anything other than natural causes.[97] Catherine herself reportedly read the wild accusations recounted in the *Discours* but dismissed them – much as a modern celebrity might dismiss hate mail on social media today.[98]

Catherine's reputation for evil continued to mushroom after her death: the lurid claims in the *Discours merveilleux* inspired countless authors over the centuries. Christopher Marlowe included the story of the poisoned gloves in his play *The Massacre at Paris*, which was first performed in London in January 1593, just two decades after the event. It also made its way into Alexandre Dumas' *La Reine Margot* (1845), a novel based on the life of Catherine's daughter Marguerite, in which Catherine is depicted as a power-crazed, overweight mother, one of the greatest monsters in history, whose court was notorious for debauchery. The nineteenth-century artist Édouard Debat-Ponsan's image of the morning after the massacre showed Catherine coldly surveying the bodies of the Protestants she had had murdered, a chilling contrast to the horror etched on the faces of her ladies-in-waiting. And her reputation has been further entrenched with the film *La Reine Margot* (1994), based on Dumas' novel, and the Amazon television series about Catherine herself, *The Serpent Queen* (2022).

Few modern authors bother with the voices raised at the time in Catherine's defence. One of these was the loyal abbé Brantôme, who insisted that, far from being 'the instigator of all our wars', she had in fact 'spent her pains and labour in striving to extinguish them, abhorring to see so many of the nobles and men of honour die'.[99] On the St Bartholomew's Day massacres, he stuck to the story promoted by the crown, blaming 'three or four' unnamed people who 'made her believe ... that the king was to be killed with her and all her children', a plot which had to be forestalled.[100] Another supporter refuting the wild claims of the *Discours merveilleux* was the poet Jean-Antoine de Baïf, who dedicated a book of poems to Catherine, describing her as 'the most dignified and most virtuous princess' and celebrating her role as royal peacemaker.[101]

After four centuries of heated debate on the issue, some modern scholars have finally begun to question the assumption of Catherine's guilt.[102] One makes the cogent point: 'far from seeing Charles IX and Catherine de' Medici as responsible for the massacre, on the contrary I would make them the first victims.'[103] The argument that Catherine was so insanely jealous of Coligny's influence over the king that she arranged his murder is far from convincing: the admiral was at court for a matter of just five weeks between the summer of 1568, the start of the third war, and June 1572.[104] Moreover, why would she plan to eliminate the Protestant leaders after a wedding that had been negotiated with such difficulty in order to unite the two sides? The accusations make a mockery of her stubborn determination over the past two decades to pursue a policy of toleration and conciliation, in the face of considerable opposition both at home and abroad, designed specifically to avoid violent confrontation between Catholics and Protestants. Catherine was, above all things, loyal to the crown; for me the succession of events in August 1572 only make sense if she believed sincerely that the crown was under threat.

Truth, however, matters little here; what is important is how it was perceived at the time. It is crucial for Catherine's story to understand that the massacre of St Bartholomew's Day* marked the point at which she became a figure of hate in France. Denounced as the wicked queen, she was blamed for masterminding the failed attack on Coligny and the brutal elimination of the Protestant leaders, as well as for the unspeakably cruel murder of thousands of innocent men, women and children in the days that followed. In the aftermath of the killings her reputation underwent a sea change as both Protestants and Catholics turned against her. In particular, she was no longer trusted by Protestants who feared that her policy of toleration had been merely an attempt to lure them into a trap; they believed that her political allegiance was with the pope in Rome and with Spain, a rumour that had been festering ever since 1565 when they were excluded from the meeting at Bayonne. The Massacre was a watershed moment in the history of France; for Catherine, it would colour and dictate much of what happened to her in the last decades of her life.

---

* To avoid the cumbersome repetition of the full title I shall follow Joseph Bergin, the translator of Jouanna's book on the events of St Bartholomew's Day, and refer to them simply as the Massacre.

10

Jealousies
1572–1577

As the horrendous events of the Massacre caused mayhem at court, Catherine must have been cheered by one positive piece of news: the pregnancy of her daughter-in-law the queen was progressing smoothly and she was expected to give birth later in the autumn. Although no final decision would be made until the child was born, Catherine began to think about godparents for the prince or princess. The choices were significant: they would reflect her political priorities, and those of the French crown, in the aftermath of the Massacre. On 23 October she wrote to La Mothe-Fénelon, the French ambassador in England, suggesting that Elizabeth I should send high-ranking courtiers – she mentioned the earl of Leicester and the treasurer Lord Burghley – to Paris to attend the queen's confinement.[1] 'I also desire you,' she asked him, 'using as much subtlety and dexterity as you can, and without mention of the king my son or myself', to find out how the queen would react if asked to be godmother.

The baby, born on 27 October, was named Marie Elisabeth; three days later Catherine announced to Philip II that the queen had given birth to 'a beautiful girl, both are in good health, God be thanked'.[2] To her aunt Renée of France she was more candid: 'although it is not a son, I hope that now it has started there will be both sons and daughters.'[3] The christening on 2 February 1573, the Feast of Candelmas, was attended by the entire court though the papal nuncio was absent, apparently 'indisposed'.[4] Possibly his malady had more to do with the choice of godparents: empress Maria, the baby's grandmother, and Duke Emanuele Filiberto, two staunch Catholics; the third was Elizabeth I, who had sent William Somerset, earl of Worcester, to represent her at the ceremony.

Rome and Madrid had greeted the Massacre with wild enthusiasm, taking at face value Catherine's explanation that it had been the king's decision to execute the Protestant chiefs and, significantly, her reassuring news that 'the king of Navarre has returned to our religion' – with no mention that the alternative had been the death penalty.[5] By the autumn, however, Gregory XIII and Philip II had realized that, far from eliminating the new religion and joining their Catholic alliance, Catherine and Charles IX had no intention of doing so; indeed, they refused to abandon their policy of entente with Europe's Protestant leaders. In late August, before he knew of the Massacre, Gregory XIII appointed Cardinal Flavio Orsini as legate to Charles IX with instructions to negotiate a closer alignment between France and Rome in order to implement the reforms of the Council of Trent and to prevent war between France and Spain. Soon after leaving Rome in early September he was informed by a royal courier that the king would not receive him, obliging Orsini to take refuge in the papal city of Avignon. Eventually, after much discussion, the cardinal was allowed to proceed north to Paris but when he arrived in late November he had to wait a fortnight before Charles gave him an audience – and was then asked to leave France immediately.[6]

In her desire for reconciliation between the two religions,

Catherine now took steps to repair the damage done to relations with the Protestants. Although intolerant of those who
rejected the authority of the king, she made a point of offering public support not only to loyal Protestants but also to
moderate Catholics who supported her efforts towards peace.
One of these was Montmorency's brother Damville, the governor of Languedoc, who reported in late September that he
had received a letter 'from the king whose wish and intention
is none other than to keep and maintain his edict'.[7] Abroad
she made plans for alliances with Protestant rulers with offers
of marital ties. In Spain, where Jean de Vivonne, seigneur of
Saint-Goard, had replaced Fourquevaux as ambassador earlier
that year, she suggested a betrothal between her son Anjou
and Philip II's daughter Isabella (her granddaughter). She
also hoped to tempt Elizabeth I into an alliance; not only did
she invite the queen to be godmother to the baby princess,
she also continued to press Elizabeth to agree to marry her
son Alençon. In early September she asked La Mothe-Fénelon
to assure the queen of her 'earnest desire for peace' and suggested a meeting between the queen, Alençon and herself,
which could take place at sea 'on a good day'; a few days
later she suggested that if the queen did not like that idea of
meeting at sea then perhaps Jersey or Guernsey 'which are her
possessions' would be better.[8] She took advantage of Marie
Elisabeth's christening to have extensive discussions with the
earl of Worcester on the subject.[9]

In a further sign that Catherine had no wish to align France
exclusively with Catholic Europe – and, it must be said, to
gratify the regal ambitions of Anjou – she nominated him as
a candidate for the Polish throne, vacant since July and the
death of the last of the Jagiellon dynasty. This election had a
significant political context: not only did the Poles insist on
neutrality towards the Turks, they also wanted a ruler who
would be tolerant of the country's sizeable Protestant minority, a policy enshrined in the country's constitution. The other
candidates, some ten in all, included Tsar Ivan the Terrible of

Russia, King Johan III of Sweden and Duke Alfonso of Ferrara, the eldest son of Renée of France and cousin to Henri of Anjou. Anjou's main opponent was the Habsburg archduke Ernst of Austria, whose candidacy was supported by two very influential figures: Emperor Rudolf, who was his brother, and Gregory XIII, whose priority was to halt the spread of Protestantism in northern Europe.

Catherine appointed one of her trusted allies, Jean de Monluc, bishop of Valence, to lead the delegation lobbying for Anjou. A well-known Protestant sympathizer, Monluc was an astute choice; Pius V had declared him a heretic and deprived him of his benefices, though she had protected him from prosecution and continued to address him as 'Monsieur de Valence'. Monluc left Paris on 17 August, a week before the Massacre, but was arrested at Verdun on suspicion of being a Protestant. He was freed thanks to Catherine's influence: she apologized for his inappropriate treatment, assuring him that he was valued as a loyal servant and urging him 'to continue your journey as we desire you to do'.[10] She was lavish in providing funds for Monluc's campaign, forwarding large sums via the French ambassador in Venice, Arnaud du Ferrier: in February, for example, he sent 10,000 écus to Poland.[11] Much of Monluc's campaign focused on scotching the rumours that Anjou had been directly involved with the Massacre. He wrote a pamphlet, *Vera et brevis descriptio*, which was printed in Cracow in 1573, to refute the claim.[12] Purporting to give a 'true' account of the events of August 1572, it repeated the official line that the king had taken the decision to execute the Protestant chiefs in order to forestall a conspiracy and he blamed the duke of Guise for the violence that followed.[13]

Despite the lurid rumours sweeping Europe in the autumn of 1572 that enormous numbers of Protestants had been butchered by bloodthirsty Catholics, it has been estimated by some modern scholars that only some 5,000 lost their lives in the violence.[14] Some of the huge drop in the Protestant population was due to those fleeing France to find sanctuary in Germany, England and the Netherlands, but by far the greatest loss were the thousands who defected back to the Catholic fold in its aftermath: many in Rouen, for example, voiced their belief that the massacres had been a sign of God's anger.[15] However, the rumours encouraged Catholics to believe that they had put an end to the heresy, with unfortunate results. Although weakened by death and emigration, as well as the elimination of their leaders, the Protestants were far from defeated. Moreover, in a direct response to the crown's admission of guilt in the killings, they began to question the nature of the loyalty they owed to the king. Several towns with Protestant majorities rebelled: La Rochelle, for example, refused to allow Charles IX's governor, Armand de Gontaut, baron of Biron and a marshal of France, to enter the city. In Languedoc Protestants replaced the cumbersome royal administration with local councils run by elected majors (*majeurs*), which were subject to a general assembly elected to take decisions regarding the province as a whole. Significantly, this move was supported by Languedoc's governor, marshal Damville, who lobbied hard with Catherine and sent an envoy to court 'to represent the state and disposition of affairs on the other side'.[16]

In November 1572, with his authority under threat, Charles declared war on the rebels, focusing his efforts at La Rochelle, which was soon under siege by the royal army, led by the twenty-one-year-old Anjou, assisted by marshal Biron, the port's unwelcome governor, to make up for the duke's youth and inexperience. In early 1573 Catherine fell ill: as she explained to Philip II, 'I cannot write in my own hand because of my indisposition'.[17] However, she kept up with affairs of state: on 10 January she wrote to Pomponne de Bellièvre, the French envoy to Switzerland, about raising 6,000 soldiers for the army and a week later thanked him for his services to the

king who 'is rightly extremely pleased with you, and is more
and more aware of the dexterity with which you execute his
intentions'.[18]

In early February 1573 Catherine wrote to ambassador du
Ferrier in Venice to arrange for letters of exchange for 10,000
écus for Jean de Monluc in Poland; this was in addition to
20,000 écus which had already been sent to oil the electoral
process.[19] There was a scare in the middle of February when
Catherine wrote to Monluc in Poland reporting rumours
heard from England that the Poles had decided to offer the
crown to archduke Ernest and she asked the bishop to stress
her son's toleration of Protestantism in contrast to the archduke's ultra-Catholic position.[20] She seemed to be getting
better but towards the end of February she had a relapse:
Anjou was informed on 22 February that 'for the last two or
three days she has been in great pain but is better, thanks be
to God', but 'she does not leave her room and, although she
was dressed and her hair done this morning, nevertheless she
is following her doctor's orders'.[21]

One of Catherine's worries that winter was the worsening relations between Anjou and his seventeen-year-old
brother, François, duke of Alençon, a rivalry that also involved
three other young bloods, all senior nobles: Henri of Guise
(twenty-two), and the two Bourbon princes, Henri of Navarre
(nineteen) and Henri of Condé (twenty). Navarre and
Condé, who had been forced to abjure their Protestant faith,
were proving their loyalty to the crown – and, reluctantly, the
Catholic cause – by fighting in the royal army; it was the first,
and the last, occasion when all five men would serve together
and the enmities, which were to play such an important role
in French history, were already evident. As Catholic figurehead, Anjou was conspicuous in his observance of his religious
duties and, to Catherine's horror, had appointed the Jesuit
Edmond Auger as his spiritual adviser. Auger's presence in
the camp no doubt antagonized Navarre and Condé as well as
Alençon, who was increasingly the focus of those of moderate

views. For these three, the priority was less victory over the Protestants at La Rochelle but a chance to foment rebellion against Charles IX and Anjou.[22]

It must have come as a shock to Catherine to realize quite how much her sons hated each other. Less than a month after the siege began, she wrote to marshal Cossé to thank him for the effort he was making to improve relations between Anjou and Alençon.[23] A week later she wrote to the duke of Montpensier, another of her allies at the camp, 'knowing how much [the king] and his brothers love and respect you', asking him to intervene 'as a father' to stop them quarrelling and to make Alençon understand that 'if his brother were to be wounded what heart that would give to the enemy and what disorder would it bring to the kingdom'.[24] It was not just the quarrels between her sons that worried Catherine: war was dangerous and on 8 March Duke Claude of Aumale, Henri of Guise's uncle, was killed by a cannonball. His death 'has so frightened me that I dread bad news of my children', she wrote to the duke of Nevers a few days later.[25] The following month it was the king who was injured: as she informed Anjou, 'your brother was badly hurt during a boar hunt' though he was recovering, and she added: 'I pray to God to guard you from a greater wound.'[26]

By the middle of March 1573, Catherine herself had re-covered from her illness and left Paris for Fontainebleau but the news from La Rochelle was not encouraging. The port was under fierce attack from the land by the royal army but without control of the sea it was impossible to mount an effective blockade of the city. This became clear in early April when the Venetian ambassador, Sigismondo Cavalli, reported that the French navy was forced to retire after the arrival of an English fleet of thirty-five ships and over a thousand men under the command of the count of Montgomery. The count was well known in France, where his career at court had been abruptly halted in 1559 when his lance caused the death of Henry II and he had been forced to seek refuge in England, where he converted to Protestantism.[27] Anjou's efforts to enforce the siege were made all the more difficult by the state of his army: estimates suggest that 10,700 of his men were killed or wounded during the fighting, and that more were lost through illness and desertion.[28] There was also the looming threat of financial disaster as it became ever harder to raise the huge sums needed for the war – it has been estimated that this siege cost the crown 180,000 écus a month (500,000 livres).[29]

However, Anjou's failure to defeat the Protestants was matched by their inability to defeat the royal army. Faced with military stalemate, in early May Catherine sent a secretary to La Rochelle to open peace negotiations; these became all the more urgent at the end of the month when news arrived from Poland that Anjou had been elected king. Monluc's campaign to exculpate the prince of any link with the Massacre had been highly successful but Anjou, fighting Protestants at La Rochelle, still had to give a formal promise that he would allow freedom of worship for both faiths throughout his new realm. Catherine also warned him that Auger was busy spreading the rumours that 'you have promised to eradicate all [Poles] who have ever been Protestant', rumours that 'are doing great damage'.[30]

Catherine was inordinately proud of Henri and his new status – it was widely believed that he was her favourite: she wrote an emotional letter to him that June telling him of her love for him, her desire for him to achieve 'the foremost in majesty, honour and reputation', her pride that 'at the age of twenty-one you have already shown yourself to be a great military leader' and her hopes that, by winning a victory at La Rochelle, he would be 'the restorer and conservator of the realm'.[31] She ended with a request that he should no longer sign his letters to her as 'your most affectionate servant because I want you to love me as a son and to recognize me as the most affectionate mother you could ever have'.

The siege of La Rochelle ended on 6 July, thanks not to the military prowess of her son as Catherine had hoped but the result of tough negotiations. Anjou did not surrender but it was a moral victory for the Protestants, whose defence of the port had lasted five long months. However, the Edict of Boulogne,* signed on 11 July 1573, certainly looked like a victory for the Catholics. In the aftermath of the Massacre, Protestants found their freedoms were severely curtailed: although they were granted freedom of conscience, they were only permitted freedom of worship in three towns (La Rochelle, Montauban and Nîmes) and then only in the privacy of their own homes. It is a mark of just how divisive the issue was that Philip II was reported to be infuriated by the concessions made; the Protestants themselves saw it quite differently and chose, where they could, to ignore the royal edict.[32]

The following month an official embassy from the Polish government arrived in Paris to complete the formal process of declaring the succession of Henri of Anjou as the new king. Catherine reported the news to ambassador La Mothe-Fénelon 'to let you know that the twelve ambassadors from Poland followed by two hundred gentlemen arrived in this city last Wednesday with a sufficiently impressive retinue'.[33] The visitors, equally divided between Catholics and Protestants, and tired after their long journey, requested to delay their audience with 'the king, my daughter-in-law and myself', which was rescheduled to the Friday. Catherine was optimistic that they would complete the outstanding issues relating to the election in a few days, but it was not until 9 September that Henri, after much prevarication, finally signed all the relevant documents including his promise to guarantee freedom of worship to his new Protestant and Catholic subjects alike.

On 14 September, Henri made his formal entry into Paris

---

* It was signed at the royal palace in the Bois du Boulogne, also known as the château of Madrid.

as king of Poland and the following day Catherine entertained the Polish envoys in regal style with a banquet at the Tuileries, a spectacular ballet and a lavish supper: a 'beautiful and grand ceremony', as she herself described it.[34] The banquet took place in a pavilion, where the guests listened to music from a band led by the Italian violinist Baldassare di Belgioioso (better known by his French name Balthasar de Beaujoyeux) and, according to one of the Polish envoys, the singing of 'a lady with an extraordinary and very graceful voice'; he also noted how fortunate they were not to be outside as it was pouring with rain.[35] For the envoy, as for all the guests, the highlight of the evening was the ballet, devised by Beaujoyeux as dancing master and the French poet Jean Dorat, who published a description of the event (*Magnificentissini spectaculi ... in hortis suburbanis*) later that year, which he dedicated to Catherine, who, all sources agree, was not only the patron but also the creative mind behind the event.[36]

Catherine herself chose the dancers who played the 'nymphs' that represented the sixteen provinces of France, selecting ladies of noted beauty from her own household as well as those of her daughter Marguerite and her daughter-in-law the queen, and the nobility of Paris.[37] The ballet opened with the Nymph of all France, played by a castrato, probably the famous Étienne Le Roy, singing verses by the poet Ronsard.[38] Then the nymphs, dressed in exquisite costumes, 'formed themselves into a little battalion' and, to the music of Beaujoyeux's violinists, danced a routine 'so curiously designed, with so many twists and turns, swerves and sinuosities, weaving and mingling, meeting and pulling back, that it was a surprise no lady lost her place', recorded an astonished Brantôme.[39] He judged it 'the most beautiful ballet in the world': it was certainly a major achievement in the history of dance.[40]

The ballet gave Catherine a stunning medium with which to promote her political agenda and, unlike other 'magnificences', she did not elaborate on the theme of religious reconciliation, which anyway was not relevant in the Polish context.[41] Using themes from Virgil and other classical authors, she boasted her pride in Henri's achievement, the military hero who, with his brother, had created a Valois empire in Europe. She herself was hailed as fertile Cybele, 'mother of three gods' and the dynasty's protector. The final poem spoke of her joy at his glory but her sadness at his imminent departure. This was real enough: in all likelihood she would never see him again. 'In my heart I am crying,' sang the Nymph of France, but duty came first: she understood that her pain was of no significance and she was strong (male) enough to hide her emotions (female) for the greater glory of the Valois.

Catherine had been busy with the practical aspect for Henri's departure ever since news of his election arrived in late May. On 3 July, the day after the siege of La Rochelle ended, she reminded him that 'now peace is signed you need to concentrate on ... mustering the four thousand soldiers that you have agreed to send to Poland ... and to arrange for ships to transport them'; it was 'very necessary' for the soldiers to embark 'on 12–15 August'.[42] Her bossy, controlling tone must have been irritating though presumably Henri was grateful for her readiness to take on his more tedious duties. She arranged free passage for those going to Poland, writing to Elizabeth I and the kings of Denmark and Sweden for permission for the troops to sail through the English Channel and the Baltic; she had to ask Philip II to allow the royal party to cross his territories, a favour which had proved impossible to obtain in Brussels, where, according to ambassador Mondoucet, the duke of Alba 'has never replied a single word to me and his visage shows a continuation of the same ill will'.[43]

Most importantly, there were constitutional matters to arrange in case Charles died. This was a very real possibility; although only twenty-two, he was in poor health and suffered from frequent fevers, coughs and other infections symptomatic of tuberculosis; moreover, his wife showed no sign of pregnancy a year since the birth of her first child. For the moment it was Henri who was next in line to the throne. Catherine feared that if Charles died while his brother was in Poland, then Alençon might attempt a coup, so she persuaded Charles to make a public declaration that Henri was his legitimate heir. The prospect of Henri's absence also bothered many of his courtiers; for them life at the centre of power, even in a minor household, was infinitely preferable to royal exile in distant Poland. The cardinal of Lorraine went so far as to propose sending a viceroy to Poland instead; and there were rumours that Henri himself was very reluctant to leave France.[44]

Henri finally left Paris on 28 September with Catherine and Charles escorting him on the first stage of his journey. The cavalcade was impressive with huge numbers of pack animals laden with crates and chests packed with tapestries, carpets, silver for his dining table and his chapel, bed linen and table linen, furniture, jewels and extravagant outfits. Catherine spent over 29,000 écus (40,205 livres) on jewels and silverware for her son, much of it bought from Parisian goldsmiths.[45] His retinue was equally regal as befitted his new status: gentlemen and servants of his chamber, five chaplains, an almoner, a priest and a doctor, pages in green and yellow livery, secretaries, cooks, 200 soldiers, and so on; in all some 1,500 horses had to be found for the journey.[46]

Catherine tried to exert her control over Henri's courtiers, with limited success. He had his own views on the senior nobles: he chose two dukes of the Guise family (Mayenne and Elbeuf) but refused point-blank to take any of the Montmorency clan, whom he viewed as Protestant by association, though he did include Henri of Condé, who was a prince of the blood despite his Protestant ties. Catherine did not trust many of Henri's inner circle, notably René de Villequier, whom she suspected of delaying her son's departure – ironically she herself had appointed him to Henri's household a decade earlier.[47] She did have three other allies in the suite, all Italians:

Nevers (Ludovico Gonzaga), Retz (Alberto Gondi), who was first gentleman of the chamber, and abbé Gadagne (Battista Guadagni), her Florentine almoner.[48] Retz in particular benefited from her patronage: that July he had been rewarded with the post of marshal and now received a huge pension worth over 146,000 écus (420,000 livres); by contrast Villequier, who was senior valet and a favourite, received only 3,500 écus (10,000 livres).[49] Two other appointments gave her a further measure of control over her son: the new ambassador to Poland was Bellièvre, a diplomat with the ear of both herself and Charles, while Philippe Hurault, seigneur of Cheverny and another of her allies, remained at court to take charge of Henri's French affairs.[50]

The cavalcade made slow progress towards the frontier, stopping at Montceaux and Villers-Cotterêts, and on 9 November it reached Vitry-le-François, a small town south of Châlons-en-Champagne founded by Francis I some twenty years earlier to replace one destroyed by the imperial army in 1544. Here Charles IX fell ill: 'I find myself somewhat ill-disposed with a cold', and decided to rest at Vitry 'to take some purgation which I hope will get rid of it'.[51] Henri, however, needed to continue his journey and two days later, with Catherine and Alençon, was back on the road leaving the royal council, the secretaries and the diplomatic corps behind with the king, who expected to rejoin them in a few days, a wish that proved optimistic. Fortunately, Charles's illness was not serious: by 22 November news reached Catherine that he was on the mend, well enough to give audiences to foreign ambassadors and take charge of affairs of state.

Catherine, who was now at Nancy staying with her daughter Claude and son-in-law, the duke of Lorraine, warned Charles, in a letter full of maternal admonishments, not to do anything 'I beg you, without the permission of the doctors'.[52] A few days later they left for Blamont, a town near the frontier where Catherine deputized for Charles at a meeting with the Protestant leaders Louis of Nassau and Johann Casimir, son of elector Friedrich III, at which she promised to provide them with funds and 'to embrace the affairs of the said Netherlands as much and as far as the Protestant princes may wish'.[53] As ambassador Cavalli astutely reported, 'it is not easy to understand the exact scope of these conferences', of which this was the first, 'but it seems likely that their majesties are desirous to come to an arrangement with England and Germany and thus make peace with their own Protestants'.[54]

After a tearful farewell to Henri, Catherine left Blamont on 4 December to return to Charles: ambassador Cavalli reported that 'the chancellor and members of the council are in despair at the absence of the queen mother because her majesty has to be informed of every matter of importance', and that Charles IX 'has written to his mother and entreated her to return as soon as possible'.[55] Riding with all possible speed, it took her just six days to cover the 165 miles from Blamont to Rheims, where the court was now staying, en route for Saint-Germain-en-Laye, where they celebrated New Year and Carnival.

The year 1574 did not start well for Catherine. If she had hoped that Henri's departure would put an end to the rivalries between her sons, she was to be disappointed: it merely exposed the differences between Charles and Alençon. The figurehead of moderates and Protestants at court, Alençon wanted the crown to take a more pro-Protestant line in foreign policy; the crown – or, rather, Catherine – was determined to avoid any public move that would annoy Philip II, and at worst provoke war with Spain. In January, with the project to betroth Alençon to Elizabeth I foundering, Catherine and Charles agreed to appoint Alençon to the lieutenant-generalship, vacant since Henri's departure. It was a naive decision and provoked much ill-will at court, where the ultra-Catholics feared it would give moderates like marshal Montmorency undue influence with the king; and they warned of what Alençon might do as commander of the royal army.

In mid-February, just days before the appointment was announced, one of Alençon's courtiers was attacked by Henri of Guise, who claimed the man had been paid by marshal Montmorency to kill him. Charles's response was immediate: taking Guise's side, he sent Montmorency from court and gave the coveted post of lieutenant-general to Duke Charles of Lorraine, his brother-in-law but also Guise's cousin. What had begun as a means to placate Alençon was now a public relations disaster, and one that secured Alençon's position at the head of a new generation of nobles as vendetta-prone as their fathers: the two Bourbon princes, Henri of Navarre and Henri of Condé as well as marshal Montmorency and his three younger brothers, Damville, Charles, seigneur of Méru and Guillaume, seigneur of Thoré.

The fiasco of the lieutenant-generalship was to have more serious repercussions. In late February reports reached Saint-Germain that Protestant troops had been seen near the castle and were planning to rescue Alençon and Navarre from their 'imprisonment'. The king ordered the court to move to the château in the Bois de Vincennes, south-east of Paris, a heavily fortified stronghold, used only rarely as a royal residence by Francis I or Henry II.[56] Catherine and the king also challenged Alençon about the rumour: viewed by contemporaries as ambitious, unscrupulous and deceitful, he was a tricky character but silver-tongued where his mother was concerned.[57] He persuaded her that the plot had been aimed at Guise, not the king, in revenge for the duke's attack on his man a fortnight earlier. Ambassador Cavalli claimed that Alençon admitted to mustering troops to fight the Spanish in the Netherlands not the crown; 'but it is not easy,' he continued 'to say whether his statements were in conformity with his intentions' or not.[58] He was not punished, nor was Navarre, though they were asked to sign a declaration of their loyalty to the crown and their movements were closely monitored.

Despite the failure of his first coup, Alençon continued to scheme and in early April rumours of another, more serious plot against the crown reached Catherine. Charles was ill and, according to one report, he was to be abducted from his sick bed while the court was at mass on Maundy Thursday (8 April); Alençon would then escape with Navarre and, with the help of Protestant troops, seize his brother's throne.[59] Again Alençon persuaded his mother of his innocence and remained at liberty with Navarre though still under surveillance; but this time more was known about the plotters. After a meeting of the king's council, it was decided to imprison Alençon's supporters, mostly moderate Catholics; marshal Montmorency and his cousin marshal Cossé were put in the Bastille, though his brother Damville escaped after being warned that an arrest warrant was on its way south. Two members of Alençon's household were punished more severely: his chamberlain Joseph de Boniface, count of La Mole, and the captain of his guard, the Piedmontese Annibale Radicati, count of Coconat, were both charged with treason, found guilty and executed on 30 April.

Days later Charles, who had been ill most of April, suffered a severe haemorrhage. Ambassador Cavalli reported that an Italian astrologer, Cosimo Ruggieri, had been detained under suspicion of 'having bewitched the king'; many assumed he would be executed 'and all Paris believes that after his death the king will recover'.[60] It was not to be: Charles's health declined precipitously and he died on 30 May 1574, aged only twenty-three. For Catherine it was not only a personal tragedy but also a political nightmare. Although Alençon's recent plots had all been unmasked, there was the ever-present fear of another, especially in the weeks before Henri (or Henry III as we must now call him) returned to claim his throne. Her priority was to secure the succession and shortly before he died Charles summoned Alençon and Navarre to his bedside to declare in their presence: first, that Henri of Anjou was his legal successor, and second that Catherine was to act as regent until he returned from Poland.

There are no letters from Catherine dated the day of Charles's death, though she did order one of her courtiers to leave immediately for Poland. The following day she sent another courier to Poland, by a different route, carrying a long letter for Henry.[61] 'Yesterday I sent Chémerault to you bringing the woeful news,' she wrote, 'I pray to God that he will send death to me before I have to see any more of my children die.' But she was proud of the manner of her son's death: 'nobody has ever died with more good sense, speaking to his brothers, the cardinal Bourbon, the chancellor, the secretaries, the captain of the guard, even the archers and the palace guards, commanding them to obey me as they had him.' Her sadness was tangible in a letter to her aunt Renée of France, describing Charles as 'the best king that a mother could have'.[62] Aware of the very real dangers posed by this interregnum, she urged Henry: 'do not delay your departure for any reason ... your kingdom has need of you'. She could not resist her maternal instinct to give him instructions: he should travel home via Vienna and Italy rather than across Germany, 'which I do not think would be safe for you', and she told him to send an envoy to the German princes to avoid giving offence.

Charles IX's funeral, carefully planned by Catherine, was conducted with great splendour. The king is dead! Long live the king! The lengthy obsequies were designed to demonstrate the continuity of royal authority – an issue of importance on this occasion with Henry some 1,000 miles away. Once again, as she had for the reigns of her two eldest sons, Catherine underlined Henry's descent from two powerful monarchs, Francis I and Henry II. Like his father and grandfather, Charles's death was followed by the ritual lying-in-state which lasted for forty days during which an effigy of the dead king, dressed in his royal robes and placed on a richly furnished

bed, was served his meals according to custom. Elisabeth of
Austria spent the forty days in strict mourning in 'a room lit
with candles', the traditional behaviour of a widowed queen,
though one that Catherine herself had ignored.[63]

On 8 July the dead king's heart joined that of his father
at the Célestins and three days later his funeral took place.
Charles IX's corpse, together with the effigy and the bed, were
drawn in a sumptuous procession through the streets of Paris
past houses draped in black with flaming torches at the doors,
to be buried with his father and ancestors in the royal church
of Saint-Denis.[64] The splendid cavalcade was followed by
princes of the blood, nobles, cardinals, bishops and soldiers
as well as the red-robed members of the *parlement* of Paris who
surrounded the effigy, and, according to ambassador Cavalli,
'five hundred poor men each bearing a lighted torch in his
hand'.[65]

In a nation deeply divided by religion, Charles's death
provoked strong reactions. For many Catholics he was seen
as a martyr-king and they drew parallels with the pelican who
fed its offspring (subjects) with its own blood.[66] For Théodore
de Bèze it was an occasion to celebrate God's elimination of
a tyrant; other Protestants blamed Catherine and her Italian
favourites for disposing of a puppet monarch.[67] Although it
was widely known that the young king had died of a painful
and bloody cough – symptoms of tuberculosis – there were
persistent rumours on the streets that he had been poisoned
by Alençon or, some said, by Catherine herself. To counter
these accusations she ordered the eminent surgeon Ambroise
Paré[*] to perform an autopsy the day after her son's death.

---

[*]   Ambroise Paré (*c.*1517–90), known as the father of modern surgery,
was the author of several works on the subject, on various illnesses and
on the treatment of wounds acquired in battle.

Paré's revolting description of the king's putrid lungs was convincing evidence of pulmonary disease, while the relatively good condition of the digestive system made nonsense of the accusations of poison.[68]

It must have been a relief to Catherine when her appointment as regent was confirmed without fuss by the *parlement*. Taking the helm at this difficult moment posed far greater challenges than those she had faced after the death of Francis II, when she had been heard with respect by both sides in the politico-religious divide: now she was seen as the enemy by the propaganda machines of both Protestants and Catholics. Few Frenchmen agreed with the Venetian ambassador Sigismondo Cavalli, who reported in 1574 that 'she does not live in the Italian manner but wholly like a French person'.[69] Much of the criticism focused on her foreign birth: in his report on the state of France in 1575 another Venetian envoy, Giovanni Michiel, who had been at court for many years, explained that 'she was blamed for all the misfortunes which have afflicted France; a foreigner and of Italian blood, she was little liked before but now, in truth, she is hated'.[70]

War was spreading and relations with Elizabeth I had soured, thanks to the help she was giving the rebels. In Henry's absence, Catherine was reliant on the *parlement*, which insisted on harsh punishments for Protestant rebels, unfortunately for Montgomery, who had been captured in late May. Although promised he would be treated as a prisoner of war, the *parlement* had him brought to Paris where he was tried for treason, condemned to death and executed on 26 June.[71] This was not vindictiveness on Catherine's part for the role Montgomery played in the death of her husband: as the Venetian ambassador reported, 'had it not been for the greatest pressure by the *parlement*, the queen would not have taken this step'.[72]

Catherine was diligent in informing her fellow rulers, ambassadors, governors and other officials of the legality and extent of her new powers. 'Overcome by the unremitting request made by the late king my son to take up this office for the good of this crown,' she informed François de Noailles, the French envoy to Constantinople, 'I have been constrained to accept this task, hoping that God will give me the grace, assisted by the good will of my son the duke of Alençon and my son-in-law the king of Navarre and other princes and servants of this crown, to conduct everything with moderation and with good advice so that this disaster, even though it is the worst that could happen, will not affect the peace and tranquillity of this state.'[73] In the meantime, her most urgent tasks were to prevent Alençon, or anyone else, seizing the throne and to keep secret the fact that her youngest son continued to plot against the crown, while reassuring everyone of his support for the regency, and for the new king. One of her first moves was to leave the château at Vincennes and move into the royal palace of the Louvre, where she closed all but one of the entrances to enforce security.[74]

   In fact, Alençon and Navarre were not as supportive as Catherine implied. In the days following Charles's death there were vague rumours of damage to locks on windows and doors in the Louvre and on 9 June ambassador Cavalli reported that the two princes had attempted to escape.[75] Catherine had had iron gratings fixed to the windows of Navarre's apartment, which was on the ground floor, though not in Alençon's rooms, which were on an upper floor, so not in need of this precaution. Nevertheless, Cavalli continued, despite evidence to the contrary, Catherine still believed their protestations of innocence, and insisted they should retain their liberty. Six days later, however, Cavalli reported that they had made another attempt to escape, this time while attending Charles's interment at Saint-Denis, but had been forestalled by an observant captain of the guard.[76]

In Cracow Henry III heard of his accession from the imperial ambassador on 14 June, just hours before the arrival of the

courtier despatched by Catherine. Four days later, escorted by
Villequier and his courtiers, he fled under cover of darkness
to ride the 300 miles south to Vienna. From this point on his
journey took on the appearance of a royal progress. After
ten days of lavish entertainment at the imperial court, he
crossed the Alps to Venice, where he arrived on 18 July to
a splendid reception, ferried over the lagoon in the doge's
grand *bucentaur*, specially regilded in his honour, for more
parties and pleasure in the city. He left on 27 July and still
made little effort to hurry back to France, despite Catherine's
urgent pleas. He spent several days as a guest of Alfonso II
d'Este in Ferrara, where he was entertained with tournaments,
balls and hunts, before boarding the ducal barge to travel up
the Po to Mantua for a similar round of festivities hosted by
the duke of Mantua. He then moved on to Turin where he
spent two weeks as guest of his aunt duchess Marguerite of
Savoy and Duke Emanuele Filiberto. As a particular favour,
and to the fury of his mother, he returned Pinerolo and two
other towns in Piedmont, which had been French possessions
since their capture by Francis I, to the sovereignty of the duke.

The journey was an expensive undertaking and Catherine
was busy raising funds to finance her son's extravagance, a
taste they shared. Within a week of Charles's death she had
arranged for 100,000 écus in bills of exchange to be sent from
Venice to Cracow – a safer route than the empire – asking
ambassador du Ferrier to forward 12,000 écus to the embassy
in Vienna, 'though we are still uncertain which route the king
my son will take'.[77] By the end of the month Henry wanted
more money so Catherine told du Ferrier to raise a loan of
200,000 écus, specifying an interest rate of 10 per cent.[78] After
Henry left Venice the ambassador presented a bill for 35,714
écus to cover what he had spent during the king's stay.[79] Most
of the items were the tips customarily given for services rendered: to the crew of the *bucentaur*, for example, and to the staff
who had looked after him during his stay, such as the stewards,
sommeliers, cooks and gondoliers. Among the payments were

1,125 écus to a perfumier for 'musk and other merchandise';
50 écus to the painter Tintoretto for three pictures; 40 écus
to a certain Martha and her husband for singing and playing
the lute before the king; 25 écus to the maker of thirty-nine
gilded sugar sculptures; and also 500 écus in alms to the poor.

Henry III's formal entry into his realm was to take place
at Lyons and Catherine had arranged to increase security
in the city, ordering the commissar of artillery to move six
cannons currently in Dijon, Chalon-sur-Saône and Auxonne
into Lyons 'with the greatest speed you can muster' as well
as supplies of cannonballs and saltpetre.[80] Catherine herself
left for Lyons on 8 August and that day wrote to Cheverny,
who had been in charge of Henry's affairs in France and was
now on his way to meet the king at Turin, with orders on how
her son should behave: 'I pray him to enter his kingdom like
a prince not accustomed to see our disordered ways and our
fickleness, combining the gravity God has given him with his
native gentleness, to show himself the master without an equal
and free from liars. Let not people think "he is young, we will
make him do what we like".'[81]

Travelling at night to avoid the summer heat, Catherine
took Alençon and Navarre with her, 'riding in my coach and
sleeping in my lodgings'; they were evidently on best behaviour
and she hoped 'the king will find them well-disposed to obey
and serve him'.[82] After three weeks on the road, they arrived
at Lyons, lodging at the abbey of Saint-Martin-d'Ainay to await
Henry III's arrival. While she was busy finalizing preparations
for the entry, Alençon and Navarre enjoyed themselves: the
new Venetian ambassador, Gianfrancesco Morosini, reported
that she left them 'almost entirely at liberty and daily the
duke and the king go about the city at their pleasure and
without any guard'.[83] Their good behaviour continued during
Henry's entry, which took place on 6 September in the early
evening, when the king crossed the Saône in a great barge
to the ringing of church bells, salvoes of artillery and fireworks, and a celebratory mass in the cathedral. Catherine's

brief period as regent was now over and decisions about the two princes were Henry's responsibility. Soon after the entry, Morosini reported that the king had decided, on the advice of his mother and against the warnings of chancellor Birague, to allow them to continue enjoying their freedom; 'the king of Navarre goes out hunting everyday, though a closer watch is kept on Alençon,' he observed.[84]

The interregnum had given the Protestants in southern France the opportunity to strengthen their military position and form two alliances: one negotiated by Henri of Condé with Johann Casimir, son of elector Friedrich III; the other with marshal Damville, commander of the royal army in Languedoc, Guyenne and Dauphiné, with his moderate Catholic supporters. Damville's action so enraged the ultra-Catholics that the *parlement* of Toulouse sacked him, accusing him of betraying their cause. Henry tried to diffuse the situation by ordering Damville to disband his men but he refused and on 13 November issued a declaration explaining why he was taking up arms against the king. Deeply affected by the murder of his cousin Coligny during the 'cruel, barbarous and inhuman' Massacre, he demanded freedom of worship for both faiths and an end to religious conflict.[85] He also criticized Henry for excluding French nobles from power 'and preferring foreigners before them'. It was a telling point: many of Henry's men, like Retz, Nevers and Birague, were Italian, while Damville's own family, one with a glittering tradition of service to the crown, was excluded; moreover, his brother and his cousin, both marshals of France, were still prisoners in the Bastille.

Henry was still at Lyons when Damville issued his declaration but three days later boarded a boat, heavily armed with cannon and bristling with crossbowmen, to travel down the Rhône to Avignon to hold talks with the marshal.[86] Significantly, it was

Catherine who did the negotiating while Henry spent his time attending penitential Advent services in the city's churches. Indeed, ambassador Morosini reported rumours that the king had no intention of listening to the Protestants and would prefer war to giving in to their demands.[87] In January 1575 an alliance between the Protestants and their moderate Catholic allies, with Damville as military commander and Condé in overall authority, gave them control of what was effectively a separate state in southern and central France.

Having failed to assert his authority in the south – or, rather, having decided to fight this battle at a later date – Henry III left Avignon for Rheims, where he was crowned on 13 February. The *sacre* was conducted by Louis of Guise, now the senior cardinal in the family with the title 'cardinal of Lorraine' since the death of his brother Charles in late December. Two days later he celebrated Henry's marriage to Louise, daughter of the duke of Vaudémont, a cadet branch of the house of Lorraine, whom the king had met in November 1573 at Blamont en route for Poland. The news was a shock to Catherine, who had not been consulted; indeed, she herself was hunting for a suitable bride for her son and one of her secretaries was at the Swedish court when the betrothal was announced.[88] She was particularly cross that the new queen brought no political advantage to France, unlike the partners she had chosen for her other children: queen of Scotland, king of Spain, the emperor's daughter and king of Navarre.

If Catherine was angry, she kept her emotions hidden. In a letter to Bellièvre, written while travelling north from Avignon, she masked her disapproval by pointing out the financial drawbacks of such a rushed decision: 'you know that this can only be done at great expense and not only for the many necessary costs.'[89] Lord Burghley judged astutely that although she 'knew nothing about [the marriage] before it was arranged, now she accepts it as if she had organized it herself'.[90] Whatever her views were, she certainly put on a brave face: as she informed the duke of Savoy before the wedding, Louise was 'a lovely girl from a good family, modest and well brought up' and she hoped the new queen would soon have children.[91] According to the Venetian Michiel, the twenty-one-year-old bride was blonde, delicate and very pretty and he thought that 'the king desired this marriage because he wanted a beautiful wife which, as you know, is a rare thing for a person of rank'.[92]

The past few months had been very stressful for Catherine, not least the hurt Henry caused by rejecting her involvement in his affairs. In September, while the court was still at Lyons, she heard of the sudden death of Marguerite, duchess of Savoy. It must have been a shock to Henry, who had so recently been the guest of his aunt, but above all to Catherine, who had lost one of her dearest friends. As she wrote to Renée of France, her grief for her sister-in-law who had been 'such a great friend since the day that I had the honour of arriving in this kingdom, will be too heavy to bear without the help of God'.[93] Then in February 1575 news came of the death of her daughter Claude, duchess of Lorraine: writing a few days later to Elizabeth I, she apologized for the brevity of her letter, which, she explained, was 'because I am ill and because it has pleased God to visit me again, taking to himself my daughter Claude'.[94] Like so many women of the period she had died in childbirth, aged just twenty-seven; Catherine took over the upbringing of her nine-year-old daughter Christine, who provided some consolation for Claude's death.

For Catherine this must have been a difficult time. Her son did not need her; she had lost a daughter and one of her closest friends; above all she had lost her position at court. For the past fourteen years she had held the reins of power for Charles IX, who had been very dependent on his mother: Henry, by contrast, had long ago detached himself from her apron strings and, as we have seen, he had his own agenda. In fact, she was not completely excluded from government like most dowager queens. Henry evidently held his mother's knowledge of politics at home and abroad in such high regard that he invited her to attend the daily morning meetings he held with chancellor Birague, though her role was to support and offer advice rather than dictate policy. As we shall see, she did not always find it easy to accept these limitations. Moreover, she still wielded immense power of patronage. In a very revealing letter to her cousin Francesco, grand duke of Florence, she asked him to pardon an Italian member of her household, Jacopo Ricasoli, charged with murdering a Florentine subject: her main concern was that her intervention should be made known in Florence, and in France, 'so that Ricasoli's mother, his relations and friends know that my letter was not unfruitful'.[95]

With fewer responsibilities at court Catherine channelled her energies into building projects. Contemporaries noticed that she liked to be busy: 'not only does she apply her mind to politics but also to many other things,' reported Cavalli, 'she undertakes five or six important projects at one and the same time'.[96] In the aftermath of the Massacre she had become fearful of the Parisian mob and worried that the Tuileries, which was outside the walls, was not secure. Although it provided a stunning setting in which to entertain and impress visitors, she decided on a new residence for herself inside the walls and began acquiring properties for the Hôtel de la Reine (Queen's House)* – private houses as well as a convent for reformed prostitutes – in the parish of Saint-Eustache. In 1572 she commissioned designs for the palace from the architect Jean Bullant though, as with the Tuileries, many of its features reflected her own ideas. Conceived on a truly grandiose scale, it was set in magnificent gardens, laid out on the site of the convent and ornamented with fountains and sculpture. Even while it was under construction, Parisians walking past

---

*   The Hôtel de la Reine, later renamed the Hôtel de Soissons, was demolished in 1748; it is now the site of the Bourse de Commerce by the Place des Deux-Écus.

the vast building site on the rue des Deux-Écus would have
been reminded of her prestige, if not her power.

Architecture provided a visible reminder that although
Catherine's political influence might have waned, her status at
court was as high as ever. It was no coincidence that during the
early years of Henry III's reign she added such lavish embel-
lishments to her rural retreats that they acquired the palatial
splendour more usually associated with the crown's urban
residences, a stylistic change that was widely imitated.[97] At
Saint-Maur Bullant enlarged the château with an extra storey
and a new pedimented garden façade, while at Chenonceau
he added a great gallery set on the bridge over the River Cher,
though plans for an immense courtyard were not realized.[98]
She also continued work on Charleval, a hunting lodge just
east of Rouen begun by Charles IX, transforming it, too, into
a grand residence. It is an indication of Catherine's fame as
a patron of architecture that when another of her designers,
Jacques Androuet du Cerceau – a Protestant like his predecessors Philibert Delorme and Bernard Palissy – published
his treatise in 1576, *Plus excellents bastiments de France*, he
dedicated it to her, rather than to Henry III, the more conventional choice. And he flattered her by illustrating many of her
palaces and châteaux among his 'best buildings in France'.[99]

Henry's accession brought many changes at court, not
all of which met with Catherine's approval. According to
ambassador Michiel, Henry was 'without doubt very intelligent
and has good judgement' and, moreover, 'he does not lack
ambition but by nature he is very kind and peaceful'.[100] He
satisfied the expectations of many of his subjects: aged twenty-
four, he was tall, elegant and clever, and had earned the
reputation as a military hero on the battlefields of Jarnac and
Moncontour. He had recently developed less martial tastes: he
was, apparently, a beautiful dancer and devoted to his pack of

lapdogs though 'now he never gets on a horse'.[101] As king he was hardworking and involved in the business of government, opening and reading the diplomatic correspondence, unlike his brother Charles, and exercised a greater degree of personal control than his predecessor. He slimmed down his council to include just the princes of the blood and eight others, notably chancellor Birague, Bellièvre and Cheverny, and they were to assemble 'when it pleases the king to summon them and not otherwise'.[102] The secretaries were no longer permitted to make decisions on the king's behalf and had to obtain his personal signature on all important documents.[103]

Among the men now in positions of power in Henry's regime were the favourites who had been with him in Poland, many of whom Catherine distrusted. We can guess she was happy to see that Bellièvre was in charge of the treasury (*surintendant des finances*) and that Cheverny had the prestigious role of chancellor to the royal order of St Michael; but she was furious when Henry replaced Retz as first gentleman of the chamber with Villequier, whom she disliked. On this occasion she was successful in persuading Henry, with Cheverny as intermediary, to reinstate Retz, though he had to share the post with Villequier, each serving six-month terms.[104] It was an unsatisfactory arrangement, not least because of the rivalry between the two men, and Retz was forced to retire from public life a few years later.

Within weeks of his arrival at Lyons, Henry caused chaos at court with a series of regulations designed to transform royal etiquette. As the astonished Venetian envoy reported, his food was now to be served not by his squires but by the gentlemen of his chamber and a barrier was to be erected around his dining table: 'he wants no one to speak to him, nor approach his table while he is eating'.[105] He stopped the daily ceremony of the *lever* ordering that 'no one was to enter his chamber until he was dressed'. The new regulations, which suggested a desire for privacy also reflected his intention to enhance his own majesty by emphasizing the distance between the crown and its subjects, were so unpopular that many left court in protest.

Catherine, too, deplored the new arrangements and voiced her concern in a long letter to her son in which she encouraged him to follow the example set by his grandfather and father.[106] She outlined the strict timetable of the royal day which Francis I and Henry II had both followed, starting with the *lever*, and stressed the importance they placed on being accessible to their subjects. She disapproved of the chamber staff being involved in the dining room, and warned him that his subjects were being told that 'you do not care for their preservation and you do not wish to see them'. Tradition was key: 'after dinner', she recommended, he should 'visit me or the queen, so that the manner of the court be known, something that greatly pleases the French because they are accustomed to it'.

The most significant area where Henry was to assert his complete independence from Catherine's tutelage was in his attitude to religious matters, which had been formed under the influence of the Jesuit Edmond Auger, who continued to be one of the king's trusted advisers. As duke of Anjou, Henry had championed the Catholic cause at court, but Catherine had begun to worry about his increasing religiosity since his accession. Attending mass every day during Lent, as Henry did in 1575, was expected of a king who had sworn an oath at his coronation to uphold the Catholic religion, but his decision to visit 'one parish church after another' in Paris was a more conspicuous statement of his faith; he also undertook a major programme of church restoration 'and went every day to offer alms and prayers in great devotion'.[107] Certainly Gregory XIII welcomed his succession to the throne: he sent Henry the substantial sum of 200,000 scudi in anticipation of a military campaign against the Protestants and gave him permission to raise a further two million scudi from ecclesiastical revenues.[108] Elizabeth I was less enthusiastic: in April 1575 she made him a knight of the Garter but despite this initial show of friendship she refused to commit to a date for the formal investiture.

With fighting continuing across France, Henry III began negotiations with the Protestant government in the south, who sent a delegation to Paris for talks. Their agenda was optimistic: restating Damville's declaration that they wanted freedom of worship across the realm, equal representation in the judiciary, an increase in the number of surety towns (*places de sûreté*), the release of Montmorency and Cossé, punishment of those responsible for the Massacre and a meeting of Estates-General. Henry was emollient, assuring them that he intended to treat all his subjects equally, but the delegates were unimpressed and refused to continue unless he accepted two non-negotiable demands: freedom of worship in all France and the release of Montmorency and Cossé. Henri would not negotiate further but Catherine wrote to Damville reassuring him 'of how much [the king] desires the health and tranquillity of his subjects ... and a good peace': 'I am confident,' she added, that 'you will help with all the means and authority that you have with [the Protestants] to persuade them to reach a successful end to what has been begun.'[109] Though she continued to correspond with Damville and the other Protestant leaders, she was careful to insist on her loyalty to her son; in August, for example, she refused Condé's request to free a certain Abraham because 'the death sentence has already been given against him by the *parlement* for very good reasons' (he had confessed to receiving 6,000 écus to assassinate the king).[110]

Henry's overt support for the Catholic cause was just part of a change in the political alignment at his court. While marriage to Louise of Lorraine did not bring the international benefits for which Catherine had hoped, it significantly changed the balance of power and cemented the Guise family's return to favour. Louise was not only first cousin to lieutenant-general Charles, duke of Lorraine but also second cousin to Henri of Guise. Not all approved. Catherine is silent on the issue but Michiel reported that Louise was not a popular choice: 'everyone dislikes seeing his majesty accompanied by this queen whether because they believe this union brings neither advantage nor honour to the kingdom or the king, or because they fear that, as the queen is from the house of Lorraine, all the graces and favours will fall on that house, especially on the Guise family, who are already envied and detested by other nobles.'[111] Above all, it was causing trouble in the royal family itself: the English ambassador reported in March that 'it is a very hell among them, not one content or in quiet with another, nor mother with son, nor brother with brother, nor mother with daughter'.[112]

Catherine watched impotently as her children quarrelled. Rumours of Marguerite's lovers, whether true or not, provided entertainment for the court gossips but were not the decorous behaviour expected of a sixteenth-century princess and soured her relations with Henry, and with her mother. Alençon resented Henry for his lack of freedom and vented his frustration by annoying his brother in petty ways, such as boastfully parading about the Louvre with a regal entourage. For his part Henry disliked and distrusted his brother: when he fell ill that summer, he apparently told Navarre that, if he died, his brother-in-law was to seize the throne for himself, by force if necessary.[113] The rumour underlined the reality: until the queen had a son it was the ambitious and untrustworthy Alençon who was heir to the throne.

One issue upon which Catherine and Henry agreed was the need to sort a future for Alençon. The king continued to do what he could to alienate his brother from Navarre and detach him from the Protestant cause; Alençon, a virtual prisoner in the palace, continued to make plans for flight. That summer an aide reported him missing but Catherine found him in his rooms; ambassador Morosini reported that his lutenist and poet had both been arrested on suspicion of planning his escape.[114] In early September, Henry and Catherine gave an audience to the English ambassador to discuss plans to betroth Alençon to Elizabeth I; however, the reluctant groom refused to agree unless he was named as her heir, something the queen was never likely to do.[115]

A few days later Alençon finally managed to evade his guards. Catherine must bear much of the blame: according to Morosini the duke asked his mother for permission to visit the city, which she granted; he then left his empty coach outside a friend's house and escaped through the rear entrance where another coach was waiting to take him away.[116] He left a letter for Henry, assuring him of his loyalty, and claimed that he wanted to join William of Orange's campaign in the Netherlands. Catherine's shock showed just how blind a mother can be – after all, her son had been making regular attempts to escape for years now. She expressed her incredulity to the duke of Savoy, appalled that she should 'live to see such a disastrous turn of events', news of which 'has so unhappily come to the king and myself'.[117]

At Dreux on 18 September, Alençon issued a declaration revealing his true motives: far from joining the Dutch fight, he and his Protestant allies intended taking up arms against the French crown. The country was in a parlous state, he claimed, blaming this on the heavy 'taxes, impostes and subsidies' levied by those 'who only seek to make themselves rich', singling out foreigners – by whom he meant Italians – 'who have monopolized the king and the principal offices of state'.[118] The duke proposed himself as leader 'to restore this realm to its former glory' and to protect all regardless of faith. Moreover, Protestant troops were massing in strength: in addition to La Noue's band near Dreux, Condé's army was gathering in the south and Johann Casimir's 20,000 *reiters* were poised to cross the eastern frontier.[119]

The court was in uproar. Henry tried unsuccessfully to locate his brother, so on 19 September a distraught Catherine left Paris for Dreux, but Alençon had left. Determined to prevent things from spiralling out of control, she was tireless in her search: the following day she was at Nogent; two days later at Mantes; on 24 September she was at Houdan, from where she wrote to Henry III with news of Alençon's movements since leaving court: 'he has now gone by coach to join La Noue,' she reported, and was 'sending the bishop of Mende tomorrow to see if he will talk to me'.[120] The next day she was back in Nogent, where she spent the night, and in the morning sent Henry a brief note: 'I am about to mount my horse and will sleep tonight at Courville and tomorrow go to Châteaudun where I expect news of my son.'[121] It is some 25 miles from Nogent to Courville, and another 35 miles from Courville to Châteaudun, a very exhausting few days for the fifty-six-year-old woman.

As expected, there was news from Alençon at Châteaudun: he offered to meet her at Chambord, where she arrived on 28 September, but before he would go any further he insisted on the release of marshals Montmorency and Cossé. Henry agreed to this and negotiations began in earnest: the priority for both Catherine and Henry was to prevent Alençon from joining the Protestants. On 5 October she wrote to Henry urging him to pursue a peaceful solution, once again citing the model of 'the kings, your father and grandfather'; she made the key point that 'it is of primary importance to have the kingdom and the obedience of all your subjects which, while the war lasts, you will not have'.[122] The dangers were apparent the following week when Henri of Guise defeated the German *reiters* at Dormans, just south-west of Rheims; the victory was notable for the wound which removed part of Guise's cheek, allowing him to adopt his father's nickname of Balafré, or Scarface.

Catherine did all she could to achieve peace: 'I spare nothing in order to bring my business to a successful end,' she informed Morvillier on 13 October.[123] Ten days later her secretary reported on the state of the talks: 'I am not sure what the outcome will be ... but if we are so unfortunate that nothing comes of it, it will still serve to show the world how much trouble the queen was willing to take.'[124] It took another month to finalize the details and on 21 November Catherine signed a six-month truce with Alençon at Champigny-sur-Vende, near Tours. In her determination to buy her son's favour, she made significant concessions: the Protestants were given control of the towns of Angoulême, Niort, Saumur, Bourges, La Charité and Mézières, where they were granted freedom of worship, and John Casimir was bribed with 17,000 écus (50,000 livres) to keep his *reiters* out of France.[125]

Much to Catherine's disappointment, the truce did not hold: the price of peace was too high for the Catholics; even the king himself, reported Morosini, opposed it.[126] The citizens of Angoulême and Bourges refused to cede their towns and handovers elsewhere were delayed; it was only a matter of time before fighting began again. Worryingly, as Alençon's declaration made clear, Protestants had begun to challenge the idea of obedience to the king, indeed to the exercise of absolute power. Following Bèze, who believed that it was the duty of subjects to overthrow tyrants, their tracts and pamphlets questioned the nature of royal power. The new faith, which had started as a desire to reform the Church, had become a rebellion against the crown.[127] Catherine, after the stress of the past two months, was again unwell. 'Madame my mother is slightly ill,' Henry III informed his ambassador in London, 'but, thanks be to God, she is doing very well.'[128]

The year 1576 started badly. In early January the truce broke down when Condé entered Lorraine, poised to cross the French frontier, at the head of a Protestant army of over 25,000 men including Johann Casimir's large force of *reiters*.[129] Catherine returned to Paris in early February to news that Navarre had escaped from his guards to join the rebellion, and announced that he had returned to his own faith. The following month a Protestant delegation arrived in Paris with demands for peace agreed by Alençon, Navarre, Condé and Damville: 'the free, general, public and complete exercise of the reformed religion ... without any modification or restriction to time, place or person', equal representation in the *parlements* and, they insisted, the bill for the *reiters* was to be paid by the crown.[130] Alençon, greedy as ever, demanded the title of duke of Anjou that Henry had held as heir to the throne.

Henry ignored these demands but could not shrug off the announcement made by the Protestant leaders in early April. 'We have decided,' Alençon announced, 'to win by force the peace and tranquillity we could not achieve by reason.'[131] They were in a strong position: Condé's army, which had crossed into France, was now camped near Moulins and poised to attack the towns of the Loire Valley. Faced with twice the number of troops, and without funds to muster more men, Henry was in no position to argue. He sent Catherine to lead the talks and the peace she signed on 6 May 1576 at Étigny, near Sens, was a victory for the Protestants, for their moderate Catholic allies and, above all, for Alençon.* The next day she wrote to Damville of her gladness that 'it has pleased God to arrange things after such long negotiations', and her wish for a 'good understanding between all the princes, nobles and other subjects of the king my son' that they might live together in peace.[132]

The terms of the peace – the Edict of Beaulieu – reversed the restrictive measures that had been forced on the Protestants in July 1573 after the siege of La Rochelle. Thanks to Catherine they now had freedom of worship across France, though not in Paris or in places where the court was in residence, and the edict did require them to permit the same freedoms to Catholics. For the first time they had equal representation in all the *parlements* and their surety towns increased to eight: Aigues-Mortes and Beaucaire in Languedoc; Périgueux and

---

* It is often known as the Peace of Monsieur, the courtesy title accorded to the younger brother of a king.

Verdun-sur-Garonne in Guyenne; Nyons and Serres in the
Dauphiné; Issoire in the Auvergne; and La Seyne-sur-Mer in
Provence. The use of the term 'Huguenots',* the name by
which they were more generally known in France and which
they found particularly offensive, was banned; Protestant
victims of the Massacre and those accused of crimes against
the crown, including Montgomery and Coconat, were to be
rehabilitated; and they were given senior positions in government with their leaders appointed as provincial governors.
Alençon became governor of Anjou, Touraine and Berry;
Navarre was given Guyenne, Poitiers and Angoulême; Condé
got Picardy, a province provocatively close to the border with
the Netherlands; and Damville was reinstated as governor of
Languedoc. In an attempt to persuade Alençon to support
the crown in any future battle, Catherine persuaded Henry
to grant him the duchy of Anjou and an annuity of 100,000
écus.[133] And, finally, in a nod to the critics of the king's exercise of absolute power, a meeting of the Estates-General at
Blois was to be held within six months.

The terms Catherine negotiated, especially the personal
favours for Alençon (or Anjou, as we must now call him) did
much to reconcile him with Henry but, as she could have
predicted from the failure of the truce six months earlier, it
was to be a hollow victory. On 29 June she wrote to Damville
to express her pleasure at 'the prompt start you have made in
establishing and executing this edict of pacification' and sent

*   There is a tradition that the term 'Huguenot' derived from a little-
known Swiss Calvinist named Besançon Hugues (1487–1532) but
recent scholarly research shows that the word, which was first used
around 1560, is more likely to refer to the bogyman King Hugh (*roy
Hugon*), an evil spectre who roamed the streets at night (as Protestants
were said to do), and used in the Touraine to frighten children (see
Gray, 'The Origin', passim).

a similar message to Montmorency.[134] However, as before, the ultra-Catholics ignored the edict completely, furious again at the favours extended to those who had rebelled against their lawful king. The pope was shocked to hear that, less than four years after the Massacre, Protestantism was to be rehabilitated in France, and angry as he had contributed a further 100,000 scudi to the war against them.[135] In Paris there were riots against the edict and Henry had to attend the *parlement* in person, with the princes of the blood, before it would agree reluctantly to publish the edict.

Catholics vociferously expressed their opposition to the edict; Catherine's defenders claimed she had only signed it to bring an end to the rift with Anjou.[136] When Condé, the new governor of Picardy, attempted to take possession of Péronne, the Catholic population refused him entry. Both Henry and Catherine informed the governor of the town, Jacques d'Humières, of their displeasure at his behaviour, reminding him that it was his duty to obey his king.[137] Humières, however, refused and instead he formed a league to defend his faith against the Protestant heresy, urging other Catholics to do likewise, which they did in large numbers, uniting ultra-Catholics against not only Protestants but also moderates who wanted a peaceful compromise. Militant organizations, their members swore loyalty to the crown and promised to contribute their own money and men to the war effort; 'those unwilling to enter the association will be reputed its enemies and will be hunted down'.[138] Under the leadership of the duke of Guise, the movement soon acquired the backing of Philip II and Gregory XIII, but both Catherine and Henry avoided giving their support, fearful that this would widen the rift with Anjou. The king, who continued to make a very public display of his devotion, insisted that he had no need to prove his faith by supporting the league; and he astutely exploited the unpopularity of the Guise family to persuade Anjou to support his position.

That summer of 1576, Catherine had some success in

reuniting Henry and Anjou; when she arrived at Blois in November she was pleased to see 'the duke of Anjou so well reconciled with the king'.[139] She was less successful in her efforts to reconcile the faiths. In early October she wrote to the ambassador in Vienna with an upbeat report of the state of affairs: 'thank God, the edict of pacification continues to keep the peace ... and we hope to find effective remedies to do all that needs doing at the forthcoming meeting of the Estates-General which opens at Blois on 15 November.'[140] In the meantime, she went to Cognac in the hopes of convincing Navarre and Condé to attend the assembly and help the king 'do everything necessary to establish peace and to break up the malicious plans of those who want to return us to war'. [141] Poor Catherine: she was to be cruelly disappointed.

In his opening speech to the Estates-General, Henry stressed that his primary aim was peace and praised Catherine for her untiring efforts towards this end: but the two differed on how to achieve it. For Catherine the goal, as ever, was peace through reconciliation; Henry, by contrast, was hampered by the challenge to his authority posed by the ultra-Catholics, for whom peace could only be achieved through war and the extermination of the heretics. Of the 400 delegates at Blois virtually none were Protestant thanks to a campaign to exclude them: one tactic was to make announcements about the election of delegates in Catholic churches during mass.[142] Not surprisingly, the assembly's decisions favoured the Catholics' cause: the clergy voted unanimously to eradicate the Protestant faith by war; the nobles also voted for war but with a less convincing majority; the third estate agreed to ban the faith but refused to grant any taxes to pay for war. Henry himself joined the majority, declaring his intention to abide by the oath he had sworn at his coronation to allow only one religion in his realm. When the English envoy had an audience with him in early February to convey Elizabeth I's disapproval of the decision 'taken to extirpate the unfortunate members of the reformed religion', Henry said he preferred 'to die the least of kings in the world rather than do anything against his conscience'.[143]

Catherine must have been disappointed by Henry's rejection of all she had tried so hard to achieve but her reaction, typically, was to put her loyalty to the crown before all other considerations. Even after he dismissed Sébastian de L'Aubespine and sidelined Jean de Morvillier, two of her closest allies, she refused to oppose royal policy directly, even to criticize the king, though she was more explicit in private.[144] 'I am almost sorry I gave way to my son,' she confided to one, 'he should not have committed himself so absolutely'; to another she confided that 'I am not free to do as I wish'.[145] She did, however, attempt to dissuade him from war, which she believed would destroy the kingdom, suggesting that he should talk to the opposition. In a long letter to her son dated 2 January 1577 – evidently written at his request, perhaps he could not face the conversation – she recommended sending envoys to Condé, Navarre and Damville, and gave tips on how to deal with them.[146] Condé, she thought, would follow Navarre and Damville; if Navarre was obstinate, he might be persuaded by the duke of Montpensier, who was another Bourbon; 'as to marshal Damville, it is him whom I fear the most because he has the most sense, experience and consequence'.

Catherine's analysis of the situation proved wrong; while Navarre and Condé refused to compromise, Damville changed his allegiance to support the king, after accepting the tempting bribe of the marquisate of Saluzzo. Catherine, who had built up a good relationship with Damville over the years, encouraged him: 'you can rely on the word and promise of the king my son who would rather die than fail in his promises.'[147] In early March she congratulated him on his decision and sent a personal letter to Damville's wife: 'I am so pleased that your husband has decided on this matter.'[148]

It was not just Catherine who saw the dangers of war. Writing to the king, Damville lamented that 'we have tried for sixteen years now, the great battles, endless sieges, storming of towns and slaughters perpetrated in your kingdom on both sides have served for nothing but mutual destruction'.[149] The duke of Montpensier, a fierce opponent of Protestantism for many years, surprised many by voicing similar views: war has 'neither quelled the troubles nor brought back our Catholic faith'.[150] At a meeting of the king's council on 1 March, in answer to the militant views of Guise, Nevers and their allies, Montpensier voiced the opinions of many moderates when 'he said he was a Catholic and he was minded to die in that religion but that he advised making peace because there was no money and no men'.[151] Catherine also spoke against war, arguing that it was madness at the present time because of the lack of financial resources and, ever loyal to her son, 'must be delayed until she saw more certainty for the king'. In her determination to avoid war she even wrote to Gregory XIII asking him to support a compromise with the Protestants, a request he refused.[152]

In the end the war party won and fighting started in earnest in March. Henry placed Anjou in command of the army, with the duke of Nevers to back the inexperienced twenty-two-year-old, and aimed his campaign at the Protestant surety towns. Catherine was at Chenonceau when she heard that Anjou had sacked La-Charité-sur-Loire on 2 May, his first major victory, and wrote to Nevers to thank him: 'for my part I have very great pleasure that my son the duke of Anjou is assisted by you, knowing how much your prudence and experience would be of service.'[153] At the end of May, Henry reported that Damville had 'reduced over twenty-five small towns and castles in my province of Languedoc to my obedience'.[154] Catherine thanked the marshal 'for your actions and virtuous behaviour in the service of the king,' she wrote, adding, 'I beg your wife and you will not believe anything to the contrary'.[155] In late May, Anjou and Nevers moved on to Auvergne to lay siege to Issoire, which they sacked on 12 June. Once again Catherine sent special thanks to Nevers: 'I cannot express my great pleasure,' she wrote, 'of the good and great task you performed for my son Anjou at the siege of Issoire.'[156] Less successful was Damville's siege of Montpellier, which had begun in May and was still undecided at the end of the summer.

There was little sign of victory for either side; the geo-political divide remained largely unchanged, with the north of France remaining largely Catholic, while the provinces of the south – Guyenne, Gascony, Poitou and Languedoc – were still staunchly Protestant. Neither side had the strength to defeat the other. Although ambassador Lippomano reported in July that 'the Protestants are now optimistic of victory', the reality was less positive, despite the help arriving from Elizabeth I. Nor did the royal army have much hope of success: it lacked troops, artillery, munitions and even the funds to buy food for the men.

In early June, Catherine sent secretary Villeroy to Bergerac on a secret mission to take advantage of the impasse and open peace negotiations. He returned within a month to say that Protestants had demanded freedom of worship as an absolute condition for peace.[157] The talks, which lasted three months, were fraught with pressure from both sides of the political divide. Henry needed to grant enough concessions to the Protestants in order to keep Anjou on side; he also needed to satisfy the ultra-Catholics, who objected to any favours to the enemy. The peace finally signed at Bergerac on 14 September, and the accompanying edict signed at Poitiers three days later, were yet another compromise, this time between the generous terms of the Edict of Beaulieu and the militant Catholicism of the Estates-General. The places where Protestants could worship were further limited; the equal representation of Protestants in law courts and other administrative bodies was either abolished or curtailed; and finally, in a move designed to enhance his own authority, Henry banned all religious leagues and confraternities.

Rivalries
1578–1584

There is a portrait of Catherine in a painting of around
1582 that depicts a ball at the court of Henry III. The
focus of the picture is the circle of dancers, fashionably
dressed in brightly coloured outfits, the men with elaborate
ruffs and skin-tight hose, the women in dresses that show off
their elegant busts and waists. In the background a group of
musicians play for the revellers; in the foreground two lapdogs
gambol playfully on the floor. Catherine is not part of the fun.
She stands with five other soberly dressed individuals wearing
her customary black mourning for the husband she lost more
than twenty years ago. On her right are Henry and his queen,
Louise; the king, an elegant if slightly paunchy figure, is
sporting the pointed beard imitated by his courtiers on the
dance floor. On her left is Henri, duke of Guise, whom she is
restraining with an outstretched arm from approaching the
king.[1] Her gesture is hostile and provocative; and it embodies
the growing divisions between Guise and the king.

Factional rivalries at court were nothing new; indeed, those
involving the Guise family had dogged Catherine throughout her years in France. Under Henry, however, they began
to proliferate and challenge the authority of the crown. Most
distressing for her was the enmity between her own children.

The dislike between Henry and his brother François, duke of Anjou showed no signs of abating. After Anjou returned to court early in 1578 there were daily reports of quarrels and fights between their followers; on one occasion 300 of Anjou's men challenged Henry's *mignons*, as his favourites were known, to 'fight it out unto the death', an encounter which mercifully the king banned. A few weeks later he absolved some of his men from a charge of attacking a favourite of Anjou's, Louis de Bussy d'Amboise, despite the urgent plea of their sister Marguerite, who was Bussy's mistress.[2] Marguerite was another problem: estranged from her husband, Henri of Navarre, and back at court, her affairs were causing much gossip. Henry, like Catherine, was highly critical of her infidelities, though less so of Navarre's own equally public liaisons, but the fact that this Catholic–Protestant union was in trouble also had broader political ramifications.

No one was very surprised when Anjou left court in early February without the king's permission; nor when Bussy returned to Paris in secret, though it was unclear whether this was to kill one of Henry's *mignons* or to see his mistress.[3] Without Anjou it was the rivalry between the king and his Guise in-laws that took centre stage. The scale of Guise ambition was no novelty at court; the family lost little time in exploiting their relationship to the new queen. A new generation had taken over since the death of Cardinal Charles of Lorraine, led by Henri, duke of Guise, now in his late twenties, with his younger brothers Charles, duke of Mayenne and Louis, cardinal of Guise. Boasting their role as leaders of the Catholic cause, they also claimed royal rank as descendants of the first Holy Roman Emperor, Charlemagne, morally superior to the royal houses of Valois and Bourbon.

On 27 April 1578, early in the morning in the horse market near the Bastille, three men from Guise's faction and three from Henry's were involved in the so-called 'Duel des Mignons'. Four of the six swordsmen were killed: two during the fighting, one the next day and another, the leader of Henry's men, after a month; a fifth was badly cut on his face but survived after several weeks in bed, while the sixth, Guise's champion, emerged from the fighting barely scratched.[4] Guise claimed victory and in punishment Henry expelled him and his family from court but the feud continued: when another of Henry's *mignons* was murdered in Paris that July, it was Guise's brother Mayenne who fell under suspicion.

Guise's other rival was Henri of Navarre, an enmity stoked by religious differences and by his fears that the king's agenda was not as anti-Protestant as he would like. Although the treaty of Bergerac had undone much of the anti-Protestant legislation passed at Blois in December 1576, it still imposed limits on the new faith. Behind its public face, however, were several secret clauses agreed between the king and his brother-in-law.[5] As will become clear, Henry believed his real enemies were not the Protestants but the ultra-Catholics whose views had dominated at Blois; and that Navarre's quarrel was less with the king than with Henri of Guise, a shift which would have significant repercussions.

It was early on the morning of 15 February 1578 that Catherine heard of Anjou's flight the previous night, achieved with the help of Marguerite and her lover Bussy, who also left Paris with the duke and several other favourites.[6] Later that day secretary of state Villeroy was despatched with post horses to locate the prince, followed in the afternoon by Catherine herself. Anjou had made for Angers, the capital of his duchy, where he planned to raise troops to assist William of Orange's uprising against Spanish rule in the Netherlands. She seems to have spent her spring attempting to force both Anjou and Marguerite to toe the line. Her daughter responded to pressure and on 6 May Catherine was able to inform Henry that the couple had agreed to meet.[7] Anjou, however, was less amenable. Catherine tried to change his mind, but he refused to listen to her recital of his duties – the loyalty he owed to his brother and his obligations to protect the realm – though she did persuade him to stay out of Orange's affairs until given a proper title. All she could do was prevaricate: 'it was not expedient either to assist [Anjou] or to oppose him openly but to do all that was possible to throw difficulties in his way' was the decision of the king's council in late May.[8]

One of the 'difficulties' Catherine and Henry put in Anjou's way was a revival of the project of his marriage to Elizabeth I and, with this in mind, Catherine wrote to the ambassador in England, Michel de Castelnau, sieur de Mauvissière, an experienced diplomat who had succeeded La Mothe-Fénelon, asking him to reopen discussions and do what he could to achieve 'a good and happy end'.[9] Stressing the urgency of the situation, she wrote 'any delay in this affair might be very harmful, also because I am about to escort my daughter the queen of Navarre to my son the king of Navarre, her husband, and I would not want, if possible, to be delayed'.[10] Their reconciliation, she assured him, 'mattered greatly for the good of the realm' and for 'the maintenance of the peace which we wish to safeguard and observe not only in this realm but also with all our neighbouring princes'.

Neither persuasion nor distraction had any impact on the headstrong Anjou, who left for the Netherlands in July and, having listened to this part of his mother's advice, received the courtesy title of 'Defender of the Liberties of the Low Countries' and promised to bring 12,000 troops with him to fight the Spanish.[11] Fearful of what this might do to relations with Spain, Henry sent a special envoy to Philip II, to discuss the 'prosperity of your affairs in the Netherlands'.[12] In the envoy's luggage were letters from Catherine, to be presented to Philip II and his queen in person. This was a courtesy but her fulsome tones were revealing: to Philip she wrote, 'to beg you to keep me always in your good grace' and 'the great regret I have for the youth of my son', her explanation for Anjou's desire to fight the Spanish.[13]

❧

Catherine's journey to escort her daughter to Navarre had another, more serious, purpose, one that again required her skills as a negotiator. The Treaty of Bergerac had begun to unravel: in November 1577 marshal Damville, governor of Languedoc, had written to her to say he was having difficulty maintaining the peace as 'those of the reformed religion are unwilling either to disarm or to enforce the edict'.[14] Royal authority was under threat across the south, not only in Languedoc but also in Provence, Dauphiné and Guyenne, where Henri of Navarre was governor. It was unfortunate that Navarre and his Catholic lieutenant-general, marshal Biron, detested each other and their hostility threatened to overthrow the talks right from the start.

On 11 August, Catherine wrote to Jacques de Goyon, comte de Matignon, governor of Normandy, to inform him of her impending journey to Guyenne 'where they say everything has been suspended' and that she expected to be away for two months or so.[15] She thanked him for 'the beautiful harrier (lévrier) you have sent me which I like so much', adding, 'I have never received a more beautiful greyhound'. She was characteristically optimistic about how long her mission to enforce obedience to the edict would take; in the end she was away from court for fifteen months, travelling from Bordeaux to Grenoble, often in considerable discomfort and enduring privations that must have been hard on the sixty-year-old woman.

Catherine was not short of company: in her large retinue were many of her own dames d'honneur, including the duchess d'Uzès, a close friend for many years, as well as Marguerite and her household. The entourage, however, was more for business than for show: travelling with her were high-powered advisers and members of the king's council: Saint-Sulpice, who had been ambassador in Spain, La Mothe-Fénelon, ex-ambassador to England, Jean de Monluc, who had been Henry's agent in Poland, Cardinal Bourbon, who was Navarre's uncle, and several other Bourbon cousins such as the duke and duchess of Montpensier and the dowager princess of Condé with her sons.

Catherine kept in close touch with the court: in September she heard from Elizabeth I's secretary Sir Francis Walsingham that the queen had agreed to the match with Anjou; 'the best news I have received,' she replied.[16] She sent regular letters to Pomponne de Bellièvre, minister of finance, and to the secretaries, notably Villeroy, who was entrusted by Henry with reading all her letters. This was an onerous task: her reports were often lengthy and she wrote at least twice a week, some eight letters a month and sometimes as many as fifteen. But the sheer quantity is a witness to the seriousness with which she took her task, her commitment to the goal of reconciliation and her loyalty to the crown. She evidently trusted Villeroy: 'this is my advice,' she told him, 'if it is bad throw it on the fire; if it is good show it to the king.'[17] Henry himself was not as dutiful a correspondent and she frequently had to apply to Villeroy for domestic news about her son and daughter-in-law. It was to Villeroy in particular that she confided her hopes that 'before I die I have the contentment of having played a part in bringing to this realm the peace that the king promised in his edict' and that Henry 'whom I love, would receive honour and obedience and regain his authority'.[18]

Their routine of the tour was not dissimilar to that she had undertaken with the young Charles IX in 1564–6: formal entries with speeches and processions followed by banquets, balls, fireworks, entertainments and, no doubt, some very uncomfortable accommodation, an energetic social round laced with serious political negotiations. At Cognac in mid-September Marguerite was apparently much admired by the 'grand, virtuous and beautiful women of the area who came to see her and do reverence and were charmed by her beauty'.[19] Mindful of her mission, Catherine was scrupulous about attending mass to reassure Catholics in each town that she shared their faith; she then held public meetings with them to convince them of the need for toleration, 'to live all together with each other in peace and union,' she wrote and 'as I will continue to do this in all the places I visit'.[20]

Her first meeting with Henri of Navarre took place on 2 October near La Réole, some 35 miles south-east of Bordeaux, 'in a house on its own on the road'.[21] Navarre arrived 'with a substantial escort of 150 gentlemen' and could not have been more courteous, she assured Henry, insisting on accompanying her to her chamber. But there was some trouble, which she recounted in exhausting detail, about where Marguerite should sleep: Navarre wanted his wife to share his rooms 'which were on the other side of the road' but Marguerite refused, making her husband very angry. Fortunately, Catherine had been able to distract him with the timely arrival of a letter from marshal Damville, which they discussed with Bourbon and Montpensier. Before leaving Navarre signed a preliminary agreement outlining the basis for future peace talks which were to take place at L'Îsle-Jourdain before the 'fifteenth of the present month'.[22] Aware of the tricky relations between Navarre and Biron, she organized a meeting with them both at Sainte-Bazeille, where she spent the night of 8 October. Biron arrived 'in the afternoon as I had expressly ordered,' she informed Henry; it was unfortunate that Navarre lost his temper with Biron and 'spoke so roughly to him that we thought, your sister the queen of Navarre and I, because of what has happened between them, that the said marshal would be absolutely furious', but Marguerite calmed him and saved the situation.[23]

They arrived at Agen on 11 October, where Biron had issued orders for supplies for the travellers, their mounts and pack mules: 'a great quantity of all sorts of foodstuffs as well as hay, straw, oats and other fodder' was to be gathered from within a 5-mile radius of the city and the authorities were to punish anyone who refused to comply.[24] The mission was going well, she reported to Henry, 'Navarre continues to show a strong wish for peace, and behaves towards my daughter as well as we could wish, as she does towards him'.[25] But she was less sanguine about prospects in the longer term: 'considering how great the importance of this is to you, there is not an hour day or night that I do not think of the best ways of remedying this peacefully.' Her next stop was Toulouse, a fiercely Catholic city where she expected much opposition; she had already been warned that although Toulouse was loyal to the king's edict, the diocesan clergy were 'unanimous' its terms were 'completely against the duty of all good and loyal subjects'.[26] After two weeks they left for L'Îsle-Jourdain without Marguerite, who said she was not well enough to accompany her mother: that afternoon Catherine sent a footman to the duchess of Uzès asking her to 'send him back to me tomorrow with news of how Marguerite is behaving herself'.[27] At L'Îsle-Jourdain later the same day Navarre also sent his excuses, claiming to be confined to his bed 'with a boil on the buttock', and sent his loyal lieutenant Henri de La Tour d'Auvergne, viscount Turenne, a distant cousin of Catherine's and, reputedly, another of Marguerite's lovers.[28]

After a fortnight at L'Îsle-Jourdain, Catherine moved to Auch, where she arrived on 20 November; Marguerite arrived the following day and Navarre, recovered from his boil, the day after.[29] At a ball one evening, staged for their entertainment, Navarre was informed that Catholics had launched a surprise attack on La Réole, one of the surety towns ceded to the Protestants in the recent treaty. Leaving the ball with a few of his men, he rode north not in the direction of La Réole but to Fleurance, a small Catholic town some 15 miles away, which they seized without difficulty, and returned to Auch. Catherine had much to do to ensure that the incident did not wreck the peace process but on 26 November she wrote to Damville with the news that Navarre wanted 'a prompt resolution to secure peace' and four days later she informed him that 'we have decided on the advice of those members of the king's council who are here with me that we will hold our conference on 10 December at Nérac where, I am assured, the Protestant delegates will attend without using any other excuse to delay'.[30]

Catherine crossed the Garonne into Navarre and arrived at Nérac on 15 December, where Marguerite made her formal entry as queen. 'My son the king of Navarre,' Catherine informed Henry, 'arranged for everything possible to be done to welcome us', though she added that there were many in Navarre's suite who were reluctant to join in the peace talks.[31] A week later, with the talks clearly inconclusive, they crossed back into France and stayed at Porte-Sainte-Marie, some 12 miles north of Nérac, for six weeks, lodged in an abbey outside the walls known as 'Paradise'.[32] Catherine's letters, of which some fifty have survived, twenty for Henry, record the daily meetings she held with Navarre, Turenne and other Protestants, as well as marshal Biron and his Catholics. They were far from cordial, both sides refusing any concession; one meeting in her chamber with Navarre and Biron turned so violent she had to intervene to calm them down.[33] Claude Pinart, one of the secretaries of state, witnessed how hard she worked and reported to Bellièvre that 'there is nothing that she has not tried'.[34]

There was also disturbing news of her sons. Anjou had failed to take Mons in late December, while Henry had left court a month earlier for Ollainville, the château he had built for the queen south-west of Paris, with none of his advisers or the diplomatic corps eager to report his every move. He was back at Ollainville soon after the New Year celebrations 'with a few courtiers, to remain there to the end of the month, perhaps more'.[35] In January 1579, Villeroy urged the king to take more interest in affairs of state and to write to Catherine more often: 'I beg you to consider how distressed the queen your mother will be, amidst so many other things in which she is immersed for your service, to remain so long without hearing from you'.[36] She evidently did miss her son and asked the duchess d'Uzès, who was now back in Paris, 'if you see the king and queen send me their news immediately; I am very envious of you seeing them rather than me', signing the letter affectionately, 'you know the hand of the most trustworthy friend you could ever have'. [37]

Catherine returned to Nérac on 3 February and the conference opened in earnest the next day. There followed three weeks of hard bargaining and, at least on her part, the skilful use of the tricks of the negotiator's trade, many of which were recorded in the diary of Damville's secretary.[38] She kept people waiting and kept meetings going on long after they were supposed to have finished; on one occasion she refused to break for food; on another she had mass celebrated at 6 a.m., forcing her councillors out of bed much earlier than usual; one went on so long that Monluc, who was over seventy years old, had to go to bed. On one occasion, taking Navarre for a walk in the garden, she managed to make him agree to talk to all the deputies that evening to persuade them of the importance of preserving peace; another afternoon 'after dining, the queen of Navarre went down to the park to watch her husband tilting at the ring with several members of his suite, while the queen mother was at vespers'. The truce was finally signed at Nérac on 28 February and it was an indication of just how far she had compromised with the Protestants that an infuriated Gregory XIII threatened to cut diplomatic links with France.[39] Henry, however, according to Catherine, was very pleased with what she had achieved: as she informed the duchess of Uzès, 'I have not felt such great joy for a long time to hear how contented the king is with my hard work'.[40]

After Nérac, Catherine travelled back to Agen, where she spent most of March recovering from the rigours of the past five months, before taking to the road again in early April for the arduous journey back to court. On 14 April she told the duchess of Uzès that she expected to be home 'with my wishes fulfilled, the country stable, my son returned to his duty'; she would spend Easter at Castelnaudary 'and after that straight to Paris to see those I love most in the world'.[41] She looked forward to seeing Anjou, who had returned to court somewhat chastened after his failure at Mons: 'I am so pleased,' she told him, 'to hear your news after so long and of your good and sincere intention never to do anything which might alter the friendship which should exist, for reason and for nature, between the king your brother and yourself.'[42] After his disappointment in the Netherlands, he was more amenable to the idea of marriage with Elizabeth and sent an envoy to Catherine in Agen to discuss the project; Henry, however, urged his mother to discourage him from making any firm commitment.

Catherine parted from Marguerite at Castelnaudary on 7 May before setting out for Carcassonne, from where she wrote to the duchess of Uzès: 'yesterday morning I said goodbye to my daughter, which gave me great sadness, but when I think that it is nine and one half months since I saw the king my son I am comforted to know that in a month I will have that pleasure.'[43] She apologized for not visiting the duchess's castle at Uzès, north of Nîmes: 'if it were not for the plague I would bring you news of your estates but Uzès and all around is so pestiferous that even the birds are dying.' She herself was well 'except that the catarrh which irritated me at Porte-Sainte-Marie has developed into a sciatica (*une sciatique*) that does not stop me travelling but I need to have a small mule to take me for a walk if I want one; I think the king would laugh if he saw me', and asked the duchess to 'send me news of everything, especially the king and the queen'.

However, Catherine's hopes were soon dashed, as were those of the secretaries for whom Henry's lack of interest in affairs of state meant much extra work.[44] The wars had brought desperate famine to parts of Languedoc, Provence and Dauphiné, which were now suffering violent unrest, and it was decided that Catherine and her advisers should delay their return to deal with the problem. This was not a religious issue but a struggle between rich and poor. In Aubenas in the

Ardèche, for example, peasants had been forced to sell the tiles and beams from their houses in order to buy food to keep them alive and the poor of the area had sent Henry a petition against 'the insolence, authority and power of the nobles, captains and soldiers and the atrocities committed by them'.[45] Instead of travelling up the Rhône Valley from Marseilles, where Catherine spent most of June 1579, she and her entourage continued east through Provence, where she spent July negotiating the end to the local conflicts, and on to Grenoble, capital of Dauphiné, where the mountain air must have been a welcome relief.

Back at court Henry and Anjou had fallen out yet again, this time over plans for Anjou's marriage. In October the previous year Elizabeth I had issued orders regulating the betrothal which required not only that the wedding would be conducted 'according to the rites of the religion of the queen' but that Anjou must visit England before it could take place.[46] On 6 June the Venetian ambassador Girolamo Lippomano reported that Anjou's trip to England would be delayed until 'after the arrival of the queen-mother, without whose advice he could not and ought not to act'.[47] Anjou was too impatient to wait and asked Henry for permission to go before Catherine's return. The king refused so, as was his wont, Anjou went anyway, pretending – so Lippomano reported – that he was going to Grenoble to see his mother.[48] Instead he crossed the Channel in August to meet the queen, who nicknamed him the Frog, but his stay was cut short by the news that Bussy d'Amboise had been killed in a duel.

In September, Lippomano reported that Henry was ill with a headache 'from which he ordinarily suffers' but the king worried that it 'should turn into an abscess like that which affected his brother king Francis; and last night he was seized with such grave symptoms that many of his attendants were moved to tears'.[49] The king was better the next morning but then developed a fever; fortunately this too cleared up but he was reluctant to get back to work. The ambassador reported on

18 September that he 'pretends not to be aware' of the problems regarding Anjou's marriage and 'is assiduously pressing the queen mother to return as soon as possible'.[50] Catherine, too, was worried: on her way home she wrote to Villeroy to say, 'it is already almost fifteen days since my son sent me a letter', adding in a postscript in her own hand, 'I beg you to send me news of the king more often'.[51]

Catherine was back in Paris in October: 'it is easy to see that the queen mother is king and queen of this country and has lost none of her authority,' commented one ambassador.[52] But much had changed at court during her absence, though not the hostility between her sons. Henry had made more alterations to court etiquette, adding several new features designed to enhance his authority.[53] The court was now largely based in Paris: Henry II had averaged just forty-four days each year in the capital but his son spent over half the year there.[54] In the palace the unpopular barrier around his dining table was removed but he replaced it with archers to discourage courtiers from approaching him. His daily routine became more formal: after dressing in his chamber with his valets and barber, he 'announced he was awake' at which point he moved to his cabinet to chair the daily discussions of affairs of state, marking the end of the meeting by 'asking for his wine', when he was given his cape and sword for the walk to chapel for mass. Admission to the various rooms in his apartments was now graded according to rank with only the most important figures allowed into the inner core, so very different from his grandfather's policy of open access to the crown.[55]

In a further move to bolster the crumbling authority of the crown, Henry founded a new order dedicated to the Holy Ghost (*Saint-Esprit*), to unite the nobility behind their 'Most Christian King'. Replacing the knights of St Michael, who had become so numerous that membership was no longer a credible sign of royal favour, it was designed to be the premier royal order, its membership strictly limited to preserve its exclusivity.[56] Its letters patent were explicit, asking God 'to grant us the grace of soon seeing all our subjects reunited in the Catholic faith'. The knights were to dedicate themselves to 'the defence of our faith and religion, and of our person and state'. They were also given a visibly close relationship to the king at daily audiences and occasionally sitting at his dining table.

The first parade of the order had taken place on New Year's Day 1579, its members walking in procession from the Louvre to the church of the Grands-Augustins on the left bank of the Seine, dressed in their distinctive robes displaying the brilliant flames of the Holy Ghost.[57] One notable absence was the duke of Guise, who had been exiled from court the previous year. Widely seen as the leader of the ultra-Catholics, Guise was in the process of setting up Catholic leagues in Champagne and elsewhere, in direct contravention of the Edict of Poitiers which specifically banned such associations. Henry now decided that his enemy was safer within the fold and recalled Guise in March; and, to signal this return to favour, the duke was made a knight of the new order and given back his seat on the king's council.[58]

The new role for the Grands-Augustins may well have been the spur to Henry's most important architectural project, the Pont-Neuf, for which he laid the foundation stone in May 1578, though it was not finished until 1606.[59] Planned as a grand route for royal ceremonial, and to improve access across the Seine, it was part of a more ambitious project to create an imposing focus of royal power around the Louvre, which he enlarged with a new wing along the riverbank linking it to Catherine's Tuileries.[60] He spent conspicuously to provide visible evidence of his title of Most Christian King, contributing to the upkeep of religious institutions in Paris, including the city's hospital, the Hôtel Dieu, as well as churches such as Saint-Honoré, Saint-Médard, Saint-Nicolas-des-Champs and Saint-Roch, among others.[61]

Catherine's new residence, the Hôtel de la Reine, was nearing completion. In February 1580 she invited the English ambassador and his wife to dine at the palace to celebrate the end of the Carnival season but fell ill and was unable to act as host. Henry took her place: his mother had a cold, he told Lady Cobham, but 'would soon recover'.[62] During the party Henry gave Lady Cobham a tour of the palace's reception rooms, which she recorded in a letter home: they went into 'a very gallant chamber richly hung around wherein there stood a sumptuous bed' where the king showed her a portrait of his father, Henry II, 'which he said was very like him', and then 'into a very large chamber' filled with guests for the ball. After the dancing they went into another room for refreshments, laid out on a long table, where she saw 'banqueting dishes, very curiously and cunningly wrought and also a cupboard furnished with crystal glasses set in gold, so strange and so many fashions as I have not seen the like'. The behaviour of some of the guests, she observed, was not as respectful as it might have been: 'some put more into their pockets than into their bellies, so that at last all was gone.'

The construction of the Hôtel de la Reine, begun in 1572, was now largely finished: Lord Cobham described it as three storeys high and built of stone.[63] Following the standard layout of Valois palaces, it had a richly ornamented façade, a monumental staircase, a long gallery and elaborate gardens. According to the ledgers that survive from 1581, Catherine's total expenditure on buildings that year came to 10,027 écus, which included 760 écus at Saint-Maur, but the bulk was spent at the palace, notably on Catherine's sumptuous private chapel, on carved wooden doors and demolishing old structures to create her beautiful gardens.[64]

Catherine lived in some style at the palace with her grand-daughter Christine. Her household had doubled in size, from 405 in 1554 to some 800 in the mid-1580s. In addition to over one hundred *dames d'honneur*, she was attended by an army of servants: forty chambermaids, four laundresses and thirteen medical men, who included physicians, apothecaries and sur-geons; she also employed twenty singers in her chapel and sixty-five men and boys in her stables including muleteers, coachmen, saddlers, farriers and grooms.[65] Also part of the household were her painters, musicians, writers and poets, to whom she had granted the post of *valet de chambre* as a sinecure to reward their services.[66]

As Lady Cobham hinted, the palace was luxuriously fur-nished. Catherine was rich, with an income from her estates in the Auvergne as well as a large pension paid from the royal treasury, estimated by the Venetian ambassador to be 100,000 écus (300,000 livres) a year.[67] The inventory of her possessions taken after her death listed quantities of valuables, artworks, furnishings and curios: superb carpets from Turkey, Egypt and Persia, one of which measured 31 × 13 feet; tapestries, painted leather wall hangings glittering with gold, velvet and silk bed curtains embroidered with pearls and gems, damask and taffeta cushions, gilded silver vases and cups, marquetry tables, chests inlaid with ebony, ivory and mother-of-pearl, rock crystal dishes, porcelain bowls, knives and forks with coral handles, antique medals, a statue of Leda in jasper, a porphyry basin and a chandelier made of jet.[68]

She owned over 450 paintings – the inventory does not list any of the artists – including mythological and religious pictures as well as landscapes, but overwhelmingly portraits. In one room a picture of her son Francis II hung over the fireplace, while the walls were panelled with thirty-nine oval enamels and thirty-two portraits 'of various princes, lords and ladies'.[69] Next door it was a portrait of Henry II 'at the age when he was married' that sat over the fireplace with portraits of their children.[70] In another, the Cabinet of Mirrors was lined with over one hundred 'plain mirrors from Venice' and eighty-three small portraits.[71] Her most important display was in the gallery that Henry had shown Lady Cobham, a huge room, some 40 metres long, facing onto the rue des Deux-Écus, and lined with portraits of the Valois kings, their queens and their children, as well as some of their relations by marriage such as Charles V and Philip II.[72] It was evident that her French heritage mattered more than her Medici ancestors, whose portraits were relegated to a smaller room; and she gave more prominence to portraits of her French mother than to those of her father.[73] The collection, one of the largest of the period, included enamel portraits by Léonard Limousin and some 551 drawings amassed over the years of her children and of people at court, men and women, Catholics and Protestants, friends and enemies alike.

Catherine owned some 5,000 books and over 700 manuscripts of works in Greek, Latin and Hebrew.[74] She had acquired quantities of maps, the subject of much scientific interest in the sixteenth century: maps of many European countries, plans of French towns, places of French interest in the Americas and, more exotically in this age of exploration, maps of Calcutta and the Cape of Good Hope.[75] In common with other princes of the period she amassed a collection of curios, one of the hallmarks of princely prestige at courts across Europe, which she displayed in a special room, described in the inventory as the 'Fourth Storeroom-Cabinet of the Late Lady'. The items gathered, a mixture of the natural, artificial and antique, were designed to display her political prestige and intellectual knowledge.[76] Among them were ten Venetian masks, 'a number of shells from the sea to make model mountains', branches of coral, one 'large shell of a snail, painted', one 'large head of a stag', two coconuts, 'one real chameleon', the 'snout of a wild beast', seven crocodile skins, a 'buttercup-flower in crystal', two nefs cut in rock crystal, an ivory sundial, a 'model mountain made from marcasite embellished with branches of coral where there is represented the Passion', a bronze statue of Cleopatra, four 'small cannons mounted on wheels' and so on.

Arguably the most famous items owned by Catherine – and not listed in the inventory for reasons which will become clear later – were the famous Valois tapestries, a particularly expensive set of eight hangings woven in Brussels in wool and silk, lavishly shot through with gold and silver thread. Little documentary evidence has survived to throw light on these treasures: while Catherine is widely thought to have been the patron, we cannot be sure of their date or provenance; even the subject matter itself is enigmatic, and the topic of much scholarly debate.[77] The scenes show life at court: all but one depict the jousts, the mock battles, the ballets, the water-borne pageants and other entertainments for which the royal court was justly famous; the eighth, appropriately, depicts the vast cavalcade that was the court on the move. Some have been associated with the spectacular festivities staged by Catherine at Fontainebleau (1564), Bayonne (1565) and at the Tuileries (1573), not always convincingly. They offer, however, a veritable gallery of recognizable portraits of Catherine and members of her family: Charles IX, Henry III and Anjou; Henry's queen, Louise; Marguerite and her husband, Henri of Navarre. Catherine herself is present in all the scenes, a lone figure dressed in black and a striking contrast to the glittering revellers around her. And they testify to the central role she played in the political and cultural life of late sixteenth-century France.

The entente that Catherine had worked so hard to negotiate between Navarre and Biron began to break down almost as soon as she returned to court in autumn 1579 and, once again, France was at war. This time the fighting was mostly in the south, where Navarre attacked several Catholic-held castles and towns and finally took Cahors at the end of May 1580 with an unexpectedly brilliant display of military skill. His explanation was that the city was part of Marguerite's dowry which Henry still owed him – though the gossips claimed it was prompted by Marguerite's affair with Turenne (this outbreak of fighting was known as the 'Lovers' War'). Catherine wrote several times to Navarre to beg him to stop: 'my son, I cannot believe it is possible that you want to ruin this realm and your own,' she wrote; 'I will never believe that, coming from such a noble house, you aspire to be the head and commander of this kingdom's brigands, robbers and criminals.'[78] After discussions with Catherine, in late April 1580 Villeroy went to Guyenne to begin negotiations: she wrote to him before he left to say she agreed with his view of the need to avoid violence, and urged him 'to use gentleness to try and quench this fire they want to light, but also not to neglect other means if gentleness is ineffective'.[79]

Catherine was preoccupied with the problem of Anjou, who, now that he was over the shock of Bussy's death, planned to return to the Netherlands; she, once again, was doing what she could to distract him. Henry reopened discussions with Elizabeth I and her ambassador asked for an audience in mid-May to convey the queen's 'great regard and contentment' at his letter; Catherine had to take the audience alone as Henry was busy 'holding a meeting of his order'.[80] A second distraction for Anjou was to persuade him to join Villeroy negotiating a peace settlement with Navarre, and she informed Damville – now duke of Montmorency after the death of his brother – 'we still have some hopes of being able to put out this fire without violence by way of my son the duke of Anjou, who has demonstrated a great desire to do this favour for the realm and to render this service for the king'.[81] Despite Catherine's efforts, however, Anjou remained determined to join Orange's rebellion.

It was a comparatively quiet summer for Catherine though not a pleasant one. In June she caught whooping cough: she apologized to Montpensier for not writing in her own hand 'because I am ill and troubled by catarrh for the last four days, and I have not felt so weak with illness as this for a long time'.[82] Then an outbreak of the plague forced her to leave Paris in late June, when she moved to the peace and quiet of her château at Saint-Maur and only rejoined the court at Fontainebleau at the end of August. That autumn William of Orange offered Anjou the sovereignty of the United Provinces, a group of provinces of the Netherlands that had declared independence from Spanish rule earlier in the year, on condition that he brought an alliance with France to the table. Henry agreed to provide men and money but only once peace had been restored across France. It was a clever move, one that made it difficult for Anjou to refuse to take part in negotiating a truce with Navarre.

The war in the south had reached stalemate by the time Anjou arrived in Guyenne to join Villeroy, who had been asked by Catherine to keep an eye on her son, as had Bellièvre, who was also part of the negotiating team. She was optimistic about peace and in early November wrote to Villeroy expressing the hopes of herself and the king that 'with the dedication to duty and assistance of Bellièvre and yourself, that the conference will turn out well'.[83] The treaty Anjou formally signed at Fleix on 26 November was broadly the same as the one Catherine had agreed with Navarre at Nérac nearly two years earlier, and equally difficult to enforce. With this in mind, and to keep him out of mischief, Henry asked Anjou to remain in Guyenne to oversee the implementation of the treaty. Anjou was furious that Henry had not kept his promise, only agreeing with great reluctance to his brother's request; Villeroy and Bellièvre continued to keep a watchful eye on his activities.

In January 1581 Henry, who had been not been well for several months, left the court and his council behind at Blois and moved to Saint-Germain to undertake a forty-day purgation; he remained there until April, accompanied by only his favourite courtiers and a skeleton staff to look after them. He gave orders that Catherine was 'to send, command and sign everything' in his absence, while she did what she could to downplay the situation, denying he was so ill that she was now regent.[84] Rumours proliferated of various diseases: ambassador Michiel had long worried about Henry's health, reporting in 1575 that 'all France believes he cannot live long and suffers from many ailments'.[85] With the country sliding into chaos, and Henry isolated at Saint-Germain stubbornly ignoring all affairs of state, the burden of government fell squarely on Catherine's shoulders.

In early January Catherine, too, left the court at Blois to settle just 25 miles away at Chenonceau where she could be more comfortable and enjoy her gardens. It was not an easy situation: Henry's absence made the process of government very laborious. After reading all the correspondence, Catherine discussed it with the secretaries, who put notes in the margins to say what action had been taken before forwarding the letters to Saint-Germain with instructions, if any, for the king; one of Henry's *mignons* then added the king's comments to the marginal notes and returned the letters to Chenonceau.[86] Catherine kept the secretaries busy. 'I am worn out,' Pinart complained to Bellièvre in January, 'standing to write at the end of the queen's coffer, besides which it is so late that I can hardly stand up straight.'[87]

Catherine's difficulties were compounded by Anjou, who was still in Guyenne with Villeroy and Bellièvre but restless. In late December she had written to him begging him to stay out of the fighting in the Netherlands, listing all possible arguments against it, notably the dangers his actions would pose for France; even 'consider, we are in the middle of winter and it is almost impossible to fight in the Low Countries'.[88] Her most important argument was the duty that he owed to his rank as prince, 'the honour of being the brother of the king'; 'you are however his subject and you owe him complete obedience and you must also prioritize the public good of this kingdom, which is the heritage of your predecessors and of which you are the heir presumptive, before any other consideration'.

Anjou, as ever, ignored his mother's advice, stubbornly determined to fight the Spanish in the Netherlands and to force Henry to keep his promise to help now that peace had been secured. The king agreed to supply limited assistance so long as his brother remained in France but Anjou's troops, waiting for orders to cross into the Netherlands, had started to ravage the countryside around his estate at Château-Thierry where they were garrisoned. Catherine and Henry discussed what to do, by letter, and one result was to send an embassy to England to arrange Anjou's marriage. Gregory XIII, increasingly worried about what was happening in France, appointed a new nuncio, Giovanbattista Castelli, with instructions to stop the marriage and to stop any further deterioration of relations between France and Spain, which he feared, as did Catherine, might lead to all-out war.[89]

Catherine moved back to Blois, where she fell ill again. Villeroy, who returned to court in late February 1581, reported to Bellièvre that she was attempting to battle on: 'you know how courageous she is'; but she suffered a relapse and in mid-March was so unwell that she was unable to leave her bed; 'she cannot do anything but wither away,' Villeroy informed Bellièvre, so 'you can imagine how heavy my heart is'.[90] Fortunately, she was better in early April when the situation deteriorated abruptly: Anjou, bored with his role as peacemaker, left Guyenne for Normandy but his destination was clearly the frontier. On 29 April she wrote to Bellièvre of the 'extreme regret which I bear that my son has abandoned the execution of the peace to which the king his brother appointed him,'; she confided, 'as you know better than anyone, the error he is making, so you can also imagine my vexation'.[91]

A few days later Catherine climbed into her coach in pursuit of her wayward son, who was at Alençon, a 100-mile journey that, according to the Venetian envoy, took five days.[92] The mission was not a success: Bellièvre wrote to commiserate with her about 'the bad news that we have heard that Monsieur your son does not wish to obey your very revered and very reasonable wishes'.[93] Characteristically, despite the lack of response, Catherine redoubled her efforts to dissuade him. In early July she went to Mantes and the following month to La Fère; she even raised money from her own sources to help him, but her efforts were in vain. Anjou joined his troops at Château-Thierry and within weeks they had relieved Cambrai and captured Cateau-Cambrésis.

Henry's behaviour, too, was causing concern: it is hard to know what Catherine made of it; perhaps, like other indulgent mothers, she made excuses. A military hero at eighteen, he was becoming the century's least popular monarch. Lampoons for sale on the streets of Paris accused him of every kind of vice; while his reputation for evil was created by his enemies, there is no doubt that he was different from his predecessors. Put simply, he did not conform to the image of a king. He disliked hunting, jousting or the other sports favoured by his father and brothers; the English ambassador claimed Catherine was upset by this and urged her son to emulate his father's passion for strenuous games, and his habit of playing them with his courtiers.[94] Worse, he was unable to sire a child, boy or girl. 'To tell the truth,' ambassador Michiel reported, his preference for 'the soft, peaceful life has made him lose much of the good opinion of his people who had hoped he would be one of France's greatest warriors because when he was young he was in many battles and victorious in all of them.'[95]

Henry's tastes were more frivolous than military: he loved dancing and hosted balls at court twice a week; he preferred his lapdogs to the huge hunting hounds of other princes; he was a natty dresser, fond of perfume and fancy clothes to the extent that many thought him effeminate and accused him of dressing like a woman.[96] His relationship with his mother was considered too close for a grown man.[97] He was also criticized for his taste for Italian culture – ironically, here he was imitating his Italophile father and grandfather: over three-quarters of his violinists and one-quarter of his singers were Italian.[98] So, too, was his ballet master, Balthasar de Beaujoyeux, whom Catherine rewarded with the sinecure of *valet de chambre* in her household.[99] Acting troupes from Italy played regularly at court, where the *commedia dell'arte* was popular: one company of actors, the *Gelosi*, was kidnapped on the way to Blois and the king had to pay a ransom for their release.[100] He even tried to persuade his courtiers to eat with a fork, but this Italian habit was widely despised, and typical of the Italians, who were too precious to let their hands touch their food.[101]

Henry's courtiers aped his clothes and coiffure: Pierre de L'Estoile, a government official whose memoirs reveal much about the court, ridiculed their taste for 'ruffs, curls, raised crests, wigs ... powdered with scent of violet'.[102] Ambassador Lippomano was astonished at how much they spent on fashion: 'a courtier is not considered rich unless he owns twenty-five to thirty outfits, all different styles, which he has to change every day'.[103] L'Estoile was outraged at how they gambled, blasphemed, quarrelled and whored, and how they followed 'the king around everywhere and do everything to please him'.[104] It was not surprising that his close friendships with these men gave rise to rumours of homosexuality.

Henry's chief favourites were François d'O, Anne de Joyeuse d'Arques and Jean-Louis de La Valette: they were the only courtiers to accompany him to Saint-Germain in January 1581.[105] D'O was expelled from court later that year for gambling but the other two continued to enjoy Henry's favour.[106] Catherine liked Joyeuse, whom she had met when he was serving on Montmorency-Damville's staff in Languedoc, but she had little time for La Valette, whom she thought merely a '*petit galant*'.[107] Significantly neither came from the top rank of

the nobility but owed their status and wealth to Henry's indulgence. In August 1581, d'Arques was made duke of Joyeuse
and the next month La Valette became duke of Épernon. As
joint holders of the office of 'first gentleman of the chamber',
they had the power to decide who was, and who was not, permitted into the king's presence; and Henry made their status
highly visible by ordering an extra place to be laid at his dining
table, exclusively for the new dukes.

Henry has often been accused of shirking his responsibilities, but he was cleverer than that. He chose his own men to
circumvent the rivalries that had long divided the old nobility
by creating a new elite owing rank, wealth and loyalty entirely
to him. It is tempting to see that this policy of marginalization was aimed directly at the Guise family. Significantly, when
Henry created the duchies for Joyeuse and Épernon in 1581,
he assigned their titles precedence over all others at court,
including the duke of Guise, with the exception of the princes
of the blood.[108] Guise, by contrast, received no special favours
from the king; and, although he retained his rank as *Grand
Maître de France*, much of his authority was transferred to a
new post, *Grand Prévot de l'Hôtel* (provost of the household),
which was given to one of the *mignons*.[109] Guise's brothers
also lost face: Mayenne was obliged to resign his position as
admiral of France in favour of Joyeuse, and although Aumale
remained Master of the Hunt, his budget was slashed by half
and his status, in a post that had been so prestigious in previous reigns, was now negligible.[110]

The new regime was celebrated publicly in September 1581
when Joyeuse married Marguerite of Lorraine, half-sister to
the queen, a choice that not only associated him directly with
the king – they were now brothers-in-law – but also underlined
the marginalization of the Guise clan, who, despite being the
queen's cousins, could not be said to profit in any way from
the association. The wedding was a royal affair, the king and
groom both sumptuously dressed in outfits covered with pearls
and precious gems which reputedly cost the treasury 10,000

écus.[111] Henry himself devised the extravagant celebrations, spending one million écus on the banquets, jousts, masques and the other entertainments, which lasted for several weeks.[112] It was an expense that must have added considerably to his unpopularity in a realm where taxes imposed to pay for the wars were causing famine and riots.

On Sunday 15 October, Catherine attended the grand finale of the celebrations in the Louvre, *Le Ballet Comique de la Royne* – the queen in question was not Catherine but her daughter-in-law Louise, who sponsored the event and, together with the bride, was among the performers on the dance floor. The theme of the ballet was the sorceress Circe, a tale of good triumphing over evil, order over disorder: in a visual counterpart to the story, Henry sat at one end of the hall, flanked by Catherine on his right and Joyeux on his left, with Circe's bower at the other end.[113] The performance itself was devised by Beaujoyeux, who published an account of the ballet, sycophantically listing the names of the dancing court-iers with details of their superb costumes. He dedicated the performance to the king: the defeat of the sorceress Circe, as he explained, was an allegory for the peace established by Henry and Catherine, who had healed the realm from the 'maladies' from which it was suffering.[114]

With Anjou in the Netherlands, Catherine continued negotiations for his marriage to Elizabeth I, but the political difficulties were rising. Both regimes wanted an entente against Philip II but Elizabeth, not entirely trusting the French, insisted on a public alliance before she would agree to the betrothal. Moreover, her position was complicated by the fact that her heir presumptive was Mary Stuart, a Catholic, in a Protestant country where many feared that French Catholics were plotting to put Mary on the throne. In France, by contrast, Catherine and Henry worried that a public alliance with England might provoke Philip II into war; France's land borders, after all, were entirely controlled by Spain – the Netherlands, Savoy, where Philip's cousin was duke, and Spain itself. The geo-political situation, however, was of little relevance to Anjou, who, as impetuous as ever, decided to force the issue, and on 31 October he landed at Rye for his second visit to the queen.

After three weeks entertaining Anjou with the pleasures of the English court, the queen announced her intention to marry the young prince. In France speculation was rife: when questioned by the Venetian ambassador, Henry replied, 'as yet there is nothing done, or undone'.[115] Catherine acted positively, putting a full-length portrait of Elizabeth she had commissioned in England the previous year on public display. Ambassador Cobham reported that everyone was impressed by the size of the pearls on the queen's dress but above all by the fact that she was dressed 'a la Française'.[116] By the time Anjou left England at the beginning of February 1582 the match was off, but the political alliance was very much alive.

Anjou returned to the Netherlands with a large sum of money from Elizabeth for the Protestant cause and, in February, was invested in Antwerp with the titles 'Prince and Lord of the Dutch Provinces' and duke of Brabant. Catherine was not pleased: on 6 March she wrote to ambassador Mauvissière in London, 'it is to my very great regret that my son, the duke of Anjou, has decided, against my advice, to travel to Flanders'.[117] Nevertheless, she did what she could to help her son, adding funds from her own coffers to those supplied by Elizabeth. But Anjou's fight against the Spanish army was hampered by more than lack of funds, and his own lack of military talent. As Cardinal Granvelle informed Philip II, he 'can do nothing but what his mother and brother desire, since they are the ones who are paying'.[118]

Catherine also found a way to put pressure on Philip II. The king of Portugal had died in 1580 without an heir and she had claimed the throne as countess of Boulogne, the title she inherited from her mother and which, in turn, had belonged to Matilda of Boulogne, queen of Alfonso III of Portugal (died 1279). Philip, with a stronger claim and a much stronger army, conquered Portugal later that year. Once Anjou's marriage to Elizabeth was off, she offered to renounce her claim if he agreed to a betrothal between her son and one of his daughters, with the Netherlands as part of the dowry; the king did not reply. In June Catherine upped the pressure, sending the French fleet under the command of her cousin Filippo Strozzi to the Azores to free the islands from Spanish rule. It was a disaster: a month later the French were annihilated by the Spanish armada and Strozzi was killed in the fighting. The one bonus of this fiasco came from Jean Nicot, the French ambassador in Lisbon, who sent Catherine a herb from the Portuguese colonies which, he claimed, had unusual healing properties; he named it the 'queen's herb', but it was later renamed 'nicotine' in his honour.[119]

From the beginning of 1582 Henry's absences from court became more frequent as his quest for cures for his poor health and his impotence grew more urgent. Once again Catherine was left in charge with the secretaries and Villeroy worried about the shambolic state they were in, surviving only 'from day to day'.[120] In early February, after a few days at Ollainville, the king left on a Lenten pilgrimage to Chartres to pray for a son and the long walk in filthy weather caused him to fall ill. Catherine was also unwell and left Paris in early March for Chenonceau: soon after arriving she wrote to Anna d'Este, 'every day since leaving Paris I have been troubled by a dreadful headache' but it vanished at the château, 'here it is spring and everything is in flower'.[121] In late April she left for Fontainebleau to join the king, having written to approve of 'the decision you have made to take the diet with your wife', particularly because 'it is important to do everything you can to have children'.[122] Cobham reported early in May that Henry had started the 'diet' but was 'not well able to stand on his feet', nor to continue the audience, 'so he requested me to deliver him a note of the case which he would consider with his mother and his council'.[123]

A notable absentee at Fontainebleau was the duke of Guise, who had not left Paris with the court in April. There is evidence to suggest that he was putting the final touches to a plot to invade England, to be launched from his château at Eu near Dieppe, to overthrow Elizabeth I and place his niece Mary Stuart on the throne.[124] In May he attended a meeting with the papal nuncio in Paris, where he promised to take part in the invasion in person; and his qualms about breaking the oath he had sworn to the king as a knight of Saint-Esprit not to fight for another prince were put to rest by one of the other plotters, one of Henry's Jesuit confessors.[125] In May there were reports that Guise was building a college for the Jesuits at his estate at Eu; a few months later ambassador Cobham warned Walsingham that Guise was intercepting letters at Calais, and sent his via Dieppe.[126] Rumours were rife that the duke was also involved in more treasonable activities: Villeroy warned Henry that he was secretly in league with Philip II; others said that he was plotting with Philip to have Navarre deprived of his title because he was Protestant. Certainly Henry worried enough about Guise to appoint men to keep a careful eye on his activities; and Walsingham, too, had his spies at work, monitoring plots against his queen.[127]

Catherine's own problem that summer concerned her daughter Marguerite, who had returned to court the previous year, estranged again from her husband. She had infuriated Henry by showing her dislike of Joyeuse and Épernon; worse, she had taken Anjou's part in their quarrel; and she started an affair with one of the duke's men, though this remained secret. In June the king told her to dismiss a *fille d'honneur* who had had an affair with Navarre and a child by him; both Henry and Catherine expressed to her their disapproval that a girl 'of such infamy' should be allowed to remain in Marguerite's household.[128]

Henry himself was away from court for most of the autumn and Cobham's reports carry regular bulletins about his health. In mid-June he was 'not thoroughly well in health, having during his diet lost some of his teeth and feels a disposition of a fistula in an evil place'.[129] A fortnight later the diplomat had difficulties securing an audience because Henry was away but was promised that he would be back the following week, 'which is not yet so certain as I would wish'.[130] On 1 August the queen left to take the waters in the Bourbonnais and ten days later Henry left, accompanied by Joyeuse and Épernon, his Jesuit priests and his bodyguard, on a pilgrimage to Le-Puy-Notre-Dame, south of Angers, where there was a relic of the Virgin's belt, said to be particularly efficacious for those in want of a son.[131] In September he joined the queen in the Bourbonnais and was not expected back soon 'because he has sent for his violins and other musicians'.[132] But his health was no better when he returned in October and he left on another pilgrimage in November.[133]

Once again Catherine took charge of the day-to-day business of government, reading despatches and writing replies. Important letters still needed the king's signature, but he was often difficult to find and frustratingly slow to act. She was at Saint-Maur with the king's council and the secretaries for most of August and September, moving back to Paris in early October, where she remained for the next eight months. She evidently worried about Henry's health though her letters suggest that she made efforts to underplay the seriousness of this in public. At the end of September she told ambassador Mauvissière that the king 'being in a very good state of health', was on his way back to court.[134] Six weeks later she announced that the king had left 'to go hunting around Senlis five or six days ago and all was well, God be thanked'.[135] There were also problems with Anjou, who was running short of money: his extravagant lifestyle was expensive and his troops, who were dying of hunger, threatened to mutiny if they were not paid. Bellièvre was sent to Bruges to report: 'from the news you send me,' Catherine wrote in August, 'he is in great danger.'[136] She arranged for funds to be sent to her son from her own resources and, after modest additional sums from various allies, he was able to keep his hopes alive for the time being.

In December 1582 there was an upheaval of an entirely different kind: the new Gregorian calendar. That there were errors in the Julian calendar had been known since the thirteenth century, but it was not until now that serious action was taken to remedy the situation. In response to his reform commission, Gregory XIII announced that ten days must be removed from the calendar and ordered this to be implemented across the Catholic world in October 1582. Philip II complied in Spain, the Netherlands and his possessions across the Atlantic, as did most of the Italian states; in France the reform was delayed by two months, with 9 December followed by 20 December. The change caused complications for everyone, notably diplomats and bureaucrats – and for modern scholars; and it was made even more complicated by the refusal of many Protestant countries to adopt the papist revision.[*]

The year 1583 began badly for Catherine. On 17 January, Anjou launched an attack on Antwerp but failed to capture this important port city. The attack was certainly ill-judged: the duke was over-ambitious and did not possess the necessary resources nor the military skills. The result was a disaster: as Orange informed Elizabeth I, 'there was no small slaughter; of the burghers some eighty were slain and of the French about one thousand five hundred'.[137] Anjou's reign as 'prince and lord of the Dutch Provinces' had lasted less than a year; his

---

[*]   The British Parliament finally adopted the Gregorian calendar in 1752.

popularity in France had plummeted and he only avoided Spanish reprisals thanks to the intervention of Henry and William of Orange. Catherine again sent Bellièvre to the Netherlands, carrying funds to persuade to Anjou return to France.

Henry, meanwhile, had taken refuge in religion. In March 1583, under the influence of his Jesuit confessor Edmund Auger, he founded a second religious order, a confraternity of penitents dedicated to the Annunciation. Its members were known as the White Penitents from the colour of their coarse woollen robes, which also covered their heads, with slits cut for their eyes. Devoted to charity, among the brothers' duties was to accompany men condemned to their death to the scaffold.[138] Their first procession to the Grands-Augustins, where this order was also based, took place on 25 March, the Feast of the Annunciation. Henry took part in the procession: L'Estoile recorded how he 'walked unguarded and without any difference from the other confrères either as to attire or position'.[139] Cobham noted that the Parisians 'have shown themselves scandalized' at the king's behaviour.[140] The duke of Guise voiced his disapproval of Henry's desire 'to live like a monk and not a king', though he himself was a member of this confraternity, as were his brothers Mayenne and the cardinal of Guise.[141]

Guise himself was seen to be taking steps to reassert his influence at court. There were rumours that he was trying to buy Anjou's favour with offers of troops for the campaign in the Netherlands. When Catherine planned a trip to Calais to talk to Anjou about his marriage to one of her granddaughters, the children of Claude and Charles of Lorraine, Guise offered to accompany her with 1,200 of his men; Henry 'took it in very ill part', appalled that Guise could command the loyalty and devotion of so many of the king's own subjects.[142] For Guise, however, a marriage between the heir to the throne and one of his Lorraine cousins promised enormous benefits if Anjou became king. In a more sinister strategy, he continued to belittle Navarre's right, as senior prince of the blood, to inherit the throne in the event of Anjou's death: in March, Cobham sent Walsingham 'a small treatise confuting the allegations of the pretended claim of the duke of Guise to the crown of France'.[143] On the streets of Paris he was already a hero for his stand against Anjou's marriage to the Protestant queen of England and for his staunch support of the Catholic Church.

Henry was desperate for a son. At Easter he was on pilgrimage to Chartres, walking the 60 miles there, and back, while Catherine and the queen travelled by coach. In mid-April he embarked on another, which left him so exhausted that he had to rest at Ollainville on his return; in May there was talk of a third, to Notre-Dame-de-l'Épine near Verdun, though this seems to have been cancelled.[144] Catherine herself was ill that spring: ambassador Cobham reported 'the queen mother has again kept her bed these few days past constrained thereto by the swelling gout in her legs and hands, which she could not any longer dissemble'.[145] This might explain those undefined 'illnesses' from which she suffered, and the 'sciatica' she described in May 1579 that required her to ride a mule if she wanted a walk. This painful disease, which was in the Medici genes, was often fatal, though her doctors had 'comforted her with persuasions that the gout lengthens the life'. Despite the gout, she continued to keep the government going all spring and early summer with the help of the secretaries. 'If there are any urgent and important things,' Henry instructed Villeroy and his colleagues, 'you should, all of you, show them to the queen without sending them to me.'[146]

Early in June, Henry left for Mézières where he intended to take the waters – these were the waters from Spa near Liège, still famous for its mineral springs, which were bottled specially for the king, signed and sealed by a physician and carried on the backs of peasants the 100 miles to Mézières so that he could have fresh water every eighteen hours.[147] This time the court also transferred to Mézières, and Catherine herself arrived in mid-June. Soon afterwards she wrote to her friend Anna d'Este to say, 'the king takes the Spa water every day and is doing very well, the queen takes it every two days'; indeed, she added, they were so well 'that we may have the joy of seeing them with children'.[148] She also wrote to the abbess of the convent of the Murate in Florence, where she had spent some years as a child, with a gift of 6,000 scudi to add to the presents she had already given the Murate, asking the abbess 'to pray to God for the king my lord and the queen my daughter'.[149]

Leaving Henry to his waters, Catherine left with Villeroy and Pinart in early July to meet Anjou at Chaulnes in the hopes of dissuading him from raising more troops in northern France for the Netherlands campaign. She prevaricated – it was difficult to see what else she could do – and promised that Henry would help but warned that this would not happen at once. In early August, Henry left for the Bourbonnais, where the queen 'has gone to take the baths and they will return to [Paris] in September,' she reported.[150] She herself was on her way to La Fère for a second meeting with Anjou when she fell ill, worrying secretary Pinart enough to write to the king: 'your mother felt a little ill at Verneuil the day before yesterday', and was up all night with a 'looseness', probably diarrhoea.[151] Catherine's doctor diagnosed 'a very serious illness' and had her moved to Compiègne: 'she arrived here yesterday evening where she rested because she was very weak after this great evacuation,' continued Pinart, 'and after an enema this morning she is, thanks be to God, much better now and is planning to continue her journey tomorrow.' She had not lost her grasp of state matters: the rest of Pinart's letter is taken up with her instructions as to what needed Henry's attention.

Catherine's meeting with Anjou at La Fère was inconclusive and while she was there more bad news arrived from court. There were rumours that Marguerite had given birth to a son by her lover: 'the birth of the child is true,' ambassador Moro reported, in code.[152] Henry informed Navarre, who demanded

evidence, and had Marguerite's carriage searched but found
nothing. The following month Moro reported that the princess admitted that she and Anjou were plotting to assassinate
their brother, though he added that 'she is thought to have
spoken out of dread of torture'.[153] When she heard the news
of the birth, Catherine wrote at once to Bellièvre saying that
'it would be better to leave everything to the judgement and
discretion of the king'; she left the next day not for Paris but
for Gaillon, near Rouen, to convalesce.[154] Her doctor – aptly
named Vigor – wrote to the king about the state of her health
in a manner that makes alarming reading: she was 'day by
day pressed by these melancholic passions' about which he
had already sent the king three letters, augmented by 'lack
of appetite and a continual headache with heaviness and las-
situde of the whole body that are symptoms indicating fever or
another bad illness'.[155] Pinart, who also wrote to the king that
day, was more optimistic: 'I assure you Sire, that she feels well'
and intended to leave for Paris 'in four or five days'.[156]

Catherine joined the court at Saint-Germain in early October
in preparation for an Assembly of Notables which Henry was
to open on 18 November. Anjou, too, was expected to attend
but he was ill; Catherine travelled to Château-Thierry in late
October to find him with a painful throat infection, a fever
and sweating profusely, but he was better by the time she left
in early November.[157] She visited him again in late December
and in February he was well enough to join the court. This was
a joy for Catherine: 'at present he is with the king his brother,'
she wrote, and 'I praise God from the bottom of my heart to
see them so happy together, which can only be for the greater
good and prosperity of the affairs of the realm'.[158] To Bellièvre
she wrote, 'I can assure you' that the reconciliation 'has greatly
assisted my recovery and the end of my fever which was brought
on by the worry and sadness that I experienced during their

separation.'[159] Good news of her children had been in short supply during 1583 so she must have been doubly pleased in April 1584 to hear that Bellièvre, who had been sent south to mediate between Marguerite and Navarre, was successful. She thanked him effusively: 'I will start my letter to you by saying that, after God, you have returned me to health through your prudence and good conduct in achieving such good work and so important for our house and honour to have my daughter back again with her husband.'[160]

Catherine herself was ill that spring with a recurrent fever lasting for weeks; she spent much of her time at Saint-Maur. Few of her letters survive from January to April 1584 and those that do are overwhelmingly to Bellièvre and Villeroy, who kept her up to date with the news, which was not good. In February, Navarre warned Henry of a Spanish plot to overthrow him: Philip II planned to invade France from the Netherlands and his army would join with a rebellion led by the duke of Guise and his brother Mayenne.[161] In March, Henry resumed his pilgrimages, this time in the company of forty-seven penitents to pray for an heir at Chartres and Cléry.[162] This time the burden of government fell on Villeroy's shoulders: 'I am going away,' Henry informed him in early March, 'I entrust to you all my affairs ... tell your colleagues and see that no one sends me anything unless it is something really necessary [and] show everything to the queen.'[163]

In addition to her own declining health, Catherine had other worries. Anjou was ill again and she left for Château-Thierry a few days after Henry's departure on pilgrimage. For the next three months she remained nearby, either at Saint-Maur or Montceaux, watching as his health broke down and it became clear that he was in last stages of consumption. His death on 10 June 1584 at the age of only twenty-nine was a tragic end to a short life; for Catherine he was the fourth of her five sons to die young. 'I am so wretched,' she wrote the day after to Bellièvre, 'but I know that God's will must be obeyed, that everything is his and that he only lends us the children he gives us for as long as he likes.'[164] Only Henry was left: 'if I could see his children, as I hope in God he will have, this would be a great consolation for me and for all this realm,' she continued. In the meantime, the new heir to the throne was the king's brother-in-law Henri of Navarre, and he was a Protestant: the two religions were now campaigning for the crown itself.

Anguish
1584–1589

On Saturday 23 February 1585 a superb cavalcade made its way through the streets of Paris: Catholics riding alongside Protestants, it was a highly visible statement of the reconciliation between the faiths that lay at the heart of Catherine's political thinking. The riders were an English embassy, led by the earl of Derby and escorted by the knights of Henry III's order of Saint-Esprit, which was in the capital to invest the king as a knight of Elizabeth I's order of the Garter.[1] Henry had been given the honour back in 1575 but the investiture was delayed for political reasons. Now, in a new political era, it was time to celebrate the friendship between the two kingdoms – it was not quite an alliance – with due magnificence.

The court laid on two weeks of lavish entertainments: on Tuesday Joyeuse hosted a banquet; on Thursday they dined at the Louvre with the king, queen and queen mother.[2] Catherine herself hosted a banquet on the Sunday, which was followed in the evening by the king's ball, reputedly costing 40,000 écus.[3] The guests were impressed by the excellent music and singing but, above all, by Henry's elegance and skill on the dance floor. He led out a troop of twenty-four courtiers, all in white doublets and hose with hats of cloth of silver embroidered with pearls, to perform an elaborate ballet spelling out the names of 'Henry' and 'Elizabeth'. The one discordant note occurred at the investiture in the Grands-Augustins, where difficulties surfaced over the religious rites: the English refused to take part in a Catholic mass but did agree to attend evensong; and although the papal nuncio overcame his doubts to congratulate the king on the honour, the Spanish ambassador kept his eyes fixed firmly on the ground throughout the ceremony.

This display of royal friendship with Protestant England was not well received in Paris, where fear of the mob had led to an unusually high level of security: extra troops were posted at the Louvre and armed soldiers guarded the palace where the guests were lodged; the feasting and masques took place behind closed doors.[4] Catholic preachers used the visit to stir up the mob, goading their congregations to believe that Henry was plotting with the heretic Elizabeth, whose hands were already stained with the blood of Catholic martyrs, to destroy their faith. It did not take much imagination to realize how many Parisians would refuse to accept a Protestant monarch and that they would fight to defend their religion.

Within days of Anjou's death in June 1584 the palace issued a formal announcement: 'it is resolved that the king of Navarre shall be called Monsieur, as heir apparent,' reported the English resident, Sir Edward Stafford, who had replaced Lord Cobham the previous year.[5] French law dictated that, as Henry had no sons, the crown must pass to the senior prince of the blood, Henri of Navarre. Both Catherine and Henry understood the implications of a Protestant heir and sent the duke of Épernon to join Bellièvre in the south with the task of persuading Navarre to convert to Catholicism, and thus undermine the opposition. Henry's choice of envoy to the Protestant kingdom, armed with the enormous sum of

400,000 écus to cover his expenses, was not well judged.[6] Moreover, he was detested by queen Marguerite: Catherine was relieved to hear that her daughter, who could be difficult when she chose, promised to welcome Épernon.[7] But the mission was a failure. Navarre preferred to sign an alliance with Elizabeth I; secretary Villeroy feared France was heading for disaster.[8]

Catherine had been ill during the spring but was able to take charge of the government during Henry's absences that summer: always obsessed with court etiquette, in January 1585, shortly before the arrival of the English envoys, he would publish a set of radical alterations to protocol that would put even more distance between himself and his court.[9] Catherine's immediate task after Anjou's death was to delay the arrival of the Garter embassy which had been expected later that month. On 25 July 1584 she wrote to ambassador Mauvissière with news that the king was away 'to spend some days at his devotions' but that on his return 'he is allowing the court to break up for two months so he can go to Lyons for his own reasons with only a small entourage, and will return to Blois around the end of September'.[10] She continued, 'the king has asked Lord Stafford to beg the queen of England to have Lord Derby's journey bringing the order of the Garter deferred until such time as the king is able to receive it with due honour', in other words to give her time to arrange the grand ceremonial.

In mid-August, Catherine left Paris with secretary Pierre Brulart for Chenonceau, where they were joined by Pinart, though not Villeroy, who had fallen seriously ill after his hard work earlier in the year.[11] The news from abroad was depressing: the balance of power between Spain and the courts of northern Europe had begun to tip, alarmingly, in favour of Spain. A month after Anjou's death, William of Orange had been assassinated, the victim of an agent in the pay of Alessandro Farnese, prince of Parma, son of Philip II's half-sister and his new governor in the Netherlands; and his campaign to recapture the provinces was gaining ground. More evidence of this change emerged in late August when Carlo Emanuele, duke of Savoy chose Philip's daughter as his bride over the princess of Lorraine, Catherine's choice, to align himself more firmly with Spain rather than France – it should be said, both girls were her own granddaughters. More worrying, though, was the news at home.

The death of Anjou was the chance for which the unscrupulously ambitious Henri, duke of Guise had been planning, with a nexus of loyal family support: his brothers Charles, duke of Mayenne and Louis, cardinal of Lorraine; his cousins Charles, duke of Aumale and Charles, duke of Elbeuf; and their more distant relatives, Charles III, duke of Lorraine, Philippe-Emmanuel, duke of Mercoeur and Charles, cardinal of Lorraine de Vaudémont, these last two brothers to Henry's queen. The family had left Paris directly after Anjou's funeral and were not at court for the reception of Lord Derby and the Garter. In September they were guests of Lorraine at Nancy, where they took several dramatic decisions that were not only treasonable but were to have far-reaching consequences. Refusing to accept Navarre as heir to the throne, they declared the rightful heir to be his sixty-two-year-old uncle, Cardinal Charles of Bourbon; and, to acquire financial and political support for their venture, they opened negotiations with Spain and signed the Treaty of Joinville over New Year 1585, agreeing to exterminate Protestantism in France. The cardinal of Bourbon was formally declared Henry's heir; 'all princes of the blood at present heretics' were excluded from inheriting the throne; 'all practice of heresy will be banished in the kingdom of France by public edict'; and 'those who do not reconcile themselves to the obedience of the Catholic religion will be pursued to the end until they are destroyed'.[12] Philip II for his part agreed to donate an annual sum of 600,000 écus to pay for an army. However, Gregory XIII refused to add his signature to this treaty, despite the benefits for the Church; significantly, he feared a Europe dominated by Spain, which would be the result of a Franco–Spanish war, and preferred to preserve France as a major European power, and a counter-balance to Spain.

In order to marshal support across France the Nancy meeting decided to reinvigorate the leagues founded in the aftermath of the Peace of Monsieur (1576) with a new Catholic League. Initially organized by the family and their clients in northern France, it soon spread. In Paris, where its members included merchants, lawyers and officials, it was known as the Sixteen after the committees for public safety in each of the city's sixteen *quartiers*, and soon became a signifi-cant political force in the capital. The Leaguers were clever in fomenting dissatisfaction with Henry's regime, furious at the favours he heaped on his *mignons*, using the term to express their derision at the decadence of the Valois court, and at his extravagant lifestyle, which they blamed for the rising cost of living. They were also adept at using fear as a tool of control: ambassador Stafford reported rumours of a Jesuit who, after hearing a gentleman's confession, refused to grant him remis-sion of his sins 'unless he promised to defend the league of the duke of Guise to the last drop of his blood'.[13]

On 31 March, a fortnight after the Garter embassy left Paris, the Guise allies issued a manifesto at Péronne in the name of the cardinal of Bourbon, declaring 'we have all sworn and reli-giously promised to take up arms' to restore Catholicism as the sole religion in the kingdom. Despite the claim, however, this was no longer a religious affair but a battle for the throne itself. Preparations for war were already well underway. In Paris the efficient organization of the Sixteen, with its useful contacts in government, had been able to avoid capture by the police and assemble a large supply of arms. With Guise in charge of raising men and munitions, Mayenne, Elbeuf and Mercoeur had been fomenting uprisings in places where the family had influence, such as Picardy, Normandy, Brittany and Burgundy, Lyons, Bourges and Orléans, though the south-west remained loyal to the Protestant cause. By the end of May they had

25,000 infantry and 2,000 cavalry garrisoned at Châlons-en-Champagne.[14] Catherine was shocked that Guise was raising an army against the king: 'I cannot believe nor do I wish to,' she wrote angrily on hearing rumours that 'thirty companies of cavalry' from the Spanish forces under Parma's command 'are being sent to France for your service' and demanded an explanation.[15] Significantly, the Guise army was a Catholic one, not loyal to the crown but to the Catholic League, and included many foreign troops, especially mercenaries from Switzerland and Spanish soldiers from the Netherlands.

Catherine's priority in the autumn of 1584 was to rouse Henry from his lethargy, and his obsession with the revision of court etiquette, to recognize the threat posed by Guise and the League – to his survival and that of the kingdom. But his response on hearing of the Guise meeting at Nancy was to ignore it; 'the king only mocks at it and them, seeming to have them in no reputation,' reported ambassador Stafford.[16] When news arrived of the Péronne declaration he countered it with a statement calling for the League to disband, which Guise ignored. Catherine, and Villeroy, urged him to start raising troops and prepare for war. Henry did little – perhaps he knew it was hopeless. In reality it was too late: many men who would otherwise have fought for their king had enlisted in the League's army, and horses were in short supply. In truth there was little money to make a serious attempt to counter the threat posed by the League. Henry was strapped by the crippling debts left from previous wars, and by his lavish generosity to his *mignons*; beyond strengthening the existing army with his own guards, there was little practical that he could do.

Henry did take measures to increase his own security and in December set up a personal bodyguard of young men, mainly from the minor nobility, to protect the king – 'night and day' as L'Estoile put it – in the event of an uprising in Paris or a direct attack on the Louvre.[17] Known as the *Quarante-Cinq* (the Forty-five), this elite body of mercenaries earned salaries of 1,200 écus a year, three times that paid to the captain of the royal guard.[18] To counter the religious insult implied by the Sixteen, Henry founded another confraternity in Paris in March 1585, this one dedicated to Christ's Passion (*Confrérie de la Mort et Passion de Notre Seigneur*). But this attempt to unite Catholics behind the crown was derided by the leaguers, who accused him of hypocrisy with this overt display of his credentials as the Most Christian King while accepting the order of the Garter from a Protestant queen.

Characteristically keen to avoid confrontation, Henry opted to negotiate with Guise in the hope of avoiding war, asking Catherine to lead the talks. He thanked her for her help, 'which is very pleasing and gives me some hope that my cousin the duke of Guise might draw back and obey my orders'; his hope was that she could negotiate 'a good and happy peace, which can halt the great evil that we face now'.[19] On 30 March, accompanied by Pinart and members of the king's council, she left Paris for Épernay, a journey of 90 miles which must have been very uncomfortable as she was suffering from gout and troublesome pains in her side. Ill health was to dog her throughout the talks: she spent most of her time in bed from where she dictated letters to the loyal Pinart, who sat at the end of it, laboriously taking dictation.[20] The frequent letters she wrote to Henry from Épernay, mostly written by Pinart, invariably contained a report of her ailments: in one she complained of pain in her left ear which had troubled her for three days; in another she apologized for not writing herself 'but I was tormented all night by my gout'.[21] Guise must have hoped that eventually she would be too ill to continue; but Catherine was made of sterner stuff.

A day or two after her arrival Catherine summoned Guise 'to come here tomorrow so that we can begin our talks', adding her hopes for a resolution that would be 'of service to the king my son and for the peace of this realm'.[22] It was optimistic: from the start Guise proved difficult, confident of success, arrogant and demanding. Henry was equally obstinate: when she encouraged him to make concessions to Guise he replied that 'he will not be the first to accept the law from those who ought humbly to obey him'.[23] But she was comforted by the attitude of her son-in-law Lorraine: as she told Henry on 13 April, 'in two hours I have a meeting with your brother [the duke of] Lorraine who has said he will do all that is in his power to help me in this; I pray to God that all will be arranged to your satisfaction'.[24] A few days later she reported that 'my son the duke of Lorraine continues always to give me hope that I will do some good'.[25]

Catherine had much to trouble her: Pinart thought her mood was 'more angry and disturbed' than normal, though this could just have been the result of her ill health.[26] On top of her problems with Guise, her children were causing her much pain. Henry's safety was a concern: she warned him to 'take care ... especially around your person; there is so much treachery about that I die of fear'.[27] But it was Marguerite whose news was most worrying: she had fled Navarre and sought refuge in Agen, where she had started to raise troops to fight against her husband and, alarmingly, was doing this with funds supplied by Guise.[28] Catherine was appalled: her daughter had always been difficult, but this was a step too far, and treasonable. As she explained to Bellièvre, who had told her of Marguerite's actions, 'I know that God has given me this creature as punishment for my sins, an affliction that gives me pain every day; she is the thorn in my side in this world', and begged him for advice.[29]

At Épernay the talks continued. While Guise employed delaying tactics to draw out the negotiations and give him more time to muster his forces, Henry continued to ignore Catherine's pleas to prepare for war: in early May she urged him 'to gather your forces and make them as large as you can for I can well see, and they have clearly told us, that they

intend to have their own surety towns and associations until all
the towns which are held by the Protestants are taken'.[30] Still
in search of a solution to satisfy both faiths, she suggested that
he should include Protestants in his army; however, even the
optimistic Catherine understood the weakness of the crown's
position. The League held the stronger hand; 'you know that
Guise and his brother are loved and respected by the soldiers
and men of war'.[31] Two weeks later she reported that 'French
troops from all parts, infantry and cavalry' were massing
near Verdun, that they were well supplied with 'flour, bread,
wine and meat', and with artillery: 'I fear very much they are
intended for Paris.'[32]

Guise did indeed hold the stronger hand and made life
hard for Catherine by his obstinate refusal to make concessions. Pinart admitted in early June that the talks had been
a failure: they had achieved nothing because Guise refused
to negotiate and insisted on his own terms.[33] Finally on 7
July the treaty between the two sides was signed at Nemours
and it was evident that Catherine had capitulated. Henry
was forced to revoke all previous edicts of pacification, to
declare Protestantism illegal, order all heretics to convert to
Catholicism or leave France and to join the League in its fight
against the new religion. Navarre and Condé were barred
from inheriting the French throne; and this order was given
papal sanction on 9 September when they were excommunicated by Sixtus V, who had succeeded Gregory XIII that April.
One of Guise's few concessions was to drop the demand for
Joyeuse and Épernon to be replaced in key posts by his allies,
though Guise himself now became governor of several important towns in north-east France.

Guise had got his way: he wanted war with Navarre, and he
wanted the royal army on his side. Both Catherine and Henry
knew the treaty would be unacceptable to Navarre, who now
stepped up his own preparations for a war that would be a
fight for the survival of the Protestant faith. Already in March,
Navarre had held a meeting with Montmorency-Damville,

governor of Languedoc, to agree a joint policy if the talks at
Épernay went, as they suspected, against them. On 10 August
he issued a declaration at Bergerac insisting on his loyalty to
Henry – unlike the League: 'I am bound to oppose with all my
strength ... those who wish to cause the ruin of the crown and
house of France.'[34] He was prompt in putting his words into
action. As Guise was doing in the north, he began his conquest
of the south and, having consolidated his hold in Guyenne
and Languedoc, he expanded his authority into Dauphiné.
He took Montélimar in August and Die the following month,
while Condé captured the citadel of Angers, though it was
quickly retaken by the royal army under the command of
Joyeuse; the north continued to remain staunchly League
territory.

Catherine was now sixty-four years old, often ill with gout and
other ailments; the robust good health she had enjoyed for
most of her life had begun to fail. After signing the treaty
at Nemours she had returned to Paris, where, apart from a
few visits to her beloved Saint-Maur, she remained based for
the next twelve months. She found Henry again in isolation,
showing little interest in the affairs of state. Despite ratifying
the treaty, he refused to commit himself to its terms and,
in another gesture that pleased many moderate Catholics,
refused to publish Sixtus V's bull excommunicating Navarre,
arguing with reason that this was unwarranted interference in
affairs of the French crown. On Catherine's advice he sent the
bishop of Paris to Rome to repair relations with the pope, with
the result that Sixtus V agreed to a substantial loan of 800,000
écus (2,400,000 livres) to the king to prepare for war.[35]

By August, Catherine was again in charge of government
while Henry moved to the royal château in the Bois de
Vincennes, just outside Paris, where he remained based for
the rest of 1585 and much of 1586. More fortress than palace

and well-fortified against attack, it provided an ideal setting for his secluded lifestyle. He built an oratory for a new confraternity known as the Blue Penitents, dedicated to St Jerome, and gave another congregation a priory in the grounds.[36] He fasted assiduously and spent as many as twenty hours a day at his devotions; his piety – one might call it religious mania – inspired in part by the need to assert his authority in matters of religion but also by his desperate need for a son. In December, Catherine rode the seven or so miles out of Paris to the castle to see him; one of her motives was to urge him to stop fasting which, she argued, was bad for his health and for the health of his regime.[37] Another problem was money but when she suggested that he should cut back the *Quarante-Cinq* because of the expense Henry apparently retorted that he intended instead to offer them all presents of 400 écus.[38] Her appeal to him to get back to work was only briefly successful: in late December, Henry left on another pilgrimage to Chartres and, on his return to Vincennes, he refused to see not only Villeroy and Joyeuse but Catherine as well.

Catherine carried on in Henry's absence in January and February when he was ill and shut away at Vincennes, though he was well enough to receive Guise in early March to discuss plans for the war against Protestantism they had agreed in the treaty. Surrounded by an imposing entourage of 600 men, the duke made his entry into Paris, where he was given a triumphant welcome, a telling contrast to the silent streets guarded by royal troops that had marked the arrival of the Garter embassy a year earlier. Henry agreed to Guise's demands, promising to raise a powerful army; the duke, who seems to have taken the king's behaviour at face value and assumed his opponent was weak, now sensed victory. But a few weeks later Henry rescinded his offer, telling Guise he intended to negotiate with Navarre instead.[39]

Henry continued to be elusive: Filippo Cavriani, one of the king's doctors who had a secondary role as informer to the grand duke of Tuscany, reported on 14 April that the king's devotions had reached such disturbing levels that he was no longer involved in public affairs and that everything fell on Catherine's shoulders.[40] Henry ignored envoys from the Protestant rulers of Denmark, Germany and the Swiss cantons who were at court in April to urge him to make peace with Navarre: the Danish envoy was so worried about the political tension that he 'requested protection against the followers of the house of Guise' and was given an armed escort to the frontier.[41] When agents from Navarre arrived at the end of May, Henry avoided negotiating with them as well, and occupied himself hunting or with his lapdogs, a hobby almost as expensive as his indulgence of his *mignons*, wasting money that could more usefully have been put towards the war effort.[42] Although some scholars claim this behaviour was due to mental instability on the part of the king, others have argued, more convincingly, that it was a deliberate ploy on his part to gain time.

Behind the excuses, it was clear that Henry was avoiding more than diplomats: he was avoiding war, specifically the alliance with Guise, one of the cornerstones of the treaty he had signed so recently at Nemours. Trust between the two men was wearing thin: Catherine sent Guise an emollient letter, assuring him that she had 'no other object than the contentment of the king and your ease and honour'.[43] By the summer it was common knowledge that Henry intended to renege on the treaty and send Catherine to negotiate with Navarre: in early July, Villeroy informed the French ambassador in Venice that Henry wanted peace 'more than I can say'.[44] Neither mother nor son could have been very optimistic of persuading Navarre to convert to Catholicism, the prime barrier to inheriting the French throne: by doing so he would lose the support of his own subjects, and his own crown. What Catherine hoped to achieve was an end to the skirmishing between Guise and Navarre, before it turned into war.

Catherine left Paris on 24 July to spend a few days at Blois before moving on to Chenonceau to wait for arrangements for her meeting with Navarre to be finalized. In mid-August she wrote to marshal Matignon, governor of Guyenne, to advise him of her plans, and to soften his antipathy towards Navarre: 'if I can do something for the honour of God and for the peace of this poor realm, I believe that you would be very glad to see the king in complete authority', adding 'you will be advised of the day of my arrival'.[45] However, there were delays while all sides jostled for position and she remained at Chenonceau for much of the autumn, with members of the king's council and Pinart, waiting for the arrangements to be finalized. With Villeroy remaining at court, Catherine could trust the secretary to send reliable information on the state of her son's health as well as political matters. Nor was Catherine well: on one occasion she chided Navarre for expecting her to undertake a journey to La-Mothe-Saint-Héray, east of Niort, 'even though it is a place which will be very inconvenient for my health and age and the ailments I suffer, being very rheumatic'.[46]

From the south there was more bad news about Marguerite. She had been forced out of Agen by marshal Matignon the previous autumn and since then had been living with her lover the seigneur d'Aubiac at Carlat, one of her castles in the Auvergne. Plans for Catherine to spend the winter with her daughter, and persuade her to reconcile herself to her family, came to nothing. Now, a year later, Marguerite had been betrayed by one of her gentlemen, who had been tempted by Henry's offer of 10,000 écus for her capture, forcing her to flee Carlat with d'Aubiac for Ybois, a castle belonging to her mother, where she was finally caught.[47] Catherine's anger, echoed by Henry, at the shocking behaviour of the royal princess was palpable. Writing to Villeroy from Chenonceau on 23 October, Catherine described her as a 'poor, miserable creature whom God has put into this world for the torment of my old age', confiding that she 'asked the king not to lose a single hour' in having her arrested, 'or she will bring some other disgrace on us'.[48] Henry had her imprisoned in the fortress of

Usson, her estates confiscated and her household dismissed. He also ordered that d'Aubiac was to be hanged at Usson in Marguerite's presence, though in the end she was spared this brutal sight and her lover was executed elsewhere.[49]

It was not until the end of October that Catherine left Chenonceau on her quest for Navarre. Guise evidently respected her skill as a negotiator because news of her mission worried him greatly: 'I always fear the schemes of the queen-mother, who will be with the king of Navarre in a few days,' he informed the Spanish ambassador Bernardino de Mendoza; 'she wants to upset the peace of Catholics of both crowns'.[50] The place of their meeting still had to be fixed; her plan was to 'celebrate the Feast of All Saints at Champigny and leave immediately for Saint-Maixent or to La-Mothe-Saint-Hérault, in the hope of finding my son the king of Navarre'.[51] The journey was as unpleasant and uncomfortable as she had anticipated: she was often ill and suffered pain in her right arm, which made writing difficult. Pinart wrote to Villeroy from Champigny in early November to say that he was working late and, although he finished his letter at one o'clock in the morning, he still had to wait for the queen mother to finish her prayers so that he could read it back to her.[52] That day she sent a courier to Navarre with a message urging him to consider 'the conservation of this realm', and begged him 'therefore to stop playing with me and show me that you have the desire as me'.[53]

Navarre proved very adept at playing for time; possibly he had learned his tactics from Catherine herself after watching her use them to good effect during her earlier peace mission to the south. The talks finally started in December at the castle of Saint-Brice, east of Cognac, where Catherine celebrated Christmas and New Year, but proved inconclusive. It was not her fault: Navarre never had any intention of signing an alliance with Henry against Guise, or of converting to Catholicism. While the armies of the League were consolidating their hold on the northern provinces of the kingdom, he was waiting for confirmation of military aid from Protestant rulers abroad. As the Venetian ambassador Giovanni Dolfin concluded on 13 March: 'Navarre is not likely to come to terms with the king for he has received 120,000 ducats from the queen of England'; but it was the arrival of troops from the German princes that month that finally brought the talks to an end.[54]

The fighting – it was not quite war, yet – was causing chaos across France. The previous autumn the Florentine doctor Cavriani had reported his shock at the dire state of the realm, where poverty, disease and famine were all endemic: the prices of wheat and wine, he reported, had quadrupled over the summer.[55] When Henry tried to impose further taxes on his subjects, placards appeared on the streets of Paris attacking the king and his mother.[56] In November a lawyer was hanged for calling Henry a hypocrite.[57] At court the king's continued absence made for a toxic atmosphere: Cavriani feared 'some sinister accident'.[58] Ambassador Mendoza told Philip II that 'such is the confusion of this court, the vacillation of the king and the jealousy, hatred and suspicion of the courtiers … even Villeroy, who holds the helm says that such is the state of the king that it is impossible to predict whether it will be peace or war'.[59] The Spanish, and the League, wanted war; it was Catherine and Henry who wanted peace.

Others reported daily squabbles and fights between courtiers. Villeroy referred to 'disunity between Catholics', a diplomatic euphemism for the growing hostility between the supporters of Henry and Guise, as between the men themselves.[60] Petty jealousies between Joyeuse and Épernon had begun to morph into hostility and the king had been obliged to admonish them in public. And behind closed doors there were other more worrying events taking place. Catherine was on her way back to court in late March after her mission to

Navarre when Villeroy interrupted her journey at Étampes, with the news that Épernon, Guise and the Paris city authorities had all been implicated in a plot against the king.[61]

With scarcely a month to draw breath, on 12 May Catherine was on the road again with Pinart, this time travelling east to Rheims in the hope of signing a truce with Guise. The duke agreed to a truce but refused to comply with the conditions, which included the return of towns recently seized by the League to royal control. Guise was resolute in pursuing his own goals at the expense of all else: as Pinart commented in a letter to Villeroy on 24 May, 'the mask of religion is lifted: it is ambition [Guise] which rules us; imprudence [Navarre] which masters us and irresolution [Henry] which is ruining us'.[62] At the talks with Guise the 'mask of religion' was highly visible: attending one meeting with Guise, Mayenne and Elbeuf were four cardinals: Bourbon, their candidate for the throne; Vendôme, the prince of Condé's younger brother; Guise, the duke's younger brother; and Vaudémont, Guise's cousin and brother of the queen. Their presence underlined the hard-line position taken by the League that made it impossible to unite French Catholics behind the crown. Villeroy summarized the position: 'I am a good Catholic,' he wrote, 'and attached to my religion as much as any man of my standing; but not to the extent of supporting those who wish to restrain the king on the pretext of piety and so deprive him of authority', in other words, the League.[63]

There was one piece of good news to cheer Catherine that May: the birth of a son to her granddaughter Catalina, duchess of Savoy. Despite her disapproval of Catalina's marriage in March 1584, she had been genuinely thrilled the previous April at becoming a great-grandmother when Catalina gave birth to her first son, Filippo Emanuele. Although she had never met Catalina, or her sister Isabella, she had established close ties with them ever since the death of their mother, her own daughter Elisabeth, when they were babies. As she wrote to Isabella after the birth of Filippo Emanuele: 'I cannot describe to you my joy that it has pleased God to give your sister a beautiful son.'[64] She heard the news of the arrival of a second boy, Vittorio Amadeo, just thirteen months later, from the duke himself: 'I pray to God that you continue to be well, all four of you, father and mother and the two little ones,' she replied, 'and I tell you the truth that one of my greatest wishes would be to have the happiness, before I die, of seeing you all.'[65]

By the middle of June 1587 Catherine was back in Paris, where she remained for the rest of the year. The atmosphere in the capital had turned even uglier in her absence, sparked by the execution of Mary Stuart, dowager queen of France, which had taken place on 18 February (8 February in England). The previous September a Catholic plot to overthrow Elizabeth I had been uncovered and papers found implicating Mary; she was sent to trial in December, found guilty and sentenced to death. Henry had sent envoys to England to intercede on his sister-in-law's behalf but to no avail; and Catherine was saddened that her son 'was not able to do more for this poor queen'.[66] News of Mary's execution finally arrived in Paris on 9 March after the English ports, which had been closed for three weeks following the execution, reopened. Three days later a solemn mass was held at Notre-Dame with a sermon on the dead queen designed to flatter the house of Guise, 'the most excellent of all those of the other princes of the land'; another sermon preached at Saint-Eustache was interrupted after the priest, and the congregation, broke down in tears.[67]

Mary's death, and Elizabeth's other crimes against the Catholic Church, provided the clergy and the Sixteen with a treasure trove of propaganda with which to stoke fears of the horrors that would be in store under a Protestant monarch, above all of the massacre of French Catholics that would follow his succession. On the streets of his capital Henry's authority was almost non-existent, eclipsed by that of the Sixteen; and his unpopularity was growing in unison with the rising prices of basic foodstuffs, which provoked famine and riots that summer. His attempts to assert his position were futile. When he heard that a curé of Saint-Benoît was preaching against reconciliation he summoned the man to the Louvre and ordered him to cease meddling in matters of state; but the Sixteen had ensured that matters of state were indivisible from those of faith. In an attempt to satisfy the League with a display of his Catholic credentials he invited a particularly strict congregation of Cistercian monks to Paris but soon after they arrived events in the capital would spiral out of his control.

That summer, finally driven to take drastic action in order to salvage what little was left of his authority, Henry took a series of unusually bold decisions. After a meeting with Guise at Meaux, where he promised to supply money and men for the fight against Navarre, he announced in August that three armies were to take to the field against the Protestants, led by Guise, Joyeuse and, astonishingly, himself – all the more astonishing after the months he had spent in isolation, avoiding any form of confrontation. One factor that helped galvanize him into action was the enemy at the gates, some 35,000 men from Switzerland and Germany, the *reiters* supplied by Johann Casimir and financed by Elizabeth I, poised to invade France across its northern frontier. Joyeuse was to march south to engage Navarre, while Guise was to face the invaders in the north; Henry himself was to ensure that Navarre did not meet up with his foreign reinforcements. It was the start of a war known colloquially as the War of the Three Henrys – Henry III, Henri of Guise and Henri of Navarre.

Catherine, as usual, was left in charge while Henry was away. When he departed Paris on 12 September he took Villeroy and Brulart with him but left behind Pinart and Bellièvre to assist his mother, as well as his council, which Catherine would chair in his absence. She wrote regularly to the camp, keeping Henry in touch with state business, reporting what went on in council meetings and sending on documents for Henry to sign. Her letters reveal how much she worried about his safety: 'I am so vexed to know you are so close to this great storm,' she wrote just four days after he left.[68] A few weeks later, after thanking Brulart for sending 'the good news about the king', she begged him 'especially at this moment as the Protestant army is approaching, you would do me great pleasure by sending me a note every day'.[69]

At the end of September she was disturbed to hear that there had been a row at camp between Villeroy and Épernon: the *mignon*, who was clearly jealous of the secretary's influence with Henry, had accused him of fraud and treason in the presence of the king. Catherine took Villeroy's side and worried that Henry might fall out with this adviser, who was one of the few men on whom she could rely to tell her the truth: 'I have heard what has happened to you and am very sorry,' she commiserated, 'I wanted to send you this note, not to comfort you for I have no doubt that the king my son has already done so ... but to beg you that this will not be the cause of preventing you from serving with the same liberty that you have always done.'[70]

On 20 October 1587 Navarre inflicted a heavy defeat on Joyeuse's army at Coutras, north-east of Bordeaux. Apparently Henry and Navarre had done what they could to avoid any sort of confrontation but Joyeuse, who had ambitions to challenge Guise for leadership of the League, had no such scruples.[71] It was a rout: over 4,000 royal troops were killed, including 250 nobles and Joyeuse himself, but Navarre chose not to follow up this victory and instead retreated back to his kingdom to conserve his strength.[72] Catherine heard the news of the defeat on 25 October and the following day she sent letters to many towns warning them 'to watch and keep guard' for the *reiters,* who were on their way back to Germany, though she was careful not to go into details for fear of provoking panic. To the mayor and aldermen of Chartres, for example, she issued orders in the name of the king's council 'to have all the wheat, oats and other grains, milled and unmilled, brought into the said city from the towns, villages, hamlets, farms and small-holdings' in the surrounding countryside in order to avoid giving help to the foreign army.[73]

The defeat at Coutras was a humiliation for Henry and it was left to his rival Guise to restore his honour. A week later he attacked the *reiters* at Vimory, near Montargis, though heavy casualties forced him to withdraw. A month later, however, on 24 November, Guise achieved a more convincing victory at Auneau, just east of Chartres, where his army captured 400 Protestants and left 2,000 dead.[74] It was a mark of Henry's desire for peace that he not only paid off the Swiss troops fighting with him but the foreign troops fighting for Navarre as well.[75] It was one of Catherine's tasks to raise this money from a very reluctant *parlement* in Paris and, having discussed the matter with the council, she wrote to Henry on 30 November, 'we will do everything possible to find the 30,000 écus that you want sent to you and be assured not a single hour will be lost'.[76] But, as she had anticipated, she encountered problems raising the funds: 'I am very disappointed we cannot do more,' she informed Villeroy a fortnight later, 'things at this point are very bad and we do not expect to have great help from either the city [Paris] or the clergy.'[77]

Catherine was much relieved that the fighting was over and that her son was safe; she was also delighted that the debacle at Coutras had turned into a victory. 'It was a "true miracle" from God,' she told marshal Matignon, 'who has shown by this coup how much he loves the king and the kingdom', but she expressed her sadness at the death of Joyeuse and others lost in 'this pitiful battle'.[78] But she was bothered by Henry's mood: 'the king is excessively happy at defeating an army of 30,000 men', she had told Matignon but the victory, as she must have known, did not belong to the crown but to Guise and the League. In her worries she wrote to the abbess of the

Murate in Florence on 3 January 1588 to tell her she wanted to donate a portrait of herself to the nunnery which 'I will give orders to have sent to your convent as I have promised, not a marble statue of myself because this is too difficult but a portrait of me from the life, done very well, which is to be placed and fixed in your chapel in a short time, recommending you to include your prayers for the health of the king my son and the queen my daughter and if it please God to give them children for the good of this country and of all Christendom'.[79]

Henry had returned to Paris on 23 December to celebrate his victory and the peace with enthusiasm, attending parties, balls and banquets throughout Carnival. On 8 March 1588 he held a sumptuous funeral for Joyeuse, parading his corpse through Paris in a huge procession of members of his religious confraternities, dressed in their penitential robes, to the Grands-Augustins where the funeral service took place. Épernon had taken advantage of Joyeuse's absence to monopolize the king; and now he took advantage of his rival's death to take Joyeuse's positions of admiral of France and governor of Normandy. The move was not popular with the League and it infuriated Guise, who had expected to be rewarded with them for his role in defeating the *reiters* at Vimory and Auneau. The animosity between Henry and Guise continued to grow.

Despite Henry's behaviour towards him, Guise remained confident that the League held the upper hand. While the king partied during Carnival 1588, the League held a meeting at Nancy where they drew up a list of demands designed to impose limits on his powers.[80] The document ordered Henry 'to adhere more openly' to the League and 'to remove those who will be named to him from his entourage and from important offices' – a clear reference to Épernon. He was ordered to establish the Inquisition in France and to station an army in Lorraine in order to prevent another foreign invasion. This army was to be financed by the sale of properties confiscated from all Protestant 'heretics' as well as anyone with Protestant sympathies – the League detested moderate Catholics almost as much the heretics themselves. The monetary value they assigned to these sympathizers was revealing: they were taxed at the same rate of 'a third or at least a quarter' of the value of all their assets as those Protestants who converted to Catholicism; while Catholics themselves only had to pay 'one-tenth of their revenue per annum only'. The confident mood of the League increased further that spring at the news that Henri, prince of Condé, Navarre's cousin and one of his closest allies among the Protestant hierarchy as well as one of his foremost military commanders, had died after a short illness.

Henry's reaction to the League's demands was to refuse to consider any of them, and he sent Bellièvre to Soissons to persuade Guise to disarm, a mission never likely to be a success. His belief in the right of a king to rule, a right sanctioned by God, was unshakeable; but it was an attitude that struck the League as arrogance. Indeed, Guise and his supporters were so furious at the king's behaviour that they started making plans to seize the throne; and they had the support of their powerful ally Philip II, who hoped the coup would provide a useful distraction from his own plans for a seaborne invasion of England that summer. Guise had already started making preparations in Paris, moving men inconspicuously into the capital, where they were stationed at the Hôtel de Guise and the houses of his supporters.[81] By the end of April, with the gardens and courtyard of the Guise palace bursting with troops, Henry was disturbed enough to take steps to increase his own security at the Louvre by moving 4,000 Swiss troops of the royal army closer to Paris. He also issued an order banning Guise from entering the city.

On 9 May, Guise defied the royal order and rode into Paris in a show of strength. Aware that there were risks in confronting Henry directly, he went to the Hôtel de la Reine, from where Catherine escorted him to the Louvre in her carriage. Over the next two days the king and the duke made a show of reconciliation but Henry, suspecting a coup was about to take place, moved his troops into the capital very early in the morning of 12 May. However, this display of royal authority did nothing to calm the situation; it was a mistake that was to have disastrous consequences. The Parisians, who traditionally had the liberty to organize their own defence, were horrified to find their streets lined with foreign troops. Henry faced not just the fury of the mob but that of ordinary citizens, and by midday they had blocked the streets of the city and barricaded them with chains. The Day of the Barricades, it was known, marked the moment when Henry lost control of his capital.

When Catherine left the Hôtel de la Reine the following morning to attend mass at Sainte-Chapelle, the barricades were opened to let her through, but she was only allowed as far as the chapel; she was forbidden to leave the city. Later that morning she attended a meeting of the king's council at the Louvre at which Henry announced his intention to escape. Catherine urged him to delay until she had seen Guise to ask him to stop the riots, but the duke refused and when she returned to the palace the king had already fled. Within days the League seized control of the capital. They purged the city administration of its moderates and royalists, replacing them with militant League members, while the leader of the Sixteen was given the post of mayor: significantly, he swore his oath of office to Guise, who represented Cardinal Bourbon, the League's heir to the throne, who was ill with gout.[82]

Henry fled to Chartres, where he set up his court and was soon joined by Épernon, who had been absent in Normandy when the trouble started. In a letter to marshal Matignon dated 17 May, he outlined the reasons for his escape: 'things had reached such a point on the thirteenth that it seemed beyond anyone's ability to control a more violent uprising, even against my castle [the Louvre]; so, not wishing to use my forces against the inhabitants,' he explained, and 'having

prayed my mother the queen to stay to see whether by prudence and authority she might quieten the tumult', he left.[83]
Catherine remained in Paris, with the queen and a part of the
king's council, for two months, acting as her son's representative in negotiations between Henry and the League.

These lengthy negotiations were conducted largely by letters
which were couriered between Paris and Chartres without hin-
drance. Catherine wrote frequently, sometimes daily, to Henry
and less often to Villeroy; she also received regular post from
them in reply. She also received a steady stream of important
visitors, men of authority with the aim of forcing her to persuade Henry to join the League. Most of her letters refer to
the arrival of someone, usually in the afternoon, 'après-diner'
to talk with her: the papal nuncio, diplomats, notably the
ambassadors of Spain and Savoy, bishops and archbishops,
Guise himself, his brothers and other senior members of the
League.

Her first visitor, made on the evening of Henry's escape, was
Guise, who had come to complain about the king's unexpected
departure – an indication that Henry's tactical withdrawal
from his capital had ruined Guise's plans for a coup. On 20
May she took Guise, Elbeuf and Pierre d'Espinac, archbishop
of Lyons and a prominent leaguer, for a walk in her garden
for discussions. Reporting the meeting in detail to her son,
she commented that 'the duke of Guise, always repeating
himself, shows himself marvellously obstinate and determined
to insist' that the violence in Paris had not been his fault but
that of the mayor and aldermen.[84] Three days later her 'après-
diner' visitor was the Spanish envoy Mendoza, who had come
to inform her 'that the king of Spain, his master, seeing so
many English pirates on the sea, which is very prejudicial to
him and his subjects, he has been forced to assemble a naval
army, which will have set sail at the beginning of this month,
to purge the sea of these pirates'.[85] In fact the armada had still
not left Lisbon, delayed by bad weather in the Bay of Biscay.

Not long after they had taken over power in the capital, the

League presented Catherine with a list of demands for the king, which were broadly similar to those drawn up at Nancy in January though with several extra requirements: Henry was to recognize Bourbon as his heir, to dismiss Épernon from all his posts, and to appoint Guise to the coveted position of lieutenant-general of France. Catherine believed, as did Villeroy, that Henry must capitulate to the League or face losing his throne; but Henry, refusing to be coerced and lulled into a false sense of security away from Paris, refused to accept his mother's advice.

Three days later she wrote to Villeroy in some distress at her son's decision: 'this morning I received the letter in the king's own hand, and that which you have written, being so very weary of so much bad news from all parts, as I have seen from the said letter; but we have to do everything, as you say, that can be done to put out the fire before it bursts into flames.'[86] Eventually Henry was forced to accept. Catherine understood how difficult this had been for him: as she wrote to Bellièvre on 2 June, 'I well know that it is a hard medicine for my son, having the heart he has, to swallow but it will be even harder for him to lose all his authority and obedience; he would be much praised by restoring himself in whatever manner he can at this stage, for time brings many things that cannot be anticipated ... never have I seen myself in such trouble or with so little light by which to escape; unless God intervenes, I do not know what will happen.'[87]

On 21 July 1588 Henry was at Rouen to sign the Edict of Union between the crown and the League, swearing an oath 'to extirpate from our kingdom ... all heresies condemned by the holy councils'.[88] He promised 'never to make peace or truce with the heretics', nor to sign any edicts in their favour and to ban Protestants from holding office or military command; he also promised to recognize the government of the Sixteen in Paris, and to hold a meeting of the Estates-General in the autumn to discuss plans for the war against the heretics; his one small achievement was to insist that all leagues and associations were to be outlawed. Once the edict was signed Catherine and the queen were free to leave Paris – her last letter from the capital was dated 29 July. Before she left she wrote to her granddaughter Isabella in Spain with her news: 'God be thanked, everything is very good, because the king your uncle and all of us are in good health, and I have been living in this city of Paris after what happened to mend everything, which God has favoured me to do.'[89]

A fortnight later Catherine, Guise, Cardinal Bourbon and an escort of 800 men made their entry into Chartres where Henry was to stage a public reconciliation with the duke.[90] The two men dined together: according to L'Estoile, the king proposed a toast to 'our good friends the Protestants' to which Guise countered with another toast, 'to our good barricades of Paris'.[91] Further signs of the League's victory emerged a few days later when Henry appointed prominent leaguers to key positions; archbishop Espinac, for example, was made Keeper of the Seals. Guise's own return to royal favour was evident in his appointment to the honour he had coveted, lieutenant-general of the royal army. While the festivities to celebrate the new friendship were being held at Chartres, Philip II's armada had sailed up the Channel and now lay in the waters off Calais. However, the troops that Parma had promised to have ready for the invasion of England were delayed: not all the men had arrived at the coast ready to board, nor had Parma been able to find enough boats to ferry them out to the galleys. The League's triumph at home was dented by the news that the armada had been decimated by Elizabeth I's navy.

Catherine arrived at Blois on 1 September with Henry and the court for the meeting of the Estates-General which was to open later in the month. A week later she was astonished and appalled to hear that Henry had sacked a large number of his officials, among them Bellièvre, Villeroy and Pinart, her stalwart aides who had always given her loyal service and been her rocks through many crises. Indeed, the whole court was in a state of shock at the news and buzzing with speculation as to Henry's motives. Ambassador Mendoza, uncharacteristically blind to rumour, failed to find any logic in the king's decision: 'the actions of this prince contradict each other to such an extent that these dismissals ... do not appear to be the result of a plan drawn up in advance'.[92] The king's doctor Cavriani claimed he had heard that officials were guilty of passing state secrets to Guise; others suggested that their fault had been their closeness to Catherine and that Henry blamed his mother for forcing him to capitulate to the League.[93] Catherine herself clearly thought that Henry's action was in some way connected to her behaviour. She felt deeply humiliated: she wrote to Bellièvre on 20 September of her shock that her son, who had been taught 'that he must love his mother and honour her, as God commands, but not to give her such authority and trust needed to prevent one from doing what one wants, for that is what he has done'.[94]

Henry went out of his way to scotch these rumours in his opening speech to the Estates-General. Speaking from his throne in the great hall at Blois on 16 September, with the queen, Catherine and Guise prominently at his side, he praised her for what she had done on behalf of the realm, saying she deserved to be called not only 'mother of the king' but also 'mother of the state and of the kingdom'.[95] In the hope that the conference would vote to raise funds for the crown, he outlined a reform programme specially tailored for his audience, which consisted overwhelmingly of members of the League. He promised to wage war against the Protestants, to root out the corruption at the heart of his regime and to make massive economies in his own expenditure: the Estates did not believe this last promise and voted to allow him just 120,000 écus, a sum that represented the salaries of just ten men of his bodyguard, the *Quarante-Cinq*.[96]

The Estates-General marked the end of Catherine's career in public life. She played no part in the discussions that took place and spent much of the time confined to her rooms with gout and rheumatism. Very few of her letters survive from this point onwards and many of those that do were concerned with a personal matter close to her heart: the marriage of her granddaughter Christine of Lorraine to her distant cousin Ferdinando de' Medici. Catherine had had dealings with Ferdinando over many years: a cardinal since January 1563 (he was given his red hat at the age of thirteen), he was an influential figure at the papal court but, on the death of his brother Francesco I in October 1587, he had inherited the title of grand duke of Tuscany. Now his most pressing task was to sire an heir in order to secure the survival of the Medici dynasty.

Catherine had written to Ferdinando a month after Francesco's death to offer her condolences but also to express her 'joy, which is so much greater, to have heard that you have succeeded with all the goodwill and friendship of the nobles and people of your state'.[97] Within weeks the French ambassador in Rome had begun the necessary negotiations with Ferdinando for his marriage to Christine and for the dowry, which was agreed at 700,000 florins, while Ferdinando himself opened discussions with Sixtus V to allow him to resign his cardinal's hat.[98] The sluggish bureaucracy of the Curia took its time, so it was not until 28 December 1588 that the pope, who was rather annoyed that the betrothal had been arranged while the groom was still a prince of the Church, finally announced his formal consent to Ferdinando's return to secular life.[99] Ten days later, on 8 December, Catherine signed the betrothal contract and celebrated the event at Blois with a ball. In celebration of the marriage itself, which took place by proxy at Blois on 25 February 1589, Catherine had given her granddaughter several valuable presents, not least the Valois tapestries and the priceless gilded-silver casket made by the Italian goldsmith Valerio Belli which Clement VII had given

Francis I on the occasion of her own marriage. Sadly, she had died before the wedding took place.

A week after the ball Catherine was back in bed, this time seriously ill with a lung infection. Fortunately, it had begun to clear up by 23 December, though she was still convalescent that morning when Henry entered her chamber with startling news. In the words of the doctor Cavriani, who was at Catherine's bedside administering medicine at the time, the king said, 'Good morning madame, please forgive me. Monsieur of Guise is dead and will no more be mentioned; I have had him killed; I have done to him what he was going to do to me. I could no longer tolerate his insolence.'[100] Henry had planned the operation with care. Earlier that day he had summoned Guise to meeting of his council, which Guise would have to attend without a guard, and the duke accepted the invitation, despite warnings that his life was in real danger. But on entering the royal apartments he was brutally killed by members of the *Quarante-Cinq* acting on the king's orders. At the same time another eight members of the family, including Cardinal Louis, Anna d'Este and the dukes of Elbeuf and Nevers, were all arrested and thrown into the castle dungeons; the following day, Christmas Eve, the cardinal was butchered in his cell. Catherine was angry with her son: 'what do you think you have done,' she rebuked him, 'you have killed two men who have left a lot of friends.' She would be proved correct.

Catherine was well enough to visit Cardinal Bourbon on 1 January, who was bitterly angry with her, blaming her for Guise's murder, but within days her fever had returned. Doctor Cavriani diagnosed a lung infection which he called 'peripneumonia', probably pleurisy.[101] On 5 January she made her will and received the last rites; she died that night. According to the Venetian ambassador 'when the body of the Most Serene Queen mother was opened, it was found to be so sound and healthy that, despite her sixty-nine years and seven months, if it not been for the inflammation of the lungs that killed her, it was thought that she would have lived on for a long while'.[102]

Her funeral took place at Blois after the forty-day mourning period accorded to French sovereigns and their queens, and she was buried there before being moved to the Valois chapel at Saint-Denis which she herself had built for Henry II and their descendants.* In her will she listed many bequests to members of her household: doctor Cavriani received 6,160 écus, but most of her estate was left to three legatees.[103] To her granddaughter Christine she left the Hôtel de la Reine with half of the palace's furnishings, rings and jewels; to her daughter-in-law queen Louise she bequeathed the estate and title of Chenonceau; and to her grandson Charles de Valois, the illegitimate son of Charles IX, she left the family titles to the counties of Clermont and Auvergne that she had inherited from her own mother.

---

*   In 1793, during the Revolution, her bones were unearthed along with those of the rest of France's monarchs and consorts and thrown into a mass grave.

EPILOGUE

Paris is Worth a Mass

I t took just seven months after Catherine's death for Henry
III's brutal murder of the Guise brothers to be avenged
when he in turn was assassinated by Jacques Clément, a
Catholic fanatic, during the night of 1–2 August. It was a tragic
end to the Valois dynasty but not to the end of Catherine's
hopes and plans. It is fitting that a personality as powerful as
hers should have continued to exert her influence over political events from beyond the grave.

The murder of the duke of Guise and his brother the cardinal had provoked a storm of protest from the League, and
a vitriolic campaign of sermons and pamphlets slandering the
king. One theologian went so far as to argue it would be lawful
not only for the Church to depose him but for his people to
do the same, with violence if necessary. Henry had no option
but to declare Navarre as his heir; and the League were jubi-
lant when he was assassinated that August. Navarre claimed
the throne as Henry IV with, significantly, a solemn promise to
uphold the Catholic faith. The League, backed by the power
of Sixtus V and Philip II, countered by declaring Cardinal
Bourbon as Charles X. In the war that followed the optimism
of the League was soon silenced as Navarre won two decisive
victories, before laying siege to Paris in the spring of 1590.

Unfortunately for Navarre 'Charles X' died that May
and Philip II claimed the throne on behalf of his daughter

Isabella, Henry II and Catherine's granddaughter, bringing his powerful army to France and successfully lifting the siege of the capital. His thinly disguised aim, after cleansing France of Protestantism, was to reduce the country to a vassal of Spain and it looked, for a time, as if he would succeed, or that all Europe would be engulfed in a war for the succession. But that August, Philip lost his main ally when Sixtus V died; and the next three popes also died in quick succession, leaving a power vacuum in Rome that lasted until January 1592 and the election of Clement VIII. In one of those coincidences of which history is so fond, Clement VIII was the son of the Florentine chancellor Silvestro Aldobrandini, who in July 1530 had escorted a reluctant Catherine out of the Murate convent in the middle of the siege of Florence, treating her with such kindness and respect that when the siege was over she intervened on his behalf and he escaped serious punishment.

In the meantime Navarre had an unexpected stroke of luck. An offer of financial and political help came from an unlikely quarter: Ferdinando de' Medici, grand duke of Tuscany, and his wife, Catherine's much-loved granddaughter Christine of Lorraine. On the face of it, Ferdinando and Christine were not obvious allies for the Protestant cause: Christine's brother Charles was given his red hat by Sixtus V in December 1589, while Ferdinando himself had been a cardinal and a prominent figure at the papal court in Rome for many years before resigning to sire an heir for the Medici dynasty. Encouraged by Christine, Ferdinando decided to promote Navarre, whose support base was increasing to include moderate Catholic opponents of the League. Not only did the duke send large sums to finance the Protestant army, he was also, perhaps more significantly, instrumental in persuading Clement VIII to withdraw his opposition to Navarre as king of France. And the king himself, with Ferdinando's encouragement, also changed tactics. On 25 July 1593, surrounded by the tombs of his predecessors in the great basilica at Saint-Denis, he formally became a Catholic: 'Paris is worth a mass', he is reputed

to have said. And on 13 April 1598 he signed the Edict of
Nantes, granting toleration to Protestants in France and
ending four decades of war. It must have come as a relief for
a nation weary of the violence and privations of war; certainly
the fanatics on both sides had lost support and, as Clement
VIII's behaviour showed, the political pendulum had swung
strongly in favour of compromise.

Henry IV owed much to Catherine's courage, determination and intelligence. Despite the claims made by her
enemies, she was a loyal Catholic, though a moderate who
failed to understand the mindset of the zealot, Protestant or
Catholic. From the moment she became regent in 1561 she
campaigned tirelessly for peace between the two faiths; she
was not always successful, but she went out of her way to seek
compromise solutions that would be acceptable to both sides.
She remained stubborn in her conviction that religious toleration was the only way forward, a position she refused to yield
except in obedience to the crown, or until the only option
was violence. It was thanks in large part to her tireless efforts
to negotiate, even in the most unpromising of circumstances,
that the kingdom Henry IV inherited was a united realm
and tolerant of both religions. That the crown rose from the
ashes of the civil wars with its authority and power intact, was
largely due to her. She had been obstinate in her insistence on
French independence in the face of overpowering opposition,
refusing to allow foreign intervention in French affairs, firmly
opposing attempts by Philip II and successive popes to dictate
their terms. Although the wars did not end until after her
death, Catherine played a key role in obstructing Philip II's
ambitions and preserving France as one of Europe's leading
powers. In all, it was an astonishing achievement.

Acknowledgements

I would like to thank the following for all their help and support during the writing of this book: Dottie Ainscough, Annabel and Philip Athill, Storm Athill, Giles Bancroft, Elisabeth de Bièvre, Sarah Carr-Gomm, Flora Dennis, Jack Edmonds, Tabitha Goldstaub, Milo Goslett, Hans Erik Havesteen, Rosamund Hollingsworth and the rest of my long-suffering family, Sally and Liam Laurence Smyth, Jo Mitchell, Isabelle Onians, John Onians, Harry Polhill, Stephen Reid, Henry Saywell, Rupert Shepherd, Robin and Jo Simon, Terry Sweeney and Geoff Williams.

Among the many scholars to whom I am indebted, I am particularly grateful to Joseph Bergin, Stuart Carroll, Monique Chatenet, Natalie Zemon Davis, Arlette Jouanna, Robert Knecht, Roy Strong and Nicola Sutherland for their assistance in negotiating the minefield of sixteenth-century French politics.

As usual it has been a pleasure to work with the team at Head of Zeus, particularly my courteous and patient editor, Richard Milbank, who had more than usual to endure with this book. Above all, I owe a huge debt to my agent, Andrew Lownie, for his unwavering encouragement and support.

Bibliography

Adams, Simon, 'Providing for a Queen: the stables under Elizabeth I', *The Court Historian* 26 (2021), 210–28.

Anglo, Sidney, *The Martial Arts of Renaissance Europe* (New Haven and London, 2000).

Baker-Bates, Piers, 'Beyond Rome: Sebastiano Del Piombo as a painter of diplomatic gifts', *Renaissance Studies* 27 (2013), 51–72.

Balsamo, Jean, '"Ses vertus l'ont assise au rang des Immortels": Catherine de Médicis et ses poètes', in ed. Sabine Frommel and Wolf, 11–38.

Bardati, Flaminia, 'Un omaggio a Caterina? Politica, poesia e architettura a Gaillon nel 1566', in ed. Sabine Frommel and Wolf, 345–67.

Bastien, Pascal, '"Aux tresors dissipez l'on cognoist le malfaict": Hiérarchie sociale et transgression des ordonnances somptuaires en France, 1543–1606', *Renaissance and Reformation* 23 (1999), 23–43.

Benedict, Philip, 'The Saint Bartholomew's Massacres in the Provinces', *The Historical Journal* 21 (1978), 205–25.

Bertrand, Pascal-François, 'A new method of interpreting the Valois Tapestries, through a history of Catherine de Médicis', *Studies in the Decorative Arts* 14 (2006–2007), 27–52.

Bèze, Théodore de, *Histoire Ecclésiastique des Églises Réformées au royaume de France*, 2 vols (Toulouse, 1882).

Bimbinet-Privat, Michèle, 'Catherine de Médicis et ses orfèvres: autorité, précision, exigence', in ed. Wilson-Chevalier, 545–55.

Blaisdell, Charmarie Jenkins, 'Calvin's letters to women: The courting of ladies in high places', *Sixteenth Century Journal* 13 (1982), 67–84.

Blunt, Anthony, *Art and Architecture in France 1500–1700* (Harmondsworth, 1982).

—, *Philibert de L'Orme* (London, 1958).

Bondois, P. M., 'Bernardo Carnesecchi, jardinier de Catherie de Médicis', *Revue du Seizième Siècle* 14 (1927), 389–92.

Boström, Antonia, 'Daniele da Volterra and the equestrian monument to Henry II of France', *Burlington Magazine* 137 (1995), 809–20.

Boucher, Jacqueline, 'Contribution à l'histoire du Duel des Mignons (1578): une lettre de Henri III à Laurent de Maugiron', *Nouvelle Revue du XVIe Siècle* 18 (2000), 113–26.

Boudon, Françoise and Monique Chatenet, 'Les logis du roi de France au XVIe siècle', in ed. Jean Guillaume, *Architecture et vie sociale. Actes du colloque tenu à Tours du 6 au 10 juin 1988* (Paris, 1994), 65–81.

Bourgeon, Jean-Louis, 'Les légendes ont la vie dure: à propos de la Saint-Barthélemy et de quelques livres récents', *Revue d'histoire moderne et contemporaine* 34 (1987), 102–16.

—, 'Un texte capital sur la Saint-Barthélemy: le "discours à la royne mere du roy" (20 août 1573)', *Bulletin de la Société de l'Histoire du Protestantism Français* 160 (2014), 709–32.

Braghi, Gianmarco, 'The Death of Charles IX Valois: an Assassin's or a Martyr's Blood? The Image of Kingship During the French Wars of Religion', *French History* 28 (2014), 303–21.

Brantôme, Pierre de Bourdeille, abbé de, *Illustrious Dames of the Court of the Valois Kings*, trans. Katharine Prescott Wormeley (New York, 1912).

Bresc-Bautier, Geneviève, 'Catherine de Médicis: la passion du marbre', in ed. Sabine Frommel and Wolf, 251–77.

Briggs, Linda, 'Presenting the Most Christian King: Charles IX's Performance of Catholic Ritual in the Royal Tour of France (1564–1566)', *French History* 32 (2018), 2–24.

Broomhall, Susan, 'Women's Little Secrets: Defining the Boundaries of Reproductive Knowledge in Sixteenth-century France', *Social History of Medicine* 15 (2002), 1–15.

—, 'The game of politics: Catherine de' Medici and chess', *Early Modern Women* 12 (2017), 104–18.

—, 'In the orbit of the king: women, power and authority at the French court 1483–1563', in ed. Broomhall, 9–38.

—, '"The king and I": Rhetorics of power in the letters of Diane de Poitiers', in ed. Broomhall, 335–56.

—, *The Identities of Catherine de' Medici* (Leiden and Boston, 2021).

Broomhall, Susan (ed.), *Women and Power at the French court, 1483–1563* (Amsterdam, 2018).

Brown, Horatio F., 'The death and funeral of Catherine de' Medici, as described by the Venetian ambassador in France', *The English Historical Review* 11 (1896), 748–50.

Brown, Judith C., 'Monache a Firenze all'inizio dell'età moderna: un'analisi demografica', *Quaderni storici* 29 (1994), 117–52.

Bryant, Lawrence M., *The King and the City in the Parisian Royal Entry Ceremony: Politics, Ritual, and Art in the Renaissance* (Geneva, 1986).

Bullard, Melissa Meriam, *Filippo Strozzi and the Medici* (Cambridge, 1980).

Calendar of State Papers, Foreign series: Elizabeth, ed. Arthur John Butler et al., 23 vols (London 1863–1950). See www.british-history. ac.uk accessed 21 February 2023.

Calendar of State Papers, Venetian, ed. R. Brown, C. Bentinck and H. Brown, 9 vols (London, 1864–98). See www.british-history.ac.uk accessed 21 February 2023.

Cameron, Keith, 'La polémique, la mort de Marie Stuart et l'assassinat de Henri III', in ed. Robert Sauzet, *Henri III et son temps* (Paris, 1992), 185–94.

Canguilhem, Philippe, 'Catherine de Médicis, la musique, l'Italie', in ed. Sabine Frommel and Wolf, 135–48.

Capodieci, Luisa, '"Il cielo in una stanza"; la camera di Enrico II e di Caterina de' Medici nel castello di Fontainebleau', in ed. Sabine Frommel and Wolf, 327–43.

—, 'Magnificentissimum spectaculum. Caterina de' Medici e le feste parigine del 1573', in ed. Strunck, 47–71.

Carroll, Stuart, *Martyrs and Murderers: The Guise family and the making of Europe* (Oxford, 2009).

—, '"Nager entre deux eaux": The princes and the ambiguities of French Protestantism', *Sixteenth Century Journal* 44 (2013), 985–1020.

Cashman, Anthony B. III, 'Performance Anxiety: Federico Gonzaga at the Court of Francis I and the Uncertainty of Ritual Action', *Sixteenth Century Journal* 33 (2002), 333–52.

Castiglione, Baldesar, *The Book of the Courtier* (Harmondsworth, 1976).

Champion, Pierre, *Catherine de Médicis présente à Charles IX son royaume 1564–1566* (Paris, 1937).

Chatenet, Monique, 'Henri III et "L'ordre de la cour". Évolution de l'étiquette à travers les règlements généraux de 1578 et 1585', in ed. Robert Sauzet, *Henri III et son temps* (Paris, 1992), 133–9.

—, *La Cour de France au XVIe Siècle* (Paris, 2002).

—, 'La reine en majesté', in ed. Sabine Frommel and Wolf, 169–82.

Cloulas, Ivan, *Catherine de' Médicis* (Paris, 1979).

Conihout, Isabelle de and Pascal Ract-Madoux, 'À la recherche de la bibliothèque perdue de Catherine de Médicis', in ed. Sabine Frommel and Wolf, 39–62.

Coope, Rosalys, 'The Château of Montceaux-en-Brie', (Chicago, 1959), 71–6.

Cooper, John, *The Queen's Agent* (London, 2011).

Cooper, Richard (ed.), *Maurice Scève. The Entry of Henry II into Lyon, September 1548* (Tempe AZ, 1997).

Cordellier, Dominique, 'Précisions sur l'activité de Francesco Primaticcio et de son entourage au temps de Catherine de Médicis', in ed. Sabine Frommel and Wolf, 229–44.

Courtright, Nicola, 'A Garden and a Gallery at Fontainebleau: Imagery of Rule for Medici Queens', *The Court Historian* 10 (2005), 55–84.

Crawford, Katherine, 'Catherine de Medici and the performance of political motherhood', *Sixteenth Century Journal* 31 (2000), 643–73.

Croizat, Yassana C., '"Living Dolls": François 1er dresses his women', *Renaissance Quarterly* 60 (2007), 94–130.

Crouzet, Denis, 'Catherine de Médicis tested by the virtue of charity (1533–1559). Discourse and metadiscourse' in ed. Broomhall, 357–76.

—, *La Nuit de la Saint-Barthélemy* (Oxford, 1996), 114.

Cummings, Anthony M., *The Politicized Muse* (Princeton NJ, 1992).

—, 'Three gigli. Medici musical patronage in the early Cinquecento', *Recercare* 15 (2003), 39–72.

Davila, H. C., *Negociations ou Lettres d'Affaires Ecclesiastiques et Politiques* (Paris, 1658).

Davis, Natalie Zemon, 'The Rites of Violence: Religious Riot in Sixteenth-Century France', reprinted in idem, *Society and Culture in Early Modern France* (Stanford, 1975), 152–87.

—, 'Women in Politics' in Natalie Zemon Davis and Arlette Farge (eds), *A History of Women. Renaissance and Enlightenment*

Paradoxes (Cambridge MA, 1993), 167–83.

—, *The Gift* (Oxford, 2000).

Dizionario Bibliografico degliItaliani, see www.treccani.it/biografie'; accessed 21 February 2023.

Droguet, Vincent, 'De l'agrément à la splendour: le goût de Catherine de Médicis pour l'architecture et les jardins', in ed. Sabine Frommel and Wolf, 305–25.

Ehrmann, Jean, 'Massacre and persecution pictures in sixteenth-century France', *Journal of the Warburg and Courtauld Institutes* 8 (1945), 195–99.

—, 'Tableaux de Massacres au XVIe siècle', *Bulletin de la Société de l'Histoire du Protestantisme Français* 118 (1972), 445–55.

Fenlon, Iain, 'From Caterina de' Medici to Maria Magdalena of Austria: The Politics of Danced Spectacle', in ed. Strunck, 73–87.

ffolliott, Sheila, 'Catherine de' Medici as Artemisia: figuring the powerful widow' in M. Ferguson, M. Gulligan and N. J. Vickers (eds), *Rewriting the Renaissance: the Discourse of Difference in Early Modern Europe* (Chicago and London, 1986), 227–41.

—, 'Casting a rival into the shade: Catherine de' Medici and Diane de Poitiers', *Art Journal* 48 (1989), 138–43.

—, 'A queen's garden of power: Catherine de' Medici', in M. A. Di Cesare (ed), *Reconsidering the Renaissance* (Binghamton, 1992), 245–55.

—, 'The Italian "training" of Catherine de' Medici: Portraits as dynastic narrative', *The Court Historian* 10 (2005), 37–53.

—, 'La reine mécène idéale de la Renaissance: Catherine de Médicis définie par elle- même

ou définie par les autres?', in ed. Wilson-Chevalier, 455–66.

—, '"La Florentine" or "la bonne Françoise": Some Sixteenth-Century Commentators on Catherine de' Medici and Her Patronage', in ed. Strunck, 17–37.

Fletcher, Catherine, *The Black Prince of Florence* (Oxford, 2016).

Forster, Philip, 'Lorenzo de' Medici's Cascina at Poggio a Caiano', *Mitteilungen des Kunsthistorischen Institutes in Florenz* 14 (1969), 47–56.

Frommel, Christoph Luitpold, 'Caterina de' Medici, commit-tente di architettura', in ed. Sabine Frommel and Wolf, 369–89.

Frommel, Sabine, 'Florence, Rome, La France', in ed. Sabine Frommel and Wolf, 281–303.

Frommel, Sabine and Gerhard Wolf (eds), *Il mecenatismo di Caterina de' Medici* (Venice, 2008).

Gaehtgens, Barbara, 'Cathérine de Médicis et *L'Histoire françoyse de nostre temps*. Des tapisseries au service de la Régence', in ed. Sabine Frommel and Wolf, 149–67.

Gebhardt, K., 'Catherine de Médicis (1519–1589) et la langue française', in R. Sauzet (ed.), *Henri III et son temps* (Paris, 1992), 21–38.

Geevers, Liesbeth, 'Ties, triangles and tangles: Catherine de' Medici as Philip II of Spain's mother-in-law', *The Court Historian* 25 (2020), 186–200.

Gnoli, Domenico, 'Un censimento della popolazione di Roma avanti il sacco borbonico', *Archivio della Reale Società di Roma di Storia Patria* 17 (1894), 375–507.

Goldberg, Victoria L., 'Graces, muses, and arts: the urns of Henry II and Francis I', *Journal of the Warburg and Courtauld Institutes* 29 (1966), 206–18.

Goldthwaite, Richard A., *The Building of Renaissance Florence* (Baltimore and London, 1980).

Graham, Victor E., 'The Triumphal Entry in sixteenth-century France', *Renaissance and Reformation* 10 (1986), 237–56.

—, 'The 1564 Entry of Charles IX into Troyes', *Bibliothèque d'Humanisme et Renaissance* 48 (1986), 105–20.

Gray, Janet G., 'The Origin of the Word Huguenot', *Sixteenth Century Journal* 14 (1983), 349–59.

Greene, Thomas M., 'The King's One Body in the Balet Comique de la Royne', *Yale French Studies* (1994), 75–93.

—, 'Labyrinth dances in the French and English Renaissance', *Renaissance Quarterly* 54 (2001), 1403–66.

Greengrass, M., 'The Sixteen. Radical politics in Paris during the League', *History* 69 (1984) 432–9.

Guillaume, Jean (ed.), *Architecture et Vie Sociale. Actes du colloque tenu à Tours du 6 au 10 juin 1988* (Paris, 1994).

Hale, John R., 'The end of Florentine liberty: the Fortezza da Basso', in Nicolai Rubinstein (ed.) *Florentine Studies. Politics and Society in Renaissance Florence* (London, 1968), 501–32.

Hall, J. T. D., 'Was Ronsard's *Bergerie* performed at Fontainebleau in 1564?', *Bibliothèque d'Humanisme et Renaissance* 51 (1989), 301–9.

Harrie, Jeanne, 'The Guises, the Body of Christ and the Body Politic', *Sixteenth Century Journal* 37 (2006), 43–57.

Herz, Alexandra, 'Vasari's "Massacre" series in the Sala Regia. The Political, Juristic, and Religious Background', *Zeitschrift für Kunstgeschichte* 49 (1986), 41–54.

Hewitt, Edith, 'An assessment of Italian benefices held by cardinals for the Turkish War of 1571', *English Historical Review* 30 (1915), 488–501.

Hollingsworth, Mary, *The Cardinal's Hat* (London, 2004).

—, *The Medici* (London, 2017).

—, *Princes of the Renaissance* (London, 2021).

—, *Conclave 1559. Ippolito d'Este and the Papal Election of 1559* (London, 2021).

Holt, Mack P., *The French Wars of Religion, 1562–1629* (Cambridge, 2005).

Hoogvliet, Margriet, 'Le cabinet de curiosités de Catherine de Médicis dans l'hôtel de la Reine à Paris', in ed. Sabine Frommel and Wolf, 205–13.

Jackson, Richard A., 'The Sleeping King', *Bibliothèque d'Humanisme et Renaissance* 31 (1969), 525–51.

Jacquot, Jean, 'Panorama des fêtes et cérémonies du règne', in ed. Jean Jacquot, *Fêtes et Cérémonies au temps de Charles Quint*, 2 vols (Paris 1960), 2: 413–491.

Jensen, De Lamar, 'French Diplomacy and the Wars of Religion', *Sixteenth Century Journal* 5 (1974), 23–46.

—, 'Catherine de Medici and her Florentine friends', *Sixteenth Century Journal* 9 (1978), 57–74.

Johnson, Eugene J., 'The theater at Lyon of 1548: a reconstruction and attribution', *Artibus et Historiae* 35 (2014), 173–202.

Johnson, Jerah, 'Bernard Palissy, Prophet of Modern Ceramics', *Sixteenth Century Journal* 14 (1983), 399–410.

Jouan, Abel, *Recueil et discours du voyage du Roy Charles IX* (Paris, 1566).

Jouanna, Arlette, *The Saint*

Bartholomew's Day Massacre, trans.
Joseph Bergin (Manchester,
2015).

Jouanna, Arlette, Jacqueline Boucher,
Dominique Biloghi and Guy Le
Thiec, *Des Guerres de Religion.
Histoire et Dictionnaire* (Paris,
1998).

Jouanna, Arlette, Philippe Hamon,
Dominique Biloghi and Guy Le
Thiec, *La France de la Renaissance.
Histoire et Dictionnaire* (Paris,
2001).

Kamen, Henry, *Philip of Spain* (New
Haven and London, 1997).

Kim, Seong-Hak, 'Dieu nous garde de
la messe du chancelier: The
religious belief and political
opinion of Michel de L'Hôpital',
Sixteenth Century Journal 24
(1993), 595–620.

Kingdon, Robert M., *Myths about the St.
Bartholomew's Day Massacres,
1572–1576* (Cambridge MA,
1988).

Knauer, Elfriede R., 'The "Battle
of Zama" after Giulio Romano:
A Tapestry in the American
Academy in Rome, Part 1',
*Memoirs of the American
Academy in Rome* 50 (2005),
221–65.

Knecht, Robert J., *Renaissance Warrior
and Patron. The Reign of Francis I*
(Cambridge, 1994).

—, 'Popular theatre and the court in
sixteenth-century France',
Renaissance Studies 9 (1995),
364–73.

—, *The French Wars of Religion
1559–1598* (London and New
York, 1996).

—, *The Rise and Fall of Renaissance
France 1483–1610* (London,
1996).

—, *Catherine de' Medici* (London and
New York, 1998).

—, *The French Renaissance Court
1483–1589* (New Haven and
London, 2008).

Kociszewaka, Ewa, 'War and seduction

in Cybele's garden: contextualiz-
ing the *Ballet des Polonais*',
Renaissance Quarterly 65 (2012),
806–63.

—, 'Woven bloodlines: the *Valois
Tapestries* in the Trousseau of
Christine de Lorraine, Grand
Duchess of Tuscany', *Artibus et
Historiae* 73 (2016), 335–63.

Kolk, Caroline zum, 'L'évolution du
mécénat de Catherine de Médicis
d'après sa correspondance,
depuis son arrivée en France
jusqu'à la mort de Charles IX', in
ed. Sabine Frommel and Wolf,
63–87.

—, 'The household of the queen of
France in the sixteenth century',
The Court Historian 14 (2009),
3–22.

—, 'Le mécénat de Catherine de
Médicis d'après sa correspondence', in ed. Wilson- Chevalier,
467–80.

Langdon, Gabrielle, *Medici Women.
Portraits of Power, Love, and
Betrayal* (Toronto and London,
2007).

Lapini, Agostino, *Diario Fiorentino di
Agostino Lapini: dal 252 al 1596*
(Florence, 1900).

Lefevre, Renato, *"Madama" Margarita
d'Austria (1522–1586)* (Rome
1986).

Le Roux, Nicolas, *La Faveur du Roi.
Mignons et courtisans au temps des
derniers Valois (vers 1547 – vers
1589)* (Paris, 2000).

Lettres de Catherine de Médicis, ed.
Hector de la Ferrière and
Gustave Baguenault de Puchesse,
10 vols (Paris 1880–1909).

*Letters and Papers, Foreign and Domestic,
of the Reign of Henry VIII*, ed. J. S.
Brewer, J. Gairdner and R. H.
Brodie, 21 vols (London,
1862–1910). See www.british-
history.ac.uk accessed 21
February 2023.

Lowe, K. J. P., 'Female strategies for
success in a male-ordered world:

the Benedictine convent of Le Murate in Florence in the fifteenth and early sixteenth centuries', in W. J. Sheils and Diana Wood (eds), *Women in the Church* (Oxford, 1990), 209–21.

—, *Chronicles and Convent Culture in Renaissance and Counter-Reformation Italy* (Cambridge, 2003).

McGowan, Margaret M., 'Form and Themes in Henri II's Entry into Rouen', *Renaissance Drama* 1 (1968), 199–251.

—, *The Vision of Rome in Late Renaissance France* (New Haven and London, 2000).

Marguerite of Navarre, *The Tales of the Heptameron*, 5 vols (London 1894), accessed 21 February 2023, online via the Project Gutenberg.

Martin, Meredith, *Dairy Queens: The Politics of Pastoral Architecture from Catherine de' Medici to Marie-Antoinette* (Cambridge MA and London, 2011).

Masi, Bartolomeo, *Ricordanze di Bartolomeo Masi calderaio fiorentino dal 1478 al 1526* (Florence, 1906).

Mears, Natalie, 'Love-making and Diplomacy: Elizabeth I and the Anjou Marriage Negotiations', *History* 86 (2001), 442–66.

Michahelles, Kerrie-rue, 'Catherine de' Medici's 1589 inventory at the Hôtel de la Reine in Paris', *Furniture History* 38 (2002), 1–39.

—, 'Apprentissage du mécénat et transmission matrilinéaire du pouvoir. Les enseignments de Catherine de Médicis à sa petite-fille Christine de Lorraine', in ed. Wilson-Chevalier, 557–76.

Miller, Naomi, 'Domain of Illusion: The Grotto in France', in Elisabeth B. MacDougall (ed.), *Fons Sapientiae. Renaissance Garden Fountains* (Washington DC, 1978), 177–206.

Montaigne, Michel de, *The Complete Works. Essays, Travel Journal, Letters* Translated by Frame, Donald M. (London, 2003).

Monter, William, 'The fate of the English and French Reformations, 1554–1563', *Bibliothèque d'Humanisme et Renaissance* 64 (2002), 7–19.

Najemy, John M., *A History of Florence 1200–1575* (Chichester, 2006).

Nevile, Jennifer, 'Dance and the garden: moving and static choreography in Renaissance Europe', *Renaissance Quarterly* 52 (1999), 805–36.

Newbiggin, Nerida, *Feste d'Oltrarno* (Florence, 1996).

Nugent, Donald, *Ecumenism in the Age of the Reformation: The Colloquy of Poissy* (Cambridge MA, 1974).

Occhipinti, Carmelo, *Carteggio d'arte degli ambasciatori Estensi in Francia (1536–1553)* (Pisa, 2001).

—, 'Disputes françaises sur les images sacrées (1561–1562): Le cardinal Hippolyte d'Este et les colloques religieux à la cour de Catherine de Médicis', *Seizième Siècle* 11 (2015), 217–30.

Odde, Laurent, 'Les coulisses du pouvoir: Châteaux, jardins et fêtes. Quelques aspects du mécénat (transgressif) de Catherine de Médicis', in ed. Wilson-Chevalier, 481–510.

—, 'Politic Magnificence: Deciphering the performance of the French and Spanish rivalry during the Entrevue at Bayonne', *Sixteenth Century Journal* 46 (2015), 29–52. Orden, Kate van, *Music, Discipline and Arms in Early Modern France* (Chicago and London, 2005).

Pacifici, Vincenzo, *Ippolito d'Este, Cardinale di Ferrara* (Tivoli, 1920).

Paranque, Estelle, 'Catherine de' Medici's grandmotherhood: the building of emotional and political intergenerational relationships', *Renaissance Studies* 34 (2020), 412–29.

Paresys, Isabelle, 'Vêtir les souverains français à la Renaissance: les garde-robes d'Henri II et de Catherine de Médicis en 1556 et 1557', *Apparence(s)* (online, accessed 20 March 2022) https://journals.openedition. org/apparences/1319

Parker, Geoffrey, *Emperor. A new life of Charles V* (New Haven and London, 2019).

—, *The Dutch Revolt* (London, 1985).

Pastor, Ludwig von, *The History of the Popes from the Close of the Middle Ages*, 29 vols. (London, 1894–1951).

Polizzotto, Lorenzo, *The Elect Nation: the Savonarolan Movement in Florence 1494–1545* (Oxford, 1994).

Potter, David, *The French Wars of Religion. Selected Documents* (London, 1997).

—, 'Politics and faction at the court of Francis I: the Duchesse D'Étampes, Montmorency and the Dauphin Henri', *French History* 21 (2007), 127–46.

—, 'The life and after-life of a royal mistress. Anne de Pisseleu, Duchess of Étampes', in ed. Broomhall, 309–33.

Potter, David and P. R. Roberts, 'An Englishman's View of the Court of Henri III, 1584– 1585; Richard Cook's "Description of the Court of France"', *French History* 2 (1988), 312–44.

Reiss, Sheryl E., 'Widow, Mother, Patron of Art: Alfonsina Orsini de' Medici', in Sheryl E. Reiss and David G. Wilkins (eds), *Beyond Isabella. Secular Women Patrons of Art in Renaissance Italy* (Kirksville MO, 2001), 125–57.

Ribier, Guillaume, *Lettres et Mémoires*

d'Estat, des Roys, Princes, Ambassadeurs, et autres Ministres, sous les règnes de François premier, Henri II et François II*, 2 vols (Blois, 1667).

Richardson, Glenn, 'Hunting at the courts of Francis I and Henry VIII', *The Court Historian* 18 (2013), 127–41.

Ridolfi, Roberto, *The Life of Francesco Guicciardini* (London, 1967).

Roberts, Yvonne, 'The Regency of 1574 in the *Discours Merveilleux* and in the poems of Jean-Antoine de Baïf', *Bibliothèque d'Humanisme et Renaissance* 63 (2001), 261–75.

Roelker, Nancy Lyman, *Queen of Navarre. Jeanne d'Albret 1528–1572* (Cambridge MA, 1968).

—, 'The appeal of Calvinism to French noblewomen in the sixteenth century', *Journal of Interdisciplinary History* 2 (1972), 391–418.

—, 'The Role of the Noblewoman in the French Reformation', *Archiv für Reformationsgeschichte* 63 (1972), 168–95.

Romier, Lucien, 'La Mort de Henri II', *Revue du Seizième Siècle* 1 (1913), 99–152.

Roth, Cecil, *The Last Florentine Republic* (London, 1925).

Rubinstein, Nicolai, 'Dalla repubblica al principato', in *Firenze e la Toscana dei Medici nell'Europa del '500*, 3 vols (Florence 1983), 1:159–76.

Russell, Joycelyne G., *Peacemaking in the Renaissance* (London, 1986).

Sandberg, Brian, 'Iconography of religious violence: Catherine de Médicis's art patronage during the French wars of religion', in ed. Sabine Frommel and Wolf, 91–112.

Sanudo, Marin, *Diarii*, ed. R. Fulin et al. (Venice, 1879–1903).

Sarti, Raffaella, *Europe at Home: Family and Material Culture 1500–1800*

(New Haven and London, 1999).

Schneider, Robert A., 'Mortification on parade: penitential processions in sixteenth- and seventeenth-century France', *Renaissance and Reformation* 10 (1986), 123–46.

Scott, Virginia and Sara Sturm-Maddox, *Performance, Poetry and Politics on the Queen's Day: Catherine de Médicis and Pierre de Ronsard at Fontainbleau* (Aldershot, 2007).

Shishkin, Vladimir, 'The court of Marguerite de Valois in rebellion, 1585–87', *The Court Historian* 21 (2016), 89–108.

Smither, James R., 'The St. Bartholomew's Day massacre and images of kingship in France 1572–1574', *Sixteenth Century Journal* 22 (1991), 27–46.

Stephens, J. N., 'L'infanzia fiorentina di Caterina de' Medici, regina di Francia', *Archivio Storico Italiano* 142 (1984), 421–36.

Strocchia, Sharon T., 'Taken into custody: girls and convent guardianship in Renaissance Florence', *Renaissance Studies* 17 (2003), 177–200.

—, *Nuns and Nunneries in Renaissance Florence* (Baltimore, 2009).

Strong, Roy, 'Festivals for the Garter embassy at the court of Henri III', *Journal of the Warburg and Courtauld Institutes* 22 (1959), 60–70.

—, *Art and Power* (Woodbridge, 1984).

—, *Feast. A History of Grand Eating* (London, 2002).

Strunck, Christine (ed.), *Artful Allies: Medici Women as Cultural Mediators (1533–1743)* (Milan, 2011).

Sturm-Maddox, Sara, 'Catherine de Medici and the Two Lilies', *The Court Historian* 10 (2005), 25–36.

Sutherland, Nicola Mary, *The French Secretaries of State in the Age of*

Catherine de Medici (London, 1962).

—, *The Massacre of St Bartholomew and the European Conflict 1559–1572* (London, 1973).

—, *Princes, Politics and Religion 1547–1589* (London, 1984).

—, 'Le massacre de la Saint-Barthélemy: la valeur des témoignages et leur interprétation', *Revue d'histoire moderne et contemporaine* 38 (1991), 529–54.

—, 'Calvinism and the Conspiracy of Amboise' (New York ,1962) 122–3.

Thomson, David, *Renaissance Paris. Architecture and Growth 1475–1600* (London, 1984).

Tomas, Natalie R., 'Alfonsina Orsini de' Medici and the "problem" of a female ruler in early sixteenth-century Florence', *Renaissance Studies* 14 (2000), 70–90.

—, *The Medici Women* (Aldershot, 2003).

Tommaseo, Niccolò, *Relations des ambassadeurs vénitiens sur les affaires de France au XVIe siècle*, 2 vols (Paris, 1838).

Turbide, Chantal, 'Catherine de Médicis (1519–1589) et le portrait: esquisse d'une collection royale au féminin', *RACAR: revue d'art canadienne/Canadian Art Review* 30 (2005), 48–58.

—, 'Catherine de Médicis, mécène d'art contemporain: l'Hôtel de la Reine et ses collections' in ed. Wilson-Chevalier, 511–26.

Vasari, Giorgio, *Le opere di Giorgio Vasari*, ed. Gaetano Milanesi, 8 vols (Florence, 1906).

Walker, Anita M. and Edmund H. Dickerman, 'The King Who Would Be Man: Henri III, Gender Identity and the Murders at Blois, 1988', *Historical Reflections/Réflexions Historique* 24 (1998) 253–81.

Watkin, David, '*Iungit amor*: royal marriage imagery in France,

1550–1750', *Journal of the Warburg and Courtauld Institutes* 54 (1991), 256–61.

Welch, Evelyn, *Shopping in the Renaissance* (New Haven and London, 2005).

Wilson-Chevalier, Kathleen, 'Art patronage and women (including Habsburg) in the orbit of king Francis I', *Renaissance Studies* 16 (2002), 474–524.

—, (ed.) with Eugénie Pascal, *Patronnes et mécènes au France à la Renaissance* (Saint-Étienne, 2007).

Wood, James B., *The King's Army: Warfare, Soldiers and Society during the Wars of Religion in France, 1562–1576* (Cambridge, 1996).

Woodward, Jennifer, 'Funeral Rituals in the French Renaissance', *Renaissance Quarterly* 9 (1995), 385–94.

Yates, Frances A., *The French Academies*

of the Sixteenth Century (London, 1947).

—, *The Valois Tapestries* (London 1959).

—, *Astraea. The Imperial Theme in the Sixteenth Century* (London, 1975).

Zerner, Henri, *Renaissance Art in France. The Invention of Classicism* (Paris, 2003).

—, 'Conspicuous Absences, Transnational Relationships in Catherine de' Medici's Portrait Collection', in ed. Strunck, 39–45.

Zimmerman, T. C. Price, *Paolo Giovio* (Princeton NJ, 1995).

Zvereva, Alexandra, '"Par commandement et selon devys d'icelle dame": Catherine de Médicis commanditaire de portraits', in ed. Sabine Frommel and Wolf, 215–28.

—, 'Catherine de Médicis et les portraitistes français', in ed. Wilson-Chevalier, 527–43.

Image Credits

Notes

Abbreviations

ASMo, CDAF   Archivio di Stato di Modena, Camera
Ducale, Ambasciatori Francia

ASMo, CDAP   Archivio di Stato di Modena, Camera
Ducale, Amministrazione Principi

ASMo, CS   Archivio di Stato di Modena, Casa e Stato

CSP Foreign   *Calendar of State Papers, Foreign*

CSP Ven   *Calendar of State Papers, Venetian*

DBI   *Dizionario Bibliografico degli italiani*

Prologue The Serpent Queen

1   C. L. Frommel, 'Caterina de'
Medici', 369.

2   Knecht, *Catherine de' Medici*, xiii.

**Chapter 1. The Little Duchess
1519–1531**

1   Baker-Bates, Beyond Rome
54–60.

2   Cashman, 'Performance anxiety',
342.

3   Ibid., 343.

4   Knecht, *French Court*, 87–8.

5   Rubinstein, 'Dalla repubblica',
164.

6   Knecht, *Catherine de' Medici*, 7;
Stephens, 'L'infanzia fiorentina',
423–4.

7   Chatenet, *Cour de France*, 231,
352–3 n. 20.

8   Hollingsworth, *Medici*, 98–101,
122–3, 172–3.

9   Bullard, *Filippo Strozzi*, 7.

10   Najemy, *History*, 429–30.

11   Bullard, *Filippo Strozzi*, 127.

12   Ibid., 81 n. 67.

13   Masi, *Ricordanze*, 235.

14   Pastor, *History of the Popes*, 7:80
n. 9

15   Reiss, 'Widow, Mother, Patron',
137.

16   Cummings, *Politicized Muse*,
102–3, 219 n. 10.

17   Ibid., 103–4

18   Cummings, *Politicized Muse*, 106.

19   Masi, *Ricordanze*, 238.

20   Najemy, *History*, 433.

21   Fletcher, *Black Prince*, 13.

22   Masi, *Ricordanze*, 239–40.

23   Fletcher, *Black Prince*, 13.

24   Masi, *Ricordanze*, 240.

25   Ibid., 241.

26   Fletcher, *Black Prince*, 14.

27   Stephens, 'L'infanzia fiorentina',
423–5.

28   Reiss, 'Widow, Mother, Patron',
138–9.

29   Stephens, 'L'infanzia fiorentina',
425.

30   Ibid., 426.

31 Ibid., 426–7.
32 Fletcher, *Black Prince*, 31.
33 Ibid., 16; Goldthwaite, *Building*, 430, 438.
34 Gnoli, 'Un censimento', 499; Bullard, *Filippo Strozzi*, 153 n. 9;
35 Stephens, 'L'infanzia fiorentina', 427; DBI, 'Ippolito de' Medici' (Irene Fosi).
36 Pastor, *History of the Popes*, 9:174–5.
37 Ibid., 9:502 (doc. 44).
38 Stephens, 'L'infanzia fiorentina', 427.
39 Strocchia, 'Taken into custody', 191 n. 52.
40 Bullard, *Filippo Strozzi*, 17.
41 Tomas, 'Alfonsina', 86.
42 Tomas, *Medici Women*, 184–5.
43 Stephens, 'L'infanzia fiorentina', 431.
44 Ibid., 432.
45 Ibid., 428–9.
46 Ibid., 434.
47 Polizzotto, *Elect Nation*, 190 n. 84.
48 Strocchia, *Nuns*, 34.
49 Stephens, 'L'infanzia fiorentina', 433–4.
50 Strocchia, *Nuns*, 29–30.
51 Ibid., 149–50.
52 Lowe, 'Female Strategies', 213–16.
53 *Lettres*, 1:v.
54 Lowe, 'Female Strategies', 219–20.
55 Ibid., 216–17; Strocchia, *Nuns*, 139–40.
56 Lowe, *Chronicles*, 175; Strocchia, *Nuns*, 104.
57 Lowe, *Chronicles*, 182.
58 Pastor, *History of the Popes*, 9:464.
59 Ibid., 9:466.
60 Stephens, 'L'infanzia fiorentina', 435.
61 Ibid., 433.
62 Roth, *Last Florentine Republic*, 155–6 n. 98.
63 Stephens, 'L'infanzia fiorentina', 435–6; *Lettres*, 1:iv.
64 *Lettres*, 1:iv–v n. 5.
65 Roth, *Last Florentine Republic*, 99.
66 Stephens, 'L'infanzia fiorentina', 433.
67 Roth, *Last Florentine Republic*, 121.
68 Sanudo, *Diarii*, 51:417–18.
69 Ibid., 51:461.
70 Roth, *Last Florentine Republic*, 174.
71 Ibid., 177.
72 Ibid., 204.
73 J. Brown, 'Monache a Firenze', 134.
74 Strocchia, *Nuns*, 35.
75 *Lettres*, 1:v n. 4.
76 Roth, *Last Florentine Republic*, 203–4.
77 Strocchia, 'Taken into custody', 191 n. 52.
78 *Lettres*, 1:viii.
79 Roth, *Last Florentine Republic*, 207.
80 *Lettres*, 1:vii n. 4.
81 Strocchia, 'Taken into custody', 192.

Chapter 2. Bride 1530–1533

1   *Lettres*, 1:xi.
2   Pastor, *History of the Popes*, 9:269–70.
3   *Lettres*, 1:xiii–xiv.
4   Pastor, *History of the Popes*, 10:162.
5   Ibid., 10:212.
6   *Lettres*, 1:xviii.
7   *Lettres*, 1:xiv.
8   Pastor, *History of the Popes*, 10:228.
9   Ibid., 10:229.
10 *CSP Ven*, 4:723 (Rome, 22 January 1532).
11 *CSP Ven*, 4:726 (London, 30 January 1532).
12 *CSP Ven*, 4:733 (London, 3 February 1532).
13 *CSP Ven*, 4:764 (Rome, 29 April 1532).
14 Parker, *Emperor*, 233.
15 *CSP Ven*, 4:848 (Paris, 6 February 1533), 876 (Melun, 22 April 1533).
16 *CSP Ven*, 4:886 (St-Amand, 7 May 1533).
17 Rubinstein, 'Dalla repubblica', 168.
18 Fletcher, *Black Prince*, 106–8.

19 Ibid., 117.
20 Lefevre, *Madama*, 67.
21 Fletcher, *Black Prince*, 138.
22 Newbiggin, *Feste*, 1–43, 212–13.
23 Gebhardt, 'Catherine de Médicis', 23.
24 Fletcher, *Black Prince*, 117.
25 *Lettres*, 1:xx.
26 Vasari, *Le opere*, 8:243–4 (doc. 8).
27 Hale, 'End of Florentine Liberty', 516–17.
28 Cloulas, *Catherine de Médicis*, 51.
29 Croizat, 'Living Dolls', 96–7; Welch, *Shopping*, 245–74.
30 *CSP Ven*, 4:893 (Moulins, 14 May 1533).
31 *CSP Ven*, 4:895 (Moulins, 16 May 1533).
32 *CSP Ven*, 4:900 (Venice, 24 May 1533).
33 *CSP Ven*, 4:901 (Lyons, 26 May 1533).
34 *CSP Ven*, 4:903 (Rome, 27 May 1533).
35 *CSP Ven*, 4:914 (Rome, 11 June 1533).
36 *CSP Ven*, 4:919 (London, 17 June 1533), 920 (Lyons, 19 June 1533).
37 *CSP Ven*, 4:934 (Lyons, 5 July 1533).
38 *CSP Ven*, 4:945 (Rome, 13 July 1533).
39 Bullard, *Filippo Strozzi*, 159 n. 31.
40 Ibid., 158–9, 166.
41 Cloulas, *Catherine de Médicis*, 53.
42 Ridolfi, *Life*, 225.
43 *Lettres*, 1:2 (12 September 1533).
44 *Lettres*, 1:2 (14 September 1533).
45 *Lettres*, 1:555 (23 September 1533).
46 Chatenet, *Cour de France*, 31–2.
47 Zimmerman, *Paolo Giovio*, 131.
48 Knecht, *Renaissance Warrior*, 300.
49 Ridolfi, *Life*, 225.
50 Knecht, *French Court*, 131.
51 Tommaseo, *Relations des ambassadeurs*, 1:108.
52 Cummings, 'Three gigli', 63.
53 Zimmerman, *Paolo Giovio*, 132.
54 *Lettres*, 1:xxx.
55 Canguilhem, 'Catherine de Médicis', 140.
56 Ibid., 141.
57 Knecht, *Catherine de' Medici*, 15.
58 Ridolfi, *Life*, 319 n. 13.
59 Bullard, *Filippo Strozzi*, 158.
60 Cloulas, *Catherine de Médicis*, 55–6.
61 Knecht, *French Court*, 133.
62 Zimmerman, *Paolo Giovio*, 132.
63 Cloulas, *Catherine de Médicis*, 56.
64 Pastor, *History of the Popes*, 10:233.
65 Ridolfi, *Life*, 228.

Chapter 3. Dauphine 1533–1547

1 Chatenet, *Cour de France*, 106.
2 Knecht, *French Court*, 125.
3 Tommaseo, *Relations des ambassadeurs*, 1:104.
4 Pastor, *History of the Popes*, 10:316.
5 *Lettres*, 1:xxviii.
6 Tommaseo, *Relations des ambassadeurs*, 1:104.
7 Ibid., 1:282–4.
8 Richardson, 'Hunting', 133.
9 Wilson-Chevalier, 'Art patronage', 507–11.
10 Chatenet, *Cour de France*, 191.
11 Carroll, *Martyrs and Murderers*, 31.
12 Hollingsworth, *Cardinal's Hat*, 207–9; Carroll, *Martyrs and Murderers*, 37–8.
13 Rubinstein, 'Dalla repubblica', 164 n. 21.
14 Knecht, *Renaissance Warrior*, 124–5.
15 Richardson, 'Hunting', 134.
16 Chatenet, *Cour de France*, 33–4.
17 Ibid., 27.
18 Kolk, 'Household', 12.
19 Knecht, *French Court*, 38.
20 Chatenet, *Cour de France*, 53.
21 Knecht, *Renaissance Warrior*, 400.
22 Chatenet, *Cour de France*, 51, 53–4.
23 Ibid., 45.
24 Ibid., 63.
25 Ibid., 77–80.
26 Ibid., 45; Knecht, *French Court*, 65.
27 Chatenet, *Cour de France*, 27–8.

28 Ibid., 127.

29 Ibid., 126–7.

30 McGowan, 'Form and Themes', 200–201.

31 Broomhall, 'Game of Politics', 107–8.

32 Michahelles, 'Catherine de' Medici', 18–19 (206, 215, 216).

33 Knecht, *Renaissance Warrior*, 452.

34 Hollingsworth, *Cardinal's Hat*, 263; Occhipinti, *Carteggio d'arte*, 47 (doc. 74).

35 ASMo, CS, 145, 1709–i/32.

36 Hollingsworth, *Cardinal's Hat*, 115–16.

37 Crawford, 'Political motherhood', 643–4.

38 Tommaseo, *Relations des ambassadeurs*, 1:424.

39 Brantôme, *Illustrious Dames*, 52.

40 Ibid., 53.

41 Ibid., 53; Tommaseo, *Relations des ambassadeurs*, 1:428.

42 *Lettres*, 1:xxxv.

43 ASMo, CS, 145, 1709–i/28 (11 November 1536).

44 Chatenet, *Cour de France*, 39.

45 Tommaseo, *Relations des ambassadeurs*, 1:30.

46 Occhipinti, *Carteggio d'arte*, 15 (doc. 22).

47 Chatenet, *Cour de France*, 50–51.

48 Ibid., 73.

49 ASMo, CDAF, 14. D11 (29 April 1537); Hollingsworth, *Cardinal's Hat*, 126–7.

50 ASMo, CS, 145, 1709–ii/16 (23 April 1537).

51 ASMo, CS, 145, 1709–ii/23 (15 June 1537).

52 ASMo, CS, 145, 1709–ii/27 (2 August 1537).

53 Chatenet, *Cour de France*, 253.

54 Vasari, *Le opere*, 7:106, 407.

55 Chatenet, *Cour de France*, 27–8.

56 Ibid., 27.

57 Croizat, 'Living Dolls', 97.

58 Ibid., 119–20.

59 Wilson-Chevalier, 'Art patronage', 476.

60 Broomhall, 'Game of Politics', 115.

61 Knecht, 'Popular theatre', 370.

62 Marguerite of Navarre, *Heptameron*, 1:prologue (accessed 21 February 2023, online via Project Gutenberg).

63 Occhipinti, *Carteggio d'arte*, 110 (doc. 165).

64 Castiglione, *Courtier*, 214; Conihout and Ract-Madoux, 'À la recherche', 43.

65 *Lettres*, 1:xxxiv.

66 Crouzet, 'Catherine de Médicis', 362.

67 Roelker, 'Appeal of Calvinism', 391–2.

68 Ibid., 398; Knecht, *Renaissance Warrior*, 309.

69 Wilson-Chevalier, 'Art patronage', 501.

70 Knecht, *Renaissance Warrior*, 467.

71 Wilson-Chevalier, 'Art patronage', 520.

72 Occhipinti, *Carteggio d'arte*, 23–4 (doc. 35).

73 Knecht, *Renaissance Warrior*, 340.

74 Tommaseo, *Relations des ambassadeurs*, 1:230.

75 Knecht, *French Court*, 39.

76 ASMo, CS, 145, 1709–iii/29 (21 June 1538).

77 Knecht, *French Court*, 134.

78 Tommaseo, *Relations des ambassadeurs*, 1:230.

79 Chatenet, *Cour de France*, 191.

80 Ibid., 218.

81 Occhipinti, *Carteggio d'arte*, 38–9 (doc. 40).

82 Jacquot, 'Panorama des fêtes', 2:435.

83 Knecht, *French Court*, 136.

84 Occhipinti, *Carteggio d'arte*, 38–9 (doc. 60).

85 Knecht, *French Court*, 136.

86 Ibid., 136–7.

87 Occhipinti, *Carteggio d'arte*, 39 (doc. 41).

88 Jacquot, 'Panorama des fêtes', 2:439.

89   Chatenet, *Cour de France*, 255.

90   Parker, *Emperor*, 265.

91   *Lettres*, 1:xxxii.

92   Occhipinti, *Carteggio d'arte*, 56–7 (doc. 89).

93   Chatenet, *Cour de France*, 224.

94   *Lettres*, 1:xxx n. 3.

95   Occhipinti, *Carteggio d'arte*, 96–7 (doc. 145).

96   Potter, 'Politics and faction', 134.

97   Occhipinti, *Carteggio d'arte*, 86–7 (doc. 128).

98   DBI, 'Strozzi, Roberto'.

99   Occhipinti, *Carteggio d'arte*, 96–7 (doc. 145); 98 (doc. 148).

100 ASMo, CS, 147, 1709–viii/23 (30 June 1543).

101 ASMo, CS, 147, 1709–viii/33 (6 September 1543).

102 Cloulas, *Catherine de Médicis*, 71.

103 *Lettres*, 1:7–8 (February 1544).

104 *Lettres*, 1:8 (6 July 1544).

105 Chatenet, *Cour de France*, 226.

106 Wilson-Chevalier, 'Art patronage', 513.

107 Cloulas, *Catherine de Médicis*, 74.

108 Occhipinti, *Carteggio d'arte*, 104–5 (doc. 158).

109 Knecht, *Renaissance Warrior*, 494.

110 Chatenet, *Cour de France*, 225.

111 Occhipinti, *Carteggio d'arte*, 142–6 (doc. 210).

112 Ibid., 146–8 (doc. 211).

113 Ibid., 133–5 (doc. 199).

114 Knecht, *Renaissance Warrior*, 495, 544.

Chapter 4. Queen 1547–1559

1   R. Cooper, *Maurice Scève*, passim.

2   Broomhall, *Identities*, 83–4.

3   Knecht, *Catherine de' Medici*, 40.

4   Carroll, *Martyrs and Murderers*, 56.

5   Knecht, *Catherine de' Medici*, 38.

6   Broomhall, 'The king and I', 346–7.

7   *Lettres*, 8:181; Knecht, *Catherine de' Medici*, 39.

8   Crawford, 'Political motherhood', 643–4.

9   Conihout and Ract-Madoux, 'À la recherche', 44–5.

10 Occhipinti, *Carteggio d'arte*, 167 (doc. 242).

11 Ibid., 198 (doc. 284).

12 Knecht, *French Court*, 111.

13 E. J. Johnson, 'The Theater', 187–8.

14 Ibid., 175 n. 5.

15 Roelker, *Queen of Navarre*, 73.

16 Ibid.

17 Ibid., 72.

18 Chatenet, 'La reine', 177–8.

19 Bryant, *Royal Entry*, 55, 227–8 (tables 2–3).

20 Ibid., 60–61.

21 Ibid., 60 n. 40.

22 Occhipinti, *Carteggio d'arte*, 226–8 (doc. 321).

23 Chatenet, *Cour de France*, 68 (fig. 23).

24 Ibid., 86.

25 Ibid., 195.

26 Ibid., 188.

27 Ibid., 217.

28 Martin, *Dairy Queens*, 32–4.

29 Coope, 'Château of Montceaux-en-Brie', 71–6.

30 Blunt, *Philibert de l'Orme*, 149–50.

31 Cordellier, 'Précisions sur l'activité', 234; Droguet, 'De l'agrément', 308; Miller, 'Domain of Illusion', 206.

32 Knecht, *Catherine de' Medici*, 36.

33 Le Roux, *La Faveur*, 37, 45.

34 ASMo, CS, 148, 1709–xiii/35 (29 November 1548).

35 Occhipinti, *Carteggio d'arte*, 189 (doc. 270).

36 Chatenet, *Cour de France*, 68–9 (figs 23–6).

37 Ibid., 133–4.

38 Boudon and Chatenet, 'Les logis du roi', 73–4.

39 Chatenet, *Cour de France*, 322 (table 5).

40 Blunt, *Art and Architecture*, 93; idem, *Philibert de l'Orme*, 65–7.

41 Anglo, *Martial Arts*, 11.

42   Conihout and Ract-Madoux, 'À la recherche', 43–6.

43   Bastien, 'Aux tresors', 25–6.

44   *Lettres*, 1:121 (25 April 1559).

45   Occhipinti, *Carteggio d'arte*, 197 (doc. 283).

46   Paresys, 'Vêtir les souverains', 6.

47   Chatenet, *Cour de France*, 191.

48   Kolk, 'The Household', 18.

49   Zvereva, 'Par commandement', passim.

50   Ibid., 223 n. 27.

51   Kolk, 'The Household', passim; Canguilhem, 'Catherine de Médicis', 136–7.

52   Kolk, 'L'évolution du mécénat', 65 n. 7.

53   Sutherland, *French Secretaries*, 23 n. 3.

54   Zvereva, 'Par commandement', 226.

55   Davis, *Gift*, 86.

56   ASMo, CS, 148, 1709–xiii/10 (10 April 1548).

57   Occhipinti, *Carteggio d'arte*, 217 (doc. 310).

58   Ibid., 271 (doc. 390).

59   Knecht, *Catherine de' Medici*, 34.

60   Chatenet, *Cour de France*, 213 (fig. 102).

61   *Lettres*, 1:22 (27 March 1548).

62   Chatenet, *Cour de France*, 213 (fig. 102).

63   *Lettres*, 1:39–40 (18 April 1551).

64   Broomhall, 'The king and I', 337.

65   Ibid., 339–40.

66   *Lettres*, 1:20 (31 July 1547).

67   *Lettres*, 1:20 (13 August 1547).

68   *Lettres*, 1:20 (23 August 1547).

69   *Lettres*, 1:40 n. 1.

70   *Lettres*, 1:40–41 (25 May 1551).

71   *Lettres*, 1:41 (28 May 1551).

72   Kolk, 'L'évolution du mécénat', 67–9.

73   *Lettres*, 1:31 (29 August 1549).

74   *Lettres*, 1:66 (18 June 1552).

75   Tommaseo, *Relations des ambassadeurs*, 1:372.

76   Broomhall, *Identities*, 96.

77   *Lettres*, 1:50–51 (21 April 1552).

78   *Lettres*, 1:60 n. 1.

79   Sutherland, *French Secretaries*, 78.

80   *Lettres*, 1:56 (20 May 1552).

81   *Lettres*, 1:64 (mid-June 1552).

82   Broomhall, *Identities*, 100–101 n. 77.

83   *Lettres*, 1:60–61 (end May 1552).

84   Knecht, *Catherine de' Medici*, 47.

85   *Lettres*, 1:74 (19 January 1552).

86   *Lettres*, 1:85 (23 September 1553).

87   Knecht, *Catherine de' Medici*, 46.

88   DBI, 'Strozzi, Roberto'.

89   Crouzet, 'Catherine de Médicis', 370–71.

90   Carroll, *Martyrs and Murderers*, 79.

91   Cloulas, *Catherine de Médicis*, 111–12.

92   Carroll, *Martyrs and Murderers*, 82–4.

93   Sutherland, *Princes, Politics and Religion*, 27–8.

94   Roelker, 'Appeal of Calvinism', 401.

95   Roelker, *Queen of Navarre*, 131.

96   Jouanna et al., *France de la Renaissance*, 344.

97   Ibid., 346.

98   Carroll, 'Nager entre deux eaux', 998.

99   Roelker, 'Appeal of Calvinism', 415.

100   Carroll, *Martyrs and Murderers*, 78.

101   Russell, *Peacemaking*, 138.

102   Ibid., 191.

103   Ibid., 165.

104   Romier, 'La mort', 100 n. 3.

105   Ibid., 101 n. 1.

106   Cloulas, *Catherine de Médicis*, 118.

Chapter 5. Widow 1559–1560

1   Chatenet, *Cour de France*, 250.

2   Knecht, *French Court*, 241–3.

3   Cloulas, *Catherine de Médicis*, 121.

4   Broomhall, *Identities*, 223–30.

5   Ibid., 213–14.

6   Ibid., 223.

7   Michahelles, 'Catherine de', 21–2 (inv. 351, 358, 362, 366, 367, 368), 38 n. 5.

8   Ibid., 27 (inv. 552); see also inv. 67, 550–51, 585–95.
9   Crawford, 'Political mother-hood', 657 n. 47.
10 *Lettres*, 1:122–3 (8 August 1559).
11 *Lettres*, 1:125–6 (11 September 1559).
12 *Lettres*, 1:lvi–lvii.
13 Carroll, *Martyrs and Murderers*, 21.
14 *CSP Ven*, 7:85 (12 July 1559).
15 Le Roux, *La Faveur*, 49.
16 Knecht, *French Court*, 26–9; idem, *Renaissance Warrior*, 49–54.
17 *CSP Ven*, 7:86 (16 July 1559).
18 On the government of France, see Knecht, *French Court*, 26–9.
19 *CSP Ven*, 7:85 (12 July 1559).
20 *CSP Ven*, 7:86 (16 July 1559).
21 *CSP Ven*, 7:89 (30 July 1559).
22 Ribier, *Lettres et Mémoires*, 2:830–1 (27 August 1559)
23 *CSP Ven*, 7:94 (21 August 1559).
24 Kolk, 'L'évolution du mécénat', 71.
25 Chatenet, *Cour de France*, 180 (fig. 85), 210; Boudon and Chatenet, 'Les logis du roi', 75.
26 Cloulas, *Catherine de' Médicis*, 129; Kolk, 'L'évolution du mécénat', 74.
27 Kolk, 'L'évolution du mécénat', 66.
28 Jouanna et al., *Guerres de religion*, 943.
29 Boström, 'Daniele da Volterra', 809–20.
30 Goldberg, 'Graces, Muses and Arts', passim.
31 Bresc-Bautier, 'Catherine de Médicis', 258.
32 Goldberg, 'Graces, Muses and Arts', 206–7.
33 Bresc-Bautier, 'Catherine de Médicis', 254.
34 Blunt, *Art and Architecture*, 95–8.
35 Zerner, *Renaissance Art*, 379–84.
36 Bresc-Bautier, 'Catherine de Médicis', 260–72.
37 Zerner, *Renaissance Art*, 382–3.
38 Crawford, 'Political mother-hood', 658–9 and n. 52.

39 Sutherland, 'Calvinism', 122–3.
40 Roelker, *Queen of Navarre*, 136.
41 *CSP Ven*, 7:90 (2 August 1559).
42 Sutherland, *Princes, Politics and Religion*, 61.
43 *CSP Ven*, 7: 94 (21 August 1559).
44 *Lettres*, 1:126 (15 September 1559).
45 *Lettres*, 1:127 (13 October 1559).
46 *Lettres*, 1:128–9 (end November 1559).
47 Carroll, 'Nager entre deux eaux', 994.
48 Diefendorf, *Beneath the Cross*, 53.
49 Carroll, *Martyrs and Murderers*, 112; Holt, *French Wars*, 40.
50 Carroll, *Martyrs and Murderers*, 111.
51 *Lettres*, 1:128 (14 November 1559).
52 Diefendorf, *Beneath the Cross*, 53–5.
53 *Lettres*, 1:lxx–lxxi.
54 Carroll, *Martyrs and Murderers*, 116.
55 Knecht, *Catherine de' Medici*, 66.
56 *Lettres*, 1:lxvi.
57 Knecht, *Catherine de' Medici*, 83.
58 Potter, *French Wars*, 24–5 (doc. 9).
59 Roelker, 'Appeal of Calvinism', 397.
60 Roelker, *Queen of Navarre*, 142.
61 *Lettres*, 1:144 (August 1560); 146 (August 1560).
62 *Lettres*, 1:146–7 (3 August 1560).
63 Knecht, *Catherine de' Medici*, 69.
64 Carroll, *Martyrs and Murderers*, 137.
65 Ibid., 137–8.
66 *Lettres*, 1:lxxxii.
67 Broomhall, 'Women's little secrets', 4.
68 *Lettres*, 1:565–6 (1 October 1560).
69 *Lettres*, 1:566 (7 November 1560).
70 Roelker, *Queen of Navarre*, 146–7.
71 Ibid., 146.
72 *Lettres*, 1:154–5 (end November 1560).

73   Crawford, 'Political mother-
     hood', 660.
74   Knecht, *Catherine de' Medici*, 72.
75   Carroll, *Martyrs and Murderers*,
     127.
76   *Lettres*, 1:161–3 (15 January
     1561).

Chapter 6. Regent 1561–1563
1   Cloulas, *Catherine de Médicis*, 155.
2   Davis, 'Women in Politics', 172.
3   Conihout and Ract-Madoux, 'À la
     recherche', 47.
4   *Lettres*, 1:158 (mid-December
     1560); Knecht, *Catherine de'
     Medici*, 73.
5   Cloulas, *Catherine de Médicis*, 154.
6   Gaehtgens, 'Cathérine de
     Médicis', passim.
7   ffolliott, 'Catherine de' Medici as
     Artemisia', 230.
8   Ibid., 231; 372 n. 15.
9   Ibid., 232.
10   Ibid., 234–5.
11   Watkin, '*Iungit amor*', passim.
12   ffolliott, 'Casting a rival', 141–2.
13   *Lettres*, 1:158 (mid-December
     1560).
14   Le Roux, *La Faveur*, 59–61.
15   Ibid., 57–8.
16   *Lettres*, 1:178n. 2.
17   Roelker, 'Appeal of Calvinism',
     400.
18   Roelker, *Queen of Navarre*, 156.
19   Ibid., 171.
20   Ibid., 157.
21   *Lettres*, 1:557–8 (31 January
     1561).
22   *Lettres*, 1:182–3 (2 April 1561).
23   Carroll, 'Nager entre deux eaux',
     1006–7.
24   Sutherland, *French Secretaries*, 114.
25   Tommaseo, *Relations des ambassa-
     deurs*, 1:418.
26   Ibid., 1:424–8.
27   Courtright, 'A Garden', 67.
28   Ibid., 62, 70–71.
29   Ibid., 61–2; S. Frommel,
     'Florence, Rome', 286.
30   Droguet, 'De l'agrément', 315.
31   Ibid., 320–21.

32   *Lettres*, 1:171 (March 1561).
33   Sutherland, *Massacre*, 17.
34   Tommaseo, *Relations des ambassa-
     deurs*, 418–20.
35   *Lettres*, 1:179 (27 March 1561).
36   *Lettres*, 1:182 (2 April 1561) and
     n. 2.
37   Bastien, 'Aux tresors', 28.
38   Cloulas, *Catherine de Médicis*, 162.
39   Jackson, 'The Sleeping King',
     535–9.
40   Knecht, *Catherine de' Medici*, 76.
41   *Lettres*, 1:191–2 (22 April 1561).
42   *Lettres*, 1:599–600 (20 June
     1561).
43   Hollingsworth, *Conclave*, 123.
44   Ibid., 6–8, 10–13.
45   Roelker, *Queen of Navarre*, 162.
46   Bèze, *Histoire Ecclésiastique*, 1:267.
47   Nugent, *Ecumenism*, 73.
48   Sutherland, *French Secretaries*,
     118–9.
49   Bèze, *Histoire Ecclésiastique*, 1:267;
     Pastor, *History of the Popes*, 16:170.
50   Nugent, *Ecumenism*, 155.
51   Bèze, *Histoire Ecclésiastique*, 1:325.
52   Nugent, *Ecumenism*, 156.
53   Roelker, *Queen of Navarre*, 166.
54   Ibid., 166, 458–9 n. 42.
55   Chatenet, *Cour de France*, 130,
     221.
56   Pacifici, *Ippolito d'Este*, 304 n. 1;
     Hollingsworth, *Conclave*, 243.
57   Roelker, *Queen of Navarre*, 165;
     Potter, 'Life and after-life', 324.
58   Roelker, *Queen of Navarre*, 163.
59   Cloulas, *Catherine de Médicis*,
     167.
60   Roelker, *Queen of Navarre*, 169.
61   Knecht, *Catherine de' Medici*, 83.
62   *Lettres*, 1:244 (November 1561).
63   Pastor, *History of the Popes*, 16:174;
     Knecht, *Catherine de' Medici*, 74.
64   Carroll, 'Nager entre deux eaux',
     1010.
65   Ehrmann, 'Massacre and
     Persecution', 197.
66   Knecht, *Catherine de' Medici*, 84–5.
67   *Lettres*, 1:272–3 (23 January
     1562).
68   *Lettres*, 1:275 (15 February 1562).

69 Potter, *French Wars*, 32.

70 Roelker, *Queen of Navarre*, 181–2.

71 Occhipinti, 'Disputes françaises', 219.

72 Davila, *Negociations*, 48–9.

73 Kim, 'Dieu nous garde', 595–6.

74 Ibid., 597.

75 Ibid., 598 n. 11.

76 *Lettres*, 1:277–8 (24 February 1562).

77 On the massacre, see Carroll, *Martyrs and Murderers*, 13–20.

78 Roelker, *Queen of Navarre*, 183.

79 Ibid., 183–4.

80 Jouanna et al., *Guerres de religion*, 111.

81 Cloulas, *Catherine de Médicis*, 170.

82 Harrie, 'The Guises', passim.

83 Davila, *Negociations*, 118–21 (16 March 1562).

84 *Lettres*, 1:281–4 (16–26 March 1562).

85 Jouanna et al., *Guerres de religion*, 112.

86 Potter, *French Wars*, 73–6.

87 Davila, *Negociations*, 154.

88 *Lettres*, 1:293–6 (11 April 1562); see also Potter, *French Wars*, 76.

89 *Lettres*, 1:327–8 (9 June 1562).

90 Sutherland, *French Secretaries*, 126.

91 *Lettres*, 1:317–18 (18 May 1562).

92 Sutherland, *French Secretaries*, 125.

93 Ibid., 126.

94 *Lettres*, 1:cxxxiii; Davila, *Negociations*, 234.

95 Davila, *Negociations*, 234–5.

96 *Lettres*, 1:333–5 (16 June 1562).

97 Holt, *French Wars*, 73.

98 Jensen, 'Catherine de Medici', 62–3.

99 Pastor, *History of the Popes*, 16:183–4.

100 ASMo, CS, 150, 1709–xxvii/23 (15 June 1562).

101 Cloulas, *Catherine de Médicis*, 173.

102 Roelker, *Queen of Navarre*, 195.

103 *Lettres*, 1:388–90 (2 September 1562).

104 Knecht, *Catherine de' Medici*, 90.

105 *Lettres*, 1:414–15 (6 October 1562).

106 *Lettres*, 1:420 (15 October 1562).

107 Roelker, *Queen of Navarre*, 199.

108 *Lettres*, 1:432–3 (7 November 1562).

109 Roelker, *Queen of Navarre*, 202.

110 *Lettres*, 1:500 (8 February 1563).

111 *Lettres*, 1:502 (11 February 1563).

112 *Lettres*, 1:512 (19 February 1563).

113 Diefendorf, *Beneath the Cross*, 71.

114 Ibid., 72.

115 *Lettres*, 2:xlv.

Chapter 7. Grand Tour 1563–1566

1 Potter, *French Wars*, 89–90.

2 Holt, *French Wars*, 58.

3 Tommaseo, *Relations des ambassadeurs*, 2:44.

4 *Lettres*, 2:79–81 (31 July 1563).

5 Balsamo, 'Ses vertus', 26.

6 Knecht, *Catherine de' Medici*, 96.

7 Carroll, *Martyrs and Murderers*, 170.

8 *Lettres*, 2:128–9 (5 January 1564).

9 Carroll, *Martyrs and Murderers*, 172–3.

10 Carroll, 'Nager entre deux eaux', 1018.

11 Tommaseo, *Relations des ambassadeurs*, 2:44.

12 *Lettres*, 2:18–20 (20 April 1563).

13 Roelker, *Queen of Navarre*, 224.

14 Jensen, 'French diplomacy', 25–6.

15 Ibid., 32.

16 *Lettres*, 2:56–8 (11 June 1563).

17 Champion, *Catherine de Médicis*, 45–7.

18 Chatenet, *Cour de France*, 244.

19 S. Frommel, 'Florence, Rome', 292.

20 C. L. Frommel, 'Caterina de' Medici', 377–80; Thomson, *Renaissance Paris*, 165–8.

21 Thomson, *Renaissance Paris*, 169–70.

22 Bondois, 'Bernardo Carnesecchi', 391 n. 3.

23 Champion, *Catherine de Médicis*, 52.

24 Chatenet, *Cour de France*, 321 table 4.

25 Ibid., 212 fig. 100; Champion, *Catherine de Médicis*, 53.

26 Hall, 'Ronsard's *Bergerie*', 301.

27 Ibid., 302; Champion, *Catherine de Médicis*, 59–60.

28 Champion, *Catherine de Médicis*, 60.

29 Hall, 'Ronsard's *Bergerie*', 305–6.

30 On the play, see Scott and Sturm-Maddox, *Performance, Poetry and Politics*, passim.

31 Hall, 'Ronsard's *Bergerie*', 307–8; Sturm-Maddox, 'Catherine de Medici', 35.

32 Champion, *Catherine de Médicis*, 63.

33 Graham, 'The 1564 Entry', 107, 109.

34 Carroll, *Martyrs and Murderers*, 22.

35 Sutherland, *French Secretaries*, 143.

36 Bèze, *Histoire Ecclésiastique*, 1:37.

37 Champion, *Catherine de Médicis*, 77.

38 Ibid., 78.

39 Jouan, *Recueil et Discours*, 10v–12r.

40 Cloulas, *Catherine de Médicis*, 191.

41 Briggs, 'Presenting the Most Christian King', 18–19.

42 Champion, *Catherine de Médicis*, 92.

43 Knecht, *Rise and Fall*, 383.

44 Holt, *French Wars*, 60.

45 Champion, *Catherine de Médicis*, 119.

46 Ibid., 124.

47 Ibid., 95.

48 Knecht, *Catherine de' Medici*, 104; Champion, *Catherine de Médicis*, 94.

49 Roelker, *Queen of Navarre*, 230.

50 Champion, *Catherine de Medicis*, 103.

51 Broomhall, *Identities*, 131.

52 Champion, *Catherine de Médicis*, 101.

53 *Lettres*, 2:196–7 (23 June 1564).

54 Cloulas, *Catherine de Médicis*, 199.

55 *Lettres*, 2:168–9 (1 April 1564).

56 Sutherland, *French Secretaries*, 158.

57 Roelker, *Queen of Navarre*, 222.

58 Ibid., 223.

59 Holt, *French Wars*, 62–3.

60 *Lettres*, 2:lii–liii.

61 *Lettres*, 2:218 n. 3.

62 Jouan, *Recueil et Discours*, 20v–21r.

63 Knecht, *Catherine de' Medici*, 221.

64 Roelker, *Queen of Navarre*, 231.

65 Jouan, *Recueil et Discours*, f. 22v.

66 Kolk, 'L'évolution du mécénat', 81.

67 Jouan, *Recueil et Discours*, 25v–26r; Cloulas, *Catherine de Médicis*, 202.

68 Bresc-Bautier, 'Catherine de Médicis', 273.

69 Ibid., 273–5.

70 *Lettres*, 2:lxiii.

71 Champion, *Catherine de Médicis*, 176–7.

72 Ibid., 176.

73 Jouan, *Recueil et Discours*, 29r.

74 Ibid., 29v.

75 Cloulas, *Catherine de Médicis*, 203–4.

76 Jouan, *Recueil et Discours*, 31r.

77 Cloulas, *Catherine de Médicis*, 205.

78 Champion, *Catherine de Médicis*, 204–5.

79 Ibid., 214–16.

80 Ibid., 228 n. 1.

81 Kim, 'Dieu nous garde', 617; Champion, *Catherine de Médicis*, 228.

82 Holt, *French Wars*, 60.

83 Champion, *Catherine de Médicis*, 229.

84 Ibid., 209.

85 Ibid., 229.

86 Knecht, *Rise and Fall*, 389.

87 Champion, *Catherine de Médicis*, 134.

88 *Lettres*, 2:236–7 (28 November 1564).

89 Carroll, *Martyrs and Murderers*, 173.

90 *Lettres*, 2:265–6 (19 February 1565).

91 *Lettres*, 2:247–8 (29 December 1564); Kolk, 'L'évolution du mécénat', 82.

92 *Lettres*, 2:273–4 (4 March 1565).

93 *Lettres*, 2:261 (2 February 1565);

2:270 (24 February 1565); Kolk, 'Lévolution du mécénat', 80.

94 Champion, *Catherine de Médicis*, 217, 224–5, 255.

95 *Lettres*, 2:lxvi; Roelker, *Queen of Navarre*, 233.

96 Roelker, *Queen of Navarre*, 234.

97 Bresc-Bautier, 'Catherine de Médicis', 273.

98 Briggs, 'Presenting the Most Christian King', 7–8.

99 Champion, *Catherine de Médicis*, 240.

100 Knecht, *Rise and Fall*, 386.

101 Champion, *Catherine de Médicis*, 259 n. 1.

102 Jouan, *Recueil et Discours*, 42r.

103 Champion, *Catherine de Médicis*, 257.

104 Jouan, *Recueil et Discours*, 46r.

105 Ibid., 47v.

106 Strong, *Art and Power*, 103.

107 Brantôme, *Illustrious Dames*, 72.

108 Ibid.

109 Strong, *Art and Power*, 106.

110 Knauer, 'Battle of Zama', 229.

111 Hollingsworth, *Princes*, 419–29.

112 Odde, 'Politic Magnificence', 34–5.

113 Ibid., 34.

114 Knauer, 'Battle of Zama', 241.

115 Odde, 'Politic Magnificence', 38–9.

116 Ibid., 46–8.

117 Strong, *Art and Power*, 107; Odde, 'Politic Magnificence', 39–41.

118 Odde, 'Politic Magnificence', 39–46.

119 Strong, *Art and Power*, 107–8; Odde, 'Politic Magnificence', 41–3.

120 Jouan, *Recueil et Discours*, 49r.

121 Brantôme, *Illustrious Dames*, 74.

122 Sutherland, *French Secretaries*, 144–5.

123 *Lettres*, 2:lxxx.

124 Sutherland, *Massacre*, 42–4.

125 Ibid., 44 n. 1.

126 Potter, *French Wars*, 94 doc. 27.

127 Sutherland, *Massacre*, 42.

128 *Lettres*, 2:298 n. 1.

129 Jouan, *Recueil et Discours*, 52r.

130 Champion, *Catherine de Médicis*, 297.

131 *Lettres*, 2:315 (30 August 1565).

132 Jouan, *Recueil et Discours*, 57r–58r.

133 Briggs, 'Presenting the Most Christian King', 11.

134 Ibid., 10.

135 Champion, *Catherine de Médicis*, 309.

136 Jouan, *Recueil et Discours*, 60r–64r.

137 Ibid., 64v–65r.

138 *Lettres*, 2:304–5 (21 July 1565).

139 Champion, *Catherine de Médicis*, 358–9.

140 *Lettres*, 2:338 (5 January 1566).

141 Potter, *French Wars*, 90–1 (doc. 24).

142 Carroll, *Martyrs and Murderers*, 175–6.

143 Carroll, 'Nager entre deux eaux', 1018.

144 Kolk, 'L'évolution du mécénat', 64 n. 2.

145 Broomhall, *Identities*, 267–9.

146 *Lettres*, 2: 360–1 (12 May 1566).

147 Broomhall, 'Women's Little Secrets', 9–11.

148 Roelker, *Queen of Navarre*, 230 n.

Chapter 8. Civil War 1567–1571

1 *Lettres*, 3:56 (4 September 1567).

2 *Lettres*, 3: 58–9 (18 September 1567).

3 *Lettres*, 3:ix–x.

4 *Lettres*, 3:61 (28 September 1567).

5 Roelker, *Queen of Navarre*, 241–2.

6 Carroll, *Martyrs and Murderers*, 178.

7 Sutherland, *Massacre*, 56–7.

8 *Lettres*, 3:52–3 (23–26 August 1567).

9 *Lettres*, 3:57 (10 September 1567).

10 *Lettres*, 3:48 (31 July 1567).

11 *Lettres*, 3:47 (26 July 1567).

12 Sutherland, *Massacre*, 57–8.

13 *Lettres*, 3:vi.

14 Knecht, *Rise and Fall*, 395.

15 Potter, *French Wars*, 102–3 doc. 3.

16 *Lettres*, 3:ix.
17 Sutherland, *French Secretaries*, 148.
18 Ibid.; Knecht, *Rise and Fall*, 398.
19 Sutherland, *Massacre*, 61.
20 Jensen, 'Catherine de Medici',
     63–4.
21 *Lettres*, 3:72 (6 November 1567).
22 *Lettres*, 3: 72–3 (11 November
     1567).
23 *Lettres*, 3:74–5 (14 November
     1567).
24 Sutherland, *Massacre*, 54.
25 Knecht, *Rise and Fall*, 401.
26 *Lettres*, 79–82 (27–28 November
     1567).
27 *Lettres*, 3:89 n. 1.
28 Sutherland, *Massacre*, 101.
29 *Lettres*, 3:xvii.
30 Knecht, *Catherine de' Medici*, 117.
31 *Lettres*, 3:xx.
32 *Lettres*, 3:113 (30 January 1568).
33 *Lettres*, 3:123–4 (13 February
     1568).
34 *Lettres*, 3:126 (21 February 1568).
35 *Lettres*, 3:132 (27 March 1568);
     Sutherland, *French Secretaries*, 164.
36 Potter, *French Wars*, 105–6 doc.
     6.
37 Ibid., 106–7 doc.7.
38 Roelker, *Queen of Navarre*, 292.
39 Sutherland, *Massacre*, 64.
40 Knecht, *Rise and Fall*, 403–4.
41 Sutherland, *Massacre*, 65.
42 Knecht, *Catherine de' Medici*, 119
     cites some examples.
43 *Lettres*, 3:xxvi.
44 *Lettres*, 3:142 (24 May 1568).
45 *Lettres*, 3:159 (26 July 1568).
46 *Lettres*, 3:xxvii–xxviii.
47 *Lettres*, 3:166–7 (5 August 1568);
     Knecht, *Catherine de' Medici*, 122.
48 *Lettres*, 3:167–8 (7 August 1568).
49 *Lettres*, 3:173–4 (26 August
     1568).
50 *Lettres*, 3:158–9 (26 July 1568).
51 *Lettres*, 3:176–9 (8 September
     1568).
52 Sutherland, *Massacre*, 89.
53 Ibid., 90.
54 *Lettres*, 3:176–9 (8 September
     1568).
55 Carroll, *Martyrs and Murderers*,
     182.
56 Potter, *French Wars*, 111–12 doc.
     11.
57 Ibid., 110–11 doc. 10.
58 Roelker, *Queen of Navarre*, 299.
59 Knecht, *Catherine de' Medici*,
     123–4.
60 *Lettres*, 3:193; Broomhall,
     'Women's Little Secrets', 7.
61 *Lettres*, 3:198–9 (28 October
     1568).
62 *Lettres*, 3:202–3 (12 November
     1568).
63 *Lettres*, 3:220–1 (20 January
     1569).
64 *Lettres*, 3:xxxviii.
65 *Lettres*, 3:xxxvii–xxxviii.
66 *Lettres*, 3:xxxvii; Knecht, *Catherine
     de' Medici*, 125.
67 *Lettres*, 3:235–6 (April 1569).
68 Potter, *French Wars*, 112–14 docs
     12, 13.
69 Knecht, *Catherine de' Medici*,
     125.
70 Jensen, 'Catherine de Medici',
     64.
71 Lapini, *Diario Fiorentino*, 162.
72 Jensen, 'Catherine de Medici',
     66.
73 Hollingsworth, *Princes*, 413–15.
74 Sutherland, *Massacre*, 99, 101.
75 *Lettres*, 3:241 (19 May 1569);
     Knecht, *Catherine de' Medici*, 127.
76 Sutherland, *French Secretaries*,
     150.
77 Ibid., 167.
78 *Lettres*, 3:242–3 (9 June 1569).
79 *Lettres*, 3:245–6 (12 June 1569).
80 Sutherland, *French Secretaries*,
     165–6.
81 Ibid., 168.
82 Knecht, *Catherine de' Medici*, 129.
83 Sutherland, *Massacre*, 103.
84 *Lettres*, 3:269 (4 September
     1469).
85 *Lettres*, 3:273–4 (20 September
     1569).
86 *Lettres*, 3:274 n. 1.
87 Pastor, *History of the Popes*,
     18:123–4.

88 *Lettres*, 3:276–8 (7 October 1569).

89 Sutherland, *French Secretaries*, 169–70.

90 *Lettres*, 3:279 (10 October 1569).

91 *Lettres*, 3:282 n. 1.

92 *Lettres*, 3:282 (8 November 1569).

93 Roelker, *Queen of Navarre*, 333.

94 *Lettres*, 3:284–5 (27 November 1569).

95 *Lettres*, 3:293 (27 January 1570).

96 *Lettres*, 3:294–5 n. 1; Potter, *French Wars*, 117 doc. 18.

97 *Lettres*, 3:294–5 (7 February 1570).

98 *Lettres*, 3:346–52 (10 February 1570).

99 Sutherland, *Massacre*, 108.

100 *Lettres*, 3:346–52 (10 February 1570); Roelker, *Queen of Navarre*, 336–7.

101 *Lettres*, 3:lxv.

102 *Lettres*, 3:305–6 (22 March 1570).

103 *Lettres*, 3:310 n. 1.

104 *Lettres*, 3:308 n. 1.

105 *Lettres*, 3:318 (22 June 1570).

106 *Lettres*, 3:319 (28 June 1570).

107 *Lettres*, 3:320 (8 July 1570).

108 *Lettres*, 3:lxv.

109 Potter, *French Wars*, 118–21 doc. 20.

110 Ibid., 117–18 doc. 19.

111 *Lettres*, 3:325–6 n.

112 *Lettres*, 3:330 n. 1.

113 Sutherland, *Massacre*, 92.

114 Roelker, *Queen of Navarre*, 339.

115 *Lettres*, 3:lxiv; Knecht, *Catherine de' Medici*, 135.

116 Kamen, *Philip of Spain*, 125.

117 *Lettres*, 3:267 (11 August 1569).

118 *Lettres*, 3:299 (28 February 1570).

119 *Lettres*, 4:1 (11 September 1570).

120 *Lettres*, 4:2 (15 September 1570).

121 *Lettres*, 4:2–3 (15 September 1570).

122 Knecht, *Catherine de' Medici*, 139.

123 Yates, *Astraea*, 130–33.

124 Strong, *Art and Power*, 110.

125 Ibid.

126 Bryant, *Royal Entry*, 147 n. 24.

127 Chatenet, 'La reine', 179 n. 28.

128 Strong, *Art and Power*, 110.

129 Yates, *Astraea*, 137–8.

130 Bryant, *Royal Entry*, 147.

131 Strong, *Feast*, 198.

132 *Lettres*, 4:78 (28 October 1571).

133 Droguet, 'De l'agrément', 305 n. 1.

134 S. Frommel, 'Florence, Rome', 293.

135 Blunt, *Art and Architecture*, 135–9.

136 Blunt, *Philibert de L'Orme*, 110–20.

137 Yates, *Astraea*, 130–31.

138 Kolk, 'Le mécénat', 474.

139 Kolk, 'L'évolution du mécénat', 83.

140 Martin, *Dairy Queens*, 59–61.

141 *Lettres*, 4:78 (28 October 1571).

142 Blunt, *Philibert de L'Orme*, 90–91.

143 Chatenet, *Cour de France*, 211, 213 fig. 101.

144 Ibid., 322 table 6.

145 Bresc-Bautier, 'Catherine de Médicis', 261–2 n. 22.

146 Knecht, *Catherine de' Medici*, 233.

147 *Lettres*, 3:45 (5–15 July 1567).

148 Odde, 'Les coulisses', 491 n. 44; Tommaseo, *Relations des ambassadeurs*, 2:592.

149 Thomson, *Renaissance Paris*, 173; Chatenet, *Cour de France*, 210–11.

150 Bresc-Bautier, 'Catherine de Médicis', 273–5.

151 *Lettres*, 3:1 (9 January 1567).

152 Michahelles, 'Catherine de' Medici', 7, 31 nn. 640–55.

153 *Lettres*, 4:43 (20 May 1571).

154 Bondois, 'Bernardo Carnesecchi', 390–91.

155 Odde, 'Les coulisses', 505.

156 Tommaseo, *Relations des ambassadeurs*, 2:592; Odde, 'Les coulisses', 505.

157 J. Johnson, 'Bernard Palissy', 403.

158 Michahelles, 'Catherine de' Medici', 8.

159 J. Johnson, 'Bernard Palissy', 404.

160 *Lettres*, 3:253–4 (20 June 1569).

161 Le Roux, *La Faveur*, 56.

162 Kolk, 'L'évolution', 83; idem, 'The household', 12.
163 Chatenet, *Cour de France*, 208.
164 Holt, *French Wars*, 78.
165 Roelker, *Queen of Navarre*, 339.
166 Holt, *French Wars*, 68.
167 *Lettres*, 4:31–3 (2 March 1571).
168 *Lettres*, 4:52 (3 July 1571).
169 *Lettres*, 4:xviii–xix.
170 *Lettres*, 3:5–6 (26 January 1567); 4:30–1 (28 February 1571).
171 *Lettres*, 4:70–1 (28 September 1571).
172 Knecht, *Catherine de' Medici*, 144.
173 Sutherland, *Massacre*, 206–7.
174 Ibid., 212.

Chapter 9. St Bartholomew's Day 1572

1 Yates, *French Acadmies*, ch. 11; Strong, *Art and Power*, 111–13.
2 Diefendorf, *Beneath the Cross*, 88–91.
3 Jouanna, *Massacre*, 87.
4 Diefendorf, *Beneath the Cross*, 86.
5 Ibid., 157.
6 Sutherland, *Massacre*, 214–15.
7 Roelker, *Queen of Navarre*, 355.
8 Ibid., 356.
9 Pastor, *History of the Popes*, 18:139–40.
10 Sutherland, *Massacre*, 219.
11 Roelker, *Queen of Navarre*, 373.
12 Ibid., 378.
13 Ibid., 392.
14 Ibid., 393.
15 Sutherland, *French Secretaries*, 176.
16 Potter, *French Wars*, 133 doc. 8.
17 Sutherland, *Massacre*, 235.
18 Pastor, *History of the Popes*, 18:143; Sutherland, *Massacre*, 238.
19 Sutherland, *Massacre*, 242–3.
20 Ibid., 273.
21 J. Cooper, *The Queen's Agent*, 74.
22 Bourgeon, 'Les légendes', 106–7.
23 Potter, *French Wars*, 134–5 doc. 10.
24 *Lettres*, 4:106–7 (3 July 1572).
25 *Lettres*, 4:107–8 (17 July 1572).
26 Sutherland, *Massacre*, 276.

27 Parker, *Dutch Revolt*, 137–8.
28 Carroll, *Martyrs and Murderers*, 202.
29 Jouanna, *Massacre*, 60, 61, 71 n. 74.
30 Sutherland, *Massacre*, 306.
31 Jouanna et al., *Guerres de religion*, 196.
32 Jouanna, *Massacre*, 61.
33 Jouanna et al., *Guerres de religion*, 195.
34 Jouanna, *Massacre*, 64.
35 Ibid., 64.
36 Roelker, *Queen of Navarre*, 380–81.
37 *Lettres*, 4:110–11 (19 August 1572).
38 *Lettres*, 4:111–12 (21 August 1572).
39 Carroll, *Martyrs and Murderers*, 208.
40 Jouanna et al., *Guerres de religion*, 198.
41 Sutherland, *Massacre*, 339–40; Jouanna, *Massacre*, 106.
42 Crouzet, 'Catherine de Médicis', 373; Jouanna, *Massacre*, 76–7.
43 Sutherland, *French Secretaries*, 177.
44 Jouanna, *Massacre*, 76.
45 Ibid., 100–101.
46 Potter, *French Wars*, 140–42 doc. 19; Jouanna, *Massacre*, 104, 118 n. 27.
47 Potter, *French Wars*, 142 doc. 20.
48 Diefendorf, *Beneath the Cross*, 95, 209 n. 9.
49 Ibid., 95; Holt, *French Wars*, 84.
50 Bourgeon, 'Les légendes', 110–11.
51 Jouanna, *Massacre*, 104–5.
52 Potter, *French Wars*, 142 doc. 20; Jouanna et al., *Guerres de religion*, 198.
53 Carroll, *Martyrs and Murderers*, 213–14.
54 Jouanna, *Massacre*, 111.
55 Jouanna et al., *Guerres de religion*, 201.
56 Diefendorf, *Beneath the Cross*, 210 n. 10.

57 Ibid., 104; Holt, *French Wars*, 90–91.
58 J. Cooper, *The Queen's Agent*, 1–2.
59 On the ritual killings, see Davis, 'Rites of Violence', passim.
60 Diefendorf, *Beneath the Cross*, 98.
61 Ibid., 99, 157.
62 Jouanna et al., *Guerres de religion*, 204.
63 Holt, *Franch Wars*, 91–2.
64 Benedict, 'Saint Bartholomew's Massacre', 214–15.
65 Crouzet, *La nuit*, 114.
66 Holt, *French Wars*, 95; Jouanna, *Massacre*, 3.
67 J. Cooper, *The Queen's Agent*, 80–81.
68 *Lettres*, 4:cxix; Parker, *Dutch Revolt*, 80.
69 Lapini, *Diario Fiorentino*, 177.
70 Pastor, *History of the Popes*, 19:499.
71 Ibid., 19:505–6.
72 Herz, 'Vasari's "Massacre"', 46, 53.
73 Sutherland, *Massacre*, 345.
74 J. Cooper, *The Queen's Agent*, 81.
75 Broomhall, *Identities*, 315–17.
76 Jouanna, *Massacre*, 101.
77 Ibid., 102.
78 Ibid., 102
79 *Lettres*, 4:113–14 (28 August 1572).
80 *Lettres*, 4:122–7 (13 September 1572).
81 Sutherland, *Massacre*, 332.
82 Ibid., 330, 544.
83 Jouanna, *Massacre*, 158.
84 Broomhall, *Identities*, 308.
85 Potter, *French Wars*, 148 doc. 30.
86 Jouanna, *Massacre*, 80.
87 Broomhall, *Identities*, 311–12.
88 Ehrmann, 'Tableaux de Massacres', 451–4.
89 Crouzet, *La nuit*, 126.
90 Ibid., 124.
91 Broomhall, *Identities*, 301–2.
92 Crouzet, *La nuit*, 110–11.
93 Sutherland, 'Le massacre', 540–42.
94 Kingdon, *Myths*, 200–11.
95 Crouzet, *La nuit*, 127–41.
96 Ibid., 127.
97 Roelker, *Queen of Navarre*, 391.
98 Sutherland, *Princes, Politics and Religion*, 237.
99 Brantôme, *Illustrious Dames*, 65.
100 Ibid., 66.
101 Roberts, 'Regency of 1574', 263–4.
102 In particular, see Sutherland, *Massacre*; Jouanna, *Massacre*; Bourgeon, 'Les légendes'; Crouzet, *La nuit*.
103 Bourgeon, 'Un texte capital', 709.
104 Sutherland, *Massacre*, 315–18.

Chapter 10. Jealousies 1572–1577

1 *Lettres*, 4:137–8 (23 October 1572).
2 *Lettres*, 4:139–40 (30 October 1572).
3 *Lettres*, 4:129–30 (October 1572).
4 *Lettres*, 4:161–2 n. 1.
5 *Lettres*, 4:134–5 (4 October 1572).
6 Pastor, *History of the Popes*, 19:516.
7 *Lettres*, 4:cvi–cvii.
8 *Lettres*, 4:117–18 (7 September 1572); 4:118–19 (11 September 1572).
9 *Lettres*, 4:164 (7 February 1573).
10 *Lettres*, 4:116–17 (5 September 1572).
11 *Lettres*, 4:162 (7 February 1573).
12 Smither, 'St Bartholomew's Day', 35.
13 Ibid.; Crouzet, *La nuit*, 104–5.
14 Holt, *French Wars*, 95.
15 Ibid., 95–6.
16 *Lettres*, 4:140–41 (11 November 1572); 4:141 (18 November 1572).
17 *Lettres*, 4:152 (3 January 1573).
18 *Lettres*, 4:155–6 (17 January 1573).
19 *Lettres*, 4:162 (7 February 1573).
20 *Lettres*, 4:169–70 (18 February 1573).
21 *Lettres*, 4:152 n. 1.

22 Sutherland, *French Secretaries*, 177–8.
23 *Lettres*, 4:160 (4 February 1573).
24 *Lettres*, 4:166 (10 February 1573).
25 *Lettres*, 4:180 (10–15 March 1573).
26 *Lettres*, 4:184–5 (20 March 1573).
27 *CSP Ven*, 7:540 (6 April 1573).
28 Wood, *The King's Army*, 268–300.
29 Holt, *French Wars*, 97.
30 *Lettres*, 4:224–5 (30 May 1573).
31 *Lettres*, 4:227 (June 1573).
32 *CSP Ven*, 7:548 (2 July 1573).
33 *Lettres*, 4:250 (22 August 1573).
34 *Lettres*, 4:254–5 (22 September 1573).
35 Kociszewska, 'War and Seduction', 852.
36 Ibid., 811, 814.
37 Ibid., 831.
38 Ibid., 816.
39 Brantôme, *Illustrious Dames*, 73; Kolk, 'L'évolution', 86, n. 104.
40 Fenlon, 'From Caterina de' Medici', 81.
41 On the interpretation of the ballet, see Greene, 'Labyrinth Dances'; Kociszewska, 'War and Seduction'.
42 *Lettres*, 4: 240–1 (3 July 1573).
43 *Lettres*, 4:254 n. 1.
44 Le Roux, *La Faveur*, 139–40.
45 Ibid., 143.
46 Ibid., 143.
47 Ibid., 139–40.
48 Ibid., 144.
49 Ibid., 141–2.
50 Ibid., 141.
51 *Lettres*, 4:264 n. 2.
52 *Lettres*, 4:266–7 (23 November 1573).
53 Knecht, *Catherine de' Medici*, 170.
54 *CSP Ven*, 7:565 (29 December 1573).
55 *CSP Ven*, 7:563 (2 December 1573).
56 Chatenet, *Cour de France*, 320–22, tables 3–6.
57 Sutherland, *French Secretaries*, 191–2.
58 *CSP Ven*, 7:573 (10 March 1574).
59 Braghi, 'The Death of Charles IX', 309.
60 *CSP Ven*, 7:586 (2 May 1574).
61 *Lettres*, 4:310–12 (31 May 1574); 5:i.
62 *Lettres*, 5:12 (11 June 1574).
63 Sandberg, 'Iconography of Religious Violence', 102.
64 Woodward, 'Funeral Rituals', 389–92.
65 *CSP Ven*, 7:598 (13 July 1574).
66 Braghi, 'The Death of Charles 1X', 312–13.
67 Ibid., 317–18.
68 Ibid., 310–12.
69 Droguet, 'De l'agrément', 306.
70 Tommaseo, *Relations des ambassadeurs*, 2:242.
71 *Lettres*, 5:1 n. 1.
72 *CSP Ven*, 7:597 (27 June 1574); for another view, see Knecht, *Catherine de' Medici*, 172.
73 *Lettres*, 5:1–2 (1 June 1574).
74 Knecht, *Catherine de' Medici*, 173.
75 *CSP Ven*, 7:592 (1 June 1574); 593 (9 June 1574).
76 *CSP Ven*, 7:598 (13 July 1574), 599 (15 July 1574).
77 *Lettres*, 5:9 (6 June 1574).
78 *Lettres*, 5:40 (29 June 1574).
79 *Lettres*, 5:xxiii–xxv n. 1.
80 *Lettres*, 5:64 (22 July 1574).
81 *Lettres*, 5:73–5 (8 August 1574); Potter, *French Wars*, 157.
82 *Lettres*, 5:72–3 (8 August 1574).
83 *CSP Ven*, 7:605 (3 September 1574).
84 *CSP Ven*, 7:607 (17 September 1574).
85 Potter, *French Wars*, 160–62 doc. 7.
86 *Lettres*, 5:xlii.
87 *CSP Ven*, 7:612 (29 December 1574).
88 Sutherland, *French Secretaries*, 190–91.
89 *Lettres*, 5:301 (5 February 1575).
90 *Lettres*, 5:112 n. 1.
91 *Lettres*, 5:112–13 (8 February 1575).

92 Tommaseo, *Relations des ambassa-deurs*, 2:240, 242.

93 *Lettres*, 5:91–2 (30 September 1574).

94 *Lettres*, 5:113–14 (3 March 1575).

95 *Lettres*, 5:124 (11 June 1575).

96 Droguer, 'De l'agrément', 306.

97 Chatenet, *Cour de France*, 60, 310–14.

98 Blunt, *Art and Architecture*, 140.

99 Chatenet, *Cour de France*, figs 44, 167, 168, 169.

100 Tommaseo, *Relations des ambassa-deurs*, 2:234–6

101 Knecht, *French Court*, 282–3; Holt, *French Wars*, 104.

102 *Lettres*, 5:85 n. 1.

103 Sutherland, *French Secretaries*, 186.

104 Le Roux, *La Faveur*, 166–7.

105 Chatenet, *Cour de France*, 135–6.

106 *Lettres*, 2:90–5; Potter, *French Wars*, 14–17 doc. 3; on the dating of this letter to 1576–67, see Le Roux, *La Faveur*, 164 and n. 1.

107 Potter, *French Wars*, 159 doc. 4.

108 Pastor, *History of the Popes*, 19:524.

109 *Lettres*, 5:120 (19 May 1575).

110 *Lettres*, 5:131 (19 August 1575).

111 Tommaseo, *Relations des ambassa-deurs*, 2:238.

112 Potter, *French Wars*, 158 doc. 3.

113 Knecht, *Catherine de' Medici*, 180.

114 *CSP Ven*, 7:628 (18 July 1575).

115 *CSP Ven*, 7:634 (11 September 1575).

116 *CSP Ven*, 7:636 (16 September 1575).

117 *Lettres*, 5:132–4 (15 September 1575).

118 Holt, *French Wars*, 104–5; Potter, *French Wars*, 162–3 doc. 8.

119 Holt, *French Wars*, 105.

120 *Lettres*, 5:138–9 (24 September 1575).

121 *Lettres*, 5:140–41 (26 September 1575).

122 *Lettres*, 5:147–9 (5 October 1575).

123 *Lettres*, 5:154 (13 October 1575).

124 Sutherland, *French Secretaries*, 193–4.

125 Knecht, *Catherine de' Medici*, 182.

126 *CSP Ven*, 7:641 (30 November 1575).

127 Holt, *French Wars*, 100–104.

128 *Lettres*: 5:161 n. 1.

129 Jouanna et al., *Guerres de religion*, 240; Holt, *French Wars*, 105.

130 Holt, *French Wars*, 150.

131 Knecht, *Catherine de' Medici*, 184.

132 *Lettres*, 5:192–3 (7 May 1576).

133 Knecht, *Catherine de' Medici*, 184.

134 *Lettres*, 5:206–7 (29 June 1576).

135 Pastor, *History of the Popes*, 19:526.

136 Knecht, *Catherine de' Medici*, 186.

137 *Lettres*, 5:201–2 n. 1; 201–3 (8 June 1576).

138 Potter, *French Wars*, 170–71 doc.13.

139 *Lettres*, 2:223 (23 November 1576).

140 *Lettres*, 5:219–20 (8 October 1576); 220 n. 1.

141 *Lettres*, 5:222 (2 November 1576).

142 Holt, *French Wars*, 107–8.

143 *CSP Ven*, 7:668 (7 February 1577).

144 Sutherland, *French Secretaries*, 196.

145 Knecht, *Catherine de' Medici*, 189.

146 *Lettres*, 5:231–6 (2 January 1577).

147 *Lettres*, 5:246–7 (7 March 1577).

148 *Lettres*, 5:247 (7 March 1577).

149 Potter, *French Wars*, 175–7 doc.16.

150 Ibid., 177–8 doc. 17.

151 Ibid., 178–9 doc. 18).

152 Pastor, *History of the Popes*, 19:531.

153 *Lettres*, 5:252–3 (13 May 1577).

154 *Lettres*, 5:254 n. 1.

155 *Lettres*, 5:261 (29 June 1577).

156 *Lettres*, 5:256 (12 June 1577).

157 Sutherland, *French Secretaries*, 197–8.

Chapter 11. Rivalries 1578–1584

1 Carroll, *Martyrs and Murderers*, 233.

2 Boucher, 'Contribution à l'histoire', 114–15.

3 Ibid., 116.

4 Ibid., 113.

5 Sutherland, *French Secretaries*, 200–201.

6   Boucher, 'Contribution à
     l'histoire', 114.
7   *Lettres*, 6:15–18 (6 May 1578).
8   *CSP Ven*, 7:712 (27 May 1578).
9   *Lettres*, 6:28–9 (6 June 1578).
10   *Lettres*, 6:28–9 (6 June 1578).
11   Parker, *Dutch Revolt*, 191.
12   *Lettres*, 6:33 (2 August 1578).
13   *Lettres*, 6:34 (8 August 1578).
14   *Lettres*, 6:i.
15   *Lettres*, 6:35 (11 August 1578).
16   *Lettres*, 6:36–7 (13 September
     1578).
17   *Lettres*, 6:59–60 (7 October
     1578).
18   *Lettres*, 6:59–60 (7 October
     1578).
19   *Lettres*, 37 n. 1.
20   *Lettres*, 6:63–6 (9 October 1578).
21   *Lettres*, 6:46–50 (2 October
     1578).
22   *Lettres*, 6:388–90 appendix doc. 3.
23   *Lettres*, 6:63–6 (9 October 1578).
24   *Lettres*, 6:397–8 (30 September
     1578).
25   *Lettres*, 6:67–79 (11–15 October
     1578).
26   *Lettres*, 6:67–79 (11–15 October
     1578).
27   *Lettres*, 6:108 (6 November 1578).
28   *Lettres*, 6:viii–ix.
29   *Lettres*, 6:ix.
30   *Lettres*, 6:136 (26 November
     1578), 139–40 (30 November
     1578).
31   *Lettres*, 6:173–7 (16 December
     1578).
32   *Lettres*, 6:xii.
33   *Lettres*, 6:xiii.
34   Sutherland, *French Secretaries*,
     208–9.
35   Chatenet, *Cour de France*, 62.
36   Sutherland, *French Secretaries*, 208.
37   *Lettres*, 6:284–5 (February 1579).
38   *Lettres*, 6:xvii, 441–8 appendix
     doc. 18.
39   Pastor, *History of the Popes*, 19:536.
40   *Lettres*, 6:325–6 (March 1579).
41   *Lettres*, 6:337–8 (14 April 1579).
42   *Lettres*, 6:315–17 (24 March
     1579).

43   *Lettres*, 6:360 (8 May 1579).
44   Sutherland, *French Secretaries*,
     208.
45   Holt, *French Wars*, 113–15.
46   *CSP Ven*, 7:732 (20 October
     1578).
47   *CSP Ven*, 7:760 (6 June 1579).
48   *CSP Ven*, 7:766 (3 August 1579).
49   *CSP Ven*, 7:773 (4 September
     1579).
50   *CSP Ven*, 7:775 (18 September
     1579).
51   *Lettres*, 7:163–4 (10 October
     1579).
52   *CSP Foreign: Elizabeth*, 14:74 (21
     October 1579).
53   Chatenet, 'Henri III', 135–6.
54   Chatenet, *Cour de France*, 322–3,
     tables 5 and 7.
55   Boudon and Chatenet, 'Les logis
     du roi', 76–7.
56   Knecht, *French Court*, 291.
57   Yates, *Astraea*, 174–5.
58   Carroll, *Martyrs and Murderers*,
     232, 236.
59   Thomson, *Renaissance Paris*,
     178–80.
60   Ibid., 166–8.
61   Knecht, *French Court*, 285,
     288–90.
62   *CSP Foreign: Elizabeth*, 14:189
     (February 1580).
63   *CSP Foreign: Elizabeth*, 14:172 (21
     February 1580).
64   Cloulas, *Catherine de Médicis*,
     328–31, 339.
65   Kolk, 'L'évolution du mécénat',
     65 n. 7; Cloulas, *Catherine de
     Médicis*, 330–31.
66   Zvereva, 'Catherine de Médicis',
     536, 538–9.
67   Ibid., 534 n. 22.
68   For the inventory, see
     Michahelles, 'Catherine de'
     Medici'; see also Turbide,
     'Mécène', 518–22.
69   Michahelles, 'Catherine de'
     Medici', 36 (inv. 841–3).
70   Ibid., 36 (inv. 844–5).
71   Ibid., 36 (inv. 846–8).
72   Ibid., 7, 32–3 (inv. 685–725).

73 Zerner, 'Conspicuous absences', 43.
74 Turbide, 'Mécène', 522.
75 Michahelles, 'Catherine de' Medici', 15–16 (inv. 76–100) and passim.
76 Hoogvliet, 'Le cabinet de curiosités', 207.
77 See, for example, Yates, *Valois Tapestries*; Bertrand, 'A New Method'; Kociszewska, 'Woven Bloodlines'; for a summary, see Knecht, *Catherine de' Medici*, 242–4.
78 *Lettres*, 7:252–3 (21 April 1580).
79 *Lettres*, 7:279–80 (27 April 1580).
80 *Lettres*, 7:261–2 (21 May 1580).
81 *Lettres*, 7:260–61 (20 May 1580).
82 *Lettres*, 7:263–4 (12 June 1580).
83 *Lettres*, 7:291 (7 November 1580).
84 Knecht, *Catherine de' Medici*, 204.
85 Tommaseo, *Relations des ambassadeurs*, 2:254–6.
86 Sutherland, *French Secretaries*, 218.
87 Ibid., 219–20.
88 *Lettres*, 7:304–9 (23 December 1580).
89 Pastor, *History of the Popes*, 19:537–8.
90 Sutherland, *French Secretaries*, 221–2.
91 *Lettres*, 7:373–4 (29 April 1581).
92 *Lettres*, 7:375 n. 1.
93 *Lettres*, 7:472–3 appendix 24 (1 June 1581).
94 Walker and Dickerman, 'The King', 270 n. 90.
95 Tommaseo, *Relations des ambassadeurs*, 2:236.
96 Walker and Dickerman, 'The King', 265–7.
97 Ibid., 259–61 and passim.
98 Knecht, *French Court*, 322.
99 Le Roux, *La Faveur*, 489.
100 Knecht, *French Court*, 314.
101 Sarti, *Europe at Home*, 152.
102 Knecht, *French Court*, 313.
103 Bastien, 'Aux tresors', 31–2.
104 Carroll, *Martyrs and Murderers*, 235.
105 Le Roux, *La Faveur*, 255.
106 Ibid., 484.
107 Ibid., 463–4.
108 Knecht, *French Court*, 292–3.
109 Carroll, *Martyrs and Murderers*, 237.
110 Ibid., 237–8.
111 Le Roux, *La Faveur*, 486.
112 Greene, 'King's One Body', 76.
113 Ibid., 84.
114 Ibid., 76–7.
115 *CSP Ven*, 8:63 (11 January 1582).
116 *CSP Foreign: Elizabeth*, 15:460–61 (22 January 1582).
117 *Lettres*, 8:10–12 (6 March 1582).
118 Knecht, *Catherine de' Medici*, 212.
119 Jensen, 'French Diplomacy', 29.
120 Sutherland, *French Secretaries*, 239.
121 *Lettres*, 8:13 (15 March 1582).
122 *Lettres*, 8:23 (26 April 1582).
123 *CSP Foreign: Elizabeth*, 16:33 (14 May 1582).
124 Carroll, *Martyrs and Murderers*, 244–8.
125 Ibid., 246.
126 *CSP Foreign: Elizabeth*, 16:33 (14 May 1582), 249 (15 August 1582).
127 Carroll, *Martyrs and Murderers*, 245.
128 *CSP Foreign: Elizabeth*, 16:113 (27 June 1582).
129 *CSP Foreign: Elizabeth*, 16:87 (13 June 1582).
130 *CSP Foreign: Elizabeth*, 16:113 (27 June 1582).
131 *CSP Foreign: Elizabeth*, 16:248 (15 August 1582).
132 *CSP Foreign: Elizabeth*, 16:286 (28 August 1582).
133 Sutherland, *French Secretaries*, 239.
134 *Lettres*, 8:64–6 (30 September 1582).
135 *Lettres*, 8:71 (13 November 1582).
136 *Lettres*, 8:50–1 (11 August 1582); Knecht, *Catherine de' Medici*, 212–13.
137 *CSP Ven*, 8:124 (14 February 1583).

138 Yates, *Astraea*, 180.

139 Ibid., 177.

140 *CSP Foreign: Elizabeth*, 17:186 (22 March 1583).

141 Carroll, *Martyrs and Murderers*, 234.

142 *CSP Foreign: Elizabeth*, 17:216 (end March 1583).

143 *CSP Foreign: Elizabeth*, 17:186 (22 March 1583).

144 *CSP Foreign: Elizabeth*, 17:293 (3 May 1583).

145 *CSP Foreign: Elizabeth*, 17:200 (29 March 1583).

146 Sutherland, *French Secretaries*, 247.

147 *CSP Foreign: Elizabeth*, 17:325 (22 May 1583).

148 *Lettres*, 8:108 (25 June 1583).

149 *Lettres*, 8:111–12 (6 July 1583).

150 *Lettres*, 8:119–20 (9 August 1583).

151 *Lettres*, 8:422–4 (12 August 1583).

152 *CSP Ven*, 8:155 (19 August 1583).

153 *CSP Ven*, 8:162 (2 September 1583).

154 *Lettres*, 8:126 (21 August 1583).

155 *Lettres*, 8:423 (5 September 1583).

156 *Lettres*, 8:424 (5 September 1583).

157 *Lettres*, 8:152 (4 November 1583).

158 *Lettres*, 8:174 (13 February 1584); Knecht, *Catherine de'Medici*, 217.

159 *Lettres*, 8:175 (29 February 1584); Knecht, *Catherine de' Medici*, 216.

160 *Lettres*, 8:180–2 (25 April 1584).

161 Sutherland, *French Secretaries*, 248.

162 Yates, *Astraea*, 182–3.

163 Sutherland, *French Secretaries*, 251.

164 *Lettres*, 8:190 (11 June 1584).

Chapter 12. Anguish 1584–1589

1 Strong, 'Festivals', 62.

2 Ibid., 64–70.

3 Ibid., 66, 67 n. 39.

4 Ibid., 63–4.

5 *CSP Foreign: Elizabeth*, 19:655 (13 June 1584).

6 Sutherland, *French Secretaries*, 253.

7 *Lettres*, 8:200–201 (30 July 1584).

8 Sutherland, *French Secretaries*, 253.

9 Chatenet, 'Henri III', 137–8.

10 *Lettres*, 8:197–9 (25 July 1584).

11 Sutherland, *French Secretaries*, 252.

12 Potter, *French Wars*, 188–9 doc. 2.

13 *CSP Foreign: Elizabeth*, 19 (1 April 1585).

14 Knecht, *Catherine de' Medici*, 247.

15 *Lettres*, 8:239–40 (February–March 1585).

16 *CSP Foreign: Elizabeth*, 19 (5 September 1584).

17 Le Roux, *La Faveur*, 519–22.

18 Ibid., 520 n. 3.

19 *Lettres*, 8:453 (1 April 1585).

20 Sutherland, *French Secretaries*, 258.

21 *Lettres*, 8:248–50 (13 April 1585), 261 (24 April 1585).

22 *Lettres*, 8:245 (9 April 1585).

23 Walker and Dickerman, 'The King', 277.

24 *Lettres*, 8:248–50 (13 April 1585).

25 *Lettres*, 8:260–1 (24 April 1585).

26 Sutherland, *French Secretaries*, 259.

27 *Lettres*, 8:290–91 (21 May 1585).

28 Shishkin, 'Court', 98–9.

29 *Lettres*, 8:318–19 (15 June 1585).

30 *Lettres*, 8:278–81 (7 May 1585).

31 *Lettres*, 8:275–7 (5 May 1585).

32 *Lettres*, 8:290–1 (21 May 1585).

33 Sutherland, *French Secretaries*, 262.

34 Knecht, *Catherine de' Medici*, 252.

35 Pastor, *History of the Popes*, 21:289–90.

36 Le Roux, *La Faveur*, 597; Knecht, *French Court*, 302–3.

37 Sutherland, *French Secretaries*, 265.

38 Le Roux, *La Faveur*, 520.

39 Sutherland, *French Secretaries*, 265.

40 *Lettres*, 9:10 n. 1.

41 *CSP Ven*, 8:347 (8 May 1586).

42 Sutherland, *French Secretaries*, 267–8.

43 *Lettres*, 9:9 (21 March 1586).

44 Sutherland, *French Secretaries*, 268.

45 *Lettres*, 9:30 (14 August 1586).

46 *Lettres*, 9:68–9 (19 October 1586).

47 Shishkin, 'Court', 103–7.

48 *Lettres*, 9:513 (23 October 1586);

Knecht, *Catherine de' Medici*, 254.

49   Knecht, *Catherine de' Medici*, 254–5.

50   *Lettres*, 9:68 n. 3.

51   *Lettres*, 9:76–7 (30 October 1586).

52   Sutherland, *French Secretaries*, 272.

53   *Lettres*, 9:79 (3 November 1586).

54   *CSP Ven*, 8:482 (13 March 1587).

55   Sutherland, *French Secretaries*, 267.

56   Knecht, *Rise and Fall*, 518.

57   Carroll, *Martyrs and Murderers*, 264.

58   Sutherland, *French Secretaries*, 267.

59   Ibid., 272.

60   Sutherland, *French Secretaries*, 273.

61   Ibid., 273–4.

62   Ibid., 275.

63   Ibid., 276.

64   *Lettres*, 9:12 (April 1586).

65   *Lettres*, 9:204 (17 May 1587).

66   *Lettres*, 9:166–7 (14 February 1587).

67   Cameron, 'La polémique', 186, 188.

68   *Lettres*, 9:229–30 (16 September 1587).

69   *Lettres*, 9:250 (15 October 1587).

70   *Lettres*, 7:405 (5 October 1587); on the misdating of this letter, see Sutherland, *French Secretaries*, 280 n. 1.

71   Sutherland, *French Secretaries*, 278.

72   Knecht, *French Court*, 330.

73   *Lettres*, 9:260–1 (26 October 1587).

74   Carroll, *Martyrs and Murderers*, 271.

75   Knecht, *Catherine de' Medici*, 258.

76   *Lettres*, 9:305–6 (30 November 1587).

77   *Lettres*, 9:316–17 (18 December 1587).

78   *Lettres*, 9:312 (12 December 1587).

79   *Lettres*, 9:321 (3 January 1588).

80   Potter, *French Wars*, 197–8 doc. 9.

81   Carroll, *Martyrs and Murderers*, 275.

82   Knecht, *Catherine de' Medici*, 331–2.

83   Potter, *French Wars*, 199–200 doc. 10.

84   *Lettres*, 9:342–4 (20 May 1588).

85   *Lettres*, 9:346–8 (23 May 1588).

86   *Lettres*, 9:348 (23 May 1588).

87   *Lettres*, 9:368 (2 June 1588).

88   Potter, *French Wars*, 201–3 doc. 13.

89   *Lettres*, 9:375–6 (July 1588).

90   Carroll, *Martyrs and Murderers*, 281.

91   Potter, *French Wars*, 205 doc. 15.

92   Sutherland, *French Secretaries*, 299–300.

93   Ibid., 298–9.

94   *Lettres*, 9:382 (20 September 1588).

95   Knecht, *Catherine de' Medici*, 265.

96   Ibid., 265.

97   *Lettres*, 9:278–9 (11 November 1587).

98   *Lettres*, 9:318–19 (26 December 1587).

99   Pastor, *History of the Popes*, 21:239.

100 Knecht, *Catherine de' Medici*, 266; Potter, *French Wars*, 208–9 doc. 20.

101 DBI, 'Cavriani, Filippo'.

102 H. Brown, 'The Death and Funeral', 749.

103 *Lettres*, 9:494–8.

Index